THE
PROPER
SPHERE

THE PROPER SPHERE

WOMAN'S PLACE IN CANADIAN SOCIETY

Edited by

Ramsay Cook

and

Wendy Mitchinson

TORONTO
Oxford University Press
1976

© Oxford University Press (Canadian Branch) 1976

Cover design by FRED HUFFMAN

Cover illustration from the
Montreal *Daily Herald*, 1913

ISBN-0-19-540272-3

1 2 3 4-9 8 7 6

Printed in Canada by
WEB OFFSET PUBLICATIONS LIMITED

CONTENTS

INTRODUCTION

'The exclusion of women from all public offices is a relic of days more barbaric than ours,' the Judicial Committee of the Privy Council proclaimed in 1929. It went on to rule that women were 'persons' eligible to hold public office on equal terms with men in Canada. While that decision was undoubtedly historic, it was only one of many developments that advanced Canadian women along the long road to political equality. During 'those days more barbarous than ours', when men monopolized public office, a combination of women's activism and changing social circumstances produced a profound alteration in the status of Canadian women. This collection of documents is designed to illustrate how, and in some instances why, women came to win recognition as 'persons'.

By the early 1920s the overwhelming majority of Canadian women had won the right to vote. Women who had relatives in the armed forces voted under the Wartime Elections Act in the 1917 federal election. Three years later the Dominion Elections Act extended the vote to all women. The first breakthrough had come at the provincial level: first Manitoba in 1916 and finally Quebec, twenty-four years later. Except in Quebec the Great War had given the suffrage movement a vigorous shove forward. The reason was simple enough: women played a notable and publicized part in winning that war. They worked in factories and on farms in increased numbers, served at the front as nurses, and formed numerous voluntary associations that aided the war effort from the home front. But even so, the first voting privilege came less as a recognition of woman's contribution to the war effort than from the expectation that the female relatives of servicemen would support a Unionist government and its policy of conscription. Such an act of political calculation was hardly a glorious victory for women's voting rights. But at least it was a beginning.

Yet it was only a beginning in the sense that women could now vote, and only the future would tell what effect that would have on the Canadian political system. But in another sense the granting of voting rights to women was a conclusion to a long debate about 'woman's sphere' in Canadian society that reached back into the last half of the nineteenth century. The history of that debate, and the changing status of women in

Canada, remains rather murky. That is because the history of women remains a seriously underdeveloped area of Canadian history, though the situation is gradually changing as women's history gains a certain, sometimes precarious, legitimacy. Certainly there is nothing particularly regrettable about the development of women's history as a separate field, since it should encourage serious study and analysis of a neglected dimension of our past. But to achieve a status of full equality women's history will eventually have to be re-integrated into the general history of the country. Since the documents presented in this volume belong almost exclusively to the history of women, it might be well to say something about the more general historical context into which they should be set if their full significance is to be understood.

During the latter part of the nineteenth century Canada entered a period of socio-economic change that radically altered the structure of the country. In the half-century between Confederation and the end of the Great War several developments of striking magnitude for a small country took place. First the vast Northwest and Pacific Coast territories were annexed to the new Dominion. Then, slowly at first but rapidly after 1896, hundreds of thousands of immigrants from nearly every corner of the earth flooded into Canada. Once the immigration gates were opened the hopes for a diversified economy that had underlain Macdonald's national developmental policies became a reality. After the turn of the century it became increasingly clear that industrial and urban growth would soon exceed the traditional agricultural economy in both population and wealth. The great divide came with the 1921 census, which revealed a country almost equally balanced between rural and urban dwellers.

These remarkable social, economic, and demographic changes almost inevitably brought with them regional unrest, class tension, ethnic conflict, and intellectual questioning. Regional unrest (though it had class connotations too) exploded in the farmers' Progressive Party in 1921, while the Winnipeg General Strike in 1919 dramatized the pent-up frustrations working people felt in early twentieth-century Canada. Cultural conflict, in its familiar French-English version, characterized much of the period between Riel's hanging in 1885 and the 1917 conscription crisis. But to those familiar ethnic tensions was added turmoil created by the tens of thousands of 'foreigners' who entered the country between 1900 and 1914. Finally there was intellectual ferment. The development of science and historical criticism in the late nineteenth century shook the precepts of traditional Christianity that formed the intellectual and ethical foundations of so much of Canadian thought. At the same time the churches and the educational system faced new demands from the inhabitants of the emerging industrial society and the newcomers settling in both urban and rural areas.

None of these developments left the position of women in Canadian society untouched. Indeed the 'woman question' formed an integral part of these changes. That question may be simply stated: what legitimate role could women play in the new society? What bothered many women was that they were hardly even asked an opinion about that question. They realized, perhaps only half-consciously, that social change challenged and even undermined their traditional role. That is why an increasing number of women, though probably never a majority, began to wonder how they might exercise more control over their own fate in a changing society. Ultimately that meant gaining a share of political power for, so it was somewhat naively believed, it was through political action that society could be controlled, reformed, altered, and even planned.

How did the new society modify the role of women? In the Canadian context the question can only be answered in general terms for it has only recently begun to be investigated. But certain aspects of the changes are plain enough. Obviously technological innovation and industrial growth impinged upon women's traditional realm, the home. On the one hand mass production removed certain household tasks from the home to the factory. With the work went the workers—fathers, sons, often daughters, and sometimes mothers too. Moreover technological change entered the home in a more direct fashion. Labour-saving devices and factory-made food and clothing meant that domestic tasks consumed less and less time, especially for middle-class women who sometimes could afford domestic help. Finally, it is important to remark that after about 1870 a declining birthrate in English-speaking Canada eased family responsibilities for many women.

Women reacted to these developments in a wide variety of ways. Some attempted to re-emphasize the virtues of traditional home life, evoking what might be called the ideal of domesticity. In this they were frequently seconded by conservative males. These same women often argued that they should organize themselves to bring their well-understood virtues to bear upon such outstanding social evils as the liquor trade and the white slave trade, which threatened home life. Others suggested that education for professional life would answer the problems of the underemployment and underevaluation of women. None of these palliatives meant much to women on the farms or in factories. For these women revisions of the legal system mattered much more. Reforms that would alleviate the burdens of long hours, unequal wages, unsanitary working conditions, inequitable marriage, inheritance, and homesteading laws, and sundry other discriminatory laws and customs were what the majority of Canadian women required.

Though some of these changes came slowly from the male-dominated legislatures of the country, many women concluded that only if their demands were backed up by votes would they receive a full and sympathetic hearing. Thus the argument for woman suffrage, which could be advanced on the simple grounds of justice and equity, came to be associated with a broader range of demands. That explains why the Woman's Christian Temperance Union advocated equal suffrage before any other large organization. The association between suffrage and social reform made the suffrage movement a part of a more general call for change that permeated significant sections of articulate, middle-class society in the second decade of the century. Women, in company with other critics of Canadian society, demanded that public policy and law be brought into closer conformity with the radically altered social relations that the socio-economic transformation of the country had produced.

For some women the right to vote symbolized the achievement of equality. For others, perhaps more realistically, it represented a means that, if effectively used, could lead to equality. For that reason the documents in this volume may be read as both a culmination and a beginning.

1. WOMAN'S PROPER SPHERE

What constitutes the proper sphere for woman? This question was asked continually throughout the nineteenth and early twentieth centuries in Canada. Why it was asked is debatable since those who insisted upon discussing the question agreed with monotonous regularity that woman's role was to be wife, mother, and homemaker. Did so much attention and rhetoric suggest that women no longer accepted their 'proper sphere'? The contention that 'woman's place was in the home' derived from the conviction that the family was the fundamental social unit and woman its centre. What affected the family had repercussions on the larger structure.

Yet woman had not always been the central focus of family life. In the early years of settlement both husband and wife had shared the responsibility. In fact the family often functioned as an economic unit in a rural setting or in small commercial towns, all members contributing to its survival. This state of affairs altered somewhat as more and more Canadians moved to towns and cities and as the demands of an emerging industrialized society were felt. Role differentiation was accentuated. Men left their place of residence to go to their place of work. Children no longer stayed at home, but were forced to attend schools. Woman remained in the home, isolated. Upon her fell the responsibility of holding the family together and instilling the moral virtues in her children. With this role division came an increasing stress upon character differentiation between men and women.

This role division was not artificial or imposed. Throughout centuries women had played a nurturing role and in the mid-to late-nineteenth century this role was of great significance. Canadian women did not question staying in the home. Child-bearing and child-rearing practices meant there were good reasons for women to perceive themselves as mothers. Because a woman gave birth to more children than a woman does today, women in the nineteenth century spent more time caring for their children. Because of a shorter life expectancy than today, woman's career in the nineteenth century was motherhood. She had time for little more. For most women the rhetoric of woman's sphere simply enhanced their prestige and confirmed their own lives. At the same time, however, it locked them into a restricted realm of endeavour.

The role division between male and female founded upon general trends, in fact, hardened into a 'natural' role for women. Deviation from it on the part of women was considered an attack on the family. Thus it was the origin of much social pressure and conformity. At the same time, of course, it was the origin of much of the social stability in Canada at a time when society was undergoing alterations resulting from urban growth and technological change.

As the image of woman in the home, dutifully caring for her children and husband, hardened into a social maxim, those women who did not conform to it became outcasts. The image was a middle-class one. Although not a reflection of reality for most working-class women, it did become the measure of respectability, and unmarried women or women who worked were to be pitied or criticized. A woman could not enter into any sphere of temporal society without being accused of being a proponent of 'woman's rights' whose ultimate goal was the destruction of the family. If women adhered to their role they became observers not participants. If they tried to participate, in fact, compete with men, they were ridiculed. As *The Christian Guardian* observed in 1872, 'Very intellectual women are seldom beautiful, their features, and particularly their foreheads, are more or less masculine.'

It would appear that women were trapped. However there was a flaw in the image of woman's role that allowed a latitude of freedom that many women recognized. Women were to create a refuge within their homes from the materialistic and selfish world. At the same time they were to prepare their children for the temptations of that world. If women remained isolated in their homes, if they remained uninformed, how were they to prepare their children adequately? This contradiction within the concept of 'true womanhood' was used by some Canadian women to advantage when, in attempting to expand their activities outside the home, they came up against the dictates of conventional wisdom.

'THE FEMALE RIGHTER', 1878

'The Female Righter', *Grip*, Saturday, 4, May 1878, vol. x, 24.

I am a Female Righter, and
    If you will list to me,
I soon shall make you understand,
    What sort of rights they be.

I want upon the lounge to sleep,
    Or read, or take my ease;
And want the right my house to keep
    As dirty as I please.

I want the right the meat to roast,
    Quite the reverse of well;
And want the right to make the toast,
    Full indigestible.

I want the right mid linen white,
    To mix the rust spots red;
And want the right on every night
    To find bugs in the bed.

I want the right to let each child
    Do just as it shall please,
Till not a soul—they've got so wild—
    Can get a minute's ease.

I want the right to make the man,
    Who chose to marry me,
Buy twice for me what buy he can,
    Or live in misery.

I want the right my walks to take,
    In silk and satin gay,
And tell my husband he can break,
    If that he cannot pay.

I want the right to make a speech,
    Before a yelling crowd,
And high upon a platform screech
    And objurgate aloud.

I want the franchise of the land
Which now the men have got,
To vote on all I understand
And all that I do not.

These are the rights of woman, and
You'd best oppose them not,
Or when we get the upper hand,
We'll teach you what is what.

WOMAN'S SPHERE, 1856

The Proper Sphere and Influence of Woman in Christian Society. A lecture delivered by Reverend Robert Sedgewick before the Young Men's Christian Association, Halifax, Nova Scotia, November 1856.

It seems somewhat strange that at this time of day there should be any necessity for discussing the subject which has just been announced, either from the pulpit or the press, or in the Lecture room, as on the present occasion. One would have thought that this at least was a settled question —that it had been decided by universal consent, and that the unanimous voice of civilized and Christian man had definitely and permanently fixed the sphere and influence of woman in Christian society; but it is not so, and at this present time, and especially on this continent, this very question is agitated with a freedom and a fierceness too which augur badly for its settlement on reasonable and scriptural grounds, by those who view it in its moral aspects.

The errors and blunders which are interwoven with the subject of woman's rights and woman's place in modern society are, as these points now engage public attention, to be traced either to the ignoring of the fact or the omission of the fact that in the economy of nature or rather in the design of God, *woman is the complement of man.* In defining her sphere and describing her influence, this fact is fundamental. Unless this fact be admitted as an axiom in every way self-evident, no reasoning on this subject is sound, and no conclusion legitimate, and the whole theme becomes little better than a mass of mere assumption, alike illogical in its progress and unsatisfactory in its conclusions.

In many respects woman is the equal of man. Save in the matter of sex, she has similar form and features. In the higher departments of human nature, she is man's fellow. Her mind comprehends similar powers—her heart similar passions and affections. Regarding woman as Shakespeare regarded man, the apostrophe is as deserved as it is descriptive.

What a piece of work is woman! How noble in reason; how infinite in faculty; in form and moving, how express and admirable; in action, how like an angel; in appearance, how like a god! It were enough to establish all this by an appeal to history. What man has done as an intellectual and an emotional being, woman has done. What man has done as an active being, woman has done also; or if there be any superiority in these respects on the side of man, the reason does not lie so much in the nature of the powers as in the opportunity furnished for their development and application; hence the stores of literature, ancient and modern, have been mightily enriched by the contributions of female genius and skill. If Greece had a Homer it had a Sappho too, each immortal in the divine art of poetry. If England had a Gibbon and a Hume, whose stately pen traced in flowing periods the story of the rise and the ruin of the kingdoms of the earth, it had a Strickland, who, with facile and graphic pen, described the faculties, the fortunes and the fate of England's Queens. If America had a Cooper whose glowing fancy bound as with an enchanter's spell, and an Irving, whose pathos in describing the pangs of a broken heart has melted into womanish tenderness the stoutest heart that ever beat in man's bosom, when reading of it, it has among the multitudes of its gentle authors a Harriet Beecher Stowe, a woman of whom the world is proud—a woman who has exalted not her sex but her race—a woman whose clear intellect has blazed out with an effulgence which shall dazzle into darkness the sorrows she reveals, and whose wide heart has rushed forth with a stream—a resistless stream—of loving kindness and tender mercy, which shall sweep the miseries of slavery from the face of the earth.

... [W]oman is the equal of man, alike in the matter of intellect, emotion, and activity, and ... she has shewn her capabilities in these respects, ... It would never do, however, from these premises, to draw the conclusion that woman behoves and is bound to exert her powers in the same direction and for the same ends as man. This were to usurp the place of man—this were to forget her position as the complement of man, and assume a place she is incompetent to fill, or rather was not designed to fill. This were to leap out of her sphere and attempt to move in another, in which, to move rightly, the whole moral relations of society would behove to be changed, and suited anew to each other, but which, because they are unchangeable, every attempt is fraught with damage, it may be with ruin, and woman becomes a wandering star, which, having left its due place, and violated its prescribed relations, dashes itself into shivers against some other planet, whose path it crossed in the eccentricity of its movements, and goes out in the blackness of darkness for ever.

Perhaps the condition of woman in savage life affords one of the best, though a melancholy illustration, of this point. Surely in a state of society, in which it is deplored as a great family calamity, when a woman child is born into the world, in which female infanticide is established by the law, in which a man sells his daughter (not having previously murdered her) to be the slave of the passions of a man as savage as himself, while he lives, and to be killed in cold blood in honour of his death, when he dies, surely in a state of society in which all this is tolerated and sanctioned, woman is not moving in her proper sphere. Surely a state of society which regards woman as a slave because she is woman, and reduces her to the level, and in some cases beneath the level, of a beast of burden, and while loading her with the cares of wife-hood and mother-hood, condemns her at the same time to the veriest *serf-hood*—tilling the land, sowing and gathering the crop—providing in short for the family, and allowing her master, not her husband, ah! no, but her master, to fatten on her toils, and in brutish laziness to spend his time, except when roused by the excitement of the chase or maddened by the conflicts of war, *cannot* furnish the proper sphere of woman; and when the rude mess is spread out on the ruder table, and when the savage in his savageism, gorging his inflamed appetite in barbaric solitude, or surrounded by his companions in laziness and in lust, frowns from his presence the woman he debases, and scarce deigns to cast her the refuse of his disgusting meal, it is manifest that somehow some sad revolution has befallen our race, and that woman is not moving in her proper sphere. And how unnatural for woman, nevertheless of the necessity of the thing or the romance of the thing, to be mixed up with the pomp and the circumstance, with the din and the strife of war. It has been that women have guided armies to battle, and by their skill and bravery led them to victory. It has been, that disguising her sex, and to gratify some fond passion or some wild curiosity, a gentle maiden has entered the ranks, and submitted to the punctilios and the severities of military discipline, but the voice of nature disapproves of the step, and at once pronounces it unbecoming and dangerous. The Amazons, that race of warlike women so famous in Grecian story and Grecian song, were but a mythic race after all; and the fact that women, as a class, have never been embodied for warlike purposes in any period of the world, or by any nation of the earth, would seem to demonstrate the incongruity which attaches to warlike women, and that female soldiers would be an outrageous anomaly in the body politic.

It must be granted indeed that woman's influence has often been the occasion of war; and when defensive wars were found to be necessary— when the aggressor had to be driven back and trodden down—when country and creed, when home and liberty, when nationality itself were in jeopardy by the invading foe, and there was nothing for it but to conquer or be destroyed, many a mother has devoted her son on the altar of their country, and hailed it as an honour, even when they fell in their country's defence, or, perchance, when they survived the campaign, and returned laden with laurels, though wearing the marks of their hard service, how has her heart beat with joy and her eye gleamed with gladness as she looked on their scars or listened to their tale of the gory struggle which secured to her and her nation, their altars and their homes.

And if the tented field be not woman's place, much less is the luxurious seraglio in which youth and beauty are prostituted under the sweet name of marriage to the pampering of the worst passions of the vilest voluptuary. A harem cannot be a home. The two words are not synonymous; and the man who should attempt to assert that they are convertible terms, no matter whether he be Turk or Christian, would be a fool for his pains. Polygamy is a violent intrusion into the sphere of woman; it displaces her from her rightful position in the constitution of nature; it is an impious improvement on the simplicity of the Divine arrangement; it is seeking for many what can only be obtained for one; it impeaches the wisdom of God, and thwarts the good of man. How can it comport with the prime principle on which the marriage relation proceeds. For this cause shall a man leave his father and his mother, and cleave *to his wife*, and they twain shall be one....

And if the tented field be not woman's sphere, nor the luxurious seraglio, so neither is the gloomy nunnery. Setting aside for the time the ecclesiastical view of the matter, and the spiritual aspect of it too, (for with these, in present circumstances, it would be improper to meddle) pray what is the social aspect of the nunnery? So far as it goes, it is a breaking up of the social compact; so far as it goes, it deprives man of his complement; so far as it goes, it lessens, by every inmate within its walls, the homes of society, for everybody must see that in other circumstances the nun might have been a wife, and that wife a mother; and thus it is the nunnery *versus* home—it is the nunnery and its seclusion against home with its openness; it is the nunnery and its thraldom against home with its freedom; it is the nunnery and its asceticism against home with its cheerfulness; it is the nunnery and its gloom against home with its gladness....

Were it not that so much is said about it in the neighboring States, it would seem utterly preposterous to assert that Parliament was the proper sphere of woman, and that she is just where she ought to be when sitting on the red benches, and is engaged as she ought to be in drawing out Bills—in explaining and defending them—in standing in the arena of angry debate, and condemning and counterworking one course of policy by justifying and furthering another, and as is thought a better. Now first of all it might be asked how are women to get there? Are they to set up as candidates for the representation and come out on the hard-shell ticket or the soft-shell ticket, on the red or the blue; and are they to appear on the hustings on the day of nomination, and, unless unanimously elected, to demand a poll? One thing is certain—he would be a sheriff indeed who succeeded in keeping the peace, on the day of election, provided the contest lay between a male and a female candidate, and much more if it lay between two female candidates. And then is it to be a mixed Assembly, are the honorable man-members and woman-members to meet together and unite their wisdom in legislating for their country, then who is to be the speaker, surely gallantry would not suffer such an insult to be perpetrated as to keep the favourite political heroine out of the chair; and think of her arrayed in her robes of office and addressed as Mrs. Speaker or Miss Speaker, as the case may be, and with what deference would honorable members acknowledge her when they crossed the chair and with what reverential obeisance would they uncover before her august presence, and when angry debate arose and crimination was met with recrimination, and when the logomachy was just at its wildest, how would the ceiling ring with the authoritative command, "order, order," not pronounced, *ore rotundo*, as in former times, but with the shrill, piercing, biting tones of female good nature; or are the women to have a separate House and to manage the public business themselves, untrammelled by the presence, unawed by the criticism of their fellow male-members? This would be a Parliament with a vengeance. This if ever would be a speaking Assembly. And what are the powers with which such a House is to be invested? Are they to be subordinate to the other House? That would never do. Or are they to be co-ordinate with them? That would be as unsatisfactory. Or, as probably the ladies would wish it, are they to be superordinate? Why, the claim would be resented as a most presumptuous invasion of the rights of men, and as utterly intolerable as fairly beyond the limits of the Constitution.

It might seem indelicate to conjecture the business to be introduced and transacted by this female Parliament. There would likely be a revival of the old sumptuary laws, a measure which they would unanimously declare was fairly within their power to introduce, and which moreover they imagined they were best fit to manage, and hence the likelihood that on some fitting afternoon of the female session some honorable member would ask to leave to introduce a bill for the better regulation of male dress and adornment, consisting of but two sections, the first bearing that no gentleman within the ages of sixteen and twenty-four be permitted to wear a moustache on his upper lip more than two inches long, and the second bearing that no gentleman within said age to wear more than three rings on his right hand.

It may be after all that ridicule is the test of truth, and that the best way of dealing with such a vagary as this is to cover it with the ludicrous. It may be that the restlessness and the folly of the men and the women, who in such a mad attempt are doing their utmost to turn the world upside down, are best exposed by subjecting them to the test of the grotesque and ridiculous. But seriously, that the question of investing woman with similar political rights with man, and demanding of her the discharge of similar political duties, should have arisen at this time of day, after such a world-wide and world-long experience, is indeed one of the wonders of the age....

... Politics at best is but a crude instrument of reform, incapable of nice discrimination, often including the good in its condemnations and in its legal justifications the bad, and furnishing endless examples, both in the persons who are condemned and in the penalties which are inflicted, how inferior in precision, justice and equity, is any human law when compared with the Divine. Even the best agents who are selected for the execution of our criminal codes are so blind that they never detect half the offenders, so slow that they never catch half whom they detect, and so subject to weakness and to every quality of human bias that justice, in passing through their hands, is sometimes sweetened into compassion and pardon, and sometimes vitriolized into vengeance, before it reaches its object. But the tribunal of a pure conscience and an enlightened reason, which the true reformer, the true mother and the true teacher can establish in the human breast, suffers no offending deed, nay, no offending thought or desire, to escape, holds the balances of justice with untrembling hands, and punishes by tale and by weight, according to self conscious accusations, rewards too for every good deed that is done. What gentle woman, pondering upon these truths, will not exclaim, I had rather be a doorkeeper in the house where such as Christ took in his arms and blessed, are gathered together, than to dwell in political tents and be crowned with all political honours. Nothing, as it seems to be, can account for the present clamour in behalf of women voters and women office-holders but the amazingly false notions which prevail respecting the intrinsic dignity and enduring importance of education, as compared with the ephemeral tinsel of political distinctions. Respecting the clean and beautiful work of the teacher, training up characters to empyrean height and purity, as compared with the noisome and bloody work of the politician, sometimes flaying and cauterizing, and sometimes amputating and beheading, to cure or cut away from the body politic those frightful gangrenes whose very existence would have been prevented by the intelligent and faithful performance of woman's earlier and holier service. As to the idea that woman has a self evident and inalienable right to assist in the government of the race, I reply she does assist in that government now, and would to heaven she would exercise a still larger share in its administration. But this great work, like all others, is naturally divided between the sexes, the nobler government of children belonging to women, the less noble government of adults to man.

But, if the Halls of Legislature and of Congress were opened to women, they would purify them it is said. The answer to this must recognize both hypotheses respecting the sexes. First, if woman is like man, why should she not do as man has done, only aggravating and multiplying his evil works, because then the competitors would be doubled and all restraints with-drawn. But secondly, as I contend, woman is unlike man, better when she is good and worse when she is bad. Then, at least, in the present state of society, I believe that her participation in political strifes, ambitions and cupidities, would rouse to tempestuous fury all the passions that ever swept her to swiftest perdition.—Men and women are yet drawn together by too many passional affinities to allow us even to hope that husbands could leave their wives, and wives their husbands, and pass for months and months, by day and by night, through all the enforced intimacies and juxta-positions of legislative life without something more than pure platonic emo-tions, and she who wishes her sex to encounter these perils has forgotten the wisest prayer that was ever made, "Lead us not into temptation." . . .

In justice, however, to the other side of this question, perhaps I ought not to omit certain collateral and incidental benefits which may be claimed to accrue should woman strip off her sex and rough it with man in the turbulence and riot of the political arena. What a beautiful school for domestic debate; prolonged not merely from morn to dewy eve, but from eve to early morn, should the father be a whig, the mother a democrat, and the daughter a third party man. On the stump, at the hustings or other bear-garden, the intimate relation of husband and wife would furnish admirable facilities for mutual impeachment and recrimi-nation, which to bachelors and marriage haters would be intensely edify-ing. If husband and wife were rivals for the same office, then, no matter which party might prevail, the honour and emoluments would still come into the family, or, if both were elected to Senate or House, they might pelt each other from the opposition benches, which would be a great relief from closer quarters. It is well known that, in every political campaign, there is a vast deal of Paul Prying and eaves-dropping to be done to learn the enemy's strategy, but in this new Utopia the husband might just as honorably get at the wife's correspondence by picking a lock, or the wife get at the husband's secrets by tickling him to talk in his sleep. As to the parents' equal right to inculcate hostile political doctrines on the minds of their children they might make a compromise, each devoting alternate les-sons on alternate days to the exposure of the other's iniquities, so that the children in the end would have a good opportunity to know the weakness of them both.

From the making of laws, and all the trouble attendant on the process, the transition is easy, in this argument, to their administration; and cer-tainly, if in the former case woman is out of her sphere, she would seem as improperly situated, whether on the bench deciding, or at the bar accusing, or in the jury-box weighing, or in the jail watching, or as a sheriff issuing a mandamus for the apprehension of some poor wight who had somehow outraged the decorum of society, or as a constable dodging him in all his doublings till he was fairly caught and lodged in limbo.

What can be more unfeminine than a woman thief-catcher? It is true she might answer somewhat ably in this department in the matter of skill and adroitness, the natural shrewdness of the woman's head would often be a match for the cunning and the craft of the housebreaker or the thief, but the constable's staff, as wielded by her arm, would scarce stand against the blow of the ruffian's practised fist, that would be very apt to come in contact with her face, and perchance paint her eye a little too darkly to comport with the lines of feminine beauty.

Even a posse of such constables might not suffice, for most assuredly might would overcome right, and thus the majesty of law would be insulted in the loss of its victim. And how think you would the jury-box look when packed with twelve honored matrons, or with an agreeable mixture of youth and beauty and age and experience, keeping out of sight the necessary absence from home, as it often happens for weeks together, and the compulsory attendance on Court, for it would never do to relax the law of attendance, and the coarse contact with all sorts of persons to which they would be exposed, and the other thousand and one annoyances connected with their situation. How would they look in the jury-box? Is it likely that there would be a sufficiently cool and unbiassed weighing of evidence as would secure an equitable and just verdict? Especially, is it likely that, on the evidence being closed and the counsel, rising in solemn grandeur, utters the usual exordium, Ladies of the Jury, where would be that staid attention and that resolute resistance against the sophistries and plausibilities which he might employ to mystify the question and entangle their minds, that are so requisite in order that the ends of justice be served and a righteous verdict brought in? But the judge has laid down the law, and, after a charge of some three hours length, they are sent into the jury room with the injunction to prepare and bring in their verdict in due course. Locked up in their apartment and told that they must be unanimous in their judgment, and that they are neither to eat nor drink, not even the solitary cup of tea, till they have decided, alas! for the verdict when it is brought in and the interests of the parties involved in the suit.

And, even though there was nothing of the incongruous and unbecoming about the thing generally, look at the kind of questions they would have to try. Take the docket of the Supreme Court, either civil or criminal, and is it to be thought that the most intelligent and wisest among our women are competent to sit on them? It would be as wise to submit the question of colour to a man that was born blind, or of harmony to a man who could not hear. What is a woman expected to know whether a drain be dug with the right inclination, or a pile of bricks be really merchantable? What is a woman to know whether the farrier has just done the right thing by the horse, or whether the jockey has not diddled the greenhorn? These are a sample of the questions which juries have to settle, and the bare mention of them is sufficient to show that they cannot be adjusted to the general satisfaction except by persons whose every day employment, or whose professional calling, brings them into contact with the business and the commerce of every day life. And, if the incongruity is obvious in the civil, much more is it obvious in the criminal department; and, as the instincts and feelings of nature are against them, on being engaged in the one case, much more are they against women being engaged in the other.

It might be useful to expand this particular to much greater length, as was indicated at the commencement of the illustration, and show how unsuitable the profession of law is to female capability and tendency and female position, but there is so much of the subject yet to overtake that a very few words must suffice.

That the legal profession is honourable, notwithstanding the vulgar prejudices against it, none will deny whose opinion is worth any thing on the subject. That this profession is necessary in the present state of society is as readily admitted. There seems to be something natural about the spirit of litigation, and that it has not merely been begotten out of the complex social relations which bind us to each other. It is not a small class of persons who have an itch for law, and to whom few things give more real pleasure, more exquisite delight, than a well gaining law plea, and thus it is that the necessity of the case demands that there be a class of persons who shall make the laws of the land their study, the due administration of them their business. Now, should woman be engaged in this profession? Does it comport with correct ideas of female character and position that there should be gentle women learned in the law? Are the questions which law behoves to settle such as women should entertain, and are the means which be necessary to settle these questions such as women should employ? Some of you know what is meant by a lawyer's letter, should women be employed to write them? Some of you know the power of a summons, should women be authorized to issue them? Some of you are aware of the functions of a barrister, should women, arrayed in legal vestments, practise at the bar? There are some magistrates before me, and, for aught I know, some of the judges of the land, would you be greatly assisted or honoured with one or more female coadjutors on the bench? Is it fitting that women should bring ugly and complex and vile cases into Court, and have their intellect, and heart too, engaged and affected, so as to make the most and the best of the case of their client? One would think that the drawing of deeds and conveyances, that arranging marriage settlements and dowager's portions, that framing issues and extending condescendences, that, in short, stating questions and getting up answers, and furnishing duplise and replies, so as best to prolong the cause and hinder it from dragging its dull slow length along, was any thing but suitable exercise either for a woman's head or a woman's heart, either for a woman's tongue or a woman's pen. There is little enough,

God wot, among us of genuine simplicity. Our factitious state has well nigh engulphed whatever of nature and heart a poor man had left him. The artificial and technical has all but absorbed the real and the true; and go where we will, with but one exception, and even that is scarce an exception, there is such a mixture of the deleterious about it—I mean into the bosom of a Christian family—go where we will, we meet with so much that is mere surface and show, so much that prevents you from seeing things and persons just as they are, that, were our daughters and our wives to give themselves to law and spend their lives in threading its mazes and applying its provisions, our homes would be metamorphosed into dingy dens where skill and craft try to outwit each other, and our parlours into scenes of moody silence or cold reserve, or of suspicion fearful of disclosure and defeat.

It would be no easy matter to decide which would be most hurtful to man at large, were women to become politicians on the one hand or lawyers on the other, but should the time come which is so ardently sought for by the fanatical advocates of Woman's Rights, that they would be both—these very parties would be the first to feel, and not the last to acknowledge, that they had raised a demon and given him a place in a sacred temple reared for another and a nobler inmate, which no mere human power would be able to exercise.

Even at the risk of being tedious on this part of the subject, there seems a necessity for stating that the public factory is not the proper sphere of woman. It is granted that physiologically the framework of the female is more delicate and fragile than that of man, and it is granted too that her mental constitution has been cast in a finer mould, and the whole texture of the mechanism of her inner nature is every way more susceptible and impressible. All this is admitted. Now, even taking this lowest possible view of the case, how detrimental to the health to be *confined*, I use the word advisedly, to be *confined* in the rooms of a factory, no matter how well ventilated, for ten hours a day, and that too for six days in the week. It has been found that, even when an ordinary amount of health was possessed, yet, in consequence of the temperature of the apartments and other circumstances, when females enter such places very young they reach womanhood prematurely, and sink down into an early old age, worn out in constitution at a period of their lives when they might have been enjoying lusty health. And how detrimental to their mental, as well as their bodily health, such confinement. The din and the whirl, the rumble and the roll, of the machinery acting on their mental and moral nature so as to destroy, or all but destroy, that fineness of feeling and gentleness of behaviour which seem connatural to woman from the very fact of her sex; a factory girl, in Scotland at least, being but another phrase for coarseness of temper and vulgarity of deportment. Other causes indeed help to produce such a result, but the one just indicated is the prime one, intensifying with much of their malignity the other deteriorating influences to which this situation subjects them.

Is there not something unnatural also in the restraints which are hereby inflicted on woman? At half-past five of early morn the chime of the factory-bell is heard, it may be, amid the dreams of a troubled sleep, rousing the child of labour to her day's weary darg; with hasty unconcern she finishes her rude toilet, and, all untaught to kneel before the Lord her Maker, to ask him either for mercy or grace, she rushes forth, no matter whether it be in sunshine or in storm, and hurries onward lest she be but a minute too late at her post and lest that minute's price be deducted from her scanty earnings at the week's end. And now the toil begins. The monster wheel or mightier engine, setting the whole house a trembling and demanding the incessant attention of eyes and hands and feet till the hour of the morning meal calls for a suspension, and that meal hastily snatched and the time expired, why the labour is renewed with the same monotony and the same fatigue as before, till, by the time the day closes, nature is well nigh exhausted, and the weary, languid child, with scarce leisure to romp with her playmates, and unable to mix in the gambols and pleasantries of buoyant youth happy in its freedom, retires to the same trundle bed to sleep the same troubled sleep, to wake to the same hard unmusical chime, to drag out the same weary day's darg, and thus—

> Work, work, work,
> While the cock is crowing aloof,
>   And work, work, work,
> 'Till the stars shine through the roof,
>   Its better to be a slave,
> Along with the turbaned Turk
> Where woman has never a soul to save
>   If this is Christian work!
>
> Work, work, work,
> Till the brain begins to swim,
>   Work, work, work,
> Till the eyes are heavy and dim,
> Shuttle and beam and lay,
> And lay, and shuttle and beam,
> Till over the loom I fall asleep,
> And still we toil on in a dream.
>
> O men with sisters dear,
> O men with mothers and wives,
> It's not factory cotton you're weaving out,
> But human creatures lives.

Clank, clank, clank,
In poverty, hunger and dirt,
Weaving at once with the weary loom,
A shroud as well as a shirt.

But we argue that the factory is not the sphere of woman on many additional grounds. It is impossible, for example, that women engaged in factories can be at all acquainted, or at any rate be expert, in household duties. How can they, when, from the time they are able, (it is something to say now, as an improvement on this, when, from the time the law allows,) they are sent to the factory, and thus are denied the opportunity of getting the information? "Can you wash?" so said one young girl to another who was working in a factory: "Can you wash?" "No, but my mother can do it." "Can you bake?" "No, but my mother can do it." "Can you darn?" "No, but my mother can do it." And yet, now-a-days, it is come to this, that even the women who have spent their teens in factories, when they become wives and mothers, are entirely ignorant of the art of housekeeping, and just because of this ignorance a vast, a very legion, of evils has sprung up in our social state, evils which are positively eradicating home, and the pleasures of home, out of the teeming working population of our large cities.

In public factories there is, to a great extent, the promiscuous mingling of the sexes. Now, though there were no other evils growing out of this fact, as alas! there is, and these neither few nor small, it leads to early, imprudent, and improvident marriages. Parties are joined in wedlock in our large manufacturing towns, who, because they work in the same factory, become acquainted, and, as they think, attached to each other. As often happens, they are young persons from the country; well, they have no home—they have no property, except their time, not even a bed they can call their own—no apparel, except what is commonly called their working clothes—nothing, in short, but their time, and the worth of their time which they get of a Saturday afternoon—yet they take it into their heads to marry, and married they are . . . .

It is now time that woman's sphere in Christian society be defined and described. It has been shown negatively what it is not. It requires to be shown positively what it is, and, after the previous statements and illustrations, this is no difficult matter. Indeed, the matter is settled in your own minds, and therefore it would seem there is little or no necessity to announce it formally. The sphere of woman is home and whatever is co-relative with home in the social economy.

And what a word is home. Compare it with the word camp—compare it with the word harem—compare it with the word convent—compare it with the word parliament—compare it with the word court—compare it with the word factory—so far as woman is concerned, and how vastly more seemly and natural are the notions we entertain of her sphere in the one case than those which we entertain of her sphere in the other? In the use of any of these words, as relating to woman, there is associated a feeling of the incongruous and misplaced; but in the use of the word home, as relating to woman, there is just as naturally associated a feeling of the fitting and the just, a feeling of the congruous and the appropriate, in social life. Now this fact, for fact it is, settles the question—what is the sphere of woman? It tells us where God intended her to move—it tells where we ought ever to find her—not in the camp roughing it with the soldier, but at home—not in the harem quarrelling with her rival, but at home—not in the nunnery wasting her young affections in sentimental pietism, but at home—not in the senate hall in stormy debate or in deep divan, but at home—not in the court of justice and dealing in the severe necessities of law, but amid the charities of home—not, in a word, in the greasy factory where dust and debris are so uncongenial with the fragility of her frame and the gentleness of her heart, but at home amid the quiet and the peace, and the purity and the love, of which she is alike the source and the recipient.

Besides, it is only at home and its co-relative situations that man finds woman to be his complement. In no other situation she can fill, in no other sphere in which she can move, will she so answer the end of her being, so far as this point goes, but at home; and this fact also, for fact it is, settles the question—what is the sphere of woman? In the camp she must either be the superior or the subordinate or the equal of man; she cannot be his complement, or, at least, she is so with multitudinous drawbacks. In the harem she is his slave. In the nunnery she has violently torn in sunder the ties which bind her to human society. And whether as a legislator or a lawyer, or a drudge at the factory wheel, why, she loses every thing of the woman but her sex and its weaknesses, and seems, like the Egyptian sphinx, to have more natures than one.

It being thus clear that home is the sphere of woman in the social economy, a question arises at this point—how is she to be adjusted to her place? It is true that there is a designed corresponding between the situation and the persons to fill it, the natural powers and capabilities of the agent suiting in the most admirable style possible the allotted region of activity, but all experience proves, indeed, the testing of the race, in its social bearings, is but the story of the perverted powers and the misdi-rected capabilities of the human being, woman as well as man, and some would say chiefly woman. Now, these perverted powers must be restored to their original functions and these misdirected capabilities to their true objects. All means and appliances must be put in requisition in order that woman may, as she is naturally capable, so in point of fact fill her place in the manner and to the extent that the social economy demands, hence the necessity of education, and of such education begun in early life, and hence the necessity too of a suitable education of the importance of her sphere. The wide and persuasive and powerful influence she exerts is such, that, on her due qualification depends the weal of the race, from its base to its summit, from its rudimental state all through its progress, till it reach step by step the point of a perfect civilization.

It is not the design of this lecture to treat on female education. It would seem that this point was taken for granted in the subject, and that it was admitted that, whatever the sphere, woman was qualified rightly to move in it, still the unity of the theme could not have been preserved unless some slight reference were had to this matter.

Now, there can be no doubt that the three r's, as the Irishman said, are important parts of female education, reading, writing and arithmetic. These lie at the foundation of all useful knowledge, indeed, without them the main instrumentality of acquiring knowledge is awanting, and there can be as little doubt also that the elegant accomplishments, when they can be acquired, may add very much to the usefulness of woman at home. Music and drawing, and painting and embroidery, and a smattering of French and Italian, of heavy German and clumsy Dutch, are all so many acquirements which, if once obtained, may serve to enliven a drawing room conversation and amuse and please for the nonce a drawing room party, and then they are easily retained, other things being equal, and may be exceedingly useful in various situations in life; nor can any body refuse to admit, who is willing to do woman justice, that it is quite competent and that it may be advantageous for her to dabble among the 'ologies and dive deep down into their dark regions. There is geology and ethnology and conchology and entomology, then biology and phrenology and astrology, if you will, all of them in their place somewhat instructive, all of them in their place somewhat profitable, even for a woman to know. Indeed, in certain circles of society, where these and cognate themes may happen to be the subject of conversation, a woman looks exceedingly small, if, by her silence or the irrevelancy of her remarks, she betrays her entire ignorance and the defective nature of her education; and hence the necessity and the propriety of introducing these departments of knowledge into the curriculum of our female academies and boarding-schools. But there are other 'ologies as well of which no woman, if she is to move in her sphere as she ought to, can afford to remain ignorant. There is the sublime science of washology and its sister bakeology. There is darnology and scrubology. There is mendology, and cookology in its wide comprehensiveness and its untellable utility, a science this the more profoundly it is studied it becomes the more palatable, and the more skilfully its principles are applied its professors acquire the greater popularity and are regarded with a proportionate degree of interest and complacency. Now, all this knowledge must be embraced in any system of female education that pretends to prepare woman for the duties of life.—

The knowledge of housekeeping is not only not beneath her notice and regard, but is essentially necessary if she is to be at home what home expects her to be, if, in a word, she is at all to fill her place with credit to herself and comfort to those with whom she may be associated, as daughter or sister, as wife or mother, as instructress or friend, or any other relationship she may sustain to general society. And, in order that these several departments of her education may be kept in their due place and pursued according to their relative importance—that they may be purified and elevated and chastened, and thus that by their union they may subserve to the grand end of manifesting in all its varied and attractive loveliness the female character, they must be baptized, nay, permeated with the spirit and power of true religion. It has been said that man, with all his irreligion, is a religious being. The paradox, if true at all, is eminently true of woman. There is a special unnaturalness existing and manifest between the doctrines and duties and delights of evangelical Christianity and the intellectual and spiritual process of her inner nature, and hence her aptitude for piety in its principles and practices and pleasures, hence too her attainments, and hence the vast influence which godliness exerts on herself and which it enables her to exert on others. Now, to complete her education, religion must come in—not to subsidize, but to regulate and control—not as subordinate, but as principal—not as mere *addenda* to what may be regarded as otherwise complete in itself, but as that without which nothing else is or can be complete—in short, the end of true religion, the glory of God as connected with the source of true religion, the sacrifice of Christ, must be exhibited every day as the grand object that is to be sought by all the essential and ornamental departments of her physical and mental and moral training, according as it is written, "Ye are not your own, but bought with a price; glorify God with your bodies and spirits, which are God's; whether therefore ye eat or drink, or whatsoever ye do, do all to the glory of God, and present your bodies living sacrifices, holy and acceptable, which is your reasonable service." ...

Having thus ascertained the sphere of woman, and adverted to the qualifications which she behoves to possess, that she may be and do what her situation demands, the way is now prepared for the consideration of the influence she exerts in Christian society.

Now, first of all the things—the qualifications just indicated being granted—this influence is extensive, nay, universal.—Where woman is she makes herself felt, but where woman is enlightened by education, and elevated and purified by piety, she makes herself felt for good through every ramification of the body-social. Like the light and heat of the sun, which diffuse themselves everywhere, so everywhere are there indications of her presence and her spirit. From the cellar to the attic there are marks of her tidy hand and her thoughtful heart. The well ordered kitchen owns her sway. The bedroom and parlour and drawing-room confess her authority. The table, and the chimney itself, are fairly within the reach of her pervasive power and must yield to the decisions of her judgment. Children smile in her approval or grieve under her frown.—Old men regard her as a ministering spirit commissioned to cheer and comfort when every other source of enjoyment has gone. She is the light of the dwelling when the dark cloud of adversity envelopes it, and when death crosses the threshhold and with ruthless hand snatches away from it the valued and the dear, it is her hand which wipes away the tear, even when her own eyes are streaming—it is her meek and quiet demeanour and calm submission which soothes and tranquillizes the bereaved mourner.

And, as has been asserted, this influence extends beyond her own proper sphere. If it be chiefly felt at home, it is nevertheless felt and acknowledged abroad. It reaches the schoolroom and college-hall. It finds its way into the workshop and the busy store. It is realized on 'Change, and even, as some of you well know, in the sweating room of the Bank. And though woman herself, as has been demonstrated, would be altogether out of her place on the red benches of the Parliament House, yet who will deny that she makes herself felt, even in these high places of the land, and helps to modify the acting of our representatives and rulers?

And then this influence is powerful, extensive. It is mighty. It may be resisted indeed, even as the pleasant light may be excluded from some dirty room lest its filth and its disorder be made manifest. It may be resisted indeed, as the genial heat may be prevented from radiating, and thus warming all within its scope. But, let it have fair play and full action, and just as light and heat, unchecked in their operation, reveal and revive all within their reach, so will this influence affect and subdue, and enlighten and raise, and purify and etherialize and sublimate, all and every one whose nature is capable of feeling this influence, all and every thing that, as an enchantress, she touches with her wonder working wand.

Besides this influence, extensive and powerful, is eminently gentle. It works silently. It is meek in its majesty. This is one of the elements of its power. Like the gentle dew it falls upon the place beneath unseen, unheard. Sometimes it happens there is a little friction, and, in working out her will in her household, or as a member of a household over which she presides, there may occasionally be a collision, but who knows not that she has an emollient in her possession, aye, and that she has the skill to use it, by the timeous application of which the friction ceases and the bruises which the collision may have caused are effectually and speedily healed. The glance of her eye—the sweet smile playing on her countenance—the kind conciliatory word falling from her lips—nay, the very look which she sometimes casts on one, more eloquent far than the softest words which ever fell from her tongue—succeed more efficaciously in maintaining family harmony where it is, and restoring it where it is not, than all other influences put together.

One more general statement. This influence is refining and polishing. It rubs down the hirsute coarseness of man. It frowns vulgarity into a corner, and abashes the impudent forwardness of the pert and assuming. Where it is unknown or trodden under foot, why there is savageism untamed, there is license unbridled, there is heartless cruelty and beastly debasement; but, where it is known and felt, the savage is a savage no more, licence and libertinism tremble and flee, kindness supplants cruelty and manly dignity beastly degradation. A well educated and godly woman can make, and has made, the bully quiet and the boor mannerly, and the brawler meek and gentle as a lamb. In the presence of such a woman the lips of the profane are sealed and the tongue of the obscene is locked in his jaws. Ribaldry and scurrility are frightened into propriety, and, in spite of all that is said to the contrary, it is nevertheless true that slander herself is reft of her weapons, and, if not, yet what is as good, she is shorn of her power to use them as she chooses.

From this general view of the influence of woman, however, but a very imperfect idea of its nature is obtained after all.—It must be contemplated in detail if it is to be correctly understood. It may be useful, therefore, to look at woman in her varied relationships, for the purpose of grasping somewhat of its nature.

She first of all appears in the relation of a daughter. Now, does not the very utterance of the word daughter suggest to the mind of every parent, whose heart is in the right place, a kind and an amount of influence alike powerful and pleasing, alike extensive and intense. In infancy she exerts, unconscious to herself of course, but still she exerts, an influence which positively bends a parent's heart around her, and draws out of that heart all it can pour of interest and love and delight. But, it is not this profuse power which deserves notice chiefly here, because the infant son has an equal, some would hold a greater, power over the parent than the infant daughter. It is the active influence she exerts in the period of after life, and amid the vicissitudes through which the family may pass. Arrived at the period of girlhood, and when, from her position in the family, she is required to apply her previous education for the family weal, why, if there be the average amount of the spirit of girlhood, and if its powers have reached but an average development, is she not the very soul, the life and the heart, of the family circle? She is her mother's companion—her father's friend and confidant. To the one she affords cheerful aid in the management of the household in the necessary absence of her father, or, when even at home, he may be engaged in the duties of his calling. To the other she ministers of the riches of her gladsome glee, of her piquant humour, of her racy conversation, of her sparkling wit, of her tender sympathy, and of her ardent devotional feelings, when at his own happy fireside he is solacing himself from the fatigues and cares, the toil and moil of this weary world. What father but can tell that all this is true?

And, much more, what father but feels almost as great a blank at home from the absence of his daughter as from the absence of his wife? What father but often as anxiously longs for the presence of the one as for the presence of the other? And thus, as she is the charm of the family in the season of joy, is she not the succour of the family in the hour of sorrow. When calamity happens, which involve the family fortunes, who so wise in expedients, who so expert in working them, as such a daughter? Who so ready to undergo self-denial, to an amount and of a kind as none else would endure, if so be the family fortunes might be revived and the family *status* regained. To achieve this end, and that her father's honour might be preserved or restored, many a daughter has consented that her hopes be blighted, and to bury them up in the recesses of her heart; and when all was unavailing, and when prison and death were the doleful issue, why such a daughter has contrived to be his inmate in his cell and nourish him with the milk drawn from her own breasts.

And even when sickness seizes on the household, and chiefly on the heads of the house, how timeous and tender her influence then. She is the ministering angel, whose presence and whose sympathy extracts more than half the evil from the disease, and mitigates and soothes where she cannot deliver. If no voice so tender and no hand so soft as those of a mother to a suffering child, O there is no sight so pleasing and no action so kindly as the face and the fondling of a daughter to a suffering parent.

How different, moreover, are the feelings of the parent on the marriage of a son and on that of a daughter. It is not asserted that, from that important hour, the parents feel that their son is their son no more, but, it is needless to dispute it, that from that hour they regard him as emphatically on his own hook, as now to all intents and purposes doing for himself; and most certainly he is a poltroon of a fellow, a poor spiritless thing, who, after he has taken a wife, chooses to depend on his father and mother. But how different are the feelings with which the daughter is regarded. The old tie is drawn tighter now that she is bound by a new one —the old feelings are tenderer now that she is no longer under their control—the old charm she threw over the family fireside is all the more enchanting now that she revisits it in her new capacity—and thus it is that the poet but gave utterance to nature, in one of her truest voices, when he sang in the person of a parent—

> "My son is my son till he gets a wife,
> But my daughter's my daughter all the days of her life."

It would be improper to leave this thought without looking at woman as a sister. And what power does she exert in this capacity, especially if she be an old sister. Why, in this respect she is in the parent's, in the mother's stead. How does she bustle about among the younger children and manage to keep them all in order. She is the depository of their property, she is the keeper of their secrets, she is the medium of intercourse in important affairs, in which they wish to have a little of their own will, between them and their parents. She hides their faults from each other and their parents, but encourages them to tell all these faults to their Father in heaven. Their persons and their food and their apparel—their health and cleanliness and comfort—their confidence and peace and joy—their holiness here and their bliss hereafter—all are embraced in the wide range of an old sister's care. What would the lads in a family do without their eldest sister, and what would they not do for their eldest sister? Next to their mother she lives in their heart. They are honoured in her honour. They are jealous of her reputation—as they are of her safety. She is their ornament, and they guard it with the most punctilious care, not even allowing, if that be possible, the breath of slander to sully the purity and dignity of her useful life. They joy in her joy, and her sorrows, in which they can share, are their sorrows. They live in her life, and when she dies it is thus they sing—

> Sister, thou wast mild and lovely,
>   Gentle as the summer's breeze,
> Pleasant as the air of evening
>   As it floats among the trees.
>
> Dearest sister, thou hast left us
>   And thy loss we deeply feel,
> But 'tis God who hath bereft us—
>   He can all our sorrows heal.
>
> Yet, again we hope to meet thee,
>   When the day of life is fled,
> In that deathless, sinless mansion,
>   Where no farewell tear is shed.

The influence which woman exerts as a lover is proverbially mighty and tender. When she has awakened, no matter how, that master emotion of the human breast, and when she reciprocates it, why, for the time being and ever afterwards, she sits as a queen in the heart of man, and rules him, not capriciously indeed—love is not capricious—but thoroughly and at will. She has got the key of his heart, and, having unlocked it and entered, she claims the mysterious domain as her own. She has bound him as with a spell, so that he thinks and feels and speaks and acts, he sleeps and dreams and wakes, as in a new world, in which she forms the most prominent object and over which she throws the loveliest hues. Love is essentially romantic. It is the ideal of human existence. It imbues the dull, cold realities of life with the spiritual element, and paints them with the beauteous colourings of imagination and of hope. Love is essentially poetic, and, in the wrapt musings which it inspires, the poetic fire glows as if beneath the bare, cold ribs of death. Its potency in this respect is felt, alike by the man of genuine refinement and severe taste, who would not for the world be thought so silly as to regard his lady-love as another angel, and by the unsophisticated mind, all untaught to dissemble or conceal, or even control, his emotion as he exclaims—

> Oh! Peggy, sweeter than the dawning day,
> Sweeter than gowany glens or new mawn hay,
> Blyther than lambs that frisk out o'er the knowes,
> Straighter than aught that in the forest grows.
> Her een the clearest blob of dew outshines,
> The lily in her breast its beauty tynes
> Her legs, her arms, her cheeks, her mouth, her een,
> Will be my death, and that will be shortly seen.

Now, let the woman who is thus beloved, and who honestly reciprocates it, bring her religious principles into fair and full play, and what an amount of influence for good may she not exert.

It happens occasionally, but how it is no easy matter to tell, that godly women love rakes. That somehow, all unlikely though it appears, unprincipled and ungodly men place their affections on women that fear God, and that, on the other hand, they meet and encourage their attentions. Surely this is one of love's great mysteries. Now, on the principle laid down, that woman in this case has entered the man's heart and sways over it her kindly sceptre, tell me if she has not the power to drive out thence those principles and passions which have debased and destroyed him? And she has done so in thousands of instances. The force, the gentle force, of her character, the purity and warmth of her heart, the preference she manifests for him in spite of his wildness, and the earnest entreaties poured into his ears by her streaming tears and bursting sighs, as well as by the thrilling tones of her voice, have so broken the power of the rakish propensity, as that, while a lover was made worthy of a woman's love, a soul was saved from perishing in its corruption. Chiefly has this happened when, asserting her dignity and submitting to the authority of the Word of God, she told him that, unless he agreed to act a manly and not devilish part, she would never be his. The majesty of the law of God, brought to tell by the mistress of his heart on his conscience, subdued him into penitence and reformation as it declared, "Be not unequally yoked with unbelievers, for what fellowship hath light with darkness, what concord hath Christ with Belial, what agreement hath she that believeth with an infidel?" Thus it is that virtuous love prevails. It were well if such influence as this were more frequently exerted by godly women, as it is thus so completely within their province. It would save themselves and their parents many a heart-pang. It would preserve and embellish their own character and secure the harmony and happiness of their families. And it would do, perhaps, more for abashing one species of iniquity out of sight of society than all other mere human instrumentality put together.

It is not easy to measure the depravity of the seducer, whose highest ambition is to revel on virgin purity and rob his victim of all that is valuable. "He," as Dr. Dwight expresses it, "who can adopt such a character has put off the character of a man and put on that of a fiend, and with the spirit of a fiend alone he pursues and accomplishes the infernal purpose. The ruin sought and achieved is immense. It is not the burning of a house. It is not the filching of property. It is not the deprivation of liberty. It is not the destruction of life.—The seducer plunders the wretched victim of character, morals, happiness, hope and heaven, enthrals her in the eternal bondage of sin, consumes her beyond the grave in endless fire, and murders her soul with an ever living death."

The success of the seducer, however, depends on gaining a ready ear and on injecting his poison into a heart that is not altogether unwilling to receive it. But ardent as woman is to listen to the talk of love, and confiding as woman is to depend on the promises of love, and sanguine as woman is to view in all their golden glittering the visions of love, were she but wise enough to be wary and to bring her godly jealousy into play, and stand on her high pre-eminence of modest purity and untouchable honour, why the flattery would fall innocuous on her ear, and, if she did not unsting the serpent that would beguile her, her heart would be proof against the virulence of its poison.

Her influence as a lover still farther is felt and seen, in its most amiable aspects, when her spell has enchanted a man of honour and of worth. Of such a man she has no fear, or, at all events, no fear of her virtue. In this case generally there is the confidence of love. To such a man, moreover, she is in point of fact, so long as they sustain this relation, the source of the *summum bonum* of this nether world, whether he knows it or not, and sometimes he does not know it. She is to him what the pole is to the needle, the helm to the ship, the rein to the horse,—his grand moving power for good. The desire to please which she awakens in the heart of man is probably the finest specimen of this influence. If ever man loses his selfishness it is when he is in love. If ever a Christian man, swayed by mundane motives, seems to get quit of this vile propensity, it is when endeavouring to secure the favour of the woman who holds his heart, but in whose heart he knows the love of God reigns.

And what shall be said of the influence of woman as a wife, and how shall it be said? It requires courage and taste and tact to deal with such a theme as it deserves. Probably, as there is no such union as that existing between husband and wife, there is no such influence as that which the one exercises over the other. It is admitted that the influence is mutual and reciprocal, and that as they are no more twain, but one, so each is to the other a pervasive, a ruling, a controlling power.

The idiosyncrasy of a wife's character determines to a great extent the nature and the amount of a wife's influence. This is a most important point, and, unless it be well understood and well weighed, much misapprehension must necessarily prevail, and, in the concerns of every day life, much injustice may be done alike to husbands and wives. It is worth while to repeat the sentiment that the idiosyncrasy of a wife's character determines to a great extent the nature and the amount of a wife's influence. . . .

. . . When a husband knows that with all his wife's managing it is his weal and his family's she is seeking—that with all her peevishness and temper she has their mutual interest at heart—when there is manifest similar ardour on her part for the beauty of spiritual adorning, as there is for external decency and order, he knows in all his soul that her vehemence and zeal against failings and crimes are set off by the unimpeachable consistency and the beauties of holiness which array her character—the knowledge makes him not only bear, but yield and please and gratify the woman who has ventured her all on his honour and his love. Solomon,—and he was a good, perhaps the best judge in the matter,—tells us that such a wife will do her husband good and not evil, all the days of his life. As an anonymous author has it, she will do him good by promoting his domestic comfort. This is indeed placed almost wholly in her hands; it rests with her to see that the fireside is the place of attraction—that home is the crystal spot on earth. And love will teach ingenuity to the faithful wife, and show to her a thousand ways by which she may endear the home circle. If she wishes to enjoy her husband's society, she must be a keeper at home, and so arrange her family, as that he, when he returns from the care and noise and contention of the world, shall find a retreat in which sweet converse shall beguile him of his cares; and peace, and love, and order, and gentle welcome, and soothing sympathy, shall form a striking contrast to the scenes he has just quitted. And she will do good to her husband by sharing his cares. On many in modern times the charge is not incumbent of labouring with the hands to provide food and rainment for the family. The different constitution of modern society from ancient has placed upon man the duty of maintaining a family, and left to woman the sweeter privilege of ordering the charities of home. Yet even now a wife may do much to lessen the cares of a husband.—She may not fully understand the nature of his employment, she cannot exactly enter into the details of his business, but she can give the attentive ear, she can endeavour to comprehend his difficulties, she can forbear mentioning any irritating domestic circumstances, she can soften down annoyances, sometimes she can cheer him by reminding him of sound consoling promises of God's Word, she can show him the command of Holy Writ, to cast his care upon the Lord. She can tell him that they that seek the Lord shall not want any good thing, and perhaps lead him to say with David, "When I am afraid I will trust in thee;" and when all these fail, and her anxious eye sees the cloud still darken over his brow, then she can pray with a firm unwavering faith that God would indeed lift up the light of his countenance upon him and give him peace. Nor is it less her duty to share his joys. If her husband have succeeded in some pursuit, with what heartiness should the wife enter into his pleasure. Never should the wandering eye betray that she listens to the details which interest him with indifference. She should value his pursuits if for no other reason than because they are *his*, and by an ever ready sympathy should do him good and not evil all the days of his life. Never should the depressing fear or the ardent hope be thrown coldly, harshly, again on him who utters it. One such repulsion will do more to alienate the love of a sensitive mind than many little acts of neglect and annoyance.

A wife will also do good to her husband by encouraging him to holiness and virtue, and warning him against sin. In the intimacy of domestic life the first tendency to evil is sometimes evident to the wife, and it is her duty to rebuke with all earnestness, and to plead with all gentleness, against conduct which may be displeasing to God and man....

Such, gentlemen, is the influence of woman as a wife, and where it is acknowledged and honored, the romance of love remains, the poetry of love throws its charm over the married pair down to their last days on earth, gilding them even more brightly than it did in the days when they first saw and loved each other. Such a husband and wife never grow old, for though the almond tree may flourish, and desire fail, and wrinkles furrow the brow, and the rosy hue leave the cheek, — though the eye does not beam with its former witchery, nor the tongue roll forth the flood of melody that was wont to thrill the recesses of their being, their hearts are young and green as ever, and the freshness and ripeness of their mutual affection, hallowed by the spirit of holiness, are a part of their preparation for their abode in the amaranthine bowers of the Paradise of God.

But if such be the influence of woman as a wife, what is it as a mother? It is in this relationship that her power for good is specially manifest, and specially blissful. The change which motherhood produces in woman herself is wonderful, and deserving of a passing notice in this illustration. That a young and delicate female, who, up to the time perhaps that she was married, had never known a care, save those which love imposes, who was a stranger to heavy toil, and had never known fatigue, whose every wish was gratified, because all around her were her willing servants or ministers, and who from the time she was married till the hour that made her a mother, was the idol of her husband's heart, now dearer to him than ever—that such a young and favoured woman should, as if by some mighty sudden power be changed to the thoughtful, careful nurse of a helpless babe, and seem to live but for it, is, indeed, another of the deep mysteries of love. Willingly does she watch it by day in its cozy crib, and drink in purer, sweeter joy from her vigil, than ever she drank from any other source. Willingly does she prevent the night watches, that its rest may be sweet and undisturbed. Forgetful of herself, her sole care is centred on this little object, and she lives, and moves, and works, and watches, and wrestles for its good. Such a change,—so sudden,—of her whole habits, business, thought, did we not witness it every day, would appear a more wonderful metamorphosis than any that Ovid has described. "Can a woman forget her sucking child, that she should not have compassion on the son of her womb." Now, as committed to her care, the child is just what the mother makes it; or, at the very least, she stamps upon it the impress of her own character. It is not too bold a use of the figure to say that it is in her hands as clay in the hands of the potter, and she can mould it at will. The power she can exert for a considerable period is well nigh absolute, for during all this time it is passive in her hand—and even when the understanding opens, and the will begins to work, and the passions to play, such is her power that she, as none other, can furnish the understanding and bend the will, and direct and control and subdue the affections.

Her influence thus exerted in early life she exerts and retains so long as life lasts, and its effects are seen in the history of her family alike in their temporal and spiritual condition. A mother's counsels, a mother's prayers, a mother's psalms, a mother's reproofs, a mother's commendations, the gentle firmness of her authority, and the warning attractions of her example, are immortal; they never die; they may for the time be forgotten, profligacy may bury them in the grave with all that was lovely and pure and ingenuous in youth; ingratitude may raze them from the table of the heart, and neglect may hide them so far in the treasures of the memory, that they may seem as if lost amid the rubbish which encumber it; but all will not do; and in an hour when he thinks not his mother's power will reclaim the prodigal, and restore the ingrate to her and to himself....

But such influence not only reclaims; it excites and confirms and establishes in the paths of honourable existence, and of holy obedience. The remark has so often been made that it is now a mere commonplace—"that great men had good mothers." And even where greatness was not realized, and where fame never had occasion to herald discoveries in science, nor deeds of daring and of benevolence, who will deny that the honest labour and the honourable wealth, and the humble piety and quiet usefulness, which mark the scenes of our every-day life, had their origin in the lessons which were learned from a mother's lips; and when the author, or rather the instrument, of all this good dies, who so ready to acknowledge her worth as the *reft* husband and the sorrowing children. . . .

Now the secret of all this influence is love. Truly did Gray say, "We can never have but one Mother." No love, not even the tenderest, can equal hers, for she will love on, though sickness should wither the flower, and turn all its beauty into decay, and fix her firmest and deepest affection on that one of her children who has the least outward grace and loveliness. Her love, unlike all others, can withstand neglect, and ingratitude, and forgetfulness. The prodigal son may stray from his home, and the world may frown on him, and frown justly, and all the love of neighbours and of friends, or even of brother or sister, may be worn out by his folly and wickedness, yet there is a stream of love in the mother's heart, ever fresh, and ever living—he is still her own loved son, and one word, perchance one look of sorrow, will win forgiveness for a life of unkindness. The love of a mother is like the bounty of God, who causes his sun to rise on the evil and on the good, and sendeth his rain on the just and on the unjust.

There is but one theme more on which something might have been said with advantage to many now hearing me. I refer to the influence of woman as a member of the Church, and as connected with society.

As a member of the Church, her influence is wide and powerful. When she justifies her connection with this wonderful society, she stirs up all her strength and might in working out the great design for which it has been organized. It is to the Gospel, as deposited in and declared by the Church, that she owes her elevation. It is to Christianity, as embodied in the Church, that she owes her restoration to her due place, and the good she does while she occupies it. Had it not been for the religion of Christ and its enlightening and purifying tendency, she had still been a slave all over the world; she had been sunken in ignorance, doomed to servitude, the sport of the passions, and the butt of the cruelty of man her master,—a mere chattel in law, a mere thing; in fact, a mere convenience which might be used or neglected or destroyed, just as it might happen according to the whim of her owner. Had it not been for the religion of Christ, she had been all this and worse: and she knows this if she knows anything, and she acknowledges it. Gratitude for the good makes her work for the Giver; and in how many instances has the Giver to record his approbation of woman's *willinghood* in her cause as he did that of Mary, when he said, "She hath done what she could; and verily I say unto you, that wherever this Gospel shall be preached in the whole world, this that she hath done shall be told as a memorial of her." It comes from all this that the contemptuous sneer has been bandied from one infidel to another that the Church stands by women, and that were it not for women it would soon die out. We take the sneer for the truth it teaches; we submit to the sarcasm for the sake of the sacred society against which it is hurled; and we will glory in the peculiarity—if peculiarity it be—till your infidel creed and your infidel companionship furnish finer samples of female character than the so-much *decried* Christian Church. And think you that the sense of her indebtedness to the blessed Saviour who has made her what she is,—which she daily feels has no weight with those who know it, that the ardours of her piety, and the warmth of her zeal, and the purity of her motives, and the self-denial of her life, have no weight? Think you that the constancy of her attachment to the cause and the people of Christ, and her wisdom and tact in persevering and perpetuating the peace and prosperity of the Church, have no weight? Oh, think you that her prayers and her pains have no weight, in which she labors night and day that men may be blessed indeed, and all nations call Him blessed? Nay, verily, they have weight, they are every year becoming more weighty, and the likelihood is, notwithstanding many a sad foreboding, that within the Church she will do still more for her spiritual nourishment and growth in grace.

And when she moves among the wicked as a messenger of mercy, as an angel visitant to the abodes of want and of woe, when the eye sees her then it blesses her, when the ear hears her then it gives witness to her, because she delivers the poor that cry and those who have no help of man at all. She is eyes to the blind, and feet to the lame, and the cause she knows not, she searches out, and the blessing of those that are ready to perish comes upon her, and she makes the heart of the widow to sing for joy.

In this city what scope for such labour, what opportunity for such deeds of Christian philanthropy. I do not know if I am prepared to endorse the opinion of one of your city missionaries, that Halifax, as compared with its population, is more wicked than most great cities in the old world, but there is room and verge enough for the labours of the whole sisterhood of charity. The poor need instruction in that which belongs alike to the useful and the ornamental—the art of *living*. The slattern housewife requires lessons on tidiness and economy, and a word fitly spoken to one such may revolutionize her whole conduct. The abandoned child who is left to grow up more carelessly than the weed by the wayside—yes, more carelessly, for the weed is sometimes useful after all—demands to be rescued from ignorance and crime, and what more fitting work for a tender-hearted woman? What work for woman's plastic hand more noble than this? And then there is the Sabbath School, with its weekly lessons in sacred truth, and there is the Ragged School, with its daily lessons in health and order, in cleanliness and truth, in knowledge and obedience. The most refined and elegant among us, the best born and the best bred, would but increase the lustre of their refinement and the purity of their blood if they adopted the Latin maxim, "I am a woman, and nothing that pertains to my kind is unsuitable for me." Oh, there is more true glory in redeeming one such wretch to order and decorum, to good citizenship and pure Christianity, than was won by the victories of Inkermann and Balaclava.

Let seige be laid to some den of filth and shame on your own Citadel Hill, and not by shell and grape, shot and a shower of brimstone fire, but by the armour of righteousness on the right and the left. Let its inmates, man or woman—nay, but one of them—be subdued to the obedience of faith, and a mightier work is done than when Sebastopol fell. Yes, and the fame of those deeds shall have died, and the page which records them shall cease to be read, oh, these mighty works of love and humanity will be held in everlasting remembrance.

Such, gentlemen, in my apprehension, is woman's sphere in Christian society—such the influence she is fitted and designed to exert. At home looking well to the ways of her household, in the Church keeping the unity of the spirit in the bond of peace. And like your Elizabeths and Marys, and Marthas and Dorcases, walking in all the commandments of the Lord, blameless, and in the world like the Master going about doing good—instructing the ignorant, reclaiming the wandering, befriending the orphan in his homelessness, and watching him in the home in which in her mercy she found him. Like the Saviour, when he was on earth, healing the sick and binding up those who are broken in heart, frowning intemperance from her own special domain, and doing her best to shut up every haunt of lewdness and of lust....

AN ARGUMENT AGAINST WOMAN'S RIGHTS, 1872

A Bystander [Goldwin Smith], 'The Woman's Rights Movement', *The Canadian Monthly and National Review*, March 1872, vol I, 3, 249-64.

A movement has been set on foot, and in England and the United States has made considerable way, the object of which is to effect a sweeping change in all the relations of the sexes—conjugal, political, legal, educational and industrial. It may safely be said, that such a revolution, if it actually takes place, will be at once unparalleled in importance and unprecedented in kind. Unparalleled in importance, because female character and domestic morality lie so completely at the root of civilization, that they may almost be said to be civilization itself; unprecedented in kind, since history affords no example of so extraordinary a change in the fundamental relations of humanity, the progress of which has hitherto been in conformity with those relations as well as comparatively gradual, though not unmarked by exceptional and momentous efforts, such as seem to rebut the idea that humanity is under the dominion of mere physical law.

In the United States a peculiar impulse has been given to all levelling movements by negro enfranchisement; and demagogism pounces, by anticipation, on the female vote. In England, the movement, though Radical in its origin, is fostered by a portion of the Conservative party in the hope that the female vote will come to the rescue of existing institutions. In Canada, exempt from these disturbing causes, we have hitherto been touched by the educational part of the movement alone, and are therefore in a position to consider the question calmly in case it should ever present itself to us in the broader and graver form.

It is desirable, in the first place, to clear away certain fallacies by which a very invidious character has been needlessly given to the discussion. The advocates of Woman's Rights, male and female, have represented woman as the victim hitherto of wilful and systematic injustice, against which she is at last about to rise in revolt; and their language is such as, if it could sink into the hearts of those to whom it is addressed, might turn all affection to bitterness and divide every household against itself. But these representations are without foundation in history, which shows that the lot, both of man and woman, has been determined from time to time by circumstances only to a very limited extent subject to the will of either sex, and which neither sex could be blamed for accepting or failing to reverse. Those who assume that the lot of woman has been through all the ages fixed by the will of man, and that man has willed that he should enjoy political rights and that woman should be a slave, have forgotten to consider the fact that in almost all countries down to a very recent period, man himself has been, and in most countries even at the present day remains, if not a slave, at least destitute of political rights. It may probably be affirmed that the number of men who have hitherto really and freely exercised the political suffrage is hardly greater than the number of those who have in different ages and in various ways sacrificed their lives in bringing the suffrage into existence. Actual slavery, where it has existed, has, it is believed, always extended to both sexes and ceased for both at the same time; and if, in Homeric times, there were more female slaves than males, this was because the men when vanquished in war were put to the sword, while the women were reserved for what, in the state of sentiment then prevailing, was morally as well as physically a milder lot.

The primeval family was a unit, the head of the family representing the whole household before the tribe, the state and all persons and bodies without; while within he exercised absolute power over all the members of his domestic circle, over his son and his men-servants, as well as over his daughters, his maid-servants and his wife. The tribe was in fact composed not of individuals but of families represented by their heads. At the death of the head of a family, his son stepped into his place and became the representative and protector of the whole family, including the widow of the deceased chief. This system was long retained at Rome, where it was the source of the respect for authority, and, by an expansion of feeling from the family to the community; of the patriotism which produced and sustained Roman greatness. But its traces have lingered far down in history. It was not male tyranny that permitted Queen Elizabeth to send members of the royal household to the Tower by her personal authority as the mistress of the family, without regard to the rule of the common law against arbitrary imprisonment. Such a constitution was essential to the existence of the family in primitive times; without it the germs of nations and of humanity would have perished. To suppose that it was instituted by man for the gratification of his own sexual tyranny would be the height of absurdity in any one, and in a philosopher unpardonable. It was as much a necessity to primeval woman as it was to primeval man. It is still a necessity to woman in those countries where the primeval type of society still exists. What would the fate of a female Bedouin if suddenly invested with Woman's Rights and emancipated from the protection of her husband or of the male head of her tribe?

The invidious theory that the subordination of wives to their husbands, or the denial of the suffrage to women, has its origin in slavery and, as a modified phase of that barbarous institution, is entirely at variance with historical facts. Even in the most primitive times, and those in which the subjection of the woman was most complete, the wife was clearly distinguished from the female slave. The authority of Hector over Andromache was absolute, yet no one could confound her position with that of her handmaidens. Whatever is now obsolete in marriage relations is a relic, not of slavery but of primitive marriage. Slavery, as we have said before, where it has existed has been the common lot of both sexes, and has been terminated by a common emancipation.

Even the Oriental seclusion of women, perhaps the most cruel rule to which the female sex has ever been subjected, has its root not in the slave-owning propensity, but in jealousy, a passion which, though extravagant and detestable in its excessive manifestation, is not without an element of affection.

If man has hitherto reserved to himself political power, he has also reserved to himself not only the duty of defending the nation in war with its attendant dangers and hardships but, generally speaking, the hardest and most perilous work of all kinds. The material civilization which women in common with men enjoy, has been produced mainly by male labour; though, of course, man could no more have continued to labour without his helpmate than he could have propagated his race without his wife. Nor have women as yet claimed a share of the harder kinds of male work. On the contrary, when they see their sex engaged in field labour, they point to the fact as a proof of the depravity of man.

A fallacious impression is apt to be produced by the rhetorical use of the terms "force" and "right of the strongest." It is said that the relation between man and woman has hitherto been based on force, whence it is inferred that the relation must, of course, be evil. Superiority of force is implied in protection; it is implied in the protection of an infant by its mother as well as in that of a woman by her husband. But neither superiority of force, nor the authority which it carries with it, is synonymous with tyranny in one case any more than it is in the other.

It cannot be denied that women have, in the course of history, suffered much wrong as men also have, both at the hands of their own sex and sometimes at the hands of women. But the assertion that there has been a systematic tyranny of one sex over the other is merely an ignorant libel on humanity. To what is woman appealing in this very "revolt," as it is exultingly called? To her own force, or to the justice and affection of men?

The main factors of the relation between the sexes have been sexual affection, the man's need of a helpmate and the woman's need of maintenance and protection, especially when she becomes a mother. The first of these factors remains undiminished in force, and will probably so continue, even if the advocates of Women's Rights should succeed in abolishing marriage and substituting in its place cohabitation at will. Only a smile can be excited by the attempts of philosophy, in dealing with sexual relations, to keep out of sight the most potent and most universal of human passions or to reduce it within the limits which theory requires, by diatribes and denunciations. It reigns and will reign, supreme over this question and all questions connected with it. Man's need of a helpmate is not alleged to have become less. Woman's need of maintenance and protection, and her duties and liabilities in respect of them, may have diminished by a change in industrial circumstances or by the increased supremacy of public law. To ascertain whether this is really the case and if so to what extent, is the rational method of dealing with the subject.

General comparisons between the moral qualities and intellectual powers of the two sexes, and attempts to settle the questions at issue by such comparisons, we must repudiate, as at once invidious and fruitless.

We must also, to get at the solid realities on which alone institutions can be based, blow away the froth of sentiment, even though it may be as beautiful as the foam round Venus when she rose from her native sea. The naughtiness of little girls is not caused wholly by the naughtiness of little boys. A very eminent champion of Woman's Rights, lecturing in our hearing on the English novels of the seventeenth and eighteenth centuries, ascribed their immorality to the exclusion of women and of female influence from the world of letters. Unluckily no novels of that period were more immoral than those of the notorious Mrs. Aphra Behn, who, however, had a worthy imitator in Mrs. Haywood. Heart to heart, in relations more than intimate, and which rendered great disparity almost impossible the two sexes have moved on together, through history, keeping on pretty much the same level of morality, and having their general ideas on all subjects pretty much in common.

The indications of physiology appear, at present, to be against an original distinction of sex, and in favour of the hypothesis that the two sexes were created out of some common germ, in which case the Mosaic narration of the creation of Eve would be roughly symbolical of the truth. But cycles of separation and of devotion to different functions may, notwithstanding, have impressed upon the moral character and the intellect of each sex differences now indelible, and in ignoring which we should be struggling against an adamantine law. Sex itself at all events, with its direct physical consequences, must be taken as an irreversible fact, not to be cancelled by calling women female men, as a lady at a social science meeting insisted on doing, or by any other rhetorical or philosophical conjuration. Under the strange military polity of ancient Sparta an attempt was made to unsex women. Some Roman ladies, in the corrupt days of the empire, having exhausted ordinary means of excitement, were seized with the lust of unsexing themselves and trained as gladiators. It is possible that, in equally morbid states of society, similar phenomena may occur. But even in the case of Sparta, nothing resulted but depravation.

Of all the questions raised by the movement perhaps the least difficult is that which, as we have said, is alone presented to us in Canada at present—the question of Education. There can be no hesitation in saying that God has opened to all His intelligent creatures the gates of knowledge and that every thought of closing them, every remnant of monopolizing tendency, every vestige of exclusiveness and jealousy, ought to be swept aside at once and for ever. If women choose to take up any studies which have hitherto been generally confined to men, let them do so; and, if the result is favourable, both sexes alike will be the gainers. Whether the result will be favourable, experiment alone can decide. To attempt to limit the range of female studies, or in any way to discourage their extension, on the strength of a presumption that certain subjects are beyond the range of feminine intellect would be impertinent and absurd.

On the other hand, if women are deciding for themselves whether they shall desert the domestic sphere for a career of intellectual ambition, the probability of success will be determined, not by compliments, but by the facts of physiology and by our previous experience of the relative powers of the male and female brain. In the case of most subjects our experience is vitiated by the traditional disabilities under which women have been placed; but there seems to be fair ground for an induction in the case of the arts, especially music, which women have practised without restraint of any kind and to a far greater extent than man.

As to the general question of female education there is little more to be said in a summary view of the subject like the present than that education is a preparation for life, the phrase being used, of course, in the most liberal sense; and that any education which is not a preparation for life, but a mere gratification of fancy, vanity or ambition, will turn in the end to bitterness and dust.

Special questions as to the use of Universities and other public institutions by women, must be decided, like all public questions of any kind, solely with reference to the public good, against which no claim of natural right can be pleaded by persons living, not in the bush, but in a community and enjoying the advantages of the social state. We once heard a Woman's Rights speaker assert that she had a natural right to force an entrance into a military academy belonging to the State if she had a fancy for a military education. She had no more a right to do this than she had to thrust her parasol through a picture in a public gallery or to amuse herself by placing obstructions on a railway track. At Oxford and Cambridge there is a high pressure system of competition not free from objection in itself, but without which it might perhaps not be possible to get out of a wealthy class of students, placed under great temptations to idleness, the amount of effort in self-training which they owe to the community. The physical inability of women to bear a strain under which men too often break down, and the unwillingness, which cannot yet be called preposterous, of men to enter into what would seem an unchivalrous race against women, might render the admission of women incompatible with the maintenance of the system; and, in that case, women would have no claim to admission. The co-education of the sexes altogether is a question of public expediency to be decided by reason and experience. There can be nothing morally unjust in the existence of a special place of final education for men any more than in the existence of a special place of final education for women, such as Vassar College, to which if a male student applied for admittance his application would be rejected as utterly indelicate and absurd.

It may be safe to send to the same day-school boys and girls living under the parental roof; it may not be so safe to unite in the same university young men and young women living at a distance from the parental roof. The same school education may be suitable to both sexes, the same university education may not. . . .

Painful scenes have occurred at more than one university in consequence of the determination of ladies to attend in company with the male students the whole of the medical course. If the opposition of the male students to this determination came from a desire of retaining a monopoly of knowledge it was blameworthy, as of course it was if it was manifested in any violent or indecent manner. But, on the other hand, no local or temporary excitement can prevent a disregard of the dictates of delicacy on the part of women from entailing a forfeiture of male respect, whatever that may be worth. Even male sympathizers with what they regard as a struggle for emancipation, while applauding in public the female champion of an equivocal right, may be glad in their hearts that she is not their own wife or daughter.

To pass to the industrial question. It is probable that women have hitherto been excluded by custom and tradition from some employments which they might pursue with advantage. But this is no proof of systematic and intentional injustice on the part of the other sex. The man has felt himself bound to maintain the woman and her children by labour; and the woman still in fact holds him to this obligation, and insists that it shall be enforced by law. As a natural consequence the professions and callings have hitherto generally been male, and, together with their schools and industrial training places have been organized and regulated on that footing. Nor is the present demand for the admission of women to new employments caused so much by a suddenly awakened sense of the injustice of the existing system as by the accumulation, in our great centres of population especially, of a large number of women unmarried and without sufficient means of subsistence: a circumstance due to physical and economical causes unconnected with anything in the relations between the sexes except the increased impediments to marriage arising from competition and the growth of expensive habits. As we may hope that this evil is itself abnormal and temporary, it ought not too much to influence our views as to the usual and permanent occupations of women. Meantime it must be remembered that we do not multiply the amount of work or the fund for the payment of wages by multiplying the number of labourers, and that for every man who is thrust out of employment by female competition, there will be a marriage the less, or a reduction of the means of support for some married woman and her children.

In addition to the large scope which may be afforded to female labour by the removal of traditional disabilities, there is good reason for supposing that, with the increased substitution of mechanical contrivance for manual strength, new industries have been developed of a kind better suited for women. This is a question which experience will decide. There appears to be no prejudice against the employment of women as telegraphists, or, indeed, in any branch of industry in which their labour is really as available as that of men. . . .

It is offensive to women to speak of them as existing only for the purpose of bearing children; but there is nothing offensive to them in suggesting that the duties of childbearing, and those of a wife and mother generally, are the woman's equivalent to the labour of the man, and entitle her, so long as she continues to perform them, to be supported by her partner's labour. The other objects of life, enjoyment and self-improvement, are common to both sexes. . . .

The legal relations between the sexes in England and in other countries where the feudal system prevailed have no doubt been affected in common with politics and the general laws of property by the surviving influences of that system, itself the natural product of an age of violence which for the time rendered the absolute supremacy of the head of the family almost as necessary as it had been in that primitive era, the habits of which were stereotyped as we have said in the domestic system of the Romans. This needed reform; but it is a different thing, historically, from wilful oppression of one sex by the other. Nor has reform been refused. Even in the old feudal countries the free will of the men, acting under those influences of morality and affection which acrimonious declaimers choose to treat as utterly inoperative, has now greatly modified the law and accorded to women extensive powers of holding property to their separate use and devising it by will. In the United States and in this country, there seems little left to be done in this direction; the proprietary rights of married women have been carried so far that settlements are now becoming a vast asylum for fraud; and an eminent American jurist assured the writer of this paper that he knew a case in which the property belonging to the wife, she was forcing her husband to work for her as a labourer at daily wages; and another case in which a wife had accomplished a practical divorce simply by shutting her husband out of the house, which was her property. Whatever the general effects of this system may be, it is likely at all events to have the good effect of discouraging mercenary marriages; especially if a lax divorce law should render unions precarious and make it possible that the wife may at any moment carry away her property, leaving to her husband nothing but an expensive family, luxurious habits, and the inability, which he will naturally have contracted, to work for his own bread.

With regard to the earnings of married women, as distinguished from realized property, legislation in England is at present in advance of legislation here; but the tendency of legislation everywhere is manifest, and it may be safely predicted that all that law can do will soon be done to prevent the tyrannical appropriation and waste of the wife's earnings by the husband. Justice requires this, since, as we have said before, the wife, while she fulfils her conjugal and maternal duties, must be held entitled to maintenance by her husband's labour, so that anything which she earns by labour of her own ought to be hers, and at her own disposal. But it must be borne in mind that her title depends upon her being a wife: if she chooses not to be a wife but a commercial partner, which is the ideal now proposed for the union of the sexes in place of marriage, the man as well as the woman will be entitled to settle all questions both of contribution to the partnership fund and of liability for the partnership debts on a commercial basis; and, with regard to all such matters, the common law of partnership will supersede the law of husband and wife. In any case it is hardly necessary to preach, as some domestic reformers seem inclined to do, that the worst use a married woman can make of her money is to spend it on the alien purposes of her home.

But marriage itself is now denounced as the chief of woman's wrongs. To substitute for a sacred and lifelong bond an unconsecrated cohabitation during the pleasure of both parties, commonly called free love, is the avowed aim of the more advanced section of the Woman's Rights party and the practical tendency, it would seem, of the doctrines of both sections. Both at least reprobate what they invidiously term "the property of one human being in another human being": that is to say, the power of a husband to oblige his wife to do anything which she does not choose to do or to live with him any longer than she pleases. Mrs. Victoria Woodhull, if we rightly interpret the statement of her biographer, actually had herself formally divorced from the partner with whom she intended to live and still lives, as a protest against the marriage tie.

The case of the discontented wife is evidently the one always contemplated, and it is specially, if not exclusively, for her relief that the abrogation of the marriage tie is designed. But equal justice must be meted to both parties. There is but one way of securing that any human connection shall never become irksome, and that is by allowing both parties to break it off at their pleasure. Nor can any limit be put to caprice and changefulness without a violation of the fundamental principle that love alone justifies the continuance of union. We must be prepared for a modern counterpart of the Thelesina of pagan antiquity with her ten successive husbands, and, as her complement, for a Thelesinus with his ten successive wives. Those who deem it morally impossible that the removal of restraint should be followed by a renewal of license must remember that we are at present under the dominion of the public sentiment created by the institution of marriage.

Political and social questions can no longer be settled by a text of Scripture, but the attempt to show that Christian marriage is not an integral part of Christian morality appears totally fallacious. It is said that the Gospel recognizes marriage, and the subordination of the wife to the husband, merely in the same sense in which it recognizes slavery, as an existing institution of the period, to which it lends no sanction, but which it is not called upon directly to assail. There is no analogy between the two cases. Rightly construed, the Gospel contains not a single word in favour of slavery; while all its social precepts tend to the subversion of the institution, as speedily appeared when they began to operate on the world. But it does lend a distinct sanction to marriage and to the headship of the husband, dwelling upon the special duties and virtues incident to the relation on both sides, and comparing it to the relation between Christ and the Church. Christ pronounces marriage indissoluble in the most emphatic terms, and it must be evident to any reader of St. Paul that the doctrine of free love and the example set before us in the biography of

Mrs. Woodhull would have appeared to him utterly subversive of his moral ideal.

It may be added that the Bible view of sex manifestly is that the man and the woman are the necessary complements of each other. Woman is created because it is not good for man to be alone. Make women "female men," and though you cannot obliterate physical sex, you will have, morally and intellectually, epicenes who will be alone.

The husband's headship appears to be as inseparable an incident of Christian marriage or of any marriage identical with the Christian in character, as the indissolubility of the tie. Indeed if there is to be unity in the family, on any theory, it would seem that there must be in the last resort a determining will, though there will be less occasion for the exertion of that will in proportion as the marriage is happy and in accordance with the Christian ideal. The state of the children at all events must be one of obedience, and if the ultimate depositary of authority is uncertain, how is the obedience of children to be secured? It has been suggested that authority over the children should be divided between the husband and the wife, and that their several shares should be defined by the marriage settlement. No specimen of such a settlement has however yet been laid before us; and the very mention of such an expedient suggests that the theorists by whom it is proposed have in their minds only the select and cultivated circle in which marriage settlements are usual, not the ordinary masses of mankind.

Perhaps this question of marriage, in common with most other questions relating to humanity, will depend in part on the solution of those deeper problems respecting the origin, estate and destiny of man to which the attention of humanity is being every day more seriously and painfully turned. If the present life is only a trial and a preparation, it may be expedient notwithstanding the unhappiness attendant on ill-assorted marriages to retain the tie, if on the whole it is favourable to purity and elevation of character, as, even in cases which most deeply move our compassion, it appears often to be. If this life is all, it may well seem hard that two persons should be condemned to spend it in the miseries of an unwilling union. . . .

We must bow, however unwillingly, to the fiat of nature. Man has in a certain sense an advantage over woman. To him the abrogation of the marriage tie, though depraving, would not be otherwise fatal; it would relieve his passions from a restraint now imposed on them. To woman it would be utterly fatal. The result would probably be that to secure a permanent protection for herself and her children she would have to reduce herself to slavery indeed. Marriage must be regarded as a restraint imposed on passion for the good of both sexes, but especially of the female. And to sustain it, it must be rendered tolerably attractive to that sex whose temptations to licence are the strongest. Woman's Rights philosophy tells us that the man is to have no right to complain if he comes home after his day's labour and finds a Jesuit established by his fireside; though the same philosophy would probably grant a divorce to a woman whose place in her husband's heart had been taken by a spiritual directress. But can we enforce contentment? The refined few will probably continue to prefer a regular union on any terms, trusting to cultivated sensibility and affection to set all right; but will not the rough working man, if he dislikes your terms, keep his neck out of the yoke, and being master of his own labour, make easier terms for himself, though to his great moral disadvantage? If he does, what will be left to the women's party but to make a law compelling men to enter the union prescribed by their philosophy, and to call upon the men to enforce this law upon themselves.

The blindness with which marriages are contracted, and which is the root of so much misery, is surely not wholly irremediable at least in its present extent. Perhaps an improved social arrangement, and a diminution of the dissipation and extravagance which narrow social intercourse, may in time lessen the strain laid by extreme domestic isolation on the union of any two persons of ordinary character and resources. That there are some happy marriages under the existing system will not be denied, and there seems to be no reason why the number should not be indefinitely increased.

The question whether it is desirable that women should take part in politics is closely connected with those relating to their domestic and industrial position. It is a question not as to the relative intelligence or virtue of the two sexes, but whether politics are or can be woman's sphere. The argument that educated women are better qualified for the suffrage than uneducated men is, therefore, irrelevant and invalid. The disqualification, if there be a disqualification, is not one of intellect but of position, or at least of intellect only so far as intellect, in regard to special functions, may be unfavourably influenced by position. White women, it is often said in the United States, are better qualified for the suffrage than black men. In the same sense, many white boys are better qualified for the suffrage than many white men or women, and they are excluded not on account of their want of intelligence, but because, as a general rule, being dependent on their parents, they are not in a responsible position. We may say that Richelieu made a mistake in meddling with the drama, and that Voltaire made a mistake in meddling with diplomacy, without disparagement to the intellect of Richelieu or Voltaire.

Supposing women to be emancipated legally, conjugally and industrially, in the Woman's Rights sense, and to have made their way completely into what has hitherto been the male sphere, the objections to their taking part in politics would obviously be diminished. At present, reigning apart in the household the woman does not directly feel those effects of good or bad government which are directly felt by the man, who goes forth to labour, and the practical sense of which, more than anything else, forms the political wisdom, such as it is, of the masses of mankind. Nor would there be anything to balance the political judgment in women, as it is balanced in men, by the variety and the mutual counteraction of practical needs and considerations. Even with a male suffrage a particular question is apt, under the influence of temporary excitement or party exaggeration, to become too predominant, excluding from view other questions of equal or superior importance and leading to the ostracism in elections of valuable public servants. But with female suffrage, the position and the practical education of women being as they now are, we should have at every general election a woman's question, very likely one of a sentimental kind, which demagogues would take care to provide and which would make a clean sweep of all other questions and of all public men who hesitated to take the woman's side. If female suffrage prevailed in England, for instance, under present circumstances, it is morally certain that the result of the next general election would turn almost exclusively on the Contagious Diseases Act, and that all the statesmen who had voted for the Act, including the men of most mark in both parties, would be driven from public life.

The abolition of the family would at once remove all objection, grounded on the fear lest political separation between man and wife should break the unity of the household. We are told, indeed, that there is no reason why domestic harmony should be disturbed by political differences any more than it is disturbed by differences of religion. But, in the first place, it can hardly be said that differences of religion do not disturb domestic harmony if the convictions of both parties are deeply seated, and if both believe that religion is an important element in the education of children; in the second place, the cases are not parallel. Difference of religion involves only separation in worship, it does not involve collision; difference in politics, where there are political parties, involves collision. Would the harmony of any ordinary marriage remain undisturbed by the appearance of the man and his wife on hostile committees, at a time perhaps of great public excitement, encountering each other in the canvass, and launching manifestoes against each other. While the family subsists, those who regard it as equal or (as some do) superior in value to the state will probably shrink from exposing it to such a strain.

There are other objections, however, which, whatever their degree of force, will survive all changes in industrial, legal and conjugal institutions, and remain so as long as sex itself remains. The mixture of the sexes in political assemblies and elections will be liable to the same dangers which have been already indicated as likely to attend the mixture of the sexes in courts of justice—dangers on which it is needless, and would be distasteful to dwell, but the existence of which no unwillingness to refer to them on the part of theorists can annul.

The incompatibility of political duties with child-bearing is a subject on which so much poor wit has been expended that we touch it with reluctance. The incompatibility exists, however, and when we are told that the difficulty would be met by never electing women likely to become mothers, we must ask whether this would not entail the exclusion of the best women and those most fitted to represent the sentiments and interests of their sex.

Man, as the cultivator of the earth, has hitherto been and is still the great tax-payer. But if woman takes to cultivating the earth also, or to any equivalent industries, she will be equally a tax-payer, and any doubt as to her claim to a vote which might arise from the connection between taxation and representation will be removed.

The military objection to female suffrage has perhaps been pressed too far. Still it remains true that if the defence of the country is an essential part of a citizen's duty, men alone can be full citizens. The defence of Germany has recently afforded a striking illustration of the fact, which in other countries is somewhat masked by the disuse of the national force, and the almost exclusive employment of professional soldiers. The argument that, though women do not give their own blood in defence of the country, they give the blood of their husbands, sons, and brothers, must be dismissed as for the purpose of the present argument little better than cant. That women, if invested with political power, would not be ready enough to vote for war is an allegation which no one acquainted with history could have made, and which, therefore, called for no elaborate confutation. The danger, as experience shows, is all the other way. The weak have always loved to wield the thunderbolt. No three contemporary rulers can be named who caused more bloodshed in their day than Maria Theresa, Catharine the second, and Madame de Pompadour. It is notorious that in the late American civil war the women on both sides were more passionately warlike than the men. Even among men the substitution of hired armies for the general duty of military service has greatly weakened the restraints on war, the male love of money notwithstanding.

But a still more serious doubt arises from the fact, as we believe it to be, that the supremacy of law rests at bottom on the force of the community compelling submission to the public will, while the force of the community resides in the male sex. The reason why the mass of mankind obey the law when it clashes with their individual will, is that they know that it will be upheld with a strong hand. No doubt this fundamental support is strengthened, while its coarseness is veiled, among the more civilized races by superinduced sentiments of expediency and reverence; but the fundamental support it still is, and it can no more be removed with impunity, than can the unsightly foundation of a beautiful and august edifice. Suppose women to become the lawgivers, would this connection between the law, and the force needed to sustain it, be always preserved? And if it were not always preserved, might not the supremacy of law be impaired or even cease? Suppose something which men deemed very unjust to their sex to be carried by female votes, would the men execute the enactment against themselves? A lady in the United States proposed the other day that all outrages committed by men upon women should be punished like murder with death, forgetting, as was justly remarked at the time, that, apart from the question as to the comparative gravity of the crime, in cases of murder there was a dead body, whereas in cases of outrage there was, generally speaking, no proof but the woman's own statement, which experience did not warrant us in assuming to be invariably true. Supposing that under the exciting influence of some recent and aggravated case, the women were to carry such an enactment as this, and supposing a female jury to convict a prisoner contrary to the male sense of justice, would the men put him to death? Supposing the women by their votes to bring on a war of which the men did not approve, would the men obediently shoulder their muskets and march to their death at the bidding of the women? If not, the supremacy of law would surely be in peril, and the supremacy of law, essential as it is to the welfare of both sexes, is pre-eminently essential to the welfare of the weaker.

Public law has in great measure relieved women since the primitive and feudal times from the necessity of individual protection, and a corresponding amount of individual emancipation has followed or is following; but the sex, collectively, still requires the protection of male force upholding public law. Whether this will always be so, is a speculative question: it certainly is so now.

As the question is not about the abstract capacity of women for politics, but about their capacity under their existing circumstances, and the possibility of their taking part in politics consistently with the unity and happiness of their families, it is needless to examine the lists of queens and female regents which are presented as proofs of the fitness of women to reign. These lists are selections made under the influence of strong pre-possession, not exhaustive enumerations on which an induction can be based. In English history, the female weilders of political power are Matilda, the mother, and Eleanor, the wife of Henry II.; Isabella, wife of Edward II.; Margaret of Anjou, Mary, Elizabeth, Henrietta Maria and Anne. The personal characters of these ladies and the personal interest attaching to them are not in question. Mary was, no doubt, a good woman, led fatally astray as a ruler by her weak and bigoted submission to her priests. To the tempers of Margaret of Anjou and of Henrietta Maria, the country was indebted in no small degree for two civil wars.

Anne dismissed the greatest of English ministers, and brought dishonour on the country under the influence partly of a favourite waiting-woman, partly of the fanatical clergy, and it is highly probable that had she lived much longer her weakness would have led to the return of the Stuarts and to another period of confusion. The reputation of Elizabeth once stood high; but since the recent inquiries and revelations, she has been abandoned by her former worshippers; and it is difficult to say whether the infirmities of the woman were more prejudicial to the policy of the ruler or the crimes and cruelties of the ruler to the character of the woman. The public service was starved even in the extremity of national peril and the best public servants were left unrewarded, while largesses and honour were heaped on Elizabeth's worthless lovers; we have a lady personally desiring that conspirators may be put to a death of protracted torture. On the other hand, it is probable that Eleanor the Queen of Edward I., the lady to whose memory the well-known crosses were erected by her husband, did much good in a feminine way; and it is certain that great services were rendered to the public by Caroline, Queen of George II., who quietly guided her husband in his choice of ministers, without herself ever overstepping the domestic sphere. The name of Queen Victoria has been cited as that of a great female ruler, but those who cite it must surely be aware that the government of England is now constitutional, and that Queen Victoria's virtues have been those of a wife, a mother and a head of society. But all these are cases of rulers under the hereditary system, placed in power without any process injurious to the female character, and surrounded by councillors who would supply any lack of wisdom in the queen. The question that we now have to consider is what the character of a woman would be when she had forced her way through the processes of popular election into a representative assembly, and was there struggling with men for the prizes of political ambition? By what kind of women is it likely that such an ordeal would be triumphantly encountered—by the grave matrons and spinsters whom philosophy imagines welcomed and honoured as representatives by philosophic constituencies, or by dashing adventuresses whose ascendancy neither philosophy nor the grave matrons and spinsters would contemplate with satisfaction?

The tone of politics under the system of party Government is low, and is always becoming lower; faction, virulence and corruption prevail and increase; therefore, it is said, let us send the women into the political arena; they are free from political vices, and they will redeem the men. But it is because women have not hitherto gone into the political arena that they are free from political vices. We have no good reason for assuming that, subjected to the same evil influences as men, who mix in politics, women could not contract the same bad habits. Such experience as we have had points decidedly the other way. Both in the Reign of Terror and in the rising of the Commune, the frenzy and atrocities of the women rivalled, if they did not surpass, those of the men. The female agitation against the Contagious Diseases Act in England has exhibited full-blown all the violence, narrowness and persecuting rancour of the worst male faction fight. When the Crusaders took a number of women with them to the siege of Acre, it might have been supposed that female gentleness would mitigate the ferocity of the war: the result was, that a number of Turks having been captured, the women begged that the prisoners might be delivered to them, not for the purpose of alleviating their lot, but for the purpose of cutting off their heads with knives. Grant that the moral nature of women is finer than that of men—though these vague comparisons are utterly worthless—still, if it is equally excitable, or more so, it may be liable to equal or more violent perturbations. The saying may be fulfilled, that the corruption of the best is the worst corruption. Men who have always stood aloof from politics are just as free from political vices as women. In highly educated communities a most powerful and salutary influence is at present exercised by women and by the society in which women reign upon the character of politicians as well as upon that of other men; and in those untainted circles an independent standard of honour and courtesy is maintained, which even the leaders of fighting factions cannot wholly disregard. We may be told that if party government makes politics unfit for women, party government ought to cease. Perhaps it ought, and not on that account only. But at present there is no prospect of its ceasing; and in the meantime it would hardly be wise to fling woman and the family, all that remains undisturbed and uncontaminated, into the gulf opened in our forum, unless we have good reason for believing that the gulf will be thereby closed.

Political influence may be really exercised without a vote, even in countries under the elective system; and has in fact been frequently exercised by writers and by leaders of society, who have hardly ever been seen at the polls. And in a broader sense who can doubt that female influence has been felt in all legislation relative to female interests for some time past—in fact, ever since women began to bestir themselves or to express any strong feelings on the subject? We have listened in the United States to the greatest orator of the Woman's Rights party. He protested in general terms that women in the present state of the laws were suffering the most monstrous injustice, which only female suffrage could remove. But when he came to specific facts, all that he had to say was, that in a particular case, for the details of which we were to take his authority, a lady had been improperly incarcerated in a lunatic asylum by a cruel husband. We afterwards identified the case, and satisfied ourselves that the speaker's account of it was rhetoric, and not history; but supposing that it had been history, this only proved that the community in which it occurred might, with advantage, adopt the system of inspection which has been instituted with results perfectly satisfactory by male legislatures elsewhere. That the administration of the law is at present unfavourable to women—that a female suitor is less likely to gain her suit or a female prisoner more likely to be convicted than a male, will hardly be asserted. Female prisoners, perhaps, are more likely to escape, especially in capital cases. There was much truth in the remark that if the Californian murderess was hanged she would be the first victim to Woman's Rights.

That there are public functions connected rather with the Church than with the State, with the spiritual than the political community, suitable to women, but from which they are at present excluded in Protestant countries at least, and the denial of which produces a craving for political action, is a growing opinion which has much reason and experience on its side; though it has hitherto not taken the form of any very practical suggestion.

It was necessary in touching on the chief points of this great subject to be succinct, and in being succinct it is difficult to avoid being dry, which, however, may not be the most mischievous defect when a question involving the dearest interests of humanity is being pressed to an irrevocable solution under the influence of sentiment and rhetoric.

Sentiment has been avoided. All sensible women will desire, in the interest of their sex, that it shall be avoided, and that the voice of reason alone shall be heard. The question is not as to the value and dignity of woman in her present sphere, but whether she can with advantage, or without ruinous results to herself and humanity, exchange her present sphere for another.

In conclusion, we have only to remind those specially interested that they cannot have the advantages at once of their present position and one entirely different. The relation between the sexes at present is one not of equality but of mutual privilege. That woman has her privileges will hardly be denied: in the United States, where everything is exaggerated, they are carried so far, and their enforcement is said to be so often accompanied by a repudiation of the corresponding duties, that some of the male supporters of the present movement may be suspected of having mainly in view the emancipation of their own sex. But if equality is established, privilege cannot be retained. Woman may be man's helpmate, or she may be his competitor: both she cannot be. Nor is it possible that man should preserve his present chivalrous sentiments towards woman when he finds himself daily jostling with her as his rival in the rude struggle for subsistence or in the still ruder conflicts of political ambition. Sentiment survives for a time the relations on which it is founded; but it does not survive long.

It is therefore a serious question which women have to decide; and they have reason to be careful how they allow a few members of their sex, under the influence of abnormal circumstances or inclinations, to compromise, as compromise they will, the position of the whole.

AN ARGUMENT FOR WOMAN'S RIGHTS, 1879

'The Woman Question', *The Canadian Monthly and National Review*, May 1879, vol. II, pp. 568-79.

One of the most interesting and important problems of modern civilization is indicated in the above title. Certainly no subject touches more numerous points of our life; or touches them more deeply and tenderly. It is a subject moreover, which has recently become quite prominent; engaging the attention of able minds of both sexes the world over, provoking the consideration of grave deliberative bodies, and awakening a very widespread and lively popular interest. In fact, whatever else it is doing, it is achieving a very general and thorough discussion. It has got itself before the world; and it will no more yield its present vantage-ground, until it has been satisfactorily investigated and rightly determined, than the unwelcome guest at the banquet would down at the bidding of the guilty king.

It cannot be said, however, that the discussion of this great subject is always conducted in a judicious and happy manner. Many baseless assumptions are made, many sophistical arguments employed, and much idle declamation indulged: and by no means all on one side. Delicate nerves are often not a little disturbed, and conservative prejudices shocked by what seem unwomanly words and ways on the one hand; and, on the other, the sense of justice is outraged by the denial of natural equality, and a deep indignation excited by stinging sarcasm and pitiless ridicule. But the discussion of what great subject since time began was ever carried on in a way to meet the entire approbation of sensitive or finical folk? What extravagance and fanaticism did the Reformation evoke? What coarseness and violence of speech and action did the strife against the English Corn Laws, and the age-long fight with American Slavery, call forth! When the waters are deeply stirred no little feculence is likely to come to the surface. Is that any sign that there is no water beneath? How unwise to judge any principle or movement by the follies of its friends, or the aspersions of its foes! Forgetting then, so far as we can, all the inconsequential arguments and sentimental appeals, all the unwarranted assumptions and vicious rhetoric which we may have heard or read on either side of the question—and that requires no little talent for forgetting —let us now look into the subject with such care and candour as we can, and as though for the first time it challenged attention.

Here then, is woman, a living, self-conscious, responsible, moral entity, endowed with all the instincts and faculties of her brother, man. Her's a bodily form, somewhat smaller upon the average, perhaps not less enduring, certainly more sensitive and more graceful than his. Her's every intellectual power, be it fancy or imagination, memory or hope, comparison or judgement. Her's too, every affectionate attribute, whether complacent benevolence or gentle pity, sublime enthusiasm or unselfish love. Her's likewise every spiritual capacity—impresssibility to the unseen and invisible, longing after the divine and immortal. No matter, to the point I now make, whether she have all these powers and capacities in equal degree with man or not. It suffices that she has them.

And what is she to do with them? That is, What is the purpose of her being? Is it, essentially, any different from that of man's? Why *he* is here, hedged about with both hindrances and helps, there seems now a pretty substantial agreement. Though the Westminster Catechism tells us that 'The chief end of man is to glorify God, and enjoy him for ever,' it is now tolerably well understood that this *means*, certainly ought to mean, that man's chief end is the complete and harmonious development of his whole nature. It means that his great object is the attainment of the highest and best that, with all providential aids and utmost self help is possible—the sound mind in the sound body, passion subordinate to reason, interest to conscience, with love transfiguring and enthroned over all. It means, in fine, the attainment of a perfect manhood. This is to glorify God, because it is to illustrate the grandeur and perfectness of his work; and it is to enjoy him by being in entire accordance with his law and spirit.

And is not precisely this the chief end of Woman? Is she not included in the generic term 'Man'? Is she not in the world to make the most of herself that her faculties will allow? Are not her life and culture intrinsically just as important, and provided for just as amply, in the nature of things, as her counterpart's? Is she not under just as imperative obligation to strive for the noblest goals of knowledge, wisdom, goodness, power, as is he? and does not her refusal or neglect to do so involve just as great guilt as his? Surely these questions carry their own answers.

But for the attainment of this end in any worthy degree, woman requires freedom of self-determination. Not freedom to do, or be, what idle caprice or blind passion may prompt; but, exercising her best faculties, and using such helps as she can command, to shape her own course and character, responsible only to her own conscience. This would seem to be the prerogative of every moral being, requiring only to be stated to be admitted. Of *man* it has never been denied, save in exceptional instances, and then only on the ground that the exceptions, though apparently, were not really, human beings—which was the stock justification of African slavery. Of *woman* it has not heretofore been, is not now fully, admitted. She has been the appendage of man; in savage and barbarous lands, his drudge and slave. Amongst all the ancient peoples, with perhaps a single exception, the ordinary form of marriage was a simple bargain between the bridegroom and the father of the bride. Thus Jacob purchased both Leah and Rachel by seven years service for each; and Shechem offered the same patriarch and his angry sons 'never so much dowry and gift' if they would consent to his espousal of Dinah. While indications are not wanting of the same custom among the Greeks, ample evidence appears of her still greater degradation than is involved in such a usage. According to Hellenic law, the daughter could not inherit her father's estate, nor was relationship traceable through females. The Roman law, while in some respects more lenient towards women, was in others much severer. Thus Cato proposed and carried a law which forbade making a woman an heiress, though she were an only child and unmarried, and forbade the willing to a woman of more than the fourth part of the patrimony. In Cicero's time, a century and a half later, a father leaving a son and daughter, could will the latter only a third of his estate, and if he left only a daughter could bequeath her but one half of his fortune. Still worse, the Roman Law vested in the husband and father the power of repudiating the wife at pleasure, and of condemning to death both wife and children. To the same effect are the laws of Menu, to which it is needless to refer in detail.

After a time, however, laws were modified. Not only was the formal sale of the daughter abandoned, but a dowry bestowed by the father for her separate use, which imparted to her somewhat more dignity and value. Still, as virtuous wife and mother, her condition was hardly above servitude. Amongst the Greeks she was disposed of in early childhood, with scarcely the least reference to her own wish; and was doomed to complete seclusion and ignorance. She occupied a retired part of her husband's house, never went abroad unaccompanied, never saw a male visitor except in her husband's presence, never sat at her own table with a male guest, blushed and beat a quick retreat if a male passer-by saw her face at the window. For the intelligent and ambitious woman who spurned this abject condition there was but one way of escape. It was by the sacrifice of what everywhere and at all times has been regarded as the glory of womanhood. How often this dread sacrifice was made need not be said. Equally needless to describe some of the women, as Aspasia and Theodote, by whom it was made—beautiful, brilliant, accomplished, centres of the intellectual and aesthetic society of Athens; to whom such men as Pericles and Socrates confess their indebtedness, and who became no contemptible adepts in all the scientific, philosophic and artistic culture of their time and country.

With Christianity came a new spirit. Then, as never before, was emphasized the grand realities of equality and brotherhood. Then the race became one family, wherein exist no primogenital, no superior rights of any sort. In its light, Jew and Greek, bond and free, male and female all vanish: human souls alone are. Yet the softening and refining tendency of Christianity was manifest in almost every other direction sooner and more decisively than in the elevation of woman. Here and there, of course, ere long appeared indications that its spirit was beginning to operate to this end. The old Jewish notion which made woman the source of all human ills, and asserted 'the badness of men to be better than the goodness of women,' began to fade away. The terrible power vested in the Roman husband was somewhat restricted, and the seclusion of the Hellenic wife was somewhat relaxed. Greater social freedom was accorded to woman; works of charity and piety were confided to her care; and in not a few instances she attested her devotion to the new religion by an endurance and heroism than which nothing is sublimer in the annals of martyrdom. Though she seems never to have been allowed to teach in the primitive orthodox church, yet she was occasionally elected to the office of deaconess, while the heretical sect of the Collyridians, which made some noise in the fourth century, admitted her to the priesthood. The new and slowly strengthening tendency in woman's favour was also evidenced by the early veneration, ere long developing into idolatry, of the mother of Jesus. The institution of chivalry likewise, notwithstanding the unworthy ideas of the womanly character which it recognized, and the extravagance to which it was carried, contributed somewhat to lessen woman's degradation, and open her way to a better future.

Still, all through the Middle Ages, the idea that a woman had any right to herself, or to determine her course in life, and was not first her father's, and then her husband's, was almost literally unheard of. Whatever opportunities for culture, or pleasure, or high employment she enjoyed were granted as *privileges*, not claimed and accorded as *rights*. And when the Reformation came, stupendous in many respects as were the changes wrought, it did little immediately for the elevation of woman. It was Luther's doctrine 'that she was created to bear children, and be the pleasure and solace of her husband.' 'God created Adam master and lord of living creatures,' said he, 'but Eve spoilt all when she persuaded him to set himself above God's will. 'Tis the women with their tricks and artifices that lead men into error.' And how deeply these ideas have been imbedded in the minds of his followers is evident both from the legislation, and the social and religious customs of all Protestant peoples. How long was it amongst these before any real power was accorded woman of shaping her own destiny, or of bestowing her own hand! How long and universally was she still supposed to have but one legitimate purpose in life, towards which all that related to her should tend! How often was she disposed of, if not openly for a sum of ready money, as in early times, yet from considerations of social influence, family convenience, political interest, and the like! Even now one of the most important questions in the marriage service of the Anglican Church is, 'Who *giveth* this woman to be married to this man?' As though her father, or nearest male relation had a divine right to make a *present* of her to whomsoever he would! Certainly as though she had no voice in determining a matter wherein she, of all others, had the profoundest interest! In the same service also, and in accordance with the same idea, is exacted the promise of obedience to the husband no matter which nature may be in the ascendant: a promise which, if it mean anything, means the total abnegation of the prerogatives of a moral being, which no such being has any right, or should dare to surrender. It means the bestowal of the sanction of relgion upon that formerly everywhere accepted atrocity of law, that the wife has no separate legal existence; and which, while making the husband and wife one, is very careful that that one shall be the husband! It is a fragment of that old barbarism which in England, so late as 1863, permitted a brutal husband to lead his wife, with a halter round her neck, into the public market-place, and sell her to the highest bidder, as though she were a sheep or a cow!

But, with the remarkable development of civilization during the last few centuries, the condition of woman has steadily and greatly improved. One burden after another has been lifted from her shoulders. New and numerous avenues to usefulness and happiness have opened to her. One right after another has been conquered by, or for her. So great a change has been effected in her position, and so differently is she now regarded that, as Mr. Mill has well observed, 'Historians and philosophers have come to adopt her condition as, on the whole, the surest test, and the most correct measure of the civilization of a people or an age.'

And now crowd upon us such questions as, What next? Is the admitted progress of woman to stop at the point now reached, or has it to go on in similar or analogous lines? Is the assimilation of her condition to her brother's to continue, or has it found, or is it soon likely to find, an impassable barrier? Is she, in fine, to become under Providential guidance and within the limits of her own nature, completely self-determining; developing herself from within, and in accordance with her own sense of need and fitness! How answer these questions? By mutual congratulations over past achievements, and wilful disregard of the disabilities under which woman still labour? By flattery of female vanity on the one hand, and denunciation of female presumption on the other? By highly wrought panegyrics of woman's influence as wife and mother, forgetful of the fact that many a woman is neither one nor the other, and that the influence of many a one holding both these relations is far enough from what it should be? All these answers have been rendered many times; and with what success everybody knows. Contemptuous of them and of all similar replies, shall we say, Of course woman's progress is not to be arrested now; that she is to be relieved of every unnatural and unwomanly burden, and to become as self-determining in her sphere as man in his; but that the moment she oversteps her sphere she will not only cease to progress but retrograde and receive infinite harm? Shall we say, Grant her every right, opportunity, privilege within that sphere, beyond which no true woman wants to go, and no unwomanly woman should be permitted to go? Very well. But who shall say, *just what woman's sphere is*? what it includes and what it excludes? Judging by the infinite deal of nonsense uttered on this subject, it would seem that every fledgling in philosophy or religion felt himself fully competent to mark out with entire precision both the general course, and the specific actions appropriate to every woman.

But aside from the fact that hardly any two definitions of woman's sphere fully agree, how impertinent in any *man*, or any *men*, to think of deciding that sphere for her. Just as impertinent as for any woman, or number of women, to determine the scope of man's sphere. How any attempt on her part to do this, analyzing his nature and dictating his position and duty, would be regarded is quite evident. Very plainly, woman herself alone can tell what her true sphere is. Nor can she *now* tell what it is. Once a thousand things which it would now be a shame for any intelligent woman not to know or do were deemed wholly outside her sphere; any attention to which it was fancied would destroy all the delicacy and charm of her character, if it did not wholly unsex her. So, doubtless, a multitude of things which are now popularly reckoned altogether beyond her sphere will hereafter be regarded just as appropriate to her as the care of household, teaching of children, or works of charity. Such has been her culture, or rather her want of culture, and her lack of opportunity, and, still more, her lack of stimulus to use her opportunity; such the suppression of her own will and judgment, and the deference to the will and judgment of others, that she herself has no adequate conception of her own powers. How greatly, therefore, does she hesitate before entering upon any untried arena? What meagre praise satisfies her for any success in genuine work? How frequently drops from her own lips the remark that she has all the facilities that she needs or wants, when the whole intellectual side of her being has been scarcely touched, and she has yet to practise the first instance of a genuine self-reliance. Let it be repeated accordingly, that woman herself does not yet know what her sphere is—does not know what she is capable of doing or becoming. To her unfolding powers her sphere is constantly widening. As the apostle exhorts to work out our salvation,' discovering what it is by achieving it, so must she cast out her sphere and find what it includes by finding what she has ability and taste for. For, with man or woman, 'the talent is the call' to do any work or take any position. Whoso has that, whatever the sex, has the providential commission to assume any place, or follow any vocation, and need have no scruples about overstepping their natural sphere, or violating the proprieties, or marring the spiritual lineaments.

I conclude then, that all the talk about 'woman's sphere,' as though it were something as accurately definable as a circle, or a triangle, is equally irrelevant and impertinent. I conclude that all fear that woman would fly off at a tangent, or describe an orbit as eccentric as a comet's, were all legal and social restrictions of her freedom removed, is equally idle and childish. I conclude that, spite of all the hindrances she has encountered, and is encountering, she is designed to be under the conditions of her own nature, a self-determining creature, shaping her own course, and working out for herself the problem of being.

And if a self-determining being, as she must be if a moral being, then all means and avenues of culture must be opened to her. To say the contrary is to say that her freedom is only nominal, and that her nature is unworthy a full development. Whether she will avail herself of all these means, and enter all these avenues is quite another question; and for a positive answer to which we have not yet perhaps, sufficient data. It is urged by many that she will not; that there are essential and uneffaceable mental and spiritual differences between woman and man; and that these differences, if they do not actually disqualify her for the successful pursuit of certain kinds of culture, do cause her to turn away from them. It is said that she stands for beauty and grace, and man for strength and wisdom; and that therefore her physical frame is smaller, her brain lighter, her intellectual fibre less tough and enduring than man's; though it is admitted that her sense of fitness is finer, her instinct purer, her moral nature nobler. It is concluded accordingly, that if any do choose the educational course, and win distinction in the paths generally supposed to belong especially to man, they are exceptional persons from whom it is entirely unsafe to generalize for the sex.

But upon what ground is this notion of intrinsic and ineradicable differences of taste and talent based! Is it human history? Is it said that, sad truth though it be, it is still true, that woman has never yet manifested the highest order of intellect, not to say genius, that she has never produced a twin soul of Homer or Shakespeare, Plato or Bacon, Newton or Humboldt, Swedenborg or Channing? Undeniably. But is there no other, and quite as satisfactory a reason for her past deficiency? Considering her position hitherto—how almost universally she has been discouraged from attempting aught beyond the beaten paths; and how persistently the means of a generous culture have been denied her—is it any marvel that she has achieved no worthier goals? Is it not rather the marvel that she has accomplished so much, and that there are so many shining female names, from Sappho and Hypatia to Browning and Marian Lewes, from Hebrew Miriam to American Lucretia Mott, that the world will not willingly forget? But to measure her capacity by her past performances is like measuring the possibilities of the freedman, to whom all doors are open, by what he did when the alphabet was to him forbidden fruit, and aspiration was treason against God and the State.

The theory of woman's intellectual inferiority is often based on the alleged smaller volume and lighter weight of her brain. But is it certain that her brain is smaller and lighter than man's? Absolutely it doubtless is: relatively to the size and weight of the body, there are reasons for believing there is a slight preponderance the other way. The average weight of man, the statisticians tell us, is 140 pounds; that of woman 124 pounds; making the ratio between them as 100 to 88.57. But the average weight of a woman's brain is said to be only ten per cent. less than man's, making the ratio between these organs as 100 to 90. Thus, proportionally to the weight of the body, there appears to be nearly 1½ per cent. of brain-weight on the average in her favour. The authority for these statements also declares that, if we take the average *minimum* bodily weights of the sexes, the relative brainweight preponderance of the female is still greater, being nearly 4 per cent over man's brain.'

Yet waiving this point, and conceding that possibly it may be demonstrable by existing, or yet to be collected statistics, that woman's brain is both absolutely and relatively smaller and lighter than man's, does that settle the question of his intellectual superiority? On the contrary how patent that some very large brains—that is, if they fill the cavities in which they are placed—are very dull and stupid brains; and that some, quite below the medium size are exceedingly active and vigorous ones! Is it not true here as elsewhere, that bulk and weight are no sure criterions of efficiency and value? 'It is curious to note,' says an author, 'the delight which Nature seems to take in iterating and reiterating the fact that a very large proportion of the great intellects of the age just passed, was lodged principally with men who fell short of the medium stature. Napoleon was so very short and slim in early life as to be nicknamed "Puss in Boots." Byron was no taller. Lord Jeffrey was not so tall; and Campbell and Moore were still shorter; while Wilberforce was a less man than any of them.' Size and weight of brain then, supposing these demonstrably in man's favour are not conclusive of his superiority; justify no theory of natural or essential differences between him and his sister. 'The profoundest knowledge of the laws of formation of character,' says Mr. Mill, 'is indispensable to entitle any one to affirm even that there is any difference, much more what the difference is, between the two sexes, considered as moral and rational beings; and since no one, as yet, has that knowledge—for there is hardly any subject which, in proportion to its importance, has been so little studied—no one thus far is entitled to any positive opinion on the subject. Conjectures are all that can at present be made; conjectures more or less probable, according as more or less authorized by such knowledge as we yet have of the laws of psychology, as applied to the formation of character.

Admitting, however, all that is urged by the most strenuous as to the essential difference between man and woman, and as to the latter's intellectual inferiority, what then? Are all, or any of the means of improvement and usefulness which man enjoys, and to which she may feel attracted, to be denied her? Is access to the same schools, pursuit of the same wide and varied culture to be prohibited her, if she yearn for it?

Because weak and poorly able to cope with the world, is she to be made weaker still? or, if not that, to be hindered from putting forth to the utmost such powers as she has? Because she cannot rise into the empyrean with equal ease and speed with man, shall her wings be clipped, and her soul so heavily weighted as to hold her, an unwilling prisoner, in the dust? The justice of such a course I will not attempt to disprove. The magnanimity of it I will not endeavour to characterize! If woman be so unlike and so unequal to man, as is sometimes alleged, then all the more reason is there for removing every hindrance, and providing every help to her development. All the more reason for encouraging her to put forth every energy for the attainment of the worthiest goal, saying, Here is the wide world, the immeasurable universe, this mysterious life, with all their boundless wealth of knowledge, wisdom, and goodness: take what you can, assimilate what you may, become what your nature will admit.

From woman's right of self-determination follows also the correlative right to enter any employment or profession for which she has the taste and qualification. Within a half century probably not one person in a thousand would have listened to such a proposition with any other feeling than mingled indignation and contempt. But who thinks of questioning it now? A few, boldly entering on other vocations than public opinion had assigned their sex, and successfully discharging their functions, have conquered the right for all others. Whoso now wishes to follow any profession finds comparatively little hindrance outside herself. Talent, tact, devotion, enlarged and directed by sound culture, are all that are needed. With these she may till the soil, practise any handicraft, traffic in any merchandize. With these she may set free the divine image slumbering in the marble, thrill all beholders by the impersonations of genius, lift all listeners on wings of song to the gates of Paradise. With these she may practise the healing art, thread the mazes of legal lore, preach the unsearchable riches of the gospel of love. But as all this is so generally admitted, has been so frequently and clearly demonstrated, nothing more need be said of it here.

Still further, woman's right of self-determination involves the right of *suffrage*. She can never shape her own career, never be the arbiter of her own destiny, so long as she has no voice in framing the laws under which she lives, and to which she is amenable. At least so much is true of man. We cannot think of him as a self-directing being working out the high purpose of his existence, subject to the domination of another person or class. But if this be true of man, why not of woman? And why has she not the same natural right, as a free moral being, to the ballot, as has man? So pertinent is this question that the Rev. Dr. Bushnell, in his "Reform against Nature," in order to avoid the conclusion it necessitates, denies that man has any *right* to suffrage. That is, he says in substance, it is expedient that some men—it may be expedient that all men—should vote.

But *right* to vote has no man. What then, becomes of our modern doctrines of 'equal rights before the law;' 'just government resting on the
consent of the governed;' 'the inseparability of representation and taxation,' and the like? They are turned summarily out of doors, as, in our
author's words, 'the cheap impostures of philosophy;' while in their place
we find the basis, not of a 'cheap,' but of a very dear and detestable
imperialism, or autocracy, or whatever form of government the strong and
cunning may impose. That there is much probability of the people of this
continent adopting this view—abandoning the idea of their *natural right* to
participate in governmental affairs, and seeking the right to do so, as Dr.
Bushnell advises, 'out of history, out of providential preparations and
causes, out of the concessions of custom, out of expediencies concluded,
and debated reasons of public benefit,' I think we need have little fear.
But if this view seem preposterous, then what other basis for the suffrage
is there than the rights of human nature?—a basis which no more excludes
one sex than the other.

Admitting the abstract right of woman to the ballot, is it expedient that
she be actually clothed with that right? Does not the concession of it
involve so many, and so stupendous changes, that it is wiser to withhold
it, even at the risk of violating abstract principle? Perhaps as good a way
to answer this question is to ask some others. Is it, then, expedient that the
true and right should everywhere prevail, and every soul be endowed with
its just prerogatives? Or is it better that there should be some wrong, some
injustice, some oppression done to some persons or class? When that
wrong touches ourselves, do we then gravely ask if it be expedient that it
be removed, or do we cry, 'Let justice be done though the heavens fall'?
And in the case under consideration shall we hesitate to say, 'Let justice
be done!' So far, however, from the heavens falling on that account, it is
on justice that their eternal pillars rest. Injustice it is that brings them
down on human heads with such results as those with which Dagon's
great temple fell, when the tortured giant wrenched away the columns
that upheld its mighty dome.

The next answer to this question of expediency is one which, it is
thought, goes to the root of the whole matter. It is the analogy of the
family, of society, and of the church. As a rule, children of both sexes are
born into the same family. Certainly the family is based upon—cannot
exist without—both the masculine and the feminine elements. And have
we not here the primal and most important of all human organizations?
Beyond question what is true of the family in this respect is true of
general society. Strike the feminine element out of that, and men are
savages and bears. Strike the masculine element out, and women are
gossips or dawdlers. There is no society where both are not found
reciprocally influencing each other. Just so in the church, the two elements find equal place and work. Eliminate the feminine element, and the

church would petrify. Eliminate the masculine element, and the church would collapse. Does not the same law hold in the state? or is the analogy good for nothing, and the state a wholly exceptional institution? Has the entire exclusion of feminity from that worked so well that every body is satisfied, and sees no room for improvement? Surely the person must be a recent arrival from some other planet who can honestly ask such a question. For how patent that our political life, from the primary meeting up to the highest legislative body, is, in the very mildest phrase, far enough from what it should be? How patent that there is infinite room for improvement alike in the methods of politics, in the tone of deliberative bodies, and in the spirit and administration of law! And is it not highly probable that an infusion of true femininity into this sphere would contribute somewhat to such improvement? Can it be doubted when we recall the changes which have followed the introduction of this element elsewhere? Not, of course, as is sometimes foolishly implied, that the extension of suffrage to woman would banish all trickery and corruption from politics. Women are not yet perfect any more than men; are subject to the same temptations; would unquestionably, just like their brothers, often cast their votes for quite unworthy purposes. Is that any reason why they should be deprived of their natural right? Do we reason thus in regard to men? Moreover, it seems to be universally admitted—is very often affirmed—that woman's moral instincts are purer and nobler than man's. If this be so, can the world afford to shut out their promptings and suggestions from all public affairs? Has it made such progress that it can safely trust all its political and civil interests, which are often intimately connected with its moral and religious interests, to the lower and coarser half of humanity?

It is said, however, and doubtless honestly thought by many, that the concession of the ballot to woman, instead of elevating public affairs, would injure herself. This has always been the argument against widening the sphere of her activity. Every change in her condition has been met with the objection, "Take care, take care; you will harm instead of helping;" as though women were a delicate porcelain vase that any removal, if not the slightest touch, would shiver to atoms. Yet who thinks her lower in the scale of existence to-day than when, 5,000 years ago, she was man's purchased slave? or than 500 years ago when she was his toy, or his idol! Who does not know that she is vastly higher, and that society is immeasurably better for her having more largely participated in its affairs? And why should not her assumption of all the rights her nature claims, and all the duties to which her nature prompts tend in the same direction?

Ask any, What gentleman would be willing to take his wife and daughter, supposing them willing to go, to the wretched places where elections are often held, and into the coarse, profane, and sometimes indecent crowd that clusters around? Evidently none; and there would be no need of it. The entrance of woman into any place, be it street-car, ferryboat, or political meeting, to which as a listener she is now sometimes invited, is a signal for every man to put himself on his good behaviour. Few are the men, on this continent at least, that in any mixed assembly would wish or dare insult, or show the least disrespect to, a woman who did not in some way invite it. Give woman the ballot, and the polling-place will soon be fit for her to enter. Even as it is, the man or the woman who does not shrink from many a public conveyance, with its filth, and vile air, and bad manners, need not be greatly shocked at the offensiveness of an ordinary election room.

But the concession of suffrage to woman, it is said, will beget different political convictions, and so endless bickering, in the family. Do differences in religion beget such discord? Between low and vulgar souls, Yes; and mainly because, amongst such, woman is not yet recognized as a self-determining being, having the right of independent convictions. Between noble and generous natures, No; and still less would different political opinions tend to domestic strife from the fact that the proposed change is based on woman's natural right to do her own thinking, and shape her own destiny. It is not found in business partnerships, the most common instance of voluntary association next to marriage, that political differences occasion serious troubles; and certainly no man would think of entering into such relationship where his freedom in this respect would be in the least danger. So, if there be any genuine respect of husband and wife for each other—if they *be* husband and wife—how much more conciliatory, and tolerant of each other's idiosyncrasies, will they be! If there be no such respect—if they be merely a couple of animals yoked together—it is doubtful if different political affiliations would render their condition any unhappier than it now is.

It may be said again, that the right to vote involves the right to hold office. Not necessarily. Many men now vote who have never been, who never expect to be, elected to any office; some of whom do not want to be, and others of whom are not fit to be so elected. But suppose no man voted, here for Mayor or Member of Parliament, or elsewhere for Governor or President, who is not qualified for, and might not properly aspire to, either of those positions, very few votes would be cast. Yet who, on that account, prizes any the less the sacred right of saying whom he prefers to have preside over the administration of city or country? Suppose, morever, the right to vote does involve the right to hold office. What then? Have not many women already held office, one sort or another, and shown themselves fully equal to their duties! Were Maria Theresa, and Catharine, and Elizabeth, any the less rulers because they were women? Who for more than forty years has reigned over the vast British Empire, and reigned in the hearts of her subjects as well, but a woman? Have the women of England and the United States, appointed as school superintendents, members of charitable boards, post-mistresses, and clerks of various grades, proved themselves, as a class, either dishonest or incompetent? They have shown themselves just the opposite—able, efficient, upright administrators. Naturally enough, the women whose tastes will lead them to desire, whose relations will justify them in accepting, and whose qualifications will fit them for high office will be very few—certainly for no inconsiderable period. Nor is it fairly supposable, as sometimes seems to be feared, that, suffrage once conceded to women, both they and their brothers will instantly turn idiots, or act in an altogether idiotic manner in selecting candidates for public places, or that official position would not then, quite as often as now, seek out those most capable of discharging its functions.

But it may be asked, still further, Is not woman to be a wife and mother? Some women, whether from choice or necessity, sustain neither of these relations. Some of these—as Frances Cobbe, Florence Nightingale, Clara Barton—are amongst the ablest, most refined, and noble women of the world, whom it would be a gross insult to liken to the great majority of masculine voters. And there are few things that others of this class—numbering in some populous centres their tens of thousands—do so much need as the stimulus that this enlarged sphere of action, with its new ideas and purposes, would give. Besides, if every woman were to be a wife and mother—if every one were to aspire to these relations as intrinsically the most desirable for her, as in many respects they unquestionably are—I know not that those would be any reasons why she should be content with being a mere over-dressed doll on the one hand, or an abject slave, doing and thinking only what her master permits on the other. They have long seemed to me additional reasons why she should enjoy, and endeavour to make the best use of, every opportunity, developing herself into

> 'A creature not too bright or good
> For human nature's daily food;
> A perfect woman, nobly planned
> To warn, to comfort, and command.'

It is objected, finally, that women do not want the right of suffrage; that they are entirely content to remain without other influence on public affairs than they now have. Of many women—perhaps the majority—this is unquestionably true. How greatly to their praise it need not be said. Certainly it is not to their praise if they could, by their votes, help the industrial, educational, and moral interests of their country. Many persons are said to be wholly satisfied in very unnatural and pernicious relations. Most of the wives of that occidental sultan, Brigham Young, were reputed to be quite content with one undivided twentieth part of their lord's time and affection. Nothing was more common, twenty-five years ago, than to hear that the American slaves were perfectly happy, and would not be persuaded by any officious intermeddlers to leave their indulgent masters. Whether either of these assertions were true need not here be discussed; and whether being true, either would reflect credit or discredit on the parties implicated, the reader shall judge.

But it is very far from true that *no* women wish to vote. Thousands, and tens of thousands, and they will soon be hundreds of thousands wait impatiently to be invested with this right. And if there were but one woman in all the land who claimed the right, with what justice could it be withheld? Is there any better reason for wronging one or a few than for wronging many? It seems quite evident moreover, that the time is not far distant when this right will be conceded in all free countries; for how rapid has been the progress of public opinion in this direction during the last twenty-five years. That length of time ago, how few—and those counted as womanish men, or manish women, fanatics, or lunatics—were willing to confess any leaning toward, or friendship for, the so-called 'Woman Movement?' Today, how many of the keenest politicians, quick to scent the coming breeze, are avowing themselves in its favour! Let us hope that it is not simply because they want votes. That there is a strong and growing feeling in England, and very considerable interest in certain circles in this Dominion, on the subject, is familiar to all intelligent persons. In the United States one territory has already placed woman, so far as the law is concerned on an entire equality with man; while many States have taken very decided steps in the same direction; among other things, endowing her with the right of suffrage on educational questions, as well as recognizing her eligibility to certain offices. During the last session of Congress a bill was passed authorizing her to practise in the Supreme Court on the same terms with man; while the Judiciary Committee of the Senate reported an amendment to the Constitution sweeping away all distinctions of sex in regard to political rights. It would seem that one risks little in predicting that another generation will see woman's claim to suffrage placed on the same basis with man's throughout the great Republic. . . .

'A GIRL OF THE PERIOD', 1880

Rose-Belford's *Canadian Monthly*, 1880, vol. IV, 624-7.

'CONFIDENCES'
BY 'A GIRL OF THE PERIOD'

In these days of 'women's rights' and even 'children's rights' I feel hopeful a little that there may be some chance for a 'girl of the period' to state what she thinks about her wrongs in the pages of such an 'advanced' publication as the *Canadian Monthly* justly claims to be. I don't care what row people make about it; for you'll keep my secret—won't you? Mr Editor—and not let anybody know who your contributor is.

'I want to know why' about a lot of things; and I don't care if some of your smart contributors think me a 'dreadful stupid' if only they will really deluge me with their wisdom.

I want to know why it is that I, a well-brought-up lady-like (excuse my self-conceit—but this is the remark people make of me) girl, am so utterly helpless and dependent. I have not been taught anything that is of the slightest earthly use to anybody in the whole world. Of course I can sing correctly; but have no special power or compass of voice. It is only soft and low—a peculiarity of voice which Milton (?), or some of these old poets, says is nice in a woman, because it keeps her from scolding, I suppose. As a pianist I am a *brilliant success*, and yet a humbug as regards the science of music. That goes without saying. I can waltz—well! 'divinely'—but no thanks to anybody for that; it comes *con amore*; I can sew—fancy work; but I could not cut out and 'build' a dress, even if I was never to have another. I can't make up a bonnet, nor even a hat; but I do know when the milliner has made a mess of either. I am self-conceited enough to think I have extremely good taste in such matters as a critic, yet I don't see how I could turn my good taste into a single solitary dollar if I had to. I just love parties, balls, concerts and—shall I confess it?—theatres, and yet, if I had to earn the money with which to gratify myself in these indulgences, I fancy I must perforce go amusementless for many a year. My dear old 'Pater' and my good kind mamma are fairly well-off, I believe (but I really don't know), and are very willing to give me a good share of all these enjoyments; but it does make me often 'feel mean' to know that I am utterly dependent on them for everything, and can't do anything to lighten their load. Why mamma won't even let me into the kitchen to learn how to do things. She says it is not lady-like.

A girl not out of her 'teens' yet can't be expected, perhaps, to have much brains, and so it puzzles me awfully to understand why it should be, that my brother Jack, aged sixteen, and Bill, aged twenty two, both work, the one as an office boy in a warehouse (he calls it sub-book-keeper), the other as traveller for a wholesale grocery house, and yet both are looked upon as quite respectable. Bill is asked out to all the parties with me. But if I, a girl, as Bill tries with much pains and wealth of oratory to explain to me, were known to work, *everybody* would 'cut' me at once; I would be just 'a work-girl, you see,' he says conclusively, as though that were any solution of the question or settled it at all. Why do not the smell of sugar and the raisin and molasses spots which adhere to the nether and upper integuments of his working apparel, adhere also socially to his full dress suit when he dons it? It is a conundrum, and I give it up; just as completely as I give up the other conundrum of why it should be that similar spots on a working suit of mine should inevitably reveal themselves socially, as he says they would, on any party dress I might don, however 'swell' it might be? I try to argue the thing out on this line with Bill sometimes, but he only gets mad; says girls don't know anything and can't be rational for five consecutive minutes, and goes off fuming with some favourite quotation of his from some nasty old philosopher, about 'women being unreasoning animals that poke the fire from the top' or light stoves with coal oil, etc. etc.

But I vow and declare I can't see that I am so irrational. Why should I be so fettered and useless? My mother only laughs when I torment her about it and tells me I'll soon drop all that nonsense when I get 'engaged' to some gentlemanly young fellow; but that interesting youth is hard to find, and when something that looks like him does turn up it invariably becomes painfully evident that it would be a shame to add to the burdens already laid upon his slender income by 'society' and social requirements. In fact I am shut up to a choice of ungentlemanly young men, who are half old and so wholly coarse or self-conceited through having 'fought their way up from the ranks' as papa puts it, that one can't help wishing they had stayed in those 'ranks' they are so eminently fitted to adorn.

It is towards one of these useful, practical, self-raised, men, that poor useless me is hintingly thrust by anxious relatives both near and distant. His usefulness is supposed to be eminently adapted to my uselessness. He, the self-raised one, is expected to raze me down to his level. I confess I don't like the prospect; and I'm not so sure that Jones does either (his name is Jones—*Mrs.* Jones fancy!!!) He and I have not a solitary taste in common. So, in self-defence, I take broad hints regarding my probable future destiny as mild attempts at jocularity, and vent my pent-up indignation on my long-suffering relatives in wicked conundrums and other pleasantries at the expense of my would-be husband; but nobody sympathises with these sallies except my good old papa. He laughs, and is severely rebuked for encouraging my folly. But with that moral support— highly moral I think—I am too much for my disinterested relatives. I don't 'make eyes' at Jones. He is getting discouraged. My relatives begin to look upon him (and me) as lost.

I feel lost a little myself too—lost, useless and mean—to think that I only dawdle around and can only look pretty—that is as pretty as I can, you know. I eat up, dress up, and spend the 'proceeds'—that's a business word isn't it?—of the labours of others without being a bit the happier for it.

And then there's another side to it, too, which I can't talk much about to sympathizing (?) relatives; but I will to you, dear Public, because some of you may be 'girls of the period' like me and will understand. There are nights when I am peculiarly disgusted with myself, and I sit up and moon and cry my eyes out, because—well, because I am miserable and feel such a little fool. For visions of Charlie—Charlie Rivers—will intrude at such times. He is so nice. He's simply splendid! Of course, I don't *care* for him particularly; but then I think if I tried hard I might get almost to like him. I think, and think, and think. He's a clerk you know, and papa says has got six hundred or eight hundred dollars—somewhere about that a year. But whatever his salary, he keeps himself quite like a gentleman. He's a great flirt they say, but he doesn't *ever* flirt with me. He and I always talk quite seriously. He says he lives in 'diggings,' and describes the royal times he has roughing it all by himself in a 'growlery' of his own; informs me what a splendid cook he is, and that he has learned it all by the light of nature. But then papa says, 'he'll never be anything. He's not sharp and has queer ideas—a good fellow, but a *soft*.' I think I know what he means by that, because Charlie talks to me sometimes—on the stairs at parties you know—like this, with an odd, puzzled, weary look in his eyes. 'I am worried, Miss Kate, I know I'll never be rich. I can't see my way to do the mean things necessary to get on. Not but that I am content enough to do so much work—good work, the best I've got in me—for so much pay all my life. But then if a fellow were to fall in love—get tumbled right into it before he knew—what is he to do about it? Is he to keep to his principles and lose his love, or is he to lose his principles, go in wild for money, gain his loved one, lose his own respect, and risk the loss of hers when she finds out what a mean money-grubbing wretch he has become in order to get her? That is *the* conundrum to me, Miss Kate. Have you any answer to it?' And then he looks, oh! so anxious and troubled that—I have to ask him to button my glove for me, just to change the subject. But it does not do it always. During the buttoning process he looks awfully solemn, says it's a shame to bother me about his little troubles, and that he won't fall in love at all if I don't want him to, etc. etc., till I don't know what to say, and he proposes—another waltz.

Why, oh! why, dear Public, should I need to be dumb? What have I done, or not done, that I should have no experience of real life such as he has, and so be unable to give him sound and rational advice?

Just at present the moon is full, and moonstruck visions assail me. How thoroughly jolly it would be if girls like myself were brought up to some form of trade, profession, or business, so that, when we come of age, we might earn enough to suffice for our real needs. These needs are not so very great after all; only neat, pretty, but not ever-varying and fanciful dress, and food and shelter. Steady, necessitated occupation would be a real blessing to most of us, and then if we did meet the awful fate portrayed by Charlie, and tumbled headlong into love, why we needn't be the least bit of a burden to the other 'tumbler' when we both came to the surface again, but might swim to shore hand in hand. Two eight hundred dollars a year to support two 'diggingses' rolled into *one*, might surely make that *one* extra cosy and comfortable, mightn't it? and neither of us need then be a bit more mean or money-grubbing than before. If each unit (scientific word, isn't it?) could maintain itself apart, would it be any more, or any less, difficult when united?

There are such heaps and heaps of things women might do if any body would show them how. Why, the Kindergarten system alone is quite a mine of wealth and of work to us, and might be extended indefinitely down to the very babies. Some of the married women, as well as the single, could attend to that, while others of the married ones who had children of their own, could leave their children at the Kindergarten during the day, and pursue other forms of labour themselves. Very pretty pictures are made of the husband and father wending his way home in the cool of the evening, certain of welcome from his loved ones. Why does no one sketch the wife and mother strolling home from her toil on the arm of her husband to their mutual home, alike joyous in anticipation of shouts of welcome, clinging kiss and sweet caresses from their little ones, just returned from the Kindergarten? Why may not such elements of happiness constitute a happy home for each and all; Father, Mother, and children? Each, with the experiences of the day spent in different ways, amid different scenes, can pour these into willing ears. Each can gladden each with the restful sympathy and endearment of true home love; all the more dear for the brief daily separation.

Probably the moon's influence, if turned strongly in such a direction, would upset the existing order of things a good deal in this mad world, and cause a tide in the affairs of men strong enough to sweep through a lot of social barriers of the pitchfork kind, but what of that? There are many things social which need upsetting badly, and although I am only 'a girl of the period,' and don't know much, I *do* know this, that the more the work of the world is wisely shared among all its denizens, both men and women, the less strain there will be on each to satisfy purely natural wants. . . .

But the moon is drawing me a little out of my depth. I must not be caught and swept away by her tide.

It's all that horrid Charlie. His worried look haunts me continually. Not that I am smitten with him at all. You must not think that, and of course his name isn't 'Charlie,' nor mine 'Kate.' But I can't help thinking often that if the world were different, so that I would not need thereby to cast such a moral and physical burden on him, I might be tempted to take a kind of interest in *him* as well as in the wrongs and woes, the rights and uses, of we poor 'girls of the period.' As it is, how can any girl who truly loves some one whom she also admires and respects, far more than she does herself, consider it a proof of real love to put such a fearful burden upon him as is meant by that peculiar and entirely abnormal development of this nineteenth century, called ' A GIRL OF THE PERIOD?'

A FRENCH-CANADIAN VIEW, 1901

Madame Joséphine Dandurand, *Nos Travers* (Montreal, 1901), pp. 218-29.

LE FÉMINISME
Conférence faite à l'Asile de la Providence

Eh! de quoi vous parlerais-je, Mesdames, si ce n'est de "nos affaires?" Je crois même que c'est le seul moyen de me faire absoudre de ma hardiesse. Il paraît que c'est une prérogative masculine que de parler haut, du moins à cet égard, l'usage fait loi, et il faut toujours respecter la loi quelque injuste, je veux dire, quelque sévère qu'elle nous paraisse.

Il me semble que tout ici autorise l'audace. Le bruit de notre voix qui nous effraie toujours un peu, trouve entre ces murs, un écho sympathique et rassurant.

Nous nous sentons presque justifiée d'oser nous affirmer à l'ombre de cette institution puissante qui est l'oeuvre de mains, surtout, de cerveaux féminins.

J'ai besoin de croire d'ailleurs que nous sommes "entre nous", et, "qu'officiellement", il n'y a ici qu'une femme s'adressant à des femmes. Si par hasard il s'était glissé dans cet auditoire quelques représentants du sexe fort, je veux l'oublier. Si pourtant leur dignité m'impose l'évidence, je me persuade qu'ils sont tous des féministes. Il ne faudrait pas qu'ils protestasent parce qu'alors je serais très dure pour eux. Je les comparerais à des paralytiques guéris disant du mal des béquilles; oui, je les appellerais des ingrats!

Féministes, Mesdames, quoi qu'ils disent, tous les hommes le furent une fois, et ils le redeviendront, n'ayez crainte. Ils le seront quelque jour, comme les vieillards qu'abrite ce toit hospitalier le sont, et quant ils ressentiront toute la vérité de cette parole de l'Esprit-Saint: "Malheur à l'infirme qui n'a que des coeurs d'hommes et des mains d'hommes autour de ses douleurs."

Ils le seront même dans l'acception la plus étendue du mot, chaque fois que par l'absence du soutien naturel, comme cela arrive si souvent, ils dépendront dans leur jeunesse pour l'existence, l'instruction et l'éducation d'une femme, cumulant dans ce cas les fonctions du père et de la mère sans que son coeur vaillant, sans que ses faibles épaules faillissent à la tâche. Et n'est-ce pas logique? Chez qui la femme recruterait-elle des partisans dévoués si ce n'est parmi ces témoins authentiques de sa valeur?

Le Canada est, sans s'en douter peut-être, un des pays où le féminisme est plus ancien et sûrement celui qui lui doit le plus.

Tenez, voulez-vous que nous disions un peu de bien des femmes? D'abord je vous avouerai que j'en meurs d'envie, et puis c'est ma manière à moi de traiter cette importante question sociale. Car il ne faut pas s'attendre à ce que j'en fasse l'historique rigoureux. En choisissant le sujet de cette petite causerie, je n'avais aucun système en vue. Je ne voulais pas non plus faire l'apologie du féminisme, qui se défend bien tout seul.

J'ai pensé qu'il serait intéressant de disserter un peu avec mes congénères, les Canadiennes-Françaises, que je savais devoir être brillamment représentées ici ce soir, sur un événement qui nous concerne et auquel elles ne pourront pas longtemps rester étrangères.

Il importe de voir ce que signifie pour notre pays ce terme vague, d'invention moderne: "Le féminisme." Il importe aussi de nous rendre compte que si le nom est nouveau, l'oeuvre qu'il représente ne l'est pas autant qu'on le pense. Il serait malaisé pourtant de le définir exactement parce qu'il n'a pas de programme fixe et que ses tendances varient selon les pays. En tous cas c'est une force qui ne demande qu'à être dirigée. En considérant ce qu'elle produit de meilleur chez les autres, nous apprendrons à la faire servir à notre plus grand bien.

Nous disions donc qu'à part les lois (dont on se plaint beaucoup), il n'y a guère de bienfaits nationaux auxquels la femme n'a pas contribué chez nous.

Faut-il rappeler son initiative, son courage égal à celui des plus vaillants, sa souveraine influence dans la fondation de la colonie? Voudrait-on que je fisse la nomenclature des innombrables institutions que son zèle diligent a fondées depuis, sur la surface de notre immense territoire? Est-il bien des formes de la misère et de la souffrance humaines, dites-moi, auxquelles elle ne se soit attaquée et qu'elle n'ait réussi à pallier?

La meilleure réponse à ces questions c'est que l'Etat, se désintéressant de l'éducation supérieure des filles, de l'assistance publique et des oeuvres de bienfaisance en général, s'en remet entièrement à l'initiative et à la compétence féminine pour tout ce qui s'y rapporte.

Tout favorise donc, en ce pays, l'expansion du féminisme! Et l'expérience du passé et les facilités que cette expérience donne à l'avenir, et la liberté dont nous jouissons, car si nous sommes bienvenues à vivre dans une complète oisiveté, selon qu'il nous plaît, on nous laisse également libres de participer, nous privilégiées, dans la mesure de nos forces, à l'amélioration du sort des moins favorisés. Un pays ne repousse pas les services de ses enfants. L'histoire, au contraire, nous montre les nations acceptant avec bonheur le salut de la main d'une femme, ce qui fait qu'il n'y a pas beaucoup d'Etats qui n'aient eu leur époque féministe également. On dirait qu'à cette lumière de l'histoire, la femme, réalisant tout à coup la virtualité de son pouvoir, a eu l'idée d'organiser, de centraliser ses forces éparses: d'où le féminisme moderne.

A quoi vise cette agitation dont le mouvement comme une marée puissante s'étend à tous les pays du monde? Que signifie cette levée volontaire d'une armée active, ardente mais pacifique?

Ce mouvement, c'est un réveil de la responsabilité féminine. Ce à quoi il tend? Par essence et dans ses manifestations générales, à rien que de juste, que de désintéressé, que de raisonnable. Son action s'effectue sous l'égide de la religion à l'ombre de la loi.

Entre l'injustice de l'aristocratie et la colère des socialistes, par ses attaches avec l'une et sa bonté envers les autres, la femme en Angleterre et aux Etats-Unis, sert de tampon. Son ministère contribuera sans doute largement à réconcilier dans le vieux monde comme dans le nôtre, deux éléments sociaux dont le choc est toujours terrible.

De fait, il existe une "Ligue internationale de la paix" recrutée parmi les plus grandes dames des deux hémisphères, lesquelles sont associées aux philosophes et aux hommes d'Etat les plus illustres. On sait que leur influence a été un puissant facteur dans cet événement récent: l'entente de deux grands Etats pour régler toute querelle, à l'avenir,—non par la guerre, non par le sang humain versé—mais au moyen d'une commission d'arbitres. Il y a des choses que l'homme, entraîné par la passion, oublie facilement. Dans la patrie comme dans la famille la voix de la femme doit faire entendre les paroles apaisantes qui rappellent au devoir et à l'humanité.

Mais, sans s'arrêter à ce rôle diplomatique, le Féminisme accomplit, surtout dans l'économie de la vie nationale, une oeuvre prodigieuse.

Il faut lire l'ouvrage de Mme Bentzon, sur la "Condition de la femme aux Etats-Unis", pour voir ce que dans la seule ville de Chicago, il fait de bien à l'âme comme au corps, et comment il peut transformer, non seulement une population, mais l'aspect d'un pays.

Ces dames—pour ne mentionner qu'un détail—ont entrepris de réaliser ce qui a toujours été déclaré impossible: elles ont résolu de débarrasser leur cité,—Reine de l'Ouest,—de la fumée qui, en toute saison, endeuille et souille sa beauté. Elles sont en train d'y réussir . . . Vous connaissez le proverbe arabe: "Ce que veut une belle est écrit dans les cieux"? Nos congénères américaines veulent découvrir le firmament, afin qu'on y puisse lire cette précieuse écriture.

En somme, la conscription spontanée de ces milliers de recrues du monde élégant, riche et heureux, met au service des autorités religieuses et civiles, une armée d'auxiliaires puissantes et intrépides, prêtes à entreprendre les plus rudes tâches; elle fournit des escouades d'ambulancières laiques qui cherchent dans les taudis, les tavernes et les cachots, les blessés du combat journalier, les mourants à la vie morale.

Cet enrôlement sous un même drapeau d'une classe où ont presque toujours régné en souveraines l'oisiveté, la frivolité et la jouissance, a pour but principal: d'être utile.

"Etre utile", Mesdames, il paraît que ce n'est pas pour autre chose que nous avons été mises sur cette planète. Si le bon Dieu nous a donné ces belles longues journées dont un nombre compté compose notre vie; s'il nous prête chaque matin sa lumière, des gens dignes de foi nous assurent que ce n'est pas pour vaquer tout bonnement au soin de notre nourriture, de notre vêtement et de notre divertissement. C'est dommage qu'il y ait d'aussi maussades commentateurs des décrets divins! Ne pourraient-ils, ces juges sévères, s'entendre avec d'autres hommes plus indulgents, qui assignent à la femme ce rôle exclusif, païen, mais charmant: "plaire?"

Asurément, les premiers ne nous commandent pas d'être déplaisantes—ce serait trop exigeant.—Ils admettent volontiers cette obligation de plaire (chère à la moins coquette), mais ils ne veulent pas démordre de l'idée de soumettre le sexe faible à la loi d'utilité morale aussi bien que matérielle. Ils nous parlent de nos responsabilités, de la nécessité d'amasser quelques mérites... et du temps qui ne revient plus... Ils nous font réaliser la "fuite formidable des instants, ce glissement de l'heure", comme dit Maupassant, "cette course imperceptible, affolante quand on y songe, ce défilé infini des petites secondes pressées qui grignotent le corps et la vie des hommes." Si bien que leurs scrupules nous gagnent à la fin et qu'on ne se sent pas la conscience en paix le soir—malgré les encouragements de quelques-uns—si, tout le jour, on n'a rien fait que de se laisser vivre. On en arrive même, le croirait-on? à n'oser plus s'ennuyer!

S'ennuyer, Mesdames! J'admets avec vous que voilà un mot ridicule. Si l'on n'a pas fait de l'ennui un péché capital, c'est qu'on devait le réserver pour la punition des ignorants et des égoïstes.

Au fait, y a t-il des femmes oisives ou des femmes fort occupées, si l'on veut, à ne rien faire d'utile? Soyons franches, Mesdames; admettons que l'Américaine, et surtout la Canadienne—dans la société aisée—est une reine à laquelle on ne demande rien; que l'on décharge presque complètement du soin d'élever ses enfants. C'est à ces riches que le Féminisme réclame les miettes de leur table,—quand leur famille a été largement servie,—c'est cette menue monnaie des minutes et des heures perdues par les mondaines, qu'il recueille pour en former un capital profitable aux malheureux.

Un grand nombre répond à son appel; c'est pourquoi l'on voit des maisons comme celle qui nous abrite en ce moment, si prospères. Mais nous sommes encore une immense majorité en dehors de ces oeuvres admirables. Or justement mille besoins réclament dans notre société, des dévouements nouveaux. Quand je dis: "nouveaux", je voudrais être bien comprise.

Ce qualificatif n'a rien d'agressif. La nouveauté ici est synonyme de "progrès", et le progrès est la seule route qui mène à la perfection. Le Féminisme ne doit donc pas être représenté comme une révolution qui bouleverse, mais comme une évolution naturelle dans l'ordre providentiel des événements. L'une de ces tendances est de cultiver les dons de l'esprit et c'est une attache de plus à la tradition chrétienne, qui, toujours,— depuis saint Jérôme jusqu'à Fénelon et jusqu'à Dupanloup,—a mis l'étude à côté de la prière.

Cela m'amène à parler des adversaires du mouvement qui nous occupe, car il en existe...qui se convertissent d'ailleurs tous les jours. Parmi eux, il s'en trouve qui croient en vouloir à la chose, et qui au fond, ne s'objectent qu'au nom; ils ont été les premiers à utiliser, hors du foyer, celles que le foyer ne réclamait pas constamment.

Il y en a d'autres qui se croient obligés de parler au nom de l'homme et du mari. Ils aperçoivent un danger pour la famille et la société dans cette apparente émancipation. Quelle raison ont-ils donc de suspecter l'amour et le dévouement maternels à ce point? Oublient-ils que le voilà le plus sincère et le plus sûr gardien du foyer: l'amour maternel! Aurait-il attendu si tard pour se démentir?

Mais, c'est en exagérant ce prétendu danger qu'on arrive à se persuader que la sécurité pour tous est dans l'obscurité, c'est-à-dire, la nullité de la femme. Quelle erreur! Plus nous serons instruites et éclairées, Mesdames, et plus nous serons de bonnes mères. Le P. Lacordaire le savait, lui qui reconnaissait à la femme une influence extrêmement puissante, surtout dans la société chrétienne et qui recommandait à l'une de ses amies de lire Homère, Plutarque, Cicéron, Platon, David, saint Paul, saint Augustin, sainte Thérèse, Bossuet, Pascal et d'autres semblables.

Cela étonnera bien certains de nos écrivains qui mettent de temps à autre devant nos yeux leur idéal de femme ménagère—et rien que ménagère.

Au fait, j'oubliais une dernière catégorie d'anti-féministes. Ceux-là sont plus amusants que sérieux et personne ne tient à les convertir. Pour mieux combattre le fléau, ils emploient et le sarcasme, et la foudre, deux armes trop opposées pour que leur alliance hybride cause grand ravage. D'ailleurs, ces gens-là ne sont pas convaincus. A leurs heures ils sont d'acharnés féministes; j'en connais parmi eux qui exigent une singulière investiture de la femme, devant laquelle ils s'inclinent. Il faut qu'elle ait eu des relations avec le diable, comme la pseudo Diana Vaughan.[1] La condition est dure. Tout cela n'empêche pas que dans les difficultés et les dangers de notre époque critique, on se tourne de plus en plus vers la femme pour lui demander aide et conseil.

M. Brunetière—l'un des premiers critiques de France, écrivain dont le nom est universellement respecté—parle de "refaire l'éducation de la femme, parce que, à titre de mères, les femmes sont avant tout, les éducatrices de la génération future." Après avoir remarqué en passant que si les "pédantes" sont insupportables, les sottes n'en sont pas pour cela d'un plus agréable commerce, il conclut ainsi: "Quand on voudra vraiment réformer nos lycées de garçons, il faudra commencer par réformer nos lycées de filles."

La France a souvent été représentée comme l'un des pays les plus opposés à l'émancipation du sexe faible, et pourtant, je connais un bien vieux féministe français:

Le bonhomme Montaigne disait, il y a trois cents ans: "Il est ridicule et injuste que l'oisiveté de nos femmes soit entretenue de notre sueur et de notre travail."

La France nous offre tous les jours le spectacle d'hommes illustres se ralliant, pour des motifs plus élevés, au mouvement féministe.

Le regretté Mgr d'Hulst a exprimé, avant de mourir, un voeu que vous me permettrez de citer en finissant.

"Vous n'avez pas oublié, Madame,—écrit-il,—l'appel ardent que Mgr Dupanloup adressait, il y a trente ans déjà, aux femmes chrétiennes pour les attirer au travail de l'esprit. Il voyait là, pour elles, un puissant moyen d'influence sur l'âme de leurs maris: non pas que la femme doive faire au même degré, ni de la même manière, toutes les études que fait l'homme; mais elle doit en faire de telles que rien de ce qui intéresse ou remplit ou surcharge la vie de son époux, rien de ce qui occupe l'intelligence de ses fils, ne reste pour elle chose étrangère et inaccessible.

D'autres peuvent ne pas partager cette manière de voir, ils peuvent croire que la femme serait mieux dans son rôle, en renonçant à l'influence intellectuelle pour s'enfermer dans le domaine de l'action purement morale. Mais qu'importe cette préférence? Elle ne changera pas la tendance du siècle. Elle n'empêchera pas qu'autour de nous, beaucoup de femmes recherchent la haute culture et que, pour leur donner satisfaction, de grands efforts se fassent, de grandes institutions se créent, des méthodes s'élaborent, qu'en un mot, tout un système de haute éducation féminine s'organise en France et ailleurs.

Cela est presque partout un fait accompli.

Or, à ne considérer que notre pays, il faut reconnaître que l'initiative est

---

[1] Allusion à un journaliste québécois fervent adepte de la pseudo Diana Vaughan et, en même temps antiféministe acharné.

partie des ennemis de notre foi. La discussion parlementaire qui a précédé l'établissement des lycées de filles en a fourni la preuve évidente. Les catholiques ont bien vu le péril, mais il ont cru le conjurer par l'abstention, en tenant leurs filles éloignées de ces centres intellectuels suspects, sans se préoccuper d'en créer de meilleurs.

Le résultat a été, pour beaucoup de femmes chrétiennes, un état d'infériorité, et, pour toutes celles qui ont voulu en sortir, la nécessité d'aller chercher, dans un milieu neutre ou hostile, ce qu'elles en trouvaient pas dans un milieu chrétien."

Qu'on s'en réjouisse ou qu'on le regrette, la haute culture est devenue un besoin pour les femmes. Une seule question désormais se pose: Convient-il que les femmes croyantes trouvent cette culture parmi nous? Ou veut-on qu'elles soient réduites à la chercher ailleurs?

La réponse ne saurait être douteuse. Il ne reste plus qu'à déterminer les moyens pratiques de satisfaire à ce besoin.

Il nous a semblé que l'Université catholique, créée pour l'instruction supérieure de la jeunesse masculine, pouvait assurer aux jeunes filles les ressources intellectuelles qu'elles réclament.

Il s'agit d'occuper utilement les quelques années qui s'écoulent d'ordinaire entre la fin des études et le mariage.

La musique, le dessin, le monde ne suffisent pas à remplir cet intervalle. Il faut que l'intelligence ait sa part, la principale, et qu'elle exerce sur tout le reste une action directrice.

Voici le programme de l'éducation nouvelle préconisée par l'illustre prélat:

—La religion: dogme, apologétique, Bible, histoire de l'Eglise:

—La philosophie dans ses grandes lignes;

—L'histoire, et particulièrement l'histoire contemporaine; l'exposé des conditions qui président à la vie des sociétés modernes;

—Les principes de l'économie politique et de la sociologie;

—Les éléments du droit civil et du droit politique;

—La littérature française, les littératures étrangères et les littératures anciennes;

—Les principales découvertes modernes dans l'ordre des sciences physiques et naturelles;

—Enfin, l'esthétique et l'histoire de l'art.

"Et quand on songe, ajoute la directrice du "Féminisme chrétien", revue française où nous avons puisé cette citation,—que ce plan d'éducation supérieure pour les jeunes filles est l'oeuvre d'un homme qui, il y a moins d'un an, se prononçait ouvertement contre le féminisme, n'est-on pas fondé à dire qu'une cause est gagnée quand elle a fait d'un adversaire de cette taille le promoteur d'une institution qui est pour le féminisme tout à la fois, une éclatante victoire et le plus précieux auxiliaire dont il ait pu souhaiter le puissant concours?"

Devant les progrès récemment accomplis en cette ville par l'Université anglaise, nous avons nous-même, il y a quelque temps, dans un article de journal, demandé la même chose à notre Université catholique.

Maintenant, on me dira peut-être que j'ai négligé le gros reproche qu'on fait au féminisme, qui est de réclamer les droits politiques.

En effet, il y a des femmes assez hardies pour aspirer à l'égalité avec leurs maîtres. Elles allèguent, pour s'excuser, qu'elles ne feraient pas du billet de scrutin, un plus mauvais usage qu'eux, à moins peut-être, qu'on ne leur octroyât, avec lui, tous les autres privilèges masculins ....

Enfin, que cette prétention n'effraie pas trop le sexe fort; d'abord elle est loin d'être partagée par toutes et puis il est absolument en son pouvoir à lui qui fait les lois, de la reconnaître ou d'y répondre par une fin de non-recevoir.

A ce propos, un prêtre éminent du clergé de Paris, en est venu à dire à nos amies du "Féminisme chrétien":—"Vous avez peut-être tort de ne pas revendiquer les droits politiques. C'est peut-être par le bulletin de vote de la femme que la France sera sauvée".

—Merci! aurions-nous répondu si cette parole nous eût addressée.

Ne brûlons pas les étapes. Nous trouvons encore dans le champ étendu de la bienfaisance à occuper nos loisirs.

Nous avons un rôle à jouer dans la société avant d'en jouer un dans le gouvernement.

Et puis ... laissez-nous préparer à l'art nécessaire de plaire, mais à celui qui, au moyen des grâces de l'esprit, attache et retient les maris au foyer; à celui qui fait aussi "trouver" des maris sérieux.

En pratiquant cet art élevé, en cultivant notre intelligence, nous exercerons indirectement l'influence politique que vous nous souhaitez, car nous serons en état d'enseigner à nos fils à bien voter.

UNDERSTANDING WOMEN

'The Liberation of Woman', Bliss Carman Papers, Lorne Pierce Collection, Douglas Library, Queen's University (undated ms.). Reprinted by permission.

The average man who tries to collect his ideas about women must always feel that there is something not a little preposterous in his attitudes. If his mind is at all honest he must have a consciousness that his effort, even if it could be brilliant, would at best be somewhat superfluous or futile. It is as if one should propose to collect one's thoughts on the subject of gravitation.

The theme is so obvious, so trite, so universally in mind, and yet so baffling, elusive, and transcendental. Science cannot say what gravity is; it is more obscure than electricity; and yet from infancy we are as familiar with it as with the air we breathe. Only intimacy blinds us to its tremendous power and inscrutable mystery. To pause and ask questions about it, is to become suddenly aware that we are living in the presence of something titanic and secret. It is so with woman; we live every day in her all-pervading influence, taking her for granted as something we are quite familiar with, until an occasion, when we come to reflect, we find we hardly understand her at all.

We can hope for little light on the subject from men. We know in advance that their estimates must be at best only partial and prejudiced, and in these profound reaches where we are most in need of enlightenment, uncomprehending. On the other hand, if we ask women themselves for light on the subject, we ought to know that such a hope is rather impossible. They doubtless do not seem mysterious to themselves. All their aims are so immediate and practical, they dwell so little in regions of speculation and fancy, that their life as they live it must appear to them simple enough in its essential purpose. What can it be about them that men do not understand? And even if they were well aware of any veiled mystery in their nature, why should they destroy their power by unveiling it? If they should attempt to explain themselves to us, we should probably not understand after all. As James Whitcomb Riley says, "Some folks don't like poetry, because they've got no liker to like it with." Just so, if we do not understand women, it is because we have no woman's understanding. We live in alien spheres under independent laws, to a great extent. The orb of woman's soul is like a bubble, radiant, expansive, magical, and frail. The orb of man's spirit is like a drop of dew, in comparison, more intense and far-glittering, but also harder and less entrancing. They may impinge and coalesce and run down into the soil to replenish the divine earth, but only after a touch of the rough world has shattered the bubble's tenuous glory and reduced it to the dimensions of a drop. What miracle is to expand the dewdrop to an airy bubble?

Men always take a mystic view of woman, it seems, and there is not much confidence in what philosophers have said about her. With the exception of the theologians, who long ago branded her in no uncertain terms as the source of all evil, just men either confer their perplexity or indulge in vague rhapsodies, half complimentary, half sceptical. Even such a clear-eyed rationalist as Santayana passes lightly over the topic, like a skater on thin ice. "There is something," he says, "mysterious and oracular about a woman's mind which inspires a certain instinctive deference and puts it out of the question to judge what she says by masculine standards. She has a kind of sibylline intuition and the right to be irrationally *à propos*." That does not help us much, it only confirms our traditional and instinctive attitude,—an amazed curiosity and resignation such as we feel toward nature and the riddle of existence. Another writer, a poet and man of the world with exceptionally wide experience and knowledge of men and women, once said to me in grave confusion, "All women are just a little bit crazy." And so I suppose they must often seem from the merely logical viewpoint.

When Greek philosophy came upon the problem, How can the finite comprehend the infinite, Plotinus solved it by pointing out that although finite mind cannot comprehend infinite mind, the finite soul can rise through ecstasy into infinite regions. It was a shrewd answer, and there is an echo of it in Emerson's phrase "the stairway of surprise." Mysteries, these reasoners would say, can never be understood by the literal force of logic. The questioner must abandon his argument, and by sheer transport of spirit pass behind the veil of thought into the sanctuary of feeling. The discussion is removed from the audience chamber of the mind to the penetralia of the heart, and adoration may learn what philosophy failed to unravel. Every man who has been in love knows something of the doctrine of Plotinus.

It is worthy of note that among modern philosophers Nietzsche, the most uncompromising of logicians, was a confirmed woman-hater, while Maeterlinck, the pronounced mystic, has written about women with unsurpassed insight and charm. Nietzsche dreamed of establishing an ideal of manhood in which there should be no weakness, nothing but triumphant energy and intelligence. There was no mercy in his Superman, as there was no love in his nature. With his surpassing brilliancy the saving tincture of sympathy seems to have been lacking in his mortal make up. He spent his life in intellectual warfare, a devotee of the cold Goddess of Reason, and passed in his prime to a living death in a mad-house, like a modern Lucifer whose ambition was light and whose end was darkness,—the most pitiable titan of the nineteenth century.

In Maurice Maeterlinck our generation possesses a very different thinker, a poet and dreamer whose life is rooted in the generous soil of a normal physicality, and whose mystic speculations, reasonable as they are, seem to be prompted by an almost womanly tenderness and intuitive wisdom. He is admirably a man in his way of life, his love of science, and his power of creative imagination. At the same time he is possessed of a psychologic insight which seems almost feminine in its deep and sympathetic brooding upon human destiny. The truths he brings us are all irradiated with a touch of glory beyond the guess of pure reason. He makes us familiar with a region where beauty and truth are transfigured into a supernal good; and this is the region where women habitually dwell.

Maeterlinck is the prophet of a new day in which spiritual ideals of life are coming to prevail more and more. He foresees the gradual unfolding of those mystic and emotional powers in humanity. Of these powers woman is the natural guardian and source, and woman's movement towards a more complete development is really part of the spiritual emancipation of the race. This does not mean that we are becoming feminized or weak, only that we are becoming wiser and happier, paying attention more obediently to the dictates of the soul, and learning to light up all our processes of reason and common life with a glow of the kindly and impassioned heart. It means that we are giving spiritual or moral forces their way, and recognizing their legitimate place in a triune world, where they must always be in the lead, yet always guided by intelligence and given effectiveness through sense.

In a civilization like that of the last century, dazed by stupendous revelations and engrossed in a coil of unexampled material welfare, it was only natural that the affairs of the human spirit, with its divine affiliations and unreckoned powers, should be forgotten or obscured. And as all these triumphs of industry and intelligence,—inventions and discovery and the arts,—are adjusted to life and take their place in the perspective of human progress, it is only natural that the eternal requirements of the heart should make themselves imperatively felt again, and be recognized as paramount needs.

If there is indeed a "stream of tendency, not ourselves, which makes for righteousness," beyond doubt that stream is making itself unmistakably felt in our generation. Our modern social unrest, our perplexed efforts to obtain a more truly equitable justice for all men, our growing sense of civic morality, our greater understanding and sympathy with all human hopes and wants, an intolerance of poverty, and our hatred of cruelty, our struggles for reform and improvement everywhere,—what are all these but evidences of the imperishable force and freshness of that stream of spiritual life, whose source is unknown, and whose trend can only be felt? We can only guess at the meaning of life, but its goodness and savor are indubitable.

In this vast struggle which our race seems to be making toward a fuller realization of its ideals of justice and its dreams of happiness, the part played by women must be incalculable. It is preeminently her concern. She has been from time out of mind the treasurer of all the spiritual wealth of the race, and now that this wealth is in demand, it is to her we must come for our supply. It is largely on her genius we must depend in readjusting the balance of humanity, in saving civilization from the extremes of rationalism and materialism. She will know how best to make use of all the material riches we have wrung from the earth and all the startling truths we have discovered. That is her hereditary province. She will know how to make comfort and knowledge serve the interests of the soul, which only asks to be made happy. Her genius is not only deeper, more mystical, more instinctive and impassioned than man's but at the same time more practical and less visionary. In her capacity as the great preserver and fosterer of the mysterious gift of life, she has passed countless ages of existence. Protectress of the immortal seed, guardian and transmitter of racial wisdom and inherited good, restricted to the cradle and the hearth, she had no opportunity for that detachment and comparative irresponsibility which developed men's wits. She could only brood upon the secret of her own heart and serve the pressing need of the day and the hour. So it happens she is at once more religious and more material than man. Relying upon intuition and fact, keeping close to the life of the senses and the life of the soul, she is content to worship without reason and to enjoy without question. With small scope for speculation or adventure, and with immense need of all actual advantages in an every day world, she has little interest in abstract problems. She acts from impulse rather than principle. She is a born pragmatist and lives to make her own desires come true. She only hits the high places of aspiration and achievement, skipping the valley of reason in her haste. In the realms of thought, of investigation, of invention and discovery and the creative arts, her genius is sterile, being without the detachment and roving curiosity which the freer mind of man has been enabled to develop. She is more essentially conservative than man, not less conventional, more spontaneous and less formal. Only the most finely cultivated women accept man's code of fair play, or those who are compelled to deal with men on equal terms.

There can be nothing of more vital importance in our advance toward racial perfection than the liberation of Women. It means the liberation and salvation of all that is most divine in human nature; for all her triumphs of mind, or science and art and trade, must remain aimless and empty if they are not absorbed and tramsmuted into happiness for the nourishment of spirit. In this process of liberation woman's genius becomes more rational and man's genius more inspired through enforced intercourse in common interests and employments. This seems to be one of the objects which the world spirit has in mind at the present time.

Religious and intellectual freedom women already have in common with men. Their economic, social, and political freedom is still in debate. Their control of their persons and actions ... is still limited. It is this control that many women are fighting for. They wish to be mistresses of their own destinies, to be set free from a position of material dependence, and to come into contact with the struggle for existence on the same terms as men.

Whatever we may think of the wisdom of this contention and its ultimate advantage, there is one direction in which women are gradually becoming emancipated which can only lead to good. I mean the direction of actual bodily freedom in the matter of dress and activity. Women's progress in this direction is surprisingly small as yet, but it is encouraging. That women should so passionately demand freedom of action in the world, and at the same time cling so decidedly to the fetters of conventional dress, which render freedom impossible, is one of those instances of unreason which leave the masculine mind in hopeless amazement. There are women who would welcome martyrdom for what they believe to be the cause of personal freedom, who would not accept the freedom of their own natural bodies as a gift. Nothing could induce them to abandon their absurd shoes and corsets. It is very strange; but fortunately this is no longer true of all women. The new woman, or she who was called the new woman a decade or so ago, the independent woman is beginning to insist on being free to move and breathe in a normal healthy way. Gown, hats, shoes, were never more comfortable than they are now. In her larger more active life, she is insisting on being unhampered and comfortable, and she is finding out that she can have that sort of freedom not only without any loss of charm, but with an actual increase of beauty and attractiveness. It was a long time in arriving, but the era of sanity in women's costume seems to have dawned. The mediaeval and oriental ideal of womanhood, man's inferior and toy to be indulged and enslaved, is passed, let us hope, forever; and with it must gradually pass the standard of women's accustomed dress, devised to emphasize and enforce women's restricted sphere. If you are only to be a doll, you do not need to walk and breathe like a human; but if you realize that you are human, with an angelic mission in a beautiful world, the doll's dress becomes intolerable.

With the physical liberation of women, and the passing of hampering dress, comes a magical increase of beauty and charm. The conventional and artificial "style" of the fashion-plate gives place to the loveliness of living figures free to move with the sorcery of rhythmical grace.

THE PLACE OF MODERN WOMEN

'The Woman's Place in Modern Life', *The Champion*, February 1914, pp. 12-14.

BREAKING-DOWN OF THE OLD DIVISION

When political life, or the practice of settling social or corporate issues, first arose, it was quite natural that it should fall exclusively into the hands of the men. The social decisions usually concerned migration, or war, or some other extradomal matter, in the execution of which woman was, from the nature of things, much less interested than man. The old division of home work and state work broke down in the nineteenth century. The industrial development made the first great breach in the old standard. The early political system was obviously founded on the early division of labor. Woman worked in and about the home, owing to the natural tie of the children, and man worked further afield. The factory system entirely discarded this old division, and encouraged women to leave their homes and work by the side of men. Long before the middle of the nineteenth century tens of thousands of women were performing the same work as men, as far from the home as men. Then workshops, shops and offices took fresh groups of women away from the home; and journalism and other professions further extended the process.

With this enormous and increasing employment of women in view, it is impossible to continue to talk of women's place being in the home, and quite ridiculous to make that threadbare phrase a ground for the limitation of women's interests. To refuse them a right that only the most desperate stretch of imagination could represent as taking them out of the home, and at the same time to acquiesce in an industrial development that effectually takes millions of them out of it, is a quaint aberration of reasoning. It would be more sensible to recognize that the phrase "woman's place is the home," belonged to an older civilization. Assuredly, it is a strange phrase to use today as an argument against the suffrage. The old division of labor has broken down. The old political division that was built on it must follow.

WOMAN'S PLACE TODAY

It may seem a bold thing to say, but I assert that woman's place in the home of today is neither more than is man's—or less. To put the same thing differently, man's place, his sphere of work, his activities—were very much more in the home half a century ago than they are today. Most of the work which used to be done at home is now done collectively, in factories, and thus a great forward step has been taken toward the Utopian socialism of Bellamy and Karl Marx.

Progress during the past twenty-five years has been so incredibly rapid, that many, even educated people, do not realize that conditions within the home have been transformed. Machinery, toiling in factories, has done away with most of the laborious work which formerly kept the women of the household busy from sunrise to sundown. Who now thinks of dipping candles? Who would spin yarn and weave cloth, and supposing such industrious women existed, what man would be sufficiently temarious to brave criticism in a suit of home-made clothes?

The weaving, spinning, sewing, preserving, canning of fruit and vegetables, making of shoes and all kinds of clothes is now done outside the home, and generally speaking, done better, but at the reduced expense always accruing from systematized work, the aid of machinery and the handling of raw materials on a large scale.

Thus we find that the communism fostered and engendered by the factory system not only brings thousands of women into the domain of commerce, but reduces the labor of those who stay at home.

THE MARCH OF PROGRESS

The march of progress has, therefore, not only eliminated the drudgery of housekeeping, but has lightened the labor entailed by the house itself.

In the first place, the houses of today are, generally speaking, much smaller than those our fathers lived in, and even they are dwindling in favor of flats. The herding together of vast numbers of people within the necessarily limited boundaries of cities has of necessity restricted the size of dwellings and the grounds surrounding them. Furthermore, housekeeping today has, at all events in comparison with that of a quarter of a century ago, become almost automatic through the time and labor-saving devices which the ingenuity of man has devised.

When oil lamps were in use, as they were a comparatively short time ago, the duty of cleaning, filling and trimming the wicks fell upon the woman of the household, and this disagreeable job frequently occupied half an hour's time. Today a twist of the fingers floods any room with light at will, and with no more attention than paying the bills as they fall due. Other improvements, such as hot water heating, the gas or electric range, hot and cold running water, bathrooms, the telephone, vacuum cleaners, etc., save hours daily for women, giving them opportunity to devote their powers to the broader interests of humanity.

WOMAN HAS BEEN LIFTED OUT OF RUT

It is the march of progress, the scope of invention, the co-operative way of doing things, which has transformed modern life and lifted woman out of the narrow rut of household duties. The man who says that "woman's place is in the home" is as much behind the times as the weavers of Lancashire who stoned Arkwright for inventing the spinning jenny; he has failed to interpret the spirit of the times.

It is a natural question to ask what benefit would accrue to the race if women entered the political arena, had the right to vote, and took, therefore, a genuine interest in state affairs.

There can be no question but that it would make them more broad-minded, liberal and tolerant, and therefore better fitted to raise and supervise the education of their children, and to fit them for the struggle of life which is every year becoming keener.

LE FÉMINISME, UN MOUVEMENT PERVERS, 1918

L.-A. Paquet, ptre., 'Le Féminisme', *Le Canada Français*, Décembre 1918, vol. I, 233-46.

Ne dirait-on pas que l'humanité est prise de vertige? Grisés par l'idée de progrès, des penseurs sans philosophie, et des rêveurs sans boussole, se jettent à la poursuite de toutes les chimères. A peine les mots suffisent-ils pour dénoncer, chaque jour, ce que la fièvre de l'erreur ou le prurit de la nouveauté invente.

Sous le nom de féminisme, un mouvement pervers, une ambition fallacieuse entraîne hors de sa voie la plus élégante moitié de notre espèce, et menace les bases mêmes de la famille et de la société. On n'a pas cru d'abord au danger, tant le succès d'une telle anomalie semblait invraisemblable. L'évidence est venue prouver que rien n'est à l'abri des emballements de l'esprit séduit par le prisme de théories captieuses.

Emanciper la femme, telle est la mission que se donnent les champions de l'idée féministe.

Certes, si l'on entend par là, soustraire la femme aux puissances qui l'oppriment et aux servitudes que la dégradent, il y a longtemps que l'Eglise a assumé ce rôle, et qu'elle s'en acquitte avec tout le zèle et tout le dévouement d'une tutrice incomparable. C'est grâce à l'Église catholique, continuatrice du ministère sacré de Jésus-Christ, que la femme, si avilie sous le régime païen, a été réintégrée dans sa dignité d'épouse et de mère, dans ses droits de compagne inséparable de l'homme auquel elle a uni ses destinées. Tout ce qui honore véritablement la femme, tout ce qui peut l'aider dans l'accomplissement des fonctions qui lui sont propres, tout ce qui peut instruire, élever, développer le sexe féminin dans le sens de sa nature, de sa vocation et de ses besoins, le catholicisme l'approuve, le bénit, et le favorise.

C'est là le vrai progrès.

Il y en a un autre, le faux, celui qui se fait au rebours des fonctions féminines, qui s'emploie à reconstruire sur un nouveau modèle le cerveau de la femme, qui tire l'épouse de son foyer pour la jeter sur la place publique, qui supprime la dissimilitude des sexes et la diversité de leurs conditions. Ce progrès prétendu, et qui n'est, en réalité, qu'une déviation non seulement de l'esprit chrétien, mais du plus vulgaire bon sens, l'Église le réprouve et le dénonce. Entendons, sur ce sujet, les Pères du Premier Concile Plénier de Québec:

> L'Eglise, assurément, n'interdit pas à la femme d'exercer son influ-
> ence pour le bien en dehors de sa demeure, ni de prendre sa part
> légitime dans l'action sociale plus nécessaire aujourd'hui que jamais;
> mais elle réprouve les théories malsaines, propagées dans ces derniers

temps, et dont nous devons tous travailler à préserver notre pays. Sous le très fallacieux prétexte de libérer la femme des servitudes que l'on dit peser sur elle, on veut tout simplement l'arracher au foyer dont elle a la garde, et la soustraire aux devoirs sacrés que la nature et la Providence lui imposent. Par une regrettable confusion, qui est le fruit de l'ignorance chez les uns, de la malice, chez les autres, on laisse entendre que l'égalité entraîne la similitude des droits, et l'on veut que la femme entre en une ridicule et odieuse rivalité avec l'homme, sur un champ d'action où ni les conditions de la lutte, ni les chances du succès ne sauraient être égales. La mise en pratique de pareilles théories serait funeste à la femme et à la famille, et amènerait à bref délai la déchéance de l'une et la ruine de l'autre.

C'est ainsi que les chefs de l'Église catholique au Canada caractérisaient, il y aura bientôt dix ans, le mouvement féministe dont ils voyaient poindre, avec appréhension, parmi nous, les symptômes. Ce mouvement, depuis lors, s'est propagé et accentué. Des influences de toutes sortes s'exercent sur la femme canadienne, qui en déforment le rôle, qui en altèrent l'esprit, qui en subvertissent l'action, les manières et les attitudes.

Que de jeunes filles veulent échapper à la tutelle de leurs parents! Que d'épouses se laissent distraire de leurs devoirs les plus pressants par des soucis étrangers! Certains programmes d'enseignement féminin se gonflent de questions oiseuses, et ne servent d'autre part qu'à gonfler les têtes, sans profit suffisant pour les coeurs. Certains écrits répandent des doctrines et préconisent des façons d'agir opposées aux meilleures traditions familiales. Certaines modes s'enhardissent au-delà de l'extrême limite et constituent un vrai défi à la décence et à la pudeur. Certaines lois sanctionnent les innovations les plus dangereuses, et ouvrent toute grande, à la femme, l'avenue des fonctions publiques.

Bref, le féminisme s'est implanté au milieu de nous; et c'est notre sentiment qu'il croît et qu'il progresse, et qu'il pousse en divers sens ses rameaux, où germent des fruits de mort.

Quelles sont donc les racines par lesquelles se nourrit cette végétation malsaine et vivace? De quelles erreurs, et de quelles ambitions est sorti ce mouvement qui prend ici une telle ampleur, qui emporte avec lui tant d'esprits, et qui envahit tant de domaines? Il n'est jamais vain, le labeur par lequel on fouille le sol, soit pour y déposer la bonne semence, soit pour en extirper une plante vénéneuse.

Le féminisme dont nous recherchons les causes, n'a pas surgi tout seul, et par une sorte de génération spontanée. Il est éclos de deux négations, et de deux penchants mauvais: de la négation de l'autorité, et de celle de la disparité, dans le corps social; du penchant de la présomption, et de celui de l'orgueil.

Le libre examen, posé en principe par la Réforme, a répandu sur le monde un large souffle d'agitation et d'indépendance. Tous les pouvoirs sociaux en ont été ébranlés. De là datent les luttes et les triomphes de l'individualisme, dans les pays protestantisés d'abord, puis dans certaines classes des pays catholiques plus atteintes par l'esprit nouveau.

En ces zones malheureuses, les croyances fondées sur l'autorité divine, ont fléchi. L'Église n'a plus eu sur la pensée de l'homme, ni sur celle de la femme, cette prise profonde qui lui assurait le contrôle souverain des consciences. L'homme, le premier, a secoué le joug des dogmes, le joug des préceptes issus de la foi, et d'où naissaient pour lui, pour le sexe le plus fort, à l'endroit du sexe le plus faible et le plus digne de tous les respects, d'impérieux devoirs. Victime du scandale, du désordre, de l'infidélité, la femme à son tour s'est raidie contre le sort qu'on lui faisait, et elle s'est abandonnée au rêve d'une destinée où rien, dans la société, ne gênerait ses désirs et ne heurterait son élan.

De ce jour, l'autorité maritale n'était plus. Toutes les autorités sont solidaires. Et si la première, celle de Dieu, est méprisée ou mise en doute, les puissances secondaires et subordonnées qui s'y appuient, chancellent. Et lorsque, dans la famille, il arrive que l'époux perde l'ascendant qui en faisait un chef obéi et vénéré, deux pouvoirs rivaux se dressent sous le même toit. La femme joue à l'homme. Elle revêt une personnalité qui n'est pas la sienne, et cela en dépouillant ce juste sentiment de soi, cette conscience de ses devoirs, de son rang, et de sa condition, qui seul peut maintenir l'ordre et la paix.

C'est le renversement de la tradition.

Nos moeurs chrétiennes, façonnées par l'Église et nées de son action la plus intime et la plus profonde, entourent le sexe féminin comme d'un rempart: rempart de foi, de grâce, de modestie, de retenue, de délicatesse, de tout ce qui fait la beauté morale de la femme, et de tout ce qui l'ennoblit à nos yeux. La femme, d'après l'idéal des siècles chrétiens, est une oeuvre de choix, le chef-d'oeuvre des mains divines qui, en créant des soeurs, des mères, des épouses, ont sculpté dans le marbre humain, avec un art infini, les vertus les plus pures, les physionomies les plus douces, les vies les plus humbles et les plus dévouées. L'esprit d'indépendance brise ce chef-d'oeuvre. Il défigure le type féminin que nous a légué le christianisme, et il y substitue un être nouveau, un type à part, le plus singulier mélange de faiblesse et d'audace, d'aménité et d'excentricité, une créature androgyne.

Cette bâtardise ne va pas sans une grave confusion d'idées. On proclame l'égalité de l'homme et de la femme, et on construit, là-dessus, le plus fragile des échafaudages. Or, "la question n'est pas de savoir si l'homme et la femme sont égaux, mais s'ils sont semblables." L'égalité, quelle qu'elle soit en face de Dieu, n'implique nullement la parité des rôles dans la société. On oublie que la femme, par son sexe même, par sa conformation physique et ses qualités morales, par ses goûts, ses talents, ses tendances, diffère absolument de l'homme, et que de cette différence radicale entre les sexes résulte une différence non moins grande dans les fonctions.

Fût-il même prouvé, écrit un professeur français, que le sexe féminin est aussi capable que le nôtre en toutes les choses de l'intelligence, il resterait que la femme n'en est pas moins femme, que l'homme n'en est pas moins homme, que chacun d'eux est voué à des fonctions physiologiques absolument incommunicables et muni conséquemment d'aptitudes forcément personnelles. De par la nature, l'homme a un rôle propre, la femme en a un autre; et quelles que soient les atténuations possibles de leurs différences organiques et de leurs disparités mentales, on ne saurait concevoir, fût-ce dans l'infinie profondeur des siècles, ni anatomiquement, ni intellectuellement, une parfaite égalisation des sexes. A supposer même que l'homme et la femme en arrivent un jour à ne plus former qu'un seul être, identique d'esprit et de corps,—ce qui serait monstrueux,—il faudrait en conclure qu'en ce temps-là l'humanité cessera d'exister.

Le mépris de l'autorité, l'oubli de la disparité des sexes, sont donc bien les causes fondamentales d'où est sorti le féminisme. Ces causes sont fortifiées par le concours qu'elles ont reçu des penchants qui sommeillent au fond de tout être humain.

Qui n'a pas son grain d'ambition, son instinct de présomption? C'est une pente où la chute est facile. Et cette chute se produit avec d'autant plus d'éclat, et un dérèglement d'autant plus grave, que l'homme s'écarte davantage des cadres naturels de son action.

On appelle présomption, dit saint Thomas, le fait de s'insurger dans ses actes contre l'ordre établi par la nature, et de s'assigner une mission trop haute, des opérations trop ardues, et en désaccord avec les facultés dont on est doué. L'humeur présomptueuse compte pour beaucoup dans le mouvement féministe. La femme nouveau genre aspire à remplacer l'homme; elle prétend du moins rivaliser avec lui dans tous les domaines de l'activité publique. Elle ne se demande pas comment elle est faite, ni ce que le Créateur attend d'elle, dans les limites où sa providence l'a placée. Elle refuse d'admettre des limites, et son regard curieux, sa pensée inquiète et pleine de désirs, vise tous les buts, et embrasse tous les horizons.

Elle jalouse les succès de l'homme, les triomphes de la virilité. Non contente de la sphère où elle domine elle-même et de ses propres triomphes dont l'homme est incapable, elle ambitionne la supériorité masculine, comme si sa tête soigneusement ajustée, était faite pour toutes les couronnes. On ne pousse pas plus lin l'orgueil.

Nous ne disons pas que toutes les femmes, prises du mal féministe, vont jusqu'à cette folie. Le féminisme a ses degrés; et il se nuance de toutes les couleurs que revêt l'envie de paraître, l'ambition de se distinguer, et de provoquer l'éloge flatteur et la réclame tapageuse. Il varie et s'intensifie selon la culture qu'il reçoit.

Cette culture se fait de plusieurs manières: par l'éducation que l'on fausse, par la propagande que l'on active, par les écrits que l'on répand, par l'atmosphère toute spéciale que la femme respire.

C'est fausser l'éducation féminine que de faire passer l'intelligence de la femme par tous les replis du moule où se forme l'intelligence de l'homme.

Il n'y a point entre l'homme et la femme simple *égalité* de capacité intellectuelle, parce que, si éminents qu'on les suppose tous deux, leur valeur respective gardera toujours un cachet propre qui les distinguera l'un de l'autre, de même qu'un homme et une femme peuvent être beaux dans leur genre, sans pour cela qu'ils le soient de la même façon … Mais s'il n'y a point, d'homme à femme, identité ou même égalité de puissance mentale, il y a *équivalence* d'utilité intellectuelle entre les sexes. Seulement, cette équivalence même suppose chez l'un et chez l'autre une certaine diversité de dons, d'aptitudes et de facultés. A se trop ressembler, ils finiraient par se moins rechercher.

Voilà des principes dont il faut tenir compte dans l'élaboration des programmes d'enseignement féminin.

La première qualité de cet enseignement, c'est d'être approprié au caractère physique et moral de la femme, à ses talents naturels et à son rôle primordial. "La science des femmes, comme celle des hommes, dit Fénelon, doit se borner à s'instruire par rapport à leurs fonctions. La différence de leurs emplois doit faire celle de leurs études." Toute instruction propre à détourner la femme de sa voie, est funeste. Sa Sainteté Benoît XV l'écrivait récemment: "Combien y a-t-il de femmes qui, se livrant outre mesure à des études trop étrangères à leur sexe, prennent des manières toutes masculines; ou qui désertant les devoirs domestiques pour lesquels elles étaient faites, se lancent témérairement au milieu des luttes de la vie! De là cette déplorable perversité des moeurs, que la licence même de la guerre a extraordinairement accrue et propagée."

Cela certes ne veut pas dire qu'il faille bannir des maisons d'instruction féminine les études sérieuses. Il s'agit de les bien choisir. Ce ne sont pas les femmes frottées de grec et d'hébreu qui répareront les brèches faites à la famille. Les Paula et les Eustochium, versées dans les commentaires bibliques, ne sont que des exceptions, très belles il est vrai, à la règle générale. Mais en dehors de certaines études abstraites et qui siéent davantage aux esprits masculins, quel vaste champ de culture s'ouvre à l'intelligence de la femme!

D'abord, la religion. On ne saurait mettre trop de soin, par de claires et fortes leçons apologétiques, à développer et à affirmer les principes et les convictions qui font les mères de famille véritablement chrétiennes. La femme, selon l'expression de Étienne Lamy, "est la réserve religieuse du genre humain." C'est par elle que commence l'orientation morale des enfants. 'L'éducation des enfants, voilà l'oeuvre immense, voilà le chef-d'oeuvre permanent de la femme." Une femme bien instruite des vérités théoriques et pratiques de sa religion, peut soutenir la vertu naissante de ses fils, la foi défaillante de son époux, et de tous ceux que son charme attire, et qui fréquentent ses salons.

Il nous semble désirable que, dans l'instruction des femmes, on évite également l'insuffisance ou l'anémie des programmes, et la congestion désordonnée des matières qu'on y entasse. Trop de science ruine les cerveaux. Un enseignement trop maigre, et des études sans relation avec le besoin des élèves, ne portent pas les fruits qu'on espère.

D'après saint Thomas d'Aquin, les mariages bien assortis sont ceux "où il y a convenance entre les époux." Le niveau intellectuel des jeunes filles doit donc s'élever avec le niveau professionnel et social des jeunes gens qui leur sont unis. Et il faut entendre par là, non l'identité d'instruction, mais la proportion des connaissances. Sur un fond commun de notions générales où entrent, en premier lieu, le catéchisme, la langue maternelle, l'histoire du pays, la tenue d'une maison, doivent s'adapter pour nos étudiantes, des études propres à leur état social respectif. La future maîtresse d'un foyer terrien ne se prépare pas, en tout point, par les mêmes leçons que la femme d'un haut magistrat. Rendons ici hommage aux esprits clairvoyants qui ont perçu la nécessité, pour toutes nos familles, d'écoles ménagères spéciales ou d'un bon enseignement ménager, et qui ont enrichi notre domaine scolaire de si utiles fondations.

Nul n'a mieux compris le caractère véritable de l'instruction qui convient aux filles, que l'illustre Fénelon. Et avec combien de raison cet éducateur expérimenté et sagace, pour mieux définir le caractère de l'instruction féminine, a écrit:

> Ne sont-ce pas les femmes qui ruinent ou qui soutiennent les maisons, qui règlent tout le détail des choses domestiques, et qui par conséquent décident de ce qui touche de plus près à tout le genre humain? Par là elles ont la principale part aux bonnes ou mauvaises moeurs de presque tout le monde. Une femme judicieuse, appliquée et pleine de religion, est l'âme de toute une grande maison; elle y met l'ordre pour les biens temporels et pour le salut. Les hommes mêmes qui ont toute l'autorité en public, ne peuvent par leurs délibérations établir aucun bien effectif si les femmes ne leur aident à l'exécuter.

On peut conclure de ces paroles, que la doctrine traditionnelle, dont nous nous faisons l'écho, laisse une place très large au rôle des femmes, et que, pour préparer ce rôle salutaire, elle ne supprime, dans les écoles, ni objets d'étude, ni méthodes, ni mesures, qui puissent en grandir le sens, et en accroître l'efficacité.

Tradition n'est pas immobilisation. L'Église reste fidèle à elle-même en se montrant partout sagement progressive. Nulle part l'on n'accueille avec plus de joie et l'on ne favorise avec plus de zèle, tout ce qui peut améliorer l'instruction, celle des femmes comme celle des hommes. Nos programmes d'enseignement, souvent remaniés et commentés avec compétence, témoignent ouvertement ce souci. La pédagogie canadienne est en bonne voie. Nos écoles normales de garçons et de filles font une oeuvre solide et justement réputée.

Cette oeuvre serait-elle meilleure, si, comme les féministes le veulent, on pratiquait, pour l'adolescence, la coéducation des sexes?

L'expérience de cette méthode a été faite dans notre libre, très libre Amérique. Aussi les Etats-Unis sont-ils devenus la terre classique des garçonnières. La morale que l'on y observe en est-elle plus pure? et les liens de la famille en sont-ils plus sacrés et plus durables? et l'instruction commune, départie par ce système, initie-t-elle plus efficacement la femme à l'intelligence et à l'accomplissement de tous ses devoirs domestiques et sociaux?

Le publiciste renommé qu'était Claudio Jannet, a fait de cette question une étude sérieuse. Ses conclusions ne s'accordent guère avec les prétentions féministes. Pour lui, la coéducation est déplorable, non seulement sous le rapport moral, mais encore au point de vue intellectuel et social. "Sous prétexte que l'intelligence des femmes vaut celle des hommes, on leur fait étudier le grec, l'algèbre, la mécanique et les hautes sciences. Le résultat de ces études est absolument nul;" et "le fruit de cette éducation est de dégoûter profondément les femmes des soins du foyer domestique et des fonctions pour lesquelles la nature les a créés."—Un autre écrivain laïque, M. Turgeon, que nous avons déjà cité, estime de son côté "que, dans la période moyenne correspondant aux études secondaires, la coéducation est mauvaise, irrationnelle, antipédagogique."

Le féminisme, pourtant, fait son chemin. Toutes les voix d'une réclame active et organisée s'emploient à hâter sa marche. D'une rive de l'océan à l'autre, ces voix se répondent et se soutiennent. Le féminisme français ne montre pas moins d'ardeur que celui d'Amérique. "Depuis quelque temps surtout, il multiplie les conférences, les publications, les groupements, les associations et les congrès. Nous avons aujourd'hui une propagande féministe, une littérature féministe, des clubs féministes, un théâtre féministe, une presse féministe et, à sa tête, un grand journal, la Fronde, dont les projectiles sifflent chaque jour à nos oreilles. On sait enfin que le féminisme a ses syndicats et ses conciles, et que, chaque année, il tient ses assises plénières dans une grande ville de l'ancien et du nouveau monde. Il est devenu international."

C'est ce qui se passait avant la guerre. Cette situation entamée par l'immense conflit, ne tardera pas sans doute à se reconstituer.

Le mouvement féministe s'apparente, sur plus d'un point, au mouvement socialiste, et la fortune de l'un fait le succès de l'autre. Les socialistes les plus hardis figurent, en tout pays, parmi les tenants les plus résolus des revendications féminines. Leurs livres propagent le poison, et en infectent les classes sociales les plus accessibles aux propos frondeurs et aux promesses révolutionnaires. D'autres écrivains, sans aller aussi loin, professent des doctrines qui flattent l'orgueil des femmes, et qui sèment et nourrissent et développent en leur esprit des illusions dangereuses.

Ces idées, grosses d'espoirs trompeurs, tombent en des cerveaux déjà remués par le choc des conditions économiques modernes.

L'industrie et le commerce dépeuplent beaucoup de foyers. Moins protégées par la vie de famille, les filles et les femmes subissent peu à peu l'influence des milieux vers lesquels l'appât du gain, ou la loi du travail, ou la force de l'exemple, les entraîne. Ces milieux sont très mêlés. Des rencontres se font, des conversations se tiennent, des contacts s'établissent, d'où naissent dans le coeur féminin des aspirations nouvelles. On veut améliorer son sort: on veut réduire la somme des maux que l'on souffre, et s'assurer une part plus large des félicités communes. Et le féminisme se présente aux yeux éblouis comme une admirable panacée.

Telles sont les causes par lesquelles s'explique, s'entretient et se propage, en Europe et en Amérique, le mouvement destiné, selon le mot de ses auteurs, à émanciper la femme, et qui produit chez les penseurs chrétiens, les sociologues, et les chefs de l'Église, une anxiété si profonde.

2. LEGAL RIGHTS

The woman's rights movement in the nineteenth and early twentieth centuries in Canada stressed the legal rights of women, the rights of women to represent themselves as free citizens of a nation state and to enjoy the liberties that that entailed. Certainly legal status is important for it is a formal recognition by society of an individual's rights. Legal rights, however, as the history of women has indicated, do not necessarily change the attitudes of society although they can reflect the principles upon which society would like to function.

The laws of Canada during the time when women were trying to achieve the franchise reflected woman's inferior status. Woman's citizenship depended on that of her husband, she was not allowed to receive a free homestead for herself, and not until 1929 did the Judicial Committee of the Privy Council declare that women were 'persons', allowing them to sit in the Senate of Canada. This lack of rights was based on the assumption that man would represent her, for it was his sphere to deal with public matters.

As can be seen in the following selections, Canadian women were concerned with more than political rights. The struggle for the suffrage has perhaps overshadowed a larger movement for control of their own property, their own future. Suffrage was only a means used by many to achieve these other ends. Certainly most Canadian women had little interest in voting rights in the early years of the woman's rights movement. Other rights were of more importance on a day-to-day basis. Although the Married Woman's Property Act in the 1880s protected a woman's right to her own property after marriage, it did not apply to wages. For example, according to the National Council of Women, in 1900 a Nova Scotia husband still had to agree before his wife could control her earnings, and in P.E.I. a wife was not even entitled to those earnings unless separated from her husband. This reveals not only discrimination but also the variation in laws across the country. The right of dower was not acknowledged west of Ontario. For those many Ontario women who had settled the new territories, this was difficult to accept. Dower was a recognition of a wife's contribution to the home, 'The right to an estate for life in one-third part of any lands which were the property of her husband during his lifetime.' To be without it made women totally dependent on their husbands.

The concern of Canadian women with property rights is not surprising. Property was highly valued in the new world and, with so much available, many considered ownership of it to be a right and not a privilege. It also reflected a value system that esteemed the commercial as opposed to the moral, a system that on the one hand women were trying to change but on the other were trying to join. Such a system imposed severe retribution for theft of property but less for theft of a woman's virtue. In fact seduction or rape was very difficult to prove and only punishable if the woman was of 'previously chaste character.'

If a woman's rights were few outside the home, what were they inside the home? This after all was her sphere. Within marriage a woman's rights were generally equal to man's, that is, she could obtain a divorce on the same grounds as a man could. However since divorce laws were under provincial jurisdiction, the laws governing marriage were not identical throughout the country. In British Columbia a man could obtain a divorce and be permitted to remarry on the grounds of adultery, whereas a woman could obtain a divorce only in the case of '(i) incestuous adultery; (ii) bigamy with adultery; or (iii) rape, sodomy, or bestiality; or (iv) adultery coupled with such cruelty as would have entitled her to a divorce; or (v) adultery coupled with desertion for two years or longer without reasonable excuse.' Even as a mother a woman had few rights, seldom being allowed to be guardian of her own children.

Woman's status and prestige were not based on any legal foundation. They were rather based on the attitudes and conventions of the time, a precarious situation at best. Women's desire to rectify this condition took two directions—the demand for individual rights, and the demand for protective legislation for women. The movement for individual rights, such as homestead laws, had as its end equality with men. The demand for protective legislation, such as better working conditions for women, assumed that women differed from men and that those differences required special consideration. The contradiction between the two demands was seldom acknowledged. Those women interested in the legal status of women were practical ladies. They simply wanted to improve woman's position and did not care about the philosophical implications of the way in which they did it.

LEGAL STATUS OF WOMEN IN CANADA, 1900

Clara Brett Martin, 'Legal Status of Women in the Provinces of the Dominion of Canada. (Except the Province of Quebec)', in *Women of Canada: Their Life and Work*, compiled by the National Council of Women of Canada (Ottawa, 1900).

A concise epitome of the laws is all that can be expected in the following article, owing to the limitation of space. The Ontario law is taken as the theme, with brief allusions to differences in other Provinces. The subject will be dealt with under the following heads:

(1) Infants—Those under 21 years of age. (2) Unmarried Women. (3) Married Women.

INFANTS.

The rights and liabilities of infants of both sexes are almost identical. They can make no valid contract except in a few instances, as for necessaries and for earning purposes. They are in the eye of the law infants until they reach the age of twenty-one years and therefore under guardianship. In Ontario only the most important contract in the lives of men or women may be made by infants of the age of eighteen years without the consent of their parents or guardians, viz., marriage.

By the Common Law of England, children belong to the father,—they are his, and his only. As Blackstone puts it: "Mothers, *as such*, are entitled to no power, only reverence and respect." The father is sole guardian of his infant children, and no contract before marriage that the mother is to have the custody and control of the children of that marriage is binding on the husband, nor will the courts enforce it. Nor will any contract before marriage that the children shall be brought up in a faith other than that of the father's be binding upon the intended husband. Even on the death of their father, the mother has no more rights in regard to the religious education of her children than a guardian appointed by the father, and should she attempt to bring them up in a religion different to that of the father, the court can and does interfere by appointing guardians.

In the Province of Nova Scotia an ante-nuptial contract as to the religion of children is valid.

A father may bind out his infant children, apprentice them, give them in adoption, educate them how and when he pleases, and in what religion he pleases. He is entitled to all their earnings until they reach their majority. In fact he has control and custody of their persons until they reach that age.

A mother stands legally in exactly the same position as a stranger.

Morally, they owe her some kind of respect and perhaps obedience. A father may appoint by will a guardian or guardians to his infant children and oust the mother altogether. By the Act of 1887 the law has been changed in Ontario in the following particulars:—The mother is guardian on the death of her husband should no testamentary guardian be appointed by him. But should he appoint a guardian or guardians or should the court do so (which has also the power where the father does not), the mother is allowed the privilege of acting in conjunction with those so appointed. Provisionally the mother may appoint by will a guardian but that guardian cannot act except the court considers the father incapable. Where a mother happens to be sole guardian on the death of her husband, she cannot apprentice her children except with the sanction of two Justices of the Peace. This is evidence that the judgment in law of a mother is not considered sound, since she cannot be trusted with the welfare of her children. In Manitoba the Court is empowered to appoint the mother sole guardian, notwithstanding the testamentary appointment by the father.

In the case of the adultery of the mother, she is not entitled even to see her children, but it is not so in the case of the father.

The criminal law for the Dominion is embodied in the Criminal Code, many sections of which aim at protecting girls and women who are infants-at-law.

In the case of seduction, consent cannot be pleaded by the Defendant, unless the girl be over the age of sixteen years.

A stranger to a girl under fourteen years is liable to imprisonment for life and to be whipped, if he procures the prostitution of such girl (see sections 61 and 269), but a mother for the same offence is punishable by fourteen years imprisonment only. Should a mother procure the prostitution of her daughter above fourteen years, she is liable to five years while a stranger is only liable to two; or, in other words, a mother is less criminal than a stranger when her daughter is less than fourteen and more criminal than a stranger when the girl is over fourteen.

Again, a guardian who is accessory to the prostitution of his seventeen year old ward is liable to five years imprisonment, but only to two years if he himself is the principal criminal.

Under the code men only are liable to be flogged. The wholesale flogging of girls and women for many centuries, and down to the year 1820, had such a demoralizing effect that the punishment was abolished in that year in respect to the sex.

UNMARRIED WOMEN OVER 21 YEARS OF AGE.

With regard to personal and property rights unmarried women are in the same position as men. Widows may, for legal purposes and without impropriety, be included for the nonce among the single.

Apart from certain civic disqualifications and professional exclusiveness, our old common law never thought fit to impose disabilities on single women, who, when of full age and of sound mind, have always been left free to manage their own property, whether real or personal, and to make and alter their wills and codicils as and when they, in their good sense or caprice, might think fit. No family council of males ventured to control them, nor was any limit placed either upon their acquisitiveness or their powers of inheritance. Single women amongst us have from time immemorial bought and sold, kept shop and farm and inn, driven to market, collected their rents, made their investments, sued their debtors, compounded with their creditors and in a word lived their life exposed to nothing worse than a good deal of time-honored and heavy jesting about their "single blessedness."

The Mines Act prohibits the employment of women and girls, and under the Factories and Workshops Acts, there are certain restrictions on their labor. Otherwise they may legally enter any profession or calling and engage in any business trade or pursuit outside the Army, although custom may exclude them from some occupations.

The only profession now closed to women in Ontario is the ministry, and probably for the reason held in two of the States of the American Union, namely:—She is too good, being an "angel," and the contrary opinion—She is too full of evil, being the cause of the fall of "man."

In the Province of Ontario only, has she full status at the Bar. Having all the rights and privileges of a Barrister, there is no legal disability to her being a Bencher, Queen's Counsel, or Judge.

All women are prohibited from sitting either as Aldermen, Councillors, or as Mayors or Members of either Houses of Parliament, but in Ontario unmarried women may vote at all municipal elections, provided they possess the same property qualifications as men.

MARRIED WOMEN.

Woman's legal position changes considerably on her marriage.

Our ancestors insisted upon treating marriage as a suspension of the independent existence of the wife, and as an absorption by the husband of the woman's person and all her belongings, of whatsoever nature or kind, notwithstanding that the husband solemnly declared at the altar:— "With all my worldly goods I thee endow."

This notion of unity of husband and wife, meaning thereby the suspension of the wife and the lordship of the husband, seems to have been particularly agreeable to the whole race of English jurists, tickling their grim humor and gratifying their very limited sense of the fitness of things. How pleasantly, how good humoredly does the great Blackstone handle the theme in the first book of these inimitable commentaries of his: "Even the disabilities that the wife lies under are for the most part intended for her protection and benefit—*so great a favorite is the female sex with the laws of England.*"

Lord Lyndhurst was the first lawyer of eminence, it is said, who denounced this unity. One instance still remains where the unity seems preserved, for example:—If $5,000.00 is bequeathed to Jane, Peter and John in equal shares, and Jane and Peter should chance to be husband and wife, the legacy is divided, not into thirds but into halves, for Jane and Peter are treated as one person, and take but one half between them, whilst the lucky John goes off with the other.

A married woman has not full contractual powers. She is capable of entering into or rendering herself liable in respect of her separate property, real or personal, on any contract, or of suing or being sued, may deal in shares, stocks, debentures, or other interests, of whatsoever nature or kind, and become a party to any mercantile paper, as bills of exchange, promissory notes, drafts, etc., and therefore bind herself as surety in exactly the same manner as if unmarried.

Her liability, though, on any contract is never personal (as in the case of a man or an unmarried woman) but proprietory, that is in respect to her separate property.

Under the Ontario Married Woman's Property Act of 1872, it has been decided that no contractual power was conferred upon her, except in respect to separate property.

Under the Act of 1884 her contractual powers, though extended in regard to her separate estate, are not enlarged; nor are they under the Act of 1897.

They may, however, be said to be extended under the latter Act in so far that the existence of free separate property at the time of entering into a contract, or incurring a liability, is not, as formerly, a condition precedent to the making of a valid contract.

A married woman may hold property without Power of Anticipation (this is Judge-made law), that is she can neither anticipate the income nor principal. As it can be attached by legal process, only in a very exceptional case, the unique advantage of the married woman's position is, "that she can use the restraint to discomfit her enemies and defeat her creditors, and when it suits her convenience get the Court to remove it."

The effect of a provision of the Act of 1897 is to make property acquired by a woman, after the death of her husband, liable to satisfy a judgment on a contract entered into while married. Under the former Acts, only separate property would be bound, and this is still the law in Manitoba.

By the Married Woman's Property Acts of Ontario and New Brunswick, any married woman may now have, hold and dispose, by will or otherwise, of all her real and personal property acquired or devolving upon her at any time in the same manner as if unmarried.

Except in Ontario, in the event that she were married on or before the 2nd of March, 1872, and the property was acquired or devolved upon her either before that date or between the 30th of December, 1877 and 1st July, 1884, when the husband's concurrence in the deed is still necessary, in order to convey his own interest in his wife's property.

The Married Woman's Property Acts were introduced into the other Provinces in different years, viz: Manitoba, 1875; New Brunswick, 1896; Nova Scotia, 1st January, 1899; Prince Edward Island, 1896; British Columbia, 1887; Northwest Territories, Jan. 1st, 1897. The law may be stated as follows:—That any married woman may have, hold and dispose of, by will or otherwise, in the same manner as if unmarried, all her real or personal property, acquired or devolving upon her, on and after the coming into force of the aforesaid Acts in each Province respectively. The consent of the husband to his wife's will is still necessary in New Brunswick and Nova Scotia.

Except in the Provinces bordering on the Atlantic Ocean, a strange anomaly of the law appears where a married woman is a trustee of an estate as an executrix. If beneficially entitled to realty she can dispose of it without her husband's consent, but if entitled in a representative capacity as trustee she cannot transfer the legal estate without his concurrence or without going through the cumbersome process under 3 and 4 William IV., Chap. 74, and while she can engage in the more important task of suing in respect of her trust estate, she cannot perform the far more simple operation of conveying the legal estate without his leave, nor can she transfer the legal property held as trustee by her without his concurrence, except it fall within one or other of the classes specified in Section 10, R.S.O., Chap. 163.

All the earnings of a married woman are her separate property, whether gained or acquired by her in any employment, trade or occupation, in which her husband has no proprietary interest, or by the exercise of any literary, artistic or scientific skill.

The old law required the consent, express or implied, of the husband to his wife's engaging in any business, occupation, &c., and as our statute is silent on that point, his consent would seem still necessary in order for a married woman to earn in the employ of another. For example, should she go out as a domestic, he could serve her employer with notice to discontinue her services, and should her employer refuse, the husband would be entitled to an action for harbouring. The reason given is that a wife might put an end to the matrimonial relationship without his consent, and for no fault of his, a power which it is said could not have been the intention of the Legislature to confer upon her.

However, it seems that, should she engage in any business, &c., or follow any profession, trade or calling, on her own account, that is, not in the employ of another, her husband is powerless, inasmuch as he has no one to take action against except herself. Therefore, although a husband cannot now confiscate his wife's earnings, yet he may in many cases paralyze her power to earn by prohibition.

In Nova Scotia the written and filed consent of the husband is necessary in order for a married woman to be entitled to her earnings from any business, and in Prince Edward Island she is not entitled to them in any case, except a separation has taken place between the spouses.

A husband has still to a limited extent custody and control of his wife's person. The custody lasts now only till he has been guilty of cruelty or a separation has taken place between them. He can commit a rape upon her and is not liable to an action, even although he communicate to her a disease of a most loathsome nature. The restraint must not endanger her life or health.

The Jackson case of 1892 abolished all decrees for the restitution of conjugal rights. Lord Esher, in a highly rhetorical judgment, simply danced upon the common law, but Lord Justice Fry, though he moved in statelier measure, being in truth encumbered with the learning on the subject, agreed with the rest of the Court that a husband has no right to restrain his wife and keep her in custody.

On the death of a wife intestate, it appears that where a husband is entitled as Tenant by the Curtesy (that is, a life interest in his wife's real estate) he may also, under 29 Charles II., Chap. 3, Sec. 24, take out letters of Administration to her personal estate, and as such administrator appropriate it to his own absolute use, even although there are children living.

A wife is entitled to Dower in her late husband's estate, except in Manitoba and the Northwest Territorities, where it has been abolished. A mother has in Ontario the same rights as a father in case of inheritance under an intestacy. But in the other Provinces, the father takes the entire estate to the exclusion of the mother.

CLARA BRETT MARTIN.

Marie Gérin Lajoie, 'Legal Status of Woman in the Province of Quebec', in *Women of Canada: Their Life and Work*, compiled by the National Council of Women of Canada (Ottawa, 1900).

The study of woman's legal status means to describe her position in civil society, enumerate her rights, gauge her sphere of activity, and define her capacity.

The law has grasped, in order to regulate, every phase of human existence. At the very dawn of our lives, like an immense net, it spreads over us for all time to encompass us. We are at once entangled in some of its meshes, and, willingly or not, we must bend before its irresistible force. The law asserts itself, and according as we are minors or majors, married or single, husbands or wives, it accords us rights and imposes obligations more or less extensive, within limits that are strictly defined.

The unmarried woman, whether maid or widow, has in private life precisely the same legal capacity as a man; like him she has control of her civil rights; she is free to act and enjoys the administration of her own property.

But, if the code declares the equality of the sexes within these limits, on the other hand it is adverse to its recognition beyond them; hence it declares women incapable of performing certain functions that are considered as public, such as tutorship and curatorship. Only the mother, and other female ascendants during widowhood, can act as tutrices of their children and grandchildren. However, by exception, the wife may become curatrix of her interdicted husband.

Has the woman, about to be married, any conception of the change about to take place in her legal status? Does she realize all that the "Yes" which she is about to pronounce implies? Once this step is taken, her freedom, her belongings, everything that concerns or interests her will undergo an immediate change.

The code runs thus: —

"A husband owes protection to his wife; a wife, obedience to her husband." And in order that this dependence of the wife may be really effective, and that the protection which the husband gives her may not be a meaningless phrase, the law makes her incapable of acting in any capacity, and deprives her of the exercise of every civil right except that of making a will, which remains inviolable. The privileges and advantages of civil life which adults, without distinction of sex, enjoy, are forbidden to the married woman. Her personality is blotted out and extinguished, and is absorbed by that of her husband to such an extent that, whether she desires to acquire or to dispose of property, to receive a donation, to take her share in a succession, to take the first step either to engage in business, or to devote herself to some industry, to make a defence in law, or to institute an action; or whether she wishes to favor some one, to incur obligations for others, to bestow gifts on her children, or to give them a start in life, etc., every act is absolutely null and void, no matter how just, reasonable, or advantageous to her. So absolutely null indeed that, even if she were willing to ratify later, during her widowhood, or with the consent of her husband, any act to which she had consented without her husband's authorization, for example, the acceptance of a donation made to her by an ascendant, she could not do it, for where nothing has existed there is nothing to ratify. Here we have then, in all its harshness, a succinct recital of the incapacity of woman during her married life.

But does the law aim at reducing her to complete inactivity; must her role remain absolutely passive? By no means. What then will lighten this burden of incapacity that oppresses her? The husband by his authorization can free her. From the moment that she receives his authorization the wife regains her capacity, and acts done by her thus authorized, are good and valid, and are sanctioned by law. If she desires to sell her immovables, to hypothecate them, to receive a succession, to accept a gift, to transfer a property to her children, she can perform all these acts of civil life provided she be authorized.

The wife duly authorized, then can incur every kind of responsibility, with the exception that she cannot bind herself for her husband. This wise disposition is an effective protection accorded by law to the wife, to guard her from the importunities of her husband, and allow her to preserve her own property intact. The law, however, allows the wife to make advances to her husband, to pay his debts, contemplating that she, in despoiling herself of her own property, will realize the consequences. But the law, in forbidding the wife to bind herself for her husband, takes care to protect her against the danger of those liberal acts which are readily performed when, without giving anything at present, one guarantees to fulfil an obligation, not expecting to be ever called upon to do so; acts, which daily observation teaches us, are the ruin of so many.

Another restriction attached to the capacity of women during married life, and one which attaches also to the husband, is that which forbids either to benefit the other so long as the union lasts. The liberalities which they may mutually bestow during this period are in principle all reimbursable upon the dissolution of the marriage.

Can the husband by a general authorization empower his wife to enjoy true freedom and thus evade the rigor of the law? Our laws have anticipated this and expressly forbidden any such general authorization. The wife's actions must be specially controlled by the husband; a general authorization by the husband is valueless, it must be special in every case.

Let us state beforehand that in certain conditions the wife can by contract of marriage reserve for herself the power of administering her property; but we shall see at the proper time and place that this power does not contradict the principle of incapacity which affects the married woman, and is otherwise felt under every matrimonial regime.

Has a wife no appeal from the decision of a husband, who refuses his authorization when she requires it? Yes, she has an appeal; she can apply to the judge, who will authorize her if he is satisfied that it is proper. In return for this surrender of her freedom, for this self-denial, what does the wife get from her husband? The answer to this question is that the husband is obliged to receive her and to supply her with all the necessaries of life, according to his means and condition. He must receive her, but she must follow him wherever he thinks fit to reside; her nationality is absorbed in that of her husband, according to that popular old adage: "Qui prend mari, prend pays." She who takes a husband takes also his nationality.

Husband and wife mutually owe each other fidelity; their vows are sacred. Their duty is reciprocal, but the law enforces it by unequal sanctions. Woman's adultery is abominable, and she who commits adultery can be punished by a condemnation pronounced by the courts. The wronged husband can always demand separation.

But if on the contrary it is the husband who is the guilty one, the wife cannot invoke this fault as a cause of separation unless he keep his concubine in their common habitation. A moment of weakness for a person in his house and an accidental fall with her, is not sufficient to bring the husband under this provision of law.

Although the principle that marriage cannot be dissolved is strongly supported by the code, the Federal Parliament has power to pass special acts of divorce.

Let us consider for an instant the situation which is brought about by the relations between a mother and her children. The civil law, in harmony with the natural and moral law, lays down this precept: A child, whatever may be his age, owes honor and respect to his father and mother. Their titles to respect and honor from their descendants are in effect the same; the power and authority given them by nature are derived from the same source; but the father alone exercises this authority during marriage, the mother surrenders hers; she gives up this right along with so many others. When the husband dies she resumes it in its entirety.

We all know how far custom modifies this arbitrary and rigorous law of paternal authority, which has so little regard for the susceptibilities of a mother. Custom allows the mother to exercise, in the education and moral training of her children, a much greater influence than is given her by law. Let us hasten to add that the legislator foresaw that it was necessary to forestall the conflicts between father and mother, while leaving as far as possible the salutary influence of the latter to be exercised over her own for the best welfare of the family. Alongside of the paternal authority he (the Legislator) has established the right of the mother to supervise her children; a right which she can exercise although she is separated from her husband and although she is refused the guardianship of her children.

To what extent has woman control of her property? We speak here of a married woman, for we know that an unmarried woman can exercise her own sweet will over her property from the moment that she attains majority. The law which regulates these powers varies with the regime under which she marries. The matrimonial regime determines the distribution of their wealth between husband and wife as well as the rights and duties which its possession implies.

The choice of a regime must be made with great discrimination, since after marriage it cannot be altered, nor can the consorts by mutual gifts remedy the defects of the regime under which they have contracted marriage. The only mitigating provision is that which permits the husband to insure his life in his wife's favor.

LEGAL COMMUNITY.

Legal community is the common law, the regime which the law establishes between consorts, by the mere fact of their marriage if the husband is domiciled in the Province of Quebec. The only way to prevent this is to establish a special regime by contract of marriage. In the legal community, as the term indicates, the consorts each contribute their share to the creation of a common fund of which the husband becomes proprietor and master, and in regard to which their rights are very unequal.

Besides the common fund the consorts may possess personal property called "propres," the administration of which belongs to the husband. However, he cannot alienate the "propres" of his wife without first obtaining her consent.

Accordingly we must divide the legal community into three parts:—

(1) That which comprises the common patrimony.

(2) The "propres" of the husband.

(3) The "propres" of the wife.

The assets of the community are composed as follows:

1. All the property acquired during marriage by either of the consorts by any title whatever; the revenues derived from the industry of the husband or the salary of the wife if she is engaged in a remunerative capacity, gifts, legacies, all fall into the community, excepting, however the immovables which accrue to the consorts from ascendants, and the moveables or immovables given by others than the latter with the express stipulation that they shall not become the property of the community.

2. All the moveable property which the consorts possess on the day when the marriage is solemnized; this includes shares in financial and commercial bodies, etc.; consequently the greater part of modern fortunes.

3. The revenues derived from the "propres" of the consorts.

To sum up then, all the revenues of the consorts of whatsoever nature they may be, fall into the community; and their "propres" comprise no more than the nude ownership, that is to say, the capital only without the revenues of the following properties.

1. Immovables, possessed by the consorts before the marriage.

2. Immovables which accrue to them from ascendants during marriage by gratuitous title.

3. Movables or immovables given or bequeathed with the express stipulation that they shall not become common property.

Now, let us see how the rights of the consorts in the common patrimony are distributed. Although, in a sense, the consorts may be considered joint proprietors, yet the husband alone has the administration of the property of the community. He can sell, hypothecate, alienate or even give them gratuitously if he pleases, without the consent of his wife and without ever being held to render her an account thereof.

The law adds; provided that he acts without fraud. This restriction of the liberty of the husband in regard to their common property, is of very little effect, in so far as the wife is concerned, since there is given to her no means of putting an end to the squandering or reckless use of the common property. It merely signifies that the husband cannot, by fraudulent investments, act in such a way that his wife will not receive her share upon the dissolution of the community; that is, at the period when the common patrimony is equally divided between the consorts or their heirs.

The wife's rights over the common property during marriage are then purely negative; and no way is provided by which she may act for its preservation, except the instituting of a suit for separation of property. She can, however, by virtue of the privileges granted to savings banks, deposit in her own name in the bank, a sum not exceeding $2,000, and draw it upon her own recognizance.

If the husband authorises his wife, common as to property, to act, he becomes responsible for her debts. It is presumed that he gives her a tacit mandate to incur all the necessary expenses of maintaining their household.

The authorization of the judge may replace that of the husband and enable the wife to act; but the obligations thus contracted with the simple authorization of a judge do not bind the husband; the wife alone bears the responsibility.

By what title then does she bind the common patrimony against the will of her husband? Is it because she has contributed to its formation? Or, is it on account of what she has brought into it? To think thus, would be to have but a slight grasp of the spirit of the law; let us remember that the wife, common as to property, is deprived of all her possessions in favour of her husband; they are no longer hers, or at least, she has only an eventual right over them.

How then are the creditors of the wife judicially authorized to be paid? Will they seize her "propres"? But let us not forget that she does not receive the revenues. Then will they be paid out of the capital? But this would deprive the husband of his right of enjoyment. The creditors must wait until the dissolution of the community in order to be paid. These principles being established, it will be easy for us to understand the following table, which gives a complete statement of the assets and liabilities of the community:

ASSETS	LIABILITIES
1. Property acquired during marriage, excepting immovables derived from ascendants and property given with the express stipulation that it shall be excluded from the community.	1. The maintenance of the consorts, the education and support of the children and all the other charges of marriage.
2. Movable property possessed by the consorts on the day of the marriage.	2. Debts of the husband before marriage.
3. Revenues of their "propres" or personal property.	3. Movable debts contracted by the wife before marriage, provided they are established by an authentic deed anterior to the marriage, or by a deed which before that event had acquired a certain date.
	4. Debts of the husband contracted during marriage.
	5. Penalties incurred by the husband.
	6. Debts contracted by the wife with the authorization of her husband.

The common patrimony then must bear the costs of supporting the family under the exclusive administration of the chief; thus the debts of the wife are paid out of the community only in so far as they are authorized by the husband. However, as we have remarked in paragraph three of our table, the community is bound to liquidate the obligations that the wife has contracted before her marriage. It is, therefore, important that the husband should be careful lest he be wrongly informed by his wife, and that the latter take no advantage of this sole gap left in the enclosure that hedges in her lost liberties, to impose debts contracted before their union upon the former. All this has been provided for; the husband is not obliged to pay the debts of his wife contracted before their marriage, except in so far as they are duly defined upon the day of its solemnization.

We have remarked above, in paragraph six, that the community bears the penalties incurred by the husband for crimes or debts. This law, to a certain degree, burdens the wife with responsibility for the faults of her husband; since the fines to which he is condemned impoverishes the patrimony by the amount thereof, and reduces the future proportion that she will derive from the patrimony upon its dissolution. There is no reciprocity is this case. If the wife is guilty of some misdeed and is condemned to a pecuniary punishment, she suffers at the dissolution of the community in respect to her personal property only, in order that the husband may not be affected in his enjoyment of the community. "Dura lex, sed lex," the law is hard, but it is the law.

So far, doubtless we have discovered that this phrase, "legal community" has a somewhat derisive signification as regards the wife.

This regime of authorization indeed, does not deserve such a title, were it to remain indefinitely as it is during marriage. We can say in very truth that the community has no true meaning until the moment of its dissolution. Then only is the wife placed upon a footing of equality with her husband in the exercise of her rights in the community. At this moment, indeed, she acquires privileges which, to a certain extent, compensate her for the obscure role that she has played during the marriage.

The dissolution of the community takes place at the death of one or other of the consorts, and also in the case of separation.

The community is then divided into two parts, one of which goes to the husband and the other to the wife, or their representatives.

The pretakings of the wife take precedence over those of the husband, and she enjoys the great privilege of choosing either to accept or to repudiate the community. In the latter case she is freed from any contributions to the debts chargeable to the community—even her own.

Rigorous as the law is for the wife during marriage, equally generous and mild does it become after the dissolution; this is manifested in the dower.

Dower is the right of survivorship enjoyed by the wife and taken out of the property of her husband. It has a place in every matrimonial regime. This right allows her as usufructuary to receive the revenues of half of the immovables which belong to the husband at the time of the marriage and of those which accrue to him during marriage from his father or mother, or other ascendants; that is to say the half of nearly all the propres of her husband. There is nothing to prevent the husband from granting to his wife a conventional dower by contract of marriage.

The immovable property subject to dower is irrevocably burdened when once the dower has been registered, and without the renunciation of her dower by the wife, the alienation of the property by the husband does not free it from that charge. The wife is always free to renounce her dower either wholly or in part, by contract of marriage or otherwise during marriage. As a matter of fact a clause is now almost invariably inserted in marriage contracts renouncing this dower; so universal is this that many now clamor for the abolition of dower altogether. Why will not the women themselves take the trouble to study a question which is of the highest importance to them?

The narrow space prescribed for us in which to cover a subject so vast will not allow me to more than mention the different matrimonial systems created by contract of marriage.

They are:—

(1) Conventional community.

(2) Exclusion of community.

(3) Separation of property.

In conventional community, the parties, while coming under the ordinary rules of legal community, stipulate at the same time certain special dispositions relating to the composition of the common patrimony.

In the case of exclusion of community, the property of the consorts is no longer blended in one, but the wife renounces the enjoyment of her portion in favour of the husband, who alone receives the fruits. For such purpose does he administer his wife's fortune and is bound to preserve the same. He cannot, however, alienate his wife's capital without her previous consent. This system is of very slight advantage to the latter.

In the case of separation of property, each of the consorts retains his or her personal property. This regime differs from the preceding one inasmuch as the wife, herein, retains the administration of her property and the ownership of whatever revenues it produces. But she cannot be party to any serious transaction, tending to the alienation of her immoveable property without previously having obtained her husband's authorization. Thus women, separated as to property, may of their own initiative increase their wealth. But their limited knowledge of financial operations, and the lack of completeness in this phase of their education, are such that in practice they always leave the administration of their fortunes to their husbands; and this by a mere tacit mandate. Accordingly the code ordains that the husband who has enjoyed the revenues of his wife's property, with her consent, is not obliged to render her any account of the fruits thereof which have been consumed.

Finally, it may be concluded from this article on the legal status of woman, that, as far as she is concerned, in all cases, except in simple administrative acts that are permitted her when she is separate as to property, the wife, without her husband's authorization is incapable of performing any acts whatsoever of importance, that might tend to the acquiring of new property, or the alienation of her capital. She cannot increase her responsibilities without the concurrence and agreement of the one to whom she has devoted her life.

In general the woman exercises her activity in a sphere of action more restricted than the limits traced by the hand of the law. In truth it is only, as it were, by exception and on isolated occasions in her existence that she touches the confines of an ever-increasing domain. But the law is unbending and only becomes more generous after reiterated assaults, and when the impression of customs make it clear that it must expand and progress.

MARIE GERIN LAJOIE.

THE HOUSEHOLD ALLOWANCE, 1910

'Model Husbands', *The Grain Growers' Guide*, 6 April 1910, vol. 4, 29.

Dear Isobel—
Of course there is no humiliation in asking a husband for money when he gives it as needed. But when—well, all husbands don't!

Mr. C. draws two hundred dollars a month. He allows his wife twenty-five to run the house, set the table for himself and buy her own clothing. If this is gone before the end of the month, he sulks, denounces her extravagance, and in general makes her life miserable. If he finds dinner inadequate, the next night he goes to Tait's, or to Louvre, and pays five dollars for a dinner to his taste. If, to get enough ahead for a good dress, she manages to save a little, and add to it by her own earnings, he cuts down her allowance, so that the savings must go to the table.

She is a highly educated woman, was a bookkeeper before marriage, and before that a teacher in a college. She had studied domestic science, and is thoroughly competent to run a large establishment on the most economical basis. He comes from a lower grade of people where it is thought that women are incompetent anyhow. She secretly takes pupils to supplement the household income. He does not save anything out of the remainder of his income. He has no vices, but he just spends it for anything he wants. For many years she has earned all of her own clothing, and most of the furniture. Her friends look upon her husband as a paragon of all the virtues, and often advise her that she ought to dress better and furnish her house better in order to keep the love and respect of such a good man. She is blamed by all for not having money to give to charity, to subscribe to clubs, etc. She has begged her husband by every device she can think of, to increase the household allowance.

Mr. B. drawing two hundred a month, refuses any allowance, finally allows five dollars a week, and when this proves inadequate, declares he will do the marketing himself. On Saturday night he brings home two pounds of round steak, ten cents' worth of sausages, two pounds of butter and a pound of tea every other week, with coffee when he needs it. Mrs. B does not drink coffee, nor eat sausages. They are for his breakfast. If there is no flour, he gives her the exact price of a ten-pound sack, which she must bring home herself, as it is too late for delivery, and he wants cakes for breakfast.

On Wednesday night he brings home meat, eggs and a small package of sugar. These provisions, with any others he may throw in for generosity, must last her for the week. He does not come home other nights, dining at expensive restaurants, paying from three to five dollars for each dinner.

Mr. B went away for a whole week, leaving his wife ten cents to live on, and not a scrap of flour, butter, meat, bread or potatoes in the house. For an absence of five weeks, he left her three dollars, out of which she had to pay $2.60 water bill, which he had neglected, or have the water shut off. She is an educated, refined woman, who earned her own living before marriage. The only shoes she has had for two years were a pair at auction for $1.40, and he sulked over that expenditure. She does not tell the neighbors why she is so shabby, and they think she does not care to dress well. He is regarded as a model husband.

I could recite hundreds of such cases. That more is not known of them is due to the pride of the woman. Mrs. A may be suffering for underwear, and her clothes shabby, but she is afraid of having her husband blamed by other women, who brag of how good and generous their husbands are, so she pretends that she doesn't care for pretty clothes. The probabilities are that the other women's husbands are just as stingy as hers, only these women, too, hide it from pride and a dread of having it known that they are not treated well. If every woman would drop this pride and tell the conditions of her life, we could all stand together and bring about a happy condition of mutual trust.

CAROLINE BLAKELY

WOMEN WANT TO SUPPORT THEMSELVES

Francis Marion Beynon, 'Women Don't Want to be Supported, Thank You', *The Grain Growers' Guide*, 17 December 1913, vol. 10, 1326.

It is not often, in this work-a-day world, that one gets more sympathy than is coming to one, and yet that is the unique condition in which your editor finds herself this week.

"Another Mere Man" feels that I am in rather a hard position and almost forced to take the woman's side re votes for women. While I thank the gentleman for his very kind sympathy I must confess that I am utterly undeserving of it. In supporting the woman's cause I am only expressing one of the deepest convictions of my own mind. If it were not so I would find another position, for I am afraid I have not much patience with those people who cut their opinions to suit their occupations.

All my life I have been a woman's woman. I do not hold with Wolf Willow and a great many other women that the Lord made the world for men and then made women to help the men. I believe that the world was made for men and women and they in turn were made to help each other.

So, instead of feeling that my position is a difficult one, it is the joy of my life to edit this department where one is allowed to advocate anything that promises to make the life of our sex easier and better.

It is all very well for someone like "Another Mere Man" to sit back smugly and say that there are very few men who will try to beat their wives out of a fair share of the property—"unless there is a good reason." But that is just the point. The man is allowed to decide what constitutes a good reason.

Undoubtedly there are thousands of families where there is never any dispute over property rights or the guardianship of the children, but laws have never been made for well-behaved citizens. I claim that where any trouble arises between a man and his wife it is only fair that they should start equal instead of the wife having a two-mile handicap, as she has today.

Again "Another Mere Man" shows that he has failed utterly to get our point of view when he says that husbands are compelled by law to support their wives and what more do we want. The attitude of mind expressed in that sentence is one of the things that is driving women to the point of utter exasperation today. He can't see that the progressive, independent woman doesn't want anybody to support her—that all the woman who isn't either mentally or physically lazy wants is a chance to support herself.

What is still more trying is that he and many thousands of people like him cannot see that you women in the country who work early and late are supporting yourselves right now often without wages, except your board and clothes.

I consider it downright impertinence for a man on a farm to talk about supporting his wife. When she cooks his meals and sews and mends for him and his children from dawn till dark what is she doing if she is not supporting herself?

In most country homes the wife not only keeps herself but often contributes the family groceries the year round through raising fowl and making butter. And then her husband talks in a lordly way about supporting her—if he is of the same mind as "Another Mere Man."

Fortunately, there are thousands of four-square men in this country who value their wives and their work at their real worth and who are glad to have them as partners and comrades in the highest sense of the word. We must not forget this fact when our blood boils up at the attitude of the unfair ones.

FRANCIS MARION BEYNON

THE DEMAND FOR DOWER RIGHTS, 1910

'Here is Progress', *The Grain Growers' Guide*, 6 April 1910, vol. 4, 28.

Editor, GUIDE:—Never having seen in your interesting pages any word from this place, will try as nearly as possible to give you the opinion of practically all in these parts, after having waited for neighbors to write, as I heard them say they were going to. But most of them have small clothes to wash, and small faces, too, so will write for them. As we have discussed at some length both the dower law and homesteads for women, and am happy to say both women and men are of one opinion, the sooner we get both the better for all humanity. One can't see what any sensible person can find in either to object to. Those who do not care to take advantage of these will not be compelled to.

I know of no less than a score of good honest, respectable girls of proper age, with some means, who would be a credit to any neighborhood or province, and who will do more to improve not only the homesteads, but the country, than all the Doukhobors in the province.

It may not be so in every part of the province, but here it is not the bachelor who is making the most rapid progress, buying land and in every way improving the country, but it is the married men—and why? One wonders if the women have nothing to do with this. Who does the economizing if not the women? And pray tell me what incentive a woman has to work longer hours every day than her husband, if she is to have no say in the selling or mortgaging of land her hard work has helped to pay for? Is it not the women who deny themselves most when the bills come due? It is not for myself that I so much want our rights as for our unfortunate sisters who, no matter how hard they toil, can never get what they merit. Several women in this neighborhood have land, and I do not know of one who is not anxious for the dower law and homesteads for women, and most of them for equal suffrage. None are, I am sure, afraid to leave what they have to their husbands for fear they marry again, as I hear a man say occasionally of the ladies. Not that I think men narrow-minded as a rule, for they are often broader than the fair sex, but I am sure that the women are very much broader-minded now than twenty years ago, and the right to vote will broaden them still more.

I see one of our sisters says, "A man likes a weak woman." I have a husband, father, five brothers, six brother-in-laws and a host of cousins and friends, but I have yet to hear one say he admires a woman weak either in body, intellect or courage. They may pity them. Who does not? But where is the man, woman or child who does not admire a broad-minded woman? And because our environment is narrow we should strive all the more to find literature and associates that will make it broader and better.

We have in our immediate neighborhood a homesteader whose wife furnished the money that brought them from the Old Country. She lives all the time at home with her five children—one who is consumptive—while her husband is every day in town and drinks incessantly. He will "prove up" this next summer. I wonder if Miss Johnson and Mrs. Baily will be glad to know this poor woman and her helpless children will be compelled to give up the only place they could ever call their home, and it is as sure to be the last.

Yes, a dower law by all means.

If all women are alike, every page in THE GUIDE is a woman's page, for I read them all.

A SASKATCHEWAN

Dundurn, Sask.   FARMERESS.

THE RIGHTS OF THE WOMEN IN B.C., 1913

Daughters, Wives and Mothers in British Columbia (Vancouver, 1913), chapters X, XI, pp. 32-6.

DOMESTIC LEGISLATION IN BRITISH COLUMBIA

Domestic legislation can scarcely be called modern or reasonable that:

1st—Permits the marriage of children of twelve and fourteen;

2nd—Frees the deserting husband and father from obligation to provide for his wife and family if his wife has sufficient means to support them, yet leaves him guardian of the children with right to their earnings for his or his creditors' benefit (unless a court order is obtained giving them to the deserted wife and mother for their support);

3rd—Gives the man a right to divorce his wife for a single act of adultery, yet refuses the wife a divorce however adulterous her husband may be. (The mother against whom adultery is proved is not entitled to the custody of her children.);

4th—Divides the estate, however small, of the childless widow of a man dying intestate with her husband's relatives, however distant. If there are absolutely none, gives the Crown a right to the other moiety;

5th—Provides no claim upon the family home that the husband may not alienate;

6th—Permits the husband to leave his widow penniless and dependent;

7th—Makes a stipulated provision for the concubine of a man, married or otherwise, dying intestate.

BETTER LAWS

Lest doubt arises as to the possibility of securing more just and equitable laws for women, it may be well to point out that in *New Zealand, *Colorado and *Washington State, mothers have been placed on an equality with the fathers both as to guardianship and responsibility, and in the latter State as to inheritance also. The child is not regarded as belonging exclusively to the father.

In New Zealand, the Family Testator's Act allows the court to cancel the provisions of the will of either a husband and father or wife and mother in so far as it does not make proper provision for the survivors.

The Destitute Persons' Act makes children, or grand-children, or brothers and sisters, responsible in so far as they are able, for the support of aged or infirm or indigent relatives.

The Maintenance Act provides not only that the wife can sue the husband for support, but may do so without leaving him, and a destitute husband may sue a well-to-do wife. (It is not to be presumed that the court would regard an able-bodied man or woman capable of working for a living as "destitute" in the sense of the Act.)

The conditions upon which divorce may be secured are equal for husband and wife.

In Washington State any person who is head of a family (husband or wife) may select a homestead to be the family dwelling, but the value may not exceed $2,000. The wife may select after her husband's death, if he has failed to do so, and before a sale, to pay debts.

If the husband or wife dies without a will, leaving separate estates, it is allotted as follows:

If there is a widow, or widower, and one child, it is divided equally; if more, the surviving spouse takes one-third and the children two-thirds. Father and mother inherit equally from an intestate, and in the case of a widow without children, she takes two-thirds and the other third is given her husband's immediate family, including only father and mother or brothers and sisters or their children. She does not divide with her husband's relatives to "the remotest degree of consanguinity." If there are none of these, she takes the whole; "the other moiety" does not belong to the State.

The Destitute Mothers' Pension Act provides that the county shall grant a woman whose husband has deserted her, or is in prison, insane or dead, $15.00 a month when she has one child, and five dollars for each other child under fifteen years of age, if by such means she is enabled to maintain a home for herself and for them.

Colorado has an equal guardianship law, the age of consent is eighteen,

*It is noticeable that in all these places women have the franchise.

the wife's signature is necessary before the home may be mortgaged, and aged and infirm parents must be supported.

The fact that other countries and states have such laws is evidence that the women of British Columbia, in asking for just and reasonable recognition of their relationship and human right to share equally with the father and husband in the guardianship and aught else regarding the children they have brought into the world, are making no extraordinary and unheard-of demand.

While the claims of the wife and mother are being acknowledged but slowly, yet in an increasing number of persons a keener sense of justice is growing up, and that way lies our hope.

WOMEN AND CITIZENSHIP, 1914

Francis Marion Beynon, 'Marriage and Nationality', *The Grain Growers' Guide*, 30 Sept. 1914, vol. 8, 1108.

A British subject today and an alien tomorrow is the experience of many women, and that because of no greater misconduct on their part than happening to marry a foreign resident of their country who has not become naturalized.

The cheerful readiness with which a country hands over the citizenship of its women to other countries is, to say the least, disconcerting.

Should a Canadian girl, born of Canadian parents, chance to marry a Dutchman, she becomes in the eyes of Canadian law a Dutch woman. . . .

If the woman were in no sense a contributor to the prosperity and culture of her country, but only an incumbent upon her men folk, then indeed there might be some justification for this arrangement, but with her marriage the woman usually enters upon what men are always pleased to describe as the highest field of usefulness to the country—that of motherhood.

It seems, then, that there is no excuse for such a discrimination against the women of the country except that it was so arranged a long time ago and men, not being the ones who feel the pinch of it, have not bothered to change this law.

Some defender of the theory that men look after women's interests better than they could do themselves, will be quick to declare that the matter has never been brought to their attention, but this is easily disproved. At the special war session of the Parliament, which has just closed, the naturalization law was amended making it possible for a married woman to remain a British subject if, after her marriage, her husband should become an alien, tho in order to do this it is necessary for her to make a declaration that she desires to remain a British subject.

It has also been made possible for a woman who has been divorced from or who is the widow of an alien to regain her British nationality if it should be the pleasure of the Secretary of State to grant her this privilege.

But if a woman, who is a British subject, marries an alien, she becomes an alien and must remain so until her husband dies or she gets a divorce from him.

So it is evident that the honorable gentlemen who make our laws have considered the matter and have come to the conclusion once again that a woman is not a person but an adjunct to some man.

It is strange, knowing with what ardor they themselves hug their nationality, that it does not occur to them that it is a little trying to their women folk to be so lightly tossed over to another country. You will observe also that this is another one of the laws which does not work both ways. Does a Canadian man who marries a French woman become a Frenchman? Most certainly not. Why should he?

THE CRIMINAL CODE UNFAIR TO WOMEN, MANITOBA, 1913

Mary E. Crawford, ed., *Legal Status of Women in Manitoba* (Winnipeg, 1913), chapter VIII, p. 37.

COMPARISONS OF PUNISHMENTS UNDER THE CRIMINAL CODE

Section 211. Seduction of girls between fourteen and sixteen previously chaste—two years' imprisonment, maximum sentence.

Compare *Section* 371: For stealing oysters, or oyster brood, liable to seven years' imprisonment, or a lesser term at discretion of magistrate.

Section 292. Indecent assault on female—two years' imprisonment, maximum sentence.

Compare *Section* 364: For stealing a post letter-bag, or a letter from a post-bag, or post-office, or any valuables from or out of a post letter, sentence liable to life imprisonment, or not less than three years.

Section 315. Abduction of girl under sixteen—sentence five years.

Compare *Section* 369: For cattle stealing—fourteen years, maximum sentence.

Section 213. For the seduction of ward, or employee, by her guardian or employer, said ward or employee being under twenty-one years, *two years*.

Compare *Section* 552: *For making counterfeit gold or silver coin, liable to imprisonment for life.*

Section 212. For seduction under promise of marriage by a male over twenty-one years of age, of a female previously chaste, and under the age of twenty-one years, maximum sentence, *two years*.

Compare *Section* 373. Liable to two years for stealing a tree, sapling or shrub of the value of twenty-five dollars, or of the value of five dollars, if growing in any park, pleasure-ground, garden, orchard, or in any ground adjoining or belonging to any dwelling-house.

Section 308. For bigamy, *seven years' imprisonment*.

Compare *Section* 384: Liable to fourteen years who steals anything in, or from any railway station or building, or from any vehicle of any kind on any railway.

Section 215. A parent or guardian procuring or a party to the defilement of a girl or woman over fourteen years of age, *five years' imprisonment*.

Compare *Section* 372: For stealing brass, woodwork, or lead, iron, copper, etc., fixed to any building, or on any building whatsoever, or anything made of metal used for a fence on public or private property or a burial ground, liable to *seven years' imprisonment*.

Section 216. Procuring a girl under twenty-one, and not of known immoral character, liable to *five years' imprisonment, with hard labor*.

Compare *Section* 379: For stealing from the person any chattel, money, or valuable security, liable to a sentence of *fourteen years' imprisonment*.

A WESTERN FARM WOMAN DEMANDS EQUALITY, 1910

'Membership for Women in Grain Growers' Association', *The Grain Growers' Guide*, 9 March 1910, vol. 4, 26.

After some delay in receiving THE GUIDE of January 19, I was somewhat surprised to see my hasty protest against light stories appearing on the Women's page. But since it was an expression of my principle, I will take advantage of the privilege offered to still further express my views. These pages have given us many inspiring articles, and since many women turn first to this department—and there, either from lack of time or disinclination, "skip" subjects throughout THE GUIDE that stand for all that makes for good—it would seem the better policy to keep those things intended to help women where they will reach the greatest number.

Perhaps with many of us our earliest recollections were that we stood equal with our brothers in all that concerned home and school life, both physically and mentally. We cannot forget the time when the difference was first shown—that important day when the son of the home casts his first vote. Important to him because he has gained his right to full citizenship. Important to the daughter because she felt within her the full power to think and act; but from now on her powers are put on the same basis with those of the criminal and idiot. Her confining place is to be the home, where she will be expected to teach and foster independence, freedom, and liberty. Truly, a teacher without knowledge or experience.

Why, when by every act of those around us, up to maturity, we are made to feel that we have rights with our brothers, should those rights be taken from us, dwarfing our powers to deal with the more weighty problems of life?

We feel sure the dower law will not reclaim our rights. And why ask so little? Would it be right to hamper others because we are hampered? It would be no more right, then, to say that because a woman has a homestead and can also act independently, her desire for home life will be obliterated. The possession of a homestead by a man generally increases his desire for home life, and since our needs and aims are alike, in other things, it is only fair to conclude that the possession of a homestead by a woman will have the same effect.

The physical part of man calls for domesticity. Shall we much longer act the part of mere domestic creatures, or shall we call for equal rights and equal responsibilities?

Would it not be worth the time for the women of this great Dominion to join forces, concentrate their powers to bring about such a condition so that the same opportunities be given them that are given to the hordes of men with less ability than theirs, and who are pouring into this country every year?

Are we and our daughters always to be held in the light of imbeciles in this matter of making laws that touches every vital condition under which we live? Surely we understand the needs of our sex better than men do, and since we are considered human and come under the dictum of laws controlling humans, why not have a voice in the making of these laws?

Must we go on giving birth to daughters whose fate will be the same as ours have been, and are we to continue to give our sons to help swell the number of toilers so that the product of their labors will increase the gluttonous demands for wealth of the men behind the great political web. To be sure, these men are allowing the government to give us help in the way of lectures and bulletins fresh from the brains of able men and women. They are even thinking it to their decided advantage to teach our girls in public schools (using public money) how to better look after the physical needs of their male toilers.

The key-note of all these helps ring with more and better merchantable products. All of this would be a great step in the right direction if all things were equal.

It is just possible that these men know that better enlightened boys and girls, cleaner men and voting women, will be deterrent to the satisfying of their ravenous appetites for money! In that case are we to bow our heads and respectfully obey when told, "Your place is at home"? For those of us who have taken the responsibilities of home, we have no right or desire to neglect them, no more than our husbands have to neglect their business and there is no equal for neglect in either case.

The business man must give some time and thought to the outside conditions under which his business is carried on, if he expects success. So with the business wife and mother; if her work is to bring her the results she is striving for. It is more her duty to keep clean and control the conditions under which she gives birth than it is to give birth to children under demoralizing conditions.

And what of the army of women who have no homes? Whatever the cause, have they not a right to live by their own efforts? Who has a right to say that they shall not develop their natural inclinations on these broad prairies if they do not care to, or are not fitted to enter the commercial world?

Our opportunity is at hand. The G.G.A. and U.F.A. have turned their kindly faces toward us and I move that we join in one great body of western farm women to study, to learn, our duty and our true places in the development of the west, and in national affairs, regardless of our former education as to the proper place of woman. Let us look at the situation as it stands and as it concerns us, stating our views clearly, not merely expressing our opinions in a hasty manner without thought, as is the fashion with many of our sex.

I am sure our editor will help by throwing light on our darkness. It may not be an elegant comparison, but serves our purpose, to say that the home is like a great departmental store, inasmuch as it has many departments, each of which must be treated with equal skill and care, if the one grand whole is to be a success.

I have put the motion and I hope to get a seconder, while THE GUIDE will tally the votes.

We are proud of the success of the organized farmer but still more proud of the attitude that they hold toward us in these questions concerning us. And while they are filling the nest with good eggs, we respectfully ask that the fertile egg of equal rights be placed in with the others, and we promise to faithfully care for the future chicks.

MRS. L. LANGSTON
Wetaskiwin, Alta.

3. EDUCATION

There was little controversy over whether women should be allowed to attend elementary or high schools. Canadians accepted that girls as well as boys should be educated in the rudiments of reading and writing. Controversy did develop, however, when women started demanding entrance into the institutions of higher learning. The attendance of women at universities, at an age when many educators felt they should be getting married, was a challenge to domestic sanctity. Moreover it was thought unwise, in the interest of maintaining morals, to have young women and young men in close proximity during the years of early adulthood. Extended education also challenged the traditional concept of woman's role in the home.

In the mid-nineteenth century no university opened its doors to women. Until they did, women who wanted a higher education attended ladies' academies, which usually had a religious affiliation. These academies were, needless to say, available only to those who could afford them. Thus only a minority of Canadian women actually received even this limited 'higher' education. These academies were often ambitious in their curriculum. In 1883-4 Dunham Ladies' College in Quebec taught Latin, Latin Prose, Composition, Greek Grammar, Geometry, History of Rome, Great Events in History, Logic, Rhetoric, First Principles of Natural Philosophy, Moral Philosophy, English Literature, Analysis of English Authors, French Literature, French Composition, and Christian Evidences. One cannot help wondering how intensive each study was. One girl of the period lamented that her education taught her only to be useless, and that was what society esteemed in her. Such education certainly was not intended to teach women independence. University education however held out that threat to the daughters of the middle class, the class for whom the idea of domesticity was so important as a symbol of their status in society. Public opinion only slowly moved to support university entrance for women. Lack of financing for higher education also caused delay since it prevented the establishment of separate women's institutions that might have been more readily acceptable than 'co-education'.

University classes opened to women at Mount Allison in 1862. In 1875 the first degree granted to a woman in Canada was given by Mount Allison to Grace Annie Lockhart. Interestingly enough it was a B.Sc. degree. Other universities quickly followed, in 1878 Queen's, in 1881 Dalhousie, in 1884 McGill and University College, Toronto. Not all courses, however, were open to women. For example McGill University would not permit women to enter its faculty of medicine until 1917. Nevertheless women persevered. By 1900 women composed 11 per cent of all college students. When compared with American students at the time this does not seem very remarkable. In that same year 36 per cent of the students in the universities and colleges of the United States were women. Why the difference? At least part of the answer is probably that in the United States women's colleges received much financial support and thus offered a viable alternative to co-education.

'A WOMAN'S WANT', 1880

'A Woman's Want', *Grip*, 24 January 1880, vol. XIV, 10.

"A correspondent calls attention to what many women doubtless feel to be a want—the opportunity of meeting with men for the purpose of engaging in the discussion of social topics, on a basis broader than the tittle-tattle of the tea-table or the meaningless and vipid [sic] courtesies of the drawing room."—*Evening Telegram*

"And how in the world can this result ever be brought about, unless some humanitarian angel be sent to establish among us a society for mutual benefit, and a more perfect knowledge of each other, where we might meet without reserve."—Kate *(Correspondent of the Telegram)*

How sweet it were if man and maid
  Could meet together to discuss
Great questions, wholly unafraid
  Of getting into any muss—
Society's mere fume and fuss!

Astronomy is there tabooed,
  Anatomy is little known;
One could not, without seeming rude,
  Converse of the coccygial bone
  When sitting with a man alone.

Full dearly do I love to trace
  Each page of philologic lore.
But what's the use, in this dull place,
  On sanscrit's roots for one to pore?
  Philology is thought a bore!

The other 'eve, while whirled the dance,
  To one who talked with me I said—
Thinking his pleasure to enhance—
  Have you *Fors Clavigera* read?
  He muttered audibly—"Good ged!"

Another night—'twas bright and still—
  With one who pleased me well I went,
Softened, I spoke of Stuart Mill,
  Smith, and the theory of rent—
  He yawned, and asked me what I meant!

Charmed with the intellectual face
  Of one who sat next me at whist,
I broached man's ancestry and race,
  "Come we from apes?" I asked—he hissed
  "My stock is U.E. Loyalist!"

Oh! for some place where one could meet
  Men of a much profounder kind,
  Deep subjects who would wisely treat,
  And recognize my force of mind:
  Instead of social noodles blind!

Primordial atoms, Matter, Force,
  Geology, and fossils rare,
Dawn animals, and nature's course,
  Together we would talk of there,
  All scientific labors share.

In common we would vivisect,
  Discourse of protoplasm and soul,
  All foolish social forms reject,
  Escape conventions and control,
  And go the porcine creature whole!

                                        BOZINI

'SWEET GIRL GRADUATES', 1876

Extract from *Queen's College Journal* (Kingston, 16 December 1876).
Reprinted by permission.

SWEET GIRL GRADUATES

The *Toronto Telegram*, a couple of weeks ago, gave Queen's University
the credit of having admitted ladies to its curriculum, and thereupon
launched into a eulogistic article expressive of the beneficial results likely
to ensue from the general adoption of a similar measure. We are sorry to
undeceive the *Telegram*, but the only foundation for its statement was the
attendance of one enterprising lady upon the class of logic. This could
always be done by any lady who so desired, and we presume the classes
of every college in the country are open to ladies in the same manner. We

would like to see our female friends attend in numbers, as at present there is no ladies' academy in Kingston of much higher standing than a good high school. The training of the high school, though excellent as far as it goes, is not the highest which should be open to young women, and until an institution specially adapted to the educational necessities of woman is established here, we will hail with pleasure their presence within these academic halls. We do not deem it expedient, however, that they should be admitted to all the privileges of universities, for instance to the taking of degrees, though we would desire them ever to remain Mistresses of (He)arts.

> "Prudes for proctors, dowagers for deans,
> And sweetgirl graduates in their golden hair",

or red, as the case may be, are not exactly what we sigh for. If the standard of education in ladies' colleges is at present too low, surely it may be raised till it is high enough. The degrees of a University we consider inappropriate to ladies for this reason—that they have reference solely to public life. Their conferment implies that the objects of it are to go forth to push their way in the outside world, and there acquire *ipso facto* a certain acknowledged position. They only have value when considered with reference to public life, and their bestowal upon women would be a great step towards effectuating the views of the advocates to Woman's Rights, and opening to them the professions and employments of public life, a consummation devoutly to be deprecated. If the conclusion arrived at be admitted, we are confident that among people who appreciate the delicate grace and beauty of woman's character too much to expose it to the rude influences, the bitterness and strife of the world, few will be found to advocate her admission to universities. The education which should be imparted in a ladies' college is not the same as that which always will be the curriculum of a university. Their objects are not the same. The place woman fills in society, and the peculiarities of her nature, must determine what is the proper quality of her culture. The highest ideal of society is not that in which women become logic-choppers. The severer studies which are found necessary in the training of young men would not be best suited to women. Their proper sphere of action is the domestic circle. Their highest duties they owe to the family, which also calls forth their most shining virtues. Therefore her education should be practical, fitting her to govern her household with wisdom and prudence. For her own sake her mind should be cultivated, but her mental culture should not be what is regarded as distinctively intellectual. It should be governed with reference to elegance as well as strength, to the development of the tastes and affections as well as the mere reasoning faculties. Let a woman rather acquire the modern languages than the ancient, and let her rather study music, poetry and painting than the problems of mathematics and metaphysics. We would admire the lady who, while she could bake good bread, was not unfamiliar with Corneille and Schiller, and who could give sensible opinions of the works of Beethoven and Mozart; but may the day be far distant when Canadian Lady Jane Greys shall fill up the pauses in the dance with quotations from Plotinus, and spice their drawing-room conversation with discussions on the differential calculus or transcendental idealism.

AN ENDORSEMENT OF HIGHER EDUCATION FOR WOMEN, 1879

Principal Grant of Queen's University, 'Education and Co-education', *The Canadian Monthly and National Review*, Nov.1879, vol. III,509-18. [Inaugural lecture of 9th Session of Montreal Ladies' Educational Association.]

Because the aims of your Association are modest, and therefore suited to the present condition of popular sentiment with regard to Education for ladies in this part of Canada, because they are in the right direction, and promise to lead to greater things, I had much pleasure in acceding to your request to give the Inaugural Address of this year. The higher education of women and such various questions connected with it as co-education in the recognised colleges of the country, and the fitness of women for professional and industrial careers other than those to which they have been usually limited, are now discussed everywhere. Sides have been taken, with more or less vehemence, and as usual in the heat of discussion extravagant language has been used all round. We may classify the positions taken on the whole subject into the customary three, Extreme Right, Extreme Left, and Middle. The Right wing includes those who resent all interference with use and wont. Departure from traditional views of education and life by any woman they associate with a tendency to part the hair at the side and with lax views of morals and religion. They hurtle the vigorous words 'unmaidenly,' 'unwomanly,' 'indelicate,' at the innovators, well aware that such words are offensive, perhaps not so well aware that they could be easily retorted against themselves, were retorts desirable. Is it more unwomanly to walk to college than to ride to hounds? More indelicate to sit in the same room with young men listening to lectures on philosophy or science, for two or three hours in the day time, than to dance fast dances with them all night? More unmaidenly to practise the healing art than to cultivate the art of husband-hunting? Is it less unworthy of the sex to know something than to know nothing, to do something than to do nothing, to cultivate faculties than to dwarf them? 'My daughter would like to be a physician,' said a lady to her medical man. 'I trust, madam, that you will sanction nothing so indecent,' was the immediate reply. With gentlemen the question has now got beyond this style of argument; but it is still the favourite with a few boors and not a few ladies. It is the initial stage of argument with which every step in the progress of the race has been met; and as it is admirably suited to hurt the feelings of women, I have little doubt that it will be used for some time yet against any step in advance that women may take. As usual the best allies of the Extreme Right have been the Extreme Left. Their loud cry of 'Woman's Rights' has led them to forget that there is such a thing as Woman's Duties; their contention that 'there is no sex in mind' to forget that there are undoubted mental differences corresponding to the physical differences between the sexes. I have no desire to allude to the extravagances in speech and conduct of which they have been guilty. Let the scant justice which women long received serve as their excuse. The Middle school includes all who desire to see the same thought given to the education of girls that has hitherto been given to the education of boys. What that may involve or result in they are not equally clear about. Neither are they agreed as to the practical steps that should be taken in the matter. This party has its Right Centre, and Left Centre, and Cross Sections. 'The air is thick with schemes for the education of women,' some advocating one scheme and others another. But this very variety shows how the question has advanced. Where there was formerly indifference or contempt, interest and intelligence are everywhere manifested, and these ensure that right conclusions shall eventually be reached. For the improvement in England much is due to Her Majesty, the late Prince Consort, and the Royal family,—our own gracious Princess especially. It was owing to the Queen's insistence that the first vote—the modest vote of £30,000, which has now swelled to between one and two millions—for the promotion of Common School Education in England was pressed upon Parliament. Her Majesty founded the first scholarship in Queen's College, Harley St., the first public institution opened in England for the higher education of girls. And when in 1871, a society was formed for establishing on a comprehensive scale good secondary schools where girls could be prepared for such colleges as Girton, Newnham Hall, Cambridge, and others, the Princess Louise consented to be its first President. Her Royal Highness did as much for the true education of girls in Canada by the wise words she spoke on the occasion of consenting to become the Patroness of your Association—words which have been read from the pulpit, and which should be written in letters of gold in your annual reports, and perhaps not less by the first walk she took from Rideau Hall into Ottawa, and back again, sustained only by thick soled boots and a memorable little cane.

The ground on which I advocate a thorough mental training for girls similar to that which is thought essential for boys is the equality of the sexes. That ground is given to me in the first chapters of Genesis. The account of our origin given there assigns to man a dualistic constitution both as to nature and sex. As to nature, it is two-fold, matter and spirit. Matter-day-Saints, as Matter-Evolutionists have been called, profess to evolve consciousness and conscience from protoplasm, thought from no thought, dominion over the world from the elements of the world. And in all ages ascetics have dishonoured the body. Both are wrong. Man's nature has two sides. Both sides are from God, and both are sacred. As to sex, we have also a dualistic conception of humanity. It is declared that two sexes are needed to make up the perfect type of mankind. 'Male and female created He them.' Here is the familiar truth of the equality before God of man and woman, a truth unrecognized by any other religion, but imbedded in the deepest stratum of the Christian revelation. They are different but equal, and the two make up the ideal one that was in the mind of God when He created them, and that received full expression in the Son of Mary who combined in His character all that is excellent in both. Tennyson speaking of the relation between man and woman caught this true conception, and so writes more grandly than Milton.

Here is Milton's view:

'For contemplation he and valour formed,
For softness she, and sweet attractive grace;
He for God only, she for God in him.'

Tennyson, in his *Princess*, strikes a far higher note:

'For woman is not undeveloped man,
But diverse . . . his dearest bond is this,
Not like to like, but like in difference;
Yet in the long years liker must they grow;
The man be nerve of woman, she of man;
He gain in sweetness and in moral height
Nor lose the wrestling thews that throw the world;
She mental breadth, nor fail in childward care,
Nor lose the childlike in the larger mind;
Till at the last she set herself to man,
Like perfect music until noble words.'

The figure in which the distinct creation of woman is Biblically revealed is very expressive. Much has been written on it; but nothing that seems to me better than the words of the old Commentator, Matthew Henry, I think. She was taken, not from the head, for that would have indicated that she was to rule over man; not from the feet to be trampled on by him; but from his side, under his arm and nearest his heart to show that she was to be loved and protected by him. In God's sight the two are one

'Each fulfils
Defect in each, and always thought in thought,
Purpose in purpose, will in will, they grow,
The single, pure, and perfect animal
The two-cell'd heart, bearing with one full stroke,
Life—'

There! you have just proved what I have always asserted, exclaims one of my friends on the Extreme Right. What need of a woman learning Greek or Mathematics? Her end and aim is marriage; her kingdom, a happy home; her subjects, little children clinging about her knees. Exactly so, and just because her relation to man is so close, just because her sphere is so important to man's highest welfare is she entitled to the best that education can do for her? Because of her relation to man, and because of what she is in herself, a thorough mental training is due to girls. These are the two grounds into which the first—the equality of the sexes—divides itself. ...

The great majority of women will be wives and mothers. Their influence in both relations is paramount. In the latter, there is no one to compete with them for the first ten years of the child's life, and in that time more is done towards the formation of character than in all the rest of life. Seeing that this enormous power must be in their hands, have we educated them so that it may be used to the best advantage? As a rule, we have not. Their education has been partly received in society and partly in the boarding-school, and in both cases erroneous ideals and aims have been set before them. ...

And what shall I say of most of the boarding schools that profess to give a fashionable education? Not much, for their supply is according to the demand. It is of no use in any case to rail against outcome. We must go deeper. The popular idea is that any lady, especially if she be a widow not so well off as she once was, can keep a boarding-school, and if she brings in teachers to give instruction in French, drawing, music, dancing, deportment, and fancy-work, what more can be wanted? Scraps of history and science may be thrown in, but as to the systematic study of anything, or methods of study, or mental training, it is seldom dreamed of. Why should it, if insipidity of mind and apathetic elegance of manner be considered more valuable? There has been improvement, but I fear that the complaint made by a French reviewer, a generation ago, is still too well-founded: 'Philosophers never conceived the idea of so perfect a vacuum as is found to exist in the minds of young women who are supposed to have finished in such establishments. If they marry husbands as uninformed as themselves, they fall into habits of indolent insignificance without much pain; if they marry persons more accomplished, they can retain no hold of their affections. Hence many matrimonial miseries, in the midst of which the wife finds it a consolation to be always complaining of her health and ruined nerves.' Were it not for the love that God has implanted in the hearts of women, and love, instead of being blind, is that which gives true insight, were it not for those instincts which are the inherited thought of the race, the results of such education would be unspeakable. As it is they are bad enough for women themselves, their children, and the race. Their own health and the lives of their children are often sacrificed from ignorance of elementary knowledge of anatomy and physiology; and, because of their prejudices and wrong ideas, they give a twist to the moral and intellectual nature of youth that it never completely recovers from. We are now finding out that all we have done for India avails nothing, simply because we have not reached the women. The question with statesmen and missionaries is how shall we educate or influence the women of India? Had we not better begin nearer home?

Speaking of things as they are today, and not as they were a quarter of a century ago, let us thankfully acknowledge that improvement both in the physical and mental training of women has been and is being gradually effected. Girls are more encouraged to take active exercise in the open air, to move about freely without thought of the posture-master, and to lead the same out door life as boys. And blessed be the man or woman who invented or made fashionable the game of lawn-tennis. No one can excel in it dressed in tight stays or pullbacks. I have indeed seen a young lady try to play the game so dressed, but shall not attempt to describe the ridiculous figure the poor creature cut as she hopped from court to court like a 'hobbled' donkey or a very lame and limp duck. But she was the sad and sorrowful exception that proves the rule. Physical invalidism is now not thought 'lady-like.' Perhaps Muscular Christianity has helped to dispel that idiotic notion. And for a brief comprehensive account of what has been done in Europe and America in the way of giving women means and opportunities of mental training, particularly as regards the secondary education that leads up to the University, and also in the way of opening the avenues that lead to professions from which custom, at least, formerly excluded them, let me refer you to a thoughtful paper by Mr. McHenry, Principal of the Cobourg Collegiate Institute, on 'The Higher Education of Women,' which you will find in the *Canada School Journal* of last month.

I would like to face the real question that is at the root of all the present discontent and present movements. What kind of mental training should be given to women? Should it be substantially the same as that given to men, or should it be substantially different? In order to answer this, we must first ask, what is the great object of education, whenever we get beyond that familiarity with the three R's which opens to us the gates of knowledge, and with which the mass both of men and women must for a long time rest content? It can never be too much insisted on that the aim of education is not to store the mind with facts, but to train the mind itself; to develope it in the natural order and relations of its faculties, and so aid in developing character to all its rightful issues. That is a good education which enables us to look at things in the clear light of reasoned thought, and to consider impartially all questions with which we must deal instead of seeing them under the false colourings and refractions of prejudice, emotion, or individual temperament. Education should guarantee not merely the possession of truth, stumbled into by us somehow or other, but the knowledge of how to proceed so as to attain truth, and the knowledge of what is and what is not attainable. We must be able to give a reason for the faith that is in us, for our belief that it is true, not that which has been called woman's best reason—I believe that it is just because it is—but a reason that we come to, as the result of articulated thinking. We are all biased in different ways. And that is the best education which delivers the mind from bias, sets it *in equilibro*, and enables it to act normally and vigorously. Now, it has always been thought a matter of the last importance to give such an education to men. Our methods may have been defective, but such an aim has been always professed. The whole structure of our magnificent educational systems has always had this in view. Every improvement suggested is with the view of securing this more completely.

The first question then to be asked here is, do women need such a mental training as much as men? Unless mind in women is something essentially different from what it is in men, that is, unless they do not possess minds at all, but something else they call their minds, there can be no hesitation as to the answer. We may go further. There are physiological reasons to show that women require a sound mental training more imperatively than men; and that therefore no obstacles should be placed in the way of those who are struggling to obtain its advantages.

Mr. Herbert Spencer points out ('The Study of Sociology,' p. 374) that there is a somewhat earlier arrest of individual evolution in women than in men, and that this shows itself in their physical and mental constitution. 'The mental manifestations have somewhat less of general power or massiveness; and beyond this there is a perceptible falling-short in these two faculties, intellectual and emotional, which are the latest products of human evolution—the power of abstract reasoning and that most abstract of the emotions, the sentiment of justice—the sentiment which regulates conduct irrespective of personal attachments, and the likes and dislikes felt for individuals.' If this be so, and probably most people will admit the fact, though they may not necessarily accept the cause assigned by Mr.

Spencer, it follows that the best mental training that can be had is even more indispensible in the case of women than of men. Women are already handicapped by nature. Is it necessary that they should be, in addition, artificially handicapped by unwise restrictions, by the foolish customs and opinions of a half or quarter educated society?

It being granted, then, that the best education is needed by women, the next question is, where are they to get it? Well, it is not at all likely that the great colleges and universities that have been built, equipped, and endowed in the course of centuries by pious founders and wise States, and that have hitherto been used by young men, can be duplicated at once. That is out of the question. Even if duplicates were provided, such institutions would have as a rule empty benches for many a day. We may be quite sure that we shall have no 'ugly rush' of ladies seeking higher education. Hence the so-called 'Ladies Colleges,' that are to be found in various parts of the country, must accommodate themselves to the average condition of female education, and can afford to supply only those branches and 'accomplishments' that the majority demand. Such adventure insitutions, unendowed and possibly aiming at annual dividends, cannot possibly give such an education as the old recognised institutions. We are thus driven to ask, why should not ladies, in search of a sound education, seek a regular college and university training?

Why not? It has been said or hinted that grave evils would result from allowing young men and young women to attend the same college. There is no evidence to this effect. The evidence that we have is all the other way. Surely by this time we have got far ahead of the gross idea that woman's virtue depends not on herself, her modesty, self-respect, and principle, but on thick veils, padlocks and duennas. It is best to imitate nature, and nature by sending boys and girls to the same family has ordained that they should grow up together in mutual honour and helpfulness. As a rule, boys are best when they have sisters, and girls are best when they have brothers. The two sexes now attend the same Common Schools, High Schools, Collegiate Institutes, and Normal Schools, and no one dreams of there being anything improper in their so doing. And, who would not rather trust them when they have attained the age of mutual self-respect, than in the years immediately preceding? Of course certain practical regulations would be needed, and these could easily be made; such as, not allowing both sexes to board in the same house, and in colleges where residence is enjoined, having a separate hall with a lady at its head; sitting on different benches in the class-rooms; perhaps entering or leaving by different doors; though, in my opinion, the fewer the regulations the better. The essential idea of college life is that students have attained to years of understanding, and that they are to be trusted. Professors who cannot manage students on this principle have mistaken their vocation. And students who are strangers to it should be taken or sent home as soon as possible. So far as there is evidence on the subject, it is to the effect that the influence on young men of the presence of female students is good and only good, and *vice versa*.

It is asked sometimes, with the alarm begotten of profoundest ignorance, are the subjects of a regular college course suited to ladies? A simple enumeration of these is sufficient to dispel the alarm. Take the old or any proposed new curriculum, and what subject in it is in any way objectionable? Language, literature, mental philosophy, mathematics, physical science, natural history, at which does male or female modesty or incapacity take alarm! Besides, all these subjects need not be taken by every student. Every college now allows a great measure of liberty in this respect. More and more, too, options are being allowed. Very radical proposals are being made in Britain for bifurcating or trifurcating the subjects required for a degree. And I do not see why some subjects considered specially desirable for ladies should not be allowed to rank in place of others not considered so desirable. A thorough knowledge of music, for instance, might stand for Greek or senior mathematics. As to regularity of attendance, here too, the college is not subjected to the rigid rules of the school. In most colleges it is considered sufficient if actual attendance is given from two-thirds to four-fifths of the session.

But is not excessive study injurious to young women? Very, and to young men likewise. Many of the noblest young men I have known have killed themselves. The best are apt to injure themselves. No fear of the idlers. But we do not, therefore, exclude diligent and talented young men from college. Bad results flow chiefly from entering college too soon or insufficiently prepared in the secondary school, from bad boarding-houses, from the too numerous examinations now in vogue, and from over anxiety to attain honours. These causes, the last excepted, should and could be easily guarded against. A moderate amount of regular study is physically and mentally beneficial to both young men and women. No one doubts this as far as men are concerned, and I would refer those who want testimony for it in the case of women, to an article in the *Contemporary Review* of January, 1878, by Frances Power Cobbe, on 'The Little Health of Ladies.' It is not work but worry or mental vacuity, not regular but irregular study, or study under conditions prejudicial to health, that injures.

Besides, it is a mistake almost ludicrous to suppose that excessive study is required for the ordinary B.A. examination. The knowledge represented by the possession of a pass degree, no matter from what university, is exceedingly moderate, though the value of the training received may be said to be incalculable. There is nothing like the regular university course. It is adapted to average minds, and confers benefits on the greatest.

I know of no reason that can be urged against women studying in our recognised colleges that has not been urged from time immemorial against every step in advance taken by the race, against every reform that has ever been made in the realm of thinking or of action. Of course this reform will come slowly. The mass of social prejudice to be overcome is enormous, and women are peculiarly sensitive to social opposition. At first, average young men in our colleges will be subjected to rather an unfair competition, for the young women will be a select class, chiefly those who survive the operation of a very rigid natural selection. But in time this will be righted.

Woman should have every possible opportunity of obtaining a sound mental training because of her relation to man and the importance of her position as a probable wife and mother. But to consider woman as merely a satellite of man—or, as Von Hartmann respectfully calls her, 'a moral parasite of man'—is a caricature of the truth that man is her natural head and protector. She is 'a primary existence,' owes responsibility directly to God, is bound to cultivate her faculties for her own sake, and has, in many cases, to fight her own way through the world. It is impossible to overlook the fact that there is an immense number of unmarried women, and women who are not likely to be married, or who have no disposition to waste their lives in frivolity or idleness until they meet with some man whom they can honestly marry. This class is increasing, and as civilization progresses it is sure to increase still more. The law of all progress is that the simple and homogeneous is, through a process of continuous differentiation passing into the complex and heterogeneous. Where woman is the property, and the servant, or plaything, of man, there is no woman's question. All women will be pretty much alike, and all will be provided for after a fashion. Whenever she is really recognised as his equal, variety will be seen in women as in men. All savages are alike. Converse with one savage and you have conversed with the tribe. The more advanced the civilization the greater variety among individuals. There is a higher unity, but the uniformity has gone. In an advanced civilization, then, you will be more be able to class all women as simply wives than to class all men as simply husbands. There will always be some kinds of work that men can do best; and other kinds that women can do best—but no longer can all the honourable professions be reserved for men. We may discriminate on the ground of ability or fitness, but not on the ground of sex; and before we can decide as to ability, a fair field must have been granted. Here, too, the question is solving itself. Gradually women are finding their way into new employments. We see them in railway and telegraph offices, and hear of them at bank meetings. Thousands are employed as teachers, copying-clerks, type-setters, writers, artists, house-decorators, and thousands more might be employed in dry-goods and other establishments. The medical profession has been thrown open to them in Great Britain and in the United States; and Miss Cobbe believes, and with reason, that there will soon be women-doctors and women's hospitals, attended by women-doctors, in every town in the United Kingdom. All the nineteen British medical examining bodies are now allowed to confer their licenses or diplomas upon women. In Canada, the Medical Faculty connected with Queen's University has decided to open classes for women next spring, the matriculation examination and the curriculum to be the same as for men. Of course, this means double work for the Professors, for it is generally recognised that co-education is out of the question in medical and surgical studies. Naturally enough the Professors were unwilling to undertake so much additional labour, but they could not resist the appeals made to them in letters from young women who felt impelled to devote themselves to the profession, and who were unwilling to exile themselves from their own country in order to get the necessary education. Large classes are not expected, but I understand that a sufficient number have engaged to attend to make the experiment worth trying.

But the question of higher education should be looked at apart from professional education and apart from the employments or careers to which it may lead. Culture is a good in itself, and should be sought for its own sake. If it be true that 'in this world there is nothing great but man, and in man nothing great but mind, then to neglect the proper cultivation' of the mind is a sin against our highest interests, and inexorable nature forgives no sin. What would any man who has received a thorough University training barter for it! He may have sought it at first not for its own sake, but because by that avenue only he could enter some calling that would give him honourable position as well as bread and butter. But having obtained a measure of culture, he usually values it aright. Unless he is an incurable Philistine, he has been taught to know himself, his intellectual strength and intellectual weakness, the meaning and range of his powers, and the impassable walls that hem him in. He has learned to be modest and to be confident. He looks through appearances to the heart of things; and refuses to bow down to the idols that lead the crowd astray. My only astonishment is that all such men do not resolve, as a matter of course, to give to their children that which has been their own chief solace, that which has refined and strengthened their own natures, making them independent of the accidents and changes of time by giving them unfailing resources within themselves. Why should I deny my son the highest possible training of which he is susceptible, even though he may have to earn his bread all his days by the sweat of his brow? Why should I deny my daughter the same true wealth that cannot be taken away from her, even though I see no prospect for her but to be a sempstress? If their external lot is to be circumscribed and their fare scant, the more reason that they should have compensations in themselves. Have worthier conceptions of human nature. Set high and not poor ideals before your children, and they will seek to attain to them. We talk on Sundays of the dignity of human nature, of the worth of the soul, of the sufficiency of character; and throughout the week we are materialists pure and simple. The objects set before our sons are to get money; and the prize dangled before our true-hearted girls' eyes is a husband with money. We do boys and girls grievous injustice. Too often we succeed in debasing them. They owe to us their stunted natures, their worldly minds, and the general atheism of their lives, veneered with the form of religion prevailing in their day. Can we not believe the great Teacher's words, 'the Kingdom of God is within you,' and so believing, care for that which is within rather than for that which is without?

We should, I say, value culture for itself, and not for the career it may lead to, or the external advantages it may secure. But here, as in every other similar case, the first leads to the second. What the world needs above everything else is well-qualified workers in every department. My great difficulty is, not to find positions, but to find persons qualified to fill them. Work is always needed to be done. But who shall direct us to honest and competent workers? They are at present establishing a new industry in Halifax, and they have sent two of their leading merchants to roam over the Great Republic to try and find some one fit to be entrusted with its management. I understand that it was difficult to find a person qualified to fill a situation in Montreal worth $25,000 a year. There are Professorships vacant in our Universities every year, and men competent to fill them are not easily found. When a lady applies to me for a governess, though I know of many out of work, I am thankful to find one whom I can recommend. Principals of Ladies' Colleges assure me that their difficulty is the same. We need not be alarmed at the spread and improvement of education. What the world needs, and greatly needs, is not less of it, but more and better. Depend upon it, the well-educated man and woman can always get work to do, and food and raiment, at least, as recompense. They ask for no more. In themselves they have a kingdom and an inexpugnable fortress into which they can at all times retreat, where no storms beat, and no famine threatens. 'Not by bread alone is the life of man sustained; not by raiment alone is he warmed,' writes a seer who did much for the higher life of England, in the first half of our century, 'but by the genial and vernal inmate of the breast, which at once pushes forth and cherishes; by self support and self-sufficing endeavours; by anticipations, apprehensions, and active remembrances; by elasticity under insult, and firm resistance to injury; by joy and by love; by pride, which his imagination gathers in from afar; by patience, because life wants not promises; by admiration; by gratitude—which debasing him not when his fellow-being is its object—habitually expands itself for his elevation, in complacency towards his Creator.' Every word of this is as true of women as of men. And the substance of what I have written is this, throw no obstacle in the way of those women who seek to develope and cultivate to the utmost their higher nature, intellectual, emotional, and moral. Let them know that all the avenues, and all the pages of knowledge, are open to them; and that it is not unworthy of their sex to think and to hope. For a very long time, only a small minority will seek to obtain this good thing of full-orbed culture. Among that minority may be—probably will be—some fitted to bless mankind. In the name of justice, for man's sake, let the few who seek, find; or if they fail, let them not have to blame any but themselves. Failure, both men and women must acquiesce in. Injustice, neither man nor woman can bear.

PROFESSIONS FOR WOMEN, 1879

'Letters on the Education and Employment of Women,' *The Canada Education Monthly*, 1879, vol. VI, 202-5.

Dear CLYTE,

I have not forgotten my promise to commence a correspondence with you on my return from abroad. Yes! your Agnodice (for I still keep the old name you gave me at school) is at home again with her brother and sister.

My brother has already settled down to his books and his studies, and his good, kind wife is immersed once more in her housekeeping affairs. To him, whether or not his last work will be favourable reviewed, is the most important consideration in the world; to her, the rise and fall of eggs or butter is the topic of the utmost importance. As for myself, I am still, dear Clyte, revolving in my mind the idea of following some profession. I know you are orthodox enough to be shocked at this, even in the face of the advanced views of the present day, but I shall meet your arguments, and I hope conquer them.

I am young, strong and determined. No one has a claim on my time as your delicate mother has on yours. Why should I be obliged to give up to Society, to whom, as yet, I owe nothing, the most active and vigorous part of my life? Is the aim of my education only to be accomplished by a constant round of garden-parties, balls, and receptions,—if so, why have I been taught anything else, but to read, write, dance, enter a room gracefully, and chirp a feeble song to a wandering and uncertain accompaniment? These acquirements would have been enough to have given me a footing in what is called Society. No! I cannot submit to that kind of thing; I must have a purpose, a lifework, a determined end in what I undertake. Such a purpose my sister sets before me in marriage! It is no wonder marriages are so unhappy, when they are put before girls as the end, the thing to be achieved, "the one thing needful" in their lives. When we struggle for a thing, when we fight for a prize, at least we expect, with reason, that the thing shall be worth the winning. If, in archery, we gain a golden arrow, we have a right to be disgusted if the prize turn out to be of counterfeit metal, and the arrow cannot expect to be treated with the admiration and respect that would be given it if it were genuine. This is truly the way our future husbands are held up to us, and the result must often, of course, be disappointment and despair.

Oh! the shamefulness of those odious expressions—"playing her cards well," "*making* a good match," "setting her cap," &c. I burn with anger and indignation as I write them. Do you remember what John Stuart Mill says?—"What marriage may be in the case of two persons of cultivated faculties, identical in opinions and purposes, between whom there exists the best kind of equality, similarity of powers and capacities with reciprocal superiority in them, so that each can enjoy the luxury of looking up to the other, and can have alternately the pleasure of leading and of being led in the path of development—I will not attempt to describe. To those who can conceive it there is no need; to those who cannot, it would appear the dream of the enthusiast. But I maintain, with the profoundest conviction, that this, and this only, is the ideal of marriage; and that all opinions, customs and institutions which favour any other notion of it, or turn the conceptions and aspirations connected with it into any other direction, by whatever pretences they may be coloured, are relics of primitive barbarism."

So with these opinions you will not be surprised when I tell you I seriously intend studying for a profession, and I think I have chosen the medical. I am of course aware that at present women are not admitted to degrees, and that when they practice, it can be only as quacks, but I shall go through with the regular curriculum, as so many have done, in the hope that by the time I have passed all my examinations, these disabilities will have been removed.

Now for your arguments; I believe I know them already, for how often have we discussed kindred subjects in our school-days, and I see before me now your sweet, grave, earnest face, much more persuasive than your judicious, but excuse me, not very convincing arguments.

Strong-minded, independent women are perfectly horrid, you say; they wear queer clothes, and cut their hair short, and their boots are so very, very large and thick, and they talk loudly, and stand with their hands behind them, and are altogether most objectionable. Yes! some of them are I must own, and they do a great deal of harm to the much larger class of women whose only desire, as one of them has said, is "to use the reason God has given them to form a just opinion on the circumstances around them," by exciting a prejudice against what are the supposed attributes of every thinking woman.

But you must remember that whenever there is a re-action, there will be found fanatics. It is unfair to call all Scotch clergymen Philistines, spoilers and mistaken zealots, because John Knox defaced altars, and mutilated carvings in his intemperate, yet withal lofty, because unselfish, passion for Reform. And it is equally unfair to ascribe to all earnest women who desire to work and not to talk, the rabid phraseology, such as the wish for the "painless extinction of man" &c., frequently indulged in by these *soi disant* strong-minded women.

When I was at a ball in Paris, I met a specimen of this class; she was a practising physician with a foreign diploma. She was dressed as much like the "abhorred race" as was possible. She wished to dance, but alas! there arose a difficulty in the minds of all present whether her partner should be a lady or a gentleman! This kind of thing is horrible and no one feels more strongly on the point than the true asserter of Women's rights. I must not however forget to mention that the lady in question was spoken of as *Monsieur la docteure!*

Pray believe that a woman may study any or all of the sciences, may deliver lectures and write books, and may even enter professional life, and yet may be undetected in the streets by any peculiarity in her dress or walk; she may speak and act like a lady, and even, most astonishing to relate, may order a dinner, and dispense with grace the rites of hospitality.

I see you prime your mouth now for all the world as if "prunes and prisms" were coming, but you murmur instead—womanly modesty, womanly virtue. Can a woman keep these divine attributes when she goes out into the world to fight her way and to win fame and position? I ask, why not? Are seamstresses and charwomen less virtuous and modest than their neighbours, because they have to fight their way and win their fame (such fame as it is) in the struggle for bread? Are the Turkish women, veiled and secluded as they are kept, more virtuous than those of European nations? Are we the worse for going out for a walk, when we are told to "put our virtuous indignation in our pockets," and submit to be regarded as pictures on exhibition? Are we the worse for reading our Bibles or our Shakespeares, or must these and all books written before this ultradelicate nineteenth century be Bowdlerized before being placed in our hands? Is our innate modesty so small a thing, of so frail a material, that it will bear no contact with externals? If you admit it is, I answer that I deny that a woman possesses either virtue or honour who cannot without harm read and live and work as good and holy men have read and lived and worked. Bear in mind, too, that the women who enter into public competition with men, go armed with a higher education, mental, moral and physical, than those have whose thoughts never soar above the contemplation of a comfortable home and plenty of excitement.

You think the movement is a new-fangled idea, interesting to me, perhaps, because of its novelty. Are you aware that our old friend Plato calls upon "both sexes indifferently to associate in all studies, exercises, offices and professions, military and civil, in his republic?" This is even rather farther than we go, for at present (whatever the future may give us) our physique is hardly capable of undergoing the hardships of a soldier's or a sailor's life. Montaigne affirms "that males and females are cast in the same mould; and that education and custom excepted, the difference between them is not great," and a modern poet sings,—

> "Female and male God made the man:
> His Image is the whole, not half;
> And, in our love, we dimly scan
> The love which is between Himself."

It is ridiculous to hear people exclaiming, do you want to see women in parliament? do you want to have women as judges? and the like.

We want to fit ourselves for any office; whether we shall be called upon to fill those positions is quite another question, and one thing is quite certain, that no woman is likely to be raised to any high office unless she is eminently fitted for the place. At present what women have to do is to cause their standard of education to be raised. When this has been done for some generations, then will be the time under the new *régime* to inquire what posts of importance they are capable of filling. We do not demand of a boy the strength and power of a man, or wonder why with all his potentiality of force he cannot rival at once the wisdom of an ancient, and yet the question is constantly put (with the belief that women expect all this of and for themselves), whether they do not desire *now* and *at once* to undertake work requiring intimate knowledge of the laws of political and social economy? You think, perhaps, I underrate the education of to-day. When I see hundreds of women who might vote and who do not, who might work and who do not, who have talents but hide them in a napkin, and candles, but bury them under a bushel; women who do not want to be represented in the parliament of their country, who are perfectly indifferent under the discussion of the most crying evils demanding social reform, I think I do not exaggerate the need of a higher and wider scope of thought.

Women think by their indifference and feigned humility they win admiration and affection, which is all many of them seem to require. They are not conscious of the intense selfishness that makes them shut their eyes and seek only to live and let live. For it is undoubtedly selfishness and indolence that oblige them to forget how many hundreds of women are struggling for maintenance. They call them sisters—the family likeness is not very great—and these "sisters" have their bread to earn, but also nothing to earn it with, they have been brought up to no profession, apprenticed to no trade, yet they are bound "somehow," and few care how, to rough it in the dreariest sense of the word and to support themselves and often their families.

And yet we are told there is no need for women to adopt any calling!

Does it not show that reform is much needed when so many of us are determined to face opposition, and to shock society by entering the professions?

It is not nice and pleasant to shock people, as some seem to think it is. On the contrary, it is very disagreeable, and a woman requires to be quite confident that she is doing not only *a* right and good thing, but *the* only right and good thing under the circumstances. It is far from pleasant to be called names, and to be treated with contempt, and it is still more trying for others to think that we hold ourselves superior to all around us. We do not consider ourselves justly open to this charge; true, we are forced by the very condition of things to be self-assertive, but we do not wish to be conceited.

Others who do not care to march abreast with us in our movement, may have as great or greater stores of learning, but I must say that such knowledge is of very little value unless it is made use of. It seems to me time thrown away to study sciences and arts assiduously, but never to make any account of them, and I have often wondered at men and women whom I have been told have read a great deal, and yet talk nothing but the veriest small talk. What have they done with all this acquired knowledge, I ask? But that is never discovered, till one cannot help solving the riddle by being tempted to believe that their researches have begun and ended with the titles of the books.

I shall wait impatiently for your next letter, after which I have more to say on this subject.

Till then digest this sentence from Montaigne, *à propos* of what I have just now said: — "Learning is in some hands a sceptre, in others a rattle."

Your old school-fellow,
AGNODICE.

THE NEED FOR LADIES' COLLEGES FOR HIGHER EDUCATION, 1885

T. M. MacIntyre, 'Our Ladies' Colleges in Relation to our Educational System', *The Canada Educational Monthly and School Magazine*, Feb. 1885, vol. 7, 41-6.

The question of a Provincial University has at last reached a hopeful position. Whatever other merits the present scheme may possess, not the least is found in the kind of harmony to be brought into our University Education—a harmony whose chief excellence will be in its diversity, rather than in its uniformity, obtained through the distinctive functions preserved by the Federating Colleges. If interpreted wisely the occasion has come not only to give a grand impetus to the educational interests of our country, but also to give such an impetus to the cause of religion as it may not receive for many years to come. A grave responsibility, therefore, rests upon all who have it in their power to give effect to some such scheme as is now under consideration. In the face of such possibilities as lie before us in this Province of having a thoroughly equipped system of university education, second to none on the Continent, it must be an opportune time to ask, What provision is to be made for the higher education of women? . . .

The effects of any system of education may not be seen for many years, but if present indications are keenly watched, we shall guard against making experiments where the moral character of those educated is at stake. We shall not allow ourselves to be carried away with the delusion that the acquirement of knowledge is the only or the most important part of true education. The question, so far as we are concerned, is virtually settled, and that, largely by the good sense and preference shown by our women for separate Colleges. The fact that during the past twelve years so many Ladies' Colleges have been established, and their success placed beyond a doubt, is sufficient evidence that our people are prepared to support separate Colleges for the education of their daughters. It must also be borne in mind that this preference has been shown during a period when our public education, in our High Schools and Collegiate Institutes, has been making extraordinary progress, affording the highest facilities at comparatively little or no expense.

It may be premature to draw conclusions from the results already obtained under the privileges enjoyed by our young women of attending the classes in the several Universities, yet, while it is true that the doors have just been opened, we may still note the extent to which our women are in sympathy with the movement. From the comparatively small number who avail themselves of the provisions thus made, is it not suggestive that there is something more wanted than merely to be admitted to University classes? Do not our Canadian young women value more highly the advantages of College Residence, and the mental culture and refinement, that are to be obtained by coming into contact with their instructors and superiors as well as with their fellow-students? The extent to which at present our Universities are doing the work of the higher education of women, may be gleaned from the following facts, kindly given by the Presidents of these Universities respectively:—At University College, Toronto, taking regular course in arts, seven lady students; Queen's University, Kingston, eight; Victoria University, Cobourg, two, with three occasional students; McGill University, Montreal, fourteen, with sixteen occasional students.

If any conclusion at all is drawn from the above, it must be that marked success has attended the system of separate classes established by our friends in Montreal, through the liberal gift of the Hon. Donald A. Smith in placing $50,000 at the disposal of the University for the higher education of women. That these numbers will be largely increased in this University next year there can be no doubt. On the question under consideration Sir William Dawson, in his Annual University Lecture last November, said: "I do not think it necessary to dwell on the subject of separate education for women, as at least one of the best methods in the junior years of the College Course. We already have a larger class than all those of the co-educationists of Canada united. But I may say that if I had ever entertained any doubts in this matter, they would have been dissipated by witnessing the work of our classes, and by observing how much more pleasantly and familiarly, and how much more usefully, from a purely educational point of view, it goes on than it would do in the presence of large classes of young men."

Another important feature in connection with this question which must not be lost sight of, at a time when we are paving the way to a liberal University education, is involved in the end to be kept in view, viz: Shall the aim of our Higher Education for Women be Professional Training? No mistake should be made here. We must not commit the error already made in the education of our young men. We have to deplore that there is a general tendency to undervalue the advantages of a thorough training in our Colleges and Universities unless it opens up a door to Professional life. The worthy President of University College, Toronto, whose strong views on co-education are so well known, expressed himself with equal soundness on this question. In his recent address at the Convocation of University College, he says: "But education in its highest sense means something distinct from this. It means education based on the love of knowledge for its own sake; and widely diffused so that it shall leaven the whole community and make us an educated people. For this purpose we stand peculiarly in need of highly educated women, through whom we may look for intellectual culture extending its refining influences even into the stormy arena of political contention, while it places before the rising generation a humane and ennobling standard such as we can very partially lay claim to now. This is what I understand by the Higher Education of Women; and this the present scheme tends to retard rather than to secure." While we advocate the fullest liberty in this matter to women who have the taste and the nerve to enter professional life, there is little danger that the privileges afforded them will be abused. A policy of Free Trade, however, will be the safest for our gentlemen professionals to adopt in this case, whatever their politics may be, for any effort made to protect themselves by barring out women will only create the greater desire to invade their sacred precincts. The professional tendencies of the times may be observed from the following:

At Queen's number of lady students in Medicine 14
At Toronto 10
At Victoria Medical Schools 0
At McGill 0

Let it not be supposed for a moment that there are not ample opportunities for our women to exercise their very highest gifts in mental culture and refinement. There is a Profession open to them of possibilities hitherto not dreamed of, and, up to the present, very inadequately filled— *The Profession of Teaching.*

It is undoubtedly the experience of those who have to do with Institutions for the Higher Education of Women, that the supply of teachers possessed of high scholarship and the refinement so necessary, is not equal to the demand—and the demand is becoming greater every year. In England some years ago there were two classes of female teachers, or governesses, as they were more generally styled. Both did their work badly. One class rose from the lower ranks, and by indomitable perseverance acquired an education that fitted them for imparting a certain amount of knowledge; but they were lacking in the polish that English people demanded for the drawing-room. The other class came from a very different rank. Women once in the enjoyment of comfort and ease, meeting with reverses in life, found it necessary to provide for themselves, and without the intellectual preparation undertook the management of schools or gave private instruction, and sadly failed. They left as a monument of their failure the odium that attached for a long time to the *Boarding Schools.*

We want to elevate the profession of teaching in Canada to the dignity to which it is justly entitled. What is needed is that women, who have had the advantages of the highest mental culture as well as the refining influences of our best homes, should not consider it beneath their dignity to engage in the work of education. Let women consider it their privilege as well as their duty to take a part in this work, even when they do not require to enter it for a "Living," and the cause of education will receive a *new inspiration.* We shall then have no difficulty in obtaining an Annex College in affiliation with the Provincial University, thereby securing in separate classes the advantages of a distinguished Professoriate.

Our women are specially adapted to the work of teaching. The educational success already achieved by female teachers is evidence of their adaptation for it, and gives encouragement to extend the facilities to prepare them for this particular work.

In the United States the proportion of female teachers engaged in the work of public education is seventy-five per cent. In Ontario the proportion will be over fifty per cent.

Owing in a large measure to the small remuneration paid our public school teachers there is necessarily a want of permanency in the profession. From four to five years is the average experience gained by the teacher, and his calling is made the stepping-stone to some more lucrative vocation. And who can blame him? Into what calling in life can a man enter with so discouraging an outlook? The teacher, who is prepared to remain permanently in the profession, may be described as a person who is determined to sacrifice himself on his country's altar. And, while the argument of a want of permanency applies with equal force to lady teachers, we have no hesitation in saying that, during this short period, they exercise a far more powerful influence in the moulding of character. Woman's ready sympathy, her simple and clear methods of expression, her soul power earlier developed, all tend to give her the supremacy in influencing the moral and religious life of the young. In our Kindergartens and Elementary Schools the field is hers by conquest. And when we have learned to demand qualifications of greater importance than those determined by written examinations, the supply will not be greater than the demand, and our lady teachers will be better paid for the work they do. We come now to deal more directly with the Ladies' Colleges. Their necessity has been fully implied in the foregoing remarks.

1. The distinctive character of their work.

With reference to the share of educational work entrusted to these Colleges, it may be said that they have a two-fold object in view.

(*a*) To give a liberal education, embracing a knowledge of Music and the Fine Arts. To co-operate as far as possible in the matter of University Education.

(*b*) To assist in the moulding of character, under a wisely ordered system so difficult to obtain even in the best regulated homes. To afford the refining influences which will better prepare our women for the profession of teaching.

In regard to the matter of co-education I feel called upon in this connection to enter a protest against it, based on personal experience derived under a system of co-education as well as under separate classes. The age demands of the young lady that she should know something of Music and Painting, whilst no such demands are made of her brother. The time which must be devoted to these subjects renders it impossible to compete on equal terms, otherwise we are demanding a much larger share of work from her. In order, therefore, that the young lady's literary work may be carried on in connection with these additional subjects, it becomes necessary for her to have separate classes, where satisfactory provision can be made for the differences in study. Again, the demands of social life prevent the successful accomplishment of their education along the same lines. A young lady labours under many disadvantages in attempting a heavy course of study after the age of twenty, at which time the young man is expected to begin the severer studies of his course. Exceptional cases there may be, but we must submit to the inevitable and to the general law: —

2. The relation of Ladies' Colleges to Church and State.

(a) The Ladies' Colleges to be not only in name but in fact under the direct control of their respective churches.

(b) The State to give a definite recognition and value to the higher work of education done.

It is in the interests of the Ladies' Colleges that we welcome the prospective University Confederation. The Churches relieved of some of the burdens of secular education will be able to give more attention to legitimate church work in providing for the higher education of their women, second only in importance to the efficient education of candidates for the Ministry. The denominations controlling the education of women, in addition to the influence exercised in the University of the Province, need have no fears of the safety of our State Education.

It is no credit to our Churches to be able to say that they have not the charge of a single Ladies' College in Ontario. That there is not one College for the Higher Education of Women with one dollar's endowment. Which of our denominations will be the first to set a noble example? Who will be the first benefactor in Ontario to help the endowment of these Colleges? With a liberal endowment which would lessen the actual cost to students, thus enabling them to continue longer at College, and at the same time increase the facilities for still higher work, these Colleges are destined to give an impulse to the cause of education that it has not yet received.

Owing to the denominational control here advocated, and we think wisely, no State aid can be expected. Their connection with the Provincial University along the lines already established will be found of the very greatest service. The examinations held in these Colleges, where desired, under the control of the University Senate, may be made more effective by not only recognizing them in the regular University course in proceeding to a degree, but also giving them the value of qualifications required for teachers' certificates. To complete the work undertaken by these Colleges an Annex College for women is needed, in direct affiliation with the Provincial University and Normal School. The number of women entering on a full University course may be limited, but the number demanded for the teaching profession will always be large. An Institution combining both these interests could be made a success. The women pursuing a University course and those preparing for teachers would have the safeguards of a College Residence, and in much of their work, common to both courses, they would enjoy equally the advantages provided under the scheme of University Confederation. Such Annex College would afford the advantages of separate classes, and would combine efficiency with economy.

TRAINING FOR HOUSEWORK, 1893

Helen Cameron Parker, 'Technical Schools for Women', *The Canadian Magazine*, 1893, vol. I, 634-7.

The deafening clamour for higher education for women, which for years has been heard above all other noises, is subsiding. Higher education is now an assured fact and every profession is now open to the woman who desires and has sufficient courage and strength to enter.

But our system of education for woman is not yet perfect. Two momentous facts obtrude themselves upon every thoughtful observer. First— while the intellectual standing of women in America is as high as in any other part of the world, her physical force is lower. While America produces more literary, business and professional women than any other country, she furnishes fewer "good" mothers.

Second—while for every profession which she *may* choose to enter, woman is afforded means of attaining the highest training; for the one profession which she *does* choose, no means of training is provided. For every woman who enters a profession, one hundred women enter homes, or, to put it in another way, for every woman who enters the profession of medicine or law, one hundred enter the profession of home-maker.

These two facts are so important and react so upon each other, that they demand the attention of all intelligent thinkers.

Proud as we are of our educational system, we cannot close our eyes to the truth that it is for our girls, at a certain period in their life, a most unwise one. During her earlier years, our girl is a little animal, different in kind slightly from her rollicking brother; but, as she enters her teens, a new period is reached—the first great change occurs, and of the girl is evolved slowly the woman. A birth, as full of importance and significance as the birth of an infant, takes place, requiring equal discretion, quiet and care. But see the inconsistency. When the baby girl arrives, she is cared for assiduously; her clothing, her diet, the amount of exercise, the bathing and fresh air, are regulated with great nicety, and, under the care of wise parents, all undue excitement and noise is shut out, all forcing of the dormant faculties is avoided. But when the baby-woman begins to assert her life by excessive nervousness, irritability, inactivity, and sluggishness in the erst-while active, well-poised, sweet-tempered girl, not one of the iron bands with which she is bound is relaxed. Her stand in class, her graduation is at stake; what boots it then that her pulse throbs and her nerves tingle—the prescribed work must be done. When the poor baby-woman moans in the utter agony of helplessness, she is all unheeded. When she grows up, puny and ill-fitted for her duties as wife and mother —a nervous wreck—the cause is sought for in every direction but the right one.

Not until the great physiological truth is fully apprehended, that at this period in a girl's life, mental overwork means physical wreck,—not until the fact that our present system of cram and over-work is responsible for the decline in physical force among our women, is fully realized by those at the head of our educational affairs, can we hope for a change. At present, the high pressure really begins at the age when the pressure should be lessened. For the growth of the infant-woman is required mental rest and physical exercise, and she gets mental cram and physical torpidity, and with but one result—physical declension.

For this disastrous state of affairs we would find redress. We would have a system in which, from the ages of twelve to fifteen, or later, as individual cases vary, the mental work should be less,—the physical more. After a year or two of comparative brain-rest, we could then be assured that the young woman was at an age to benefit, physically and mentally, from further study, should she desire to proceed with it. If she does not care to go further, she has secured what she requires—knowledge and skill in household affairs. The theory is easily stated: the practical application is more difficult; but we believe that in remedying the second defect, we will redress this wrong, this great wrong, which is being wrought upon our people.

The second truth now claims our attention. Society has awakened slowly to the fact that intellectual training is not the monopoly of the men. Society has seen and said—"The hand that rocks the cradle rules the world, and it is, therefore, a moral necessity that woman should receive the best intellectual training which the State can give;" and the doors of our schools and colleges have swung wide to receive her. "Not every woman marries; every woman need not marry; therefore, woman must have, with her brother, equal chances to live an independent life," it has been said; and the professions have bowed to her, and smiled upon her, and offered her the right hand as a fellow-worker.

A third truth, equally important, is now being dimly seen and whispered:—"Many women marry—the greater number of women marry; therefore, every woman shall be trained in all that pertains to wifehood and motherhood." What, but this, does the cry for schools of cookery, dress-making, etc., mean?

The fact is obtruding itself forcibly that the solution of not a few of the vexed questions of domestic, aye, and political, economy lies in the wisest education for women *by the State*. Is it a small matter to the nation that each day scores of women become wives without one idea of the true duties of a wife, of the awful responsibility of a mother, or of the practical work of a home? Would such ignorance be tolerated in any other profession? Is it of no vital importance to the nation that this unfitness of women for their great profession produces hovels instead of homes, and that each of these hovels is a breeding place for disease and crime?

Among the many reasons advanced by workers among the poor and wretched for the poverty and wretchedness so rife, is often repeated, "the thriftlessness of women." How can it be otherwise? The well-worn adage, "a wife can throw out of the window more than her husband can bring in at the door," is a positive fact.

While Government does much to neutralize the evil effect of poor homes, it has still much to do. The system of compulsory education has wrested from homes of ignorance and vice many a child, and set him on the high places. Why not provide, and compel, education for home-makers, that out of the hovels may be drawn girls who will transform the hovels into homes? If it be compulsory for woman to be able to read and write, should it not also be compulsory for her to know how to cook a meal, and to make and keep a home?

Infanticide is punishable by law, yet how many mothers, true and noble in heart, feel that they are guilty of the death, or the living death, of their children, through ignorance of the relation of a mother to her child, and of the first laws of child life? Yet the State heeds not!

We are met with the argument, "Mothers can best teach their daughters housework." An extract from an article in the *Century*, by Washington Gladden, answers this in part. What training in thrift do the children in the homes she speaks of receive from their mothers?

Especially would a little practical training in domestic economy be useful to the girls of this class. Most of them are destined to be wives and mothers, and the question whether the household shall live in pinching want or in comparative comfort often depends on the skill and thrift of the wife and mother. Here, for example, is a table with minute accounts of the expenditure for five weeks of thirty families in London; and the exhibit is a forcible illustration of the lack of thrift which accompanies poverty. One family with an income of about five dollars a week, made seventy-two different purchases of tea during the five weeks. Inasmuch as this family never took more than two meals a day at home, it is evident that they never bought more than a single drawing of tea at a time; seventy-two purchases of tea in thirty-five days is two purchases a day (Sundays included), and two extra. Of these thirty families, it is evident that quite a number went to the grocery every day of their lives—not a few of them several times a day. This hand to mouth existence is at enmity with thrift; it is scarcely possible that any family should escape from poverty until it learns wiser methods of expenditure. That many of these helpless people are pitifully ignorant of the alphabet of domestic economy is plain enough; is it not possible to give the girls in industrial schools, some practical instruction in this most important art?

She pleads for the poor. But the rich need also a pleader. In how few of our wealthy homes is the mother capable, if able, to instruct her daughter? From homes, wealthy and poor alike, go out each day into new homes girls without one truly wise idea of the work or government of a home, to say nothing of the duties of a mother.

Now that we have faced the two startling defects in our system, we come to the question of remedial measures. In the remedy of the second defect lies the remedy of the first, and the solution of the great domestic problem, the servant girl question. To remedy the first defect, we demand, for certain years in the life of our girl, less brain work—more physical work. To remedy the second, less brain work—more physical—is demanded, and it, therefore, seems the natural remedy for the first.

The missing link is between public school and high school. In every town we would establish a training school for young women, in which all the practical duties of housework should be taught professionally and done practically. This school might become partly self-supporting, if necessary, by work done for others than the pupils. We would have the course two years, with examinations, sessional and terminal, and a final test examination which should determine the diploma granted. To this school should be admitted all desirous of entering the high school further on, and those who desired to take only the practical course. We would have it a Government school, just as the public and high schools are, under Government control. We would have attendance compulsory in the same sense as that in which our present school system is compulsory.

Many objections may be raised, but they all may be answered.

Some of the advantages of these technical schools for women, other than those already pointed out, we mention. To many homes would hope and joy be born when from this school would come to the side of the toil-worn mother, a daughter intelligently enthusiastic over housework, and full of the new and best methods of work, new recipes, and new labor-saving devices. Her home would be her sphere of labor, and contentedly would she stand in her place as daughter. From homes of misery and filth would be drafted relays of girls who, under the guidance of their teachers, would become true home-makers, skilled in laundry-work, baking, cooking, housework in general, sewing and mending, and forever after benefited by the systematic training received. From these schools would go out women well fitted to rule a home, and women well fitted to serve. Instead of ignorant, thoughtless, inconsiderate mistresses, we would have an army of well-trained wives and mothers, and, side by side with them, an army of girls to whom "service" had become a science, and house work a profession.

But we cannot hope for Government to take hold of this matter quickly: that is not its way. In the meantime, let some of our philanthropic leaders, aided by our philanthropic givers, open such a school in some centre and demonstrate to the public that a school for home-makers is needed.

The men have their engineering schools, their schools of practical science, their agricultural college, and are soon to have a school for miners. Let us, as women, arise and assert our rights. We have a profession as grand and as important as any: we need training for it—and we will have it.

KINGSTON.

EDUCATION FOR DOMESTICITY, 1898

'The Labour Question and Women's Work and its Relation to Home Life', in *Women Workers of Canada*, compiled by the National Council of Women of Canada (Ottawa, 1898), pp. 254-62.

(a) Does the increase of factory, work-shop and commercial occupation amongst women tend to disintegrate domestic life?

(b) Does the education and training directly bearing on the higher development of home life, such as domestic science and all its departments, instruction in matters of health and sanitation, the care of young children and of the sick, receive the consideration its importance demands from educational authorities and organized bodies of women?

(c) Apart from the value of education in domestic and technical science in our public schools for all children, should not its importance, as bearing on the problem of domestic service, both from the Mistress' and servants' point of view, be considered?

(d) Does the higher or university education of women injure or benefit home life? . . .

When we hear bitter denunciations of political, municipal and other leaders, do we ever think that these men were once children; that their mind and character was in the hand of some woman to mould? If that early influence was one of social frivolity, sham religion, and domestic infelicity, can we expect anything very strong and upright from such a source? Upon the mother "who is a divinity" to her growing boy, and upon her early influence, must rest the foundation of her boy's character. Up to a certain age the mother has infinitely more influence over a boy than the father, and upon the character of that influence depends their future relationship. Is such mental pabulum as discussions on dress, amusements, gossip, servants, the latest novels and opera, likely to send a boy or man out into the world with a high ideal of woman's moral and mental power, or lead him to consider her as a factor in national life? If we are to have good politicians, and true, honest men, we must have a higher type of womanhood. A prominent social reformer and one who had given much thoughtful and earnest study to social problems, says, "Nothing will ever interest men unless it interests women; there are those who say that women are less intelligent than men, but who will say they are less influential." When we consider that our educational system has provided special opportunities for developing the various political, social and economic sciences, as related to man's work, leaving that phase of education which relates to woman's reponsibilities a matter of haphazard, can we wonder that woman's influence has not reached its highest point? Woman has had, from creation, distinctly defined duties, and until the power of education and influence is brought to bear upon these duties, and she has demonstrated her ability to do her own work well, she has no right to infringe on man's prerogative. In order that the questions to be discussed to-day should be presented impartially and from various points of view, I have secured the opinions of representative authorities—From the Labour Councils; from the standpoint of political and social science; and from that of noted philanthropists. The views expressed have shown a decided unanimity of thought. All deplore the tendency of girls to engage in commercial and kindred occupations, and consider that it *has* a deteriorating influence upon the home life.

The reasons given are:—That girls in factories, shops and offices have usually little time to devote to domestic occupation, the hours are so long and the work so fatiguing that any spare time must be devoted to rest and recreation. The fact of their thoughts and energies being directed to an entirely different line of work for a length of time—in some cases a number of years—must, as a natural result, unfit them for an intelligent performance of domestic duties. Too much of the "seamy" side of life is experienced and too little of the domestic to develop the higher type of womanhood. The employment of girl labour in offices, shops, and factories, deprives a girl of the refining and protecting influence of home life at a time when the character is being formed; it closes the door of occuption to many boys and not a few men, (who should be the bread-winners) driving the cream of our youth from home or leaving them "loafing" during the most critical period of their moral growth—hence the increase in juvenile crime. It tends to rob both boys and men of that protective, chivalrous element which is one of the most desirable characteristics of the sex. The subversion of the natural law, which makes man the bread-winner and woman the home-maker, cannot fail to have an injurious effect on social conditions, both morally and physically. No class of society deplores this condition of affairs more than the intelligent workingman. The trend of education, which has diverted the attention of girls from home to commercial life; the pre-eminence given to the teaching profession; the absence of any corresponding educational influence upon home duties; the indifference of women to their responsibilities has been conceded by all to have a decidedly disintegrating effect upon domestic life.

(b and c) Authorities say that "type-writing, book-keeping and short-hand are mechanical pursuits and have little tendency to develop higher intelligence or the elements of happiness." These subjects are receiving very great consideration at the hands of our educational authorities. Boys and girls are being educated on the same lines without any consideration of the special aptitude or future life of the pupil, hence girls are crowding boys and men out of the common pursuits, leaving the distinctly womanly occupations to the illiterate and untrained.

If a young woman desires—ever so earnestly—to acquire skill in womanly arts, she must either serve a long apprenticeship, which may not be under the best supervision, or go to other countries at great expenses to receive a training which should, at least, form an auxiliary to our educational system at home.

After a certain primary training there should be dividing lines in the education of boys and girls. The regular school studies and mental development should be directed to those subjects bearing upon their future occupation. Mathematics and the sciences should be applied to matters relating to home duties. It would be quite equal in mental development, and infinitely more useful, for a girl to learn the chemistry of food and its relation to the body, the science of ventilation, cleanliness, cookery and needle work, than to wear out brain tissue in puzzling out a lot of abstract questions, which will neither awaken the intelligence nor interest the pupil. Our organized bodies of women have devoted time, money and brains to the provision of work for the poor, the housing of paupers, the prevention of intemperance, missionary work, the protection of women and children, shorter hours of labour; all good and necessary, but how much attention are these bodies of women giving to the actual prevention of the evils, the result of which they are working so hard to provide. It is infinitely more difficult to secure intelligent teachers in the Sunday School, where such a powerful influence may be exercised, than it is to find members for the board of a charitable institution. We find women deeply exercised over the woes of a factory girl's long hours of labour, and yet expect their own domestics to work any number of hours, and will be among the first to join in a "scramble" around the bargain counter. We are excellent advisers in "committee," but how many of us can say we have done what we could towards promoting those interests and occupations which would tend to a higher development of home life. One of the great avenues of labour for which there is an unfailing demand is that of domestic help in the home. Who but the women are to blame if the bright intelligent girls seek occupation elsewhere, rather than accept employment which is but a relic of old time slavery?

We have been ready to re-adjust every social condition under the sun but the one bearing directly upon our own social province. Women, through perverted education, have had their mental powers developed in such a one-sided manner that they have never been able to apply them practically. Education has been on the lines of literature, music and art, to the exclusion of domestic economy. The highest pedagogical and psychological training has been provided for public school teachers, and the great underlying principle of all—without which teachers are sadly handicapped—the early development of a child's character has been left to traditional custom and haphazard instruction. Is it any wonder that we have not derived any great benefit from our "newly fledged" liberties? We must first accept the injunction, "know thyself," before we can hope to exercise the influence upon social conditions which I believe women are capable of exercising.

In order to prove our sincerity and relieve the over-crowded condition of labour in shops, factories, etc., let us at least make an attempt to re-adjust the conditions of domestic help.

Let this distinctly womanly occupation be made so attractive and remunerative that the brighter and more intelligent young women will be glad to enter the ranks. Surely it should not be any more degrading to care for the health and happiness of the family, which depends to a great extent upon the intelligence exercised in the kitchen, than to serve in the capacity of nurse in a sick room, or as type-writers, clerks, or factory operatives. We know the remedy, at least we have been told it often enough, but "there is no one so blind as the one who will not see;" it lies in a more systematic order of work, and in regular hours.

Surely the women of Canada are capable of arranging matters which are so closely related to the comfort of the home, and the condition of the wage-earning population. We owe it to humanity to adapt ourselves to existing conditions. There have been marvellous changes in business methods during the last decade; yet house-keepers have been "hugging" the delusion that they could expect menial service as a result of our advanced educational system.

Domestic work must be placed upon an intellectual basis, for "upon the health and morals of its citizens depends the prosperity of a nation, and the health and morals of the people depend mainly upon the food they

eat and the homes they live in." As stated before we must begin at the
source. After domestic work has been given the consideration its importance demands it will find its level. Method, and an intelligent arrangement of home duties, will not only simplify much that is at present
complicated, but will bring about a more systematic understanding
between employer and employee. It will be necessary for the first reforms
to run on the lines of knowledge, promptness, order and economy of time
and money. These methods which govern the office, shop, or factory,
should be brought to bear upon domestic duties. Until educational and
scientific principles are applied we shall never have social economy properly regulated; until women have learned the science of living and
properly regulating the household expenditure in proportion to the
income, wage-earners at least will be labouring under a disadvantage.

It is only a matter of education; we have been doing our best according
to our light—but it does not follow that we should consent to remain in
semi-darkness.

We have become embedded in traditional customs that generations
must pass before great results may be expected. Some influence must lead
the way, and can there be a more noble mission for the National Council
of Women than to lay the foundation of a higher ideal of homelife? The
first duty seems to be clearly defined. What we need in Canada to-day is
skilled labour, and in order to secure greater opportunities for girls to
acquire skill in the various womanly pursuits, an effort must be made to
secure for them special technical education. By developing new and remunerative industries for women, boys and men will find more steady
employment, and the present evil of girls doing their work at reduced
wages will at least be minimized. Until we have this training provided, I
can see little relief for the girls who must become wage-earners. It is not
within the scope of this paper to present an outline of the various industries which might be developed, or indeed to do more than suggest a few
points for discussion, but I trust attention may be given to this important
part of the question. "An ounce of prevention is worth a pound of cure."
Why should the pauper element be allowed to increase in a young country like Canada, when after generations of experience the older countries
have discovered their mistakes, and are now, with their millions of population, devoting enormous sums of money to the development of technical
education—which is the most direct prevention of pauperism. With their
skilled labor we must compete if we are to hold our own in manufactured
products. To no class of the community does technical education mean
more than to wage-earning girls and women.

(d) In considering the influence of university education upon the "home
life," we must bear in mind that it is a new "fledgling" and may require
to have its wings clipped. That women should receive every educational
privilege accorded to men is generally conceded, but does it follow that it

should be the *same kind* of education. Is it necessary that the higher education of women should be the same as the higher education of man or that required to fit a man for future usefulness? Surely mental development could be secured on lines bearing more directly upon matters relating to social and domestic laws, with which women must deal. That a trained mind is desirable in the proper regulation of domestic matters we must admit, but whether the solution of a problem in "Harmonical Progression" or the translation of "Bellum Gallicum" will prove more conducive to the comfort and happiness of the home than the scientific knowledge of sanitation, food values, care of the sick, artistic furnishing, the management of children, etc., remain to be proved. University graduates are "new," and the other side has not yet been developed. The danger of our present system of "higher education" lies in its being allowed to become all absorbing. The close attention to study which is necessary for many years has a tendency to develop selfishness. The absorption in study is apt to make the student indifferent to the claims of others; and when the character, to a great extent, is being formed, is not this worthy of consideration. No amount of intellectuality can compensate for the absence of that loving and unselfish consideration of others, which is woman's greatest charm. Many college girls realize this danger, and upon these it may not have any serious effect, but when we admit that the public school training has diverted girls from "home" interests, we may safely conclude that a prolonged course under existing conditions will increase that tendency. We owe a debt of gratitude to Vassar College, Leland, Stanford, Chicago, Columbia and other universities in the United States for establishing domestic science departments and recognizing that branch of study as necessary for the complete rounding out of a woman's education. With the addition of technical training, in woman's work, I should unhesitatingly say that a college education would conduce to the welfare of home life. Under present conditions it is doubtful, as there is so much attention given to developing executive ability and the "creative" faculty, the college girl must find a difficulty in adapting the theories which to a great extent have comprised her education to the actual duties of home life.

We find the "key note" of the whole matter in the words of the late Henry George: "To affect the great social improvement it is sympathy, rather than self interest, the sense of duty rather than the desire for self advancement, that must be appealed to. Social reform is not to be secured by noise, complaints, denunciation, by the formation of parties or the making of revolutions, but by the awakening of thought and the progress of ideas. Until there be correct thought there cannot be right action; and when there is correct thought right action will follow. Let no one imagine that they can have influence without work and thought, whoever they may be, and wherever he and she may be placed, the individual who thinks becomes a power. Whoever becomes imbued with a noble idea kindles a flame from which other torches are lit and influences those with whom they come in contact. How far that influence, thus perpetuated, may extend it is not given to them to see here, but it may be that the Lord of the vineyard will know."

As regard the *b* and *c*, I put these together, they really mean the same thing. One authority said in his letter, "Type-writing, book-keeping and shorthand are mechanical pursuits and have little tendency to develop higher intelligence or the elements of happiness."

When I heard Mrs. Hopkins last night speaking of "Applied Design" I thought of all it meant for a girl to go to New York and study Applied Design, and the expense of living there, which should be avoided by having opportunities at home. I hope this subject will receive the fullest discussion because it is a matter which really affects and should therefore receive the attention of every woman of our country. I will close, therefore, by moving that the earnest study and discussion of this subject be recommended to all our Local Councils. (Applause.) . . .

THE FIRST WOMEN MEDICAL STUDENTS, QUEEN'S UNIVERSITY, 1916

'Historical Sketch of Medical Education of Women in Kingston'. Read [by Elizabeth Shortt] before the Osler Club, Queen's University, 14 Sept. 1916.

Foreword. The following sketch is compiled from letters and diary written at the time of the occurrences recorded and from newspaper articles and calendars of the same period. Pardon is asked for any personal note that occurs since to a limited extent it is autobiographical.

In the Toronto newspapers of 28th May, 1879, a paragraph stated that "three ladies presented themselves before the Council of Physicians and Surgeons for matriculation examination. Two of them, Misses Augusta Stowe and Elizabeth Smith, were successful."

This was a pioneer occasion in the way of regular medical matriculation for women who were to enter on a full course of medical lectures in Canada. Previously to this, two ladies, Dr. Emily Stowe and Dr. Jennie K. Trout, practised medicine in Toronto. Both were graduates of American Colleges and were allowed to practise in Canada by virtue of having attended one session in a Canadian School of Medicine. They were given permission to attend these lectures in Toronto on condition that whatever happened they would make no fuss. From the lips of one of these ladies I heard the most staggering accounts of their experiences. Little incidents, such as having to observe their seats from a conventional loophole before entering the classroom, lest, as occurred on more than one occasion, they had to be cleared and cleaned before being occupied. Other playful activities of some members of the school were in the way of obnoxious sketches on the wall. There were so many artists, or at least sketches, that the walls of a classroom had to be whitewashed four times during that session. But more trying and more frequent were the needless objectionable stories told by 'enemy' lecturers to the class to instigate its worst element to make noisy and vulgar demonstration. It was so unbearable on one occasion that one of the ladies went to the lecturer afterwards and asked him to desist from that sort of persecution or she would go and tell his wife exactly what he had said. His lectures were more bearable after that. This same lady doctor (although wishing me to have a Canadian degree) advised me to go to Ann Arbor until such time as there should be a course open to women in Canada.

On Easter Tuesday of 1879 when the three aforementioned young ladies went up for Medical Matriculation at Toronto the examiners were the heads of Toronto and Kingston High Schools, viz., Mr. MacMurchy and Mr. A. P. Knight. They were both presiding and oral examiners and were most kind and considerate. Mr. Knight, later Dr. Knight, inquired where I meant to study, and on my explaining my reason for going to Ann Arbor, he intimated that since Queen's had that year (session '78-'79) announced that "the advantages of the University Course would henceforth be thrown open to women" (see Doomsday Book) that the Medical Faculty might be willing to have classes for women students.

The Dean of the College, Dr. Michael Lavell, was written to and he thought some arrangements might be made. This soon became an offer that if a class could be gathered the Faculty of the Royal Medical College would arrange for a summer session for women students. I then advertised in the Toronto paper and asked those women who wished to take up the study of Medicine to communicate with me. When eleven letters from would-be students had accumulated they were sent on to Dr. Lavell. . . .

From the time of our matriculation in April there began to be various sorts of evidence that higher education of women and medical education of women appealed to many. Newspapers and magazines asked for information and wrote up what had been, and what ought to be, done along this line. My mother and various others added their contributions and kept the information spreading. Among others there was a series of articles by "Agnodice" in the Educational Monthly which attracted considerable attention. Although there were a good many young women wanting to attend this first session in Medicine, many unfortunately fell out of the race for want of funds. Parents were willing to make sacrifices to send a son to college, but had not yet become convinced of any equal claim of a daughter. Also, young men were much more in the way of earning money and, having had the open door to any and all professions, went in, as years went by, whenever they were ready.

Naturally when the first chance of a separate class for women occurred comparatively suddenly, the women were not financially ready. As it came near the spring of 1880 letter after letter of despair came to announce the fact that they could not manage the financial end of it. So when the second Monday of April, 1880, came round there were only four who actually presented themselves for the course. . . .

"The days were crammed with work as we were zealous students and had literally no counter attractions. Up at six, down to the Royal at eight, practical work 1½ hours, and to Anatomy at ten. Then Physiology, Histology and Therapeutics, dinner, and back at two for Materia Medica. Then up to Queen's University for Chemistry 3.30 to 4.30, and again for a time in the early evening to the Royal for practical work and back to study till late bedtime."

An extract which might be called 'before taking' reads: "I am thinking a great deal of the coming battle . . . with everything. You may imagine that at times I feel a secret dread of what may happen and whether my nerves are equal to what it may all mean. However, I solace myself with the idea that what some not wonderful men have done perhaps I may achieve." 'After taking' the diary reads: "The reality as we find it is for the most part intensely interesting. To try to understand the huge wonder of our own bodies, our nervous systems, our functions, is to lose ourselves in wonder. Nothing has ever thrilled me into such excitement of wonder as the physiology of hearing and sight. I walk the floor with excitement and wonder." The impression was lasting and I still keep the 'incus malleus et stapes' as of the wonders of the world.

"We hear indirectly that we are much discussed as 'rara aves' and we feel directly that we are stared at. Have even noticed bareheaded men by twos and threes in shop doors staring at us as we pass up and down on our way to and from College. As Miss Dickson is a Kingstonian and lives at home, we three who are strangers and board together bear the brunt of it. It is seldom pleasant to be a pioneer. It does not worry us overmuch for we are absorbed in our work and our daily round." Still we must have felt it in some degree for about this time we christened ourselves with some sense of humor and prophecy, 'Shadrack, Mesheck and Abednego' and retained these names among ourselves to the end of the chapter.

We worked so hard that the Professors sent us off for some midsummer holidays and we returned August 1st and remained till the end of the session, just before the College opened for the winter. Since there were only four of us, with an occasional fifth, there was some talk at the end of this session of making some arrangements for a winter course. The Registrar was opposed, as he said it would crowd us too much to go straight on for the year and that it would be too difficult for the doctors to duplicate lectures in winter, but he assured us that they would keep faith with us and see us through. If a large class appeared in the spring we would probably go on as we were.

It is odd, in the light of later evolution of higher education for women in Canada, to recall some of the objections made at this time. One kind and considerate reason against a winter session was that we could never breast the snow banks going up to Queen's! (This was the first year of Queen's in the new building and of the Royal in its present quarters). And in the discussion in November, 1880, in the Senate of Toronto University one member in opposing the entrance of women into the sacred precincts of the Arts College there said, "it would be as reasonable for men to ask admission to attend a Ladies' College," etc., and evidently the majority were of like mind for they did firmly refuse the doors to women at that time.

After this summer session several ladies attended chemistry at Queen's, among them Mrs. Macgillivray, who with Miss Beatty, Miss Dickson and Miss Smith were the students of the summer session.

When April of '81 came round we returned to begin the second year's work. However, as only two new students appeared, it was mutually agreed by Faculty and students that a winter session could be arranged. We were not dissatisfied at this except that we would have saved a year had this been arranged the previous Fall. When we arrived, at the beginning of the session '82-'83, to take up the work under the new conditions, we found the Faculty had arranged a great many things to our liking: separate dissecting room, separate cloak and waiting room, and a classroom adjacent to a general classroom where we might take jurisprudence, obstetrics, anatomy, and part of physiology separately. Practical and theoretical chemistry and botany we had at Queen's University in the ordinary classes and these classes were always to our satisfaction and profit. There were six of us present in the flesh to begin this second session, backed by the goodwill of many whom we called spiritual sisters—who could only be there in thought and desire. On the opening day some of the Professors made wonderful speeches and the partly co-educational, partly separate, course was auspiciously begun. An October letter states that "the students at College are remarkably quiet and well-conducted." Later on some small outbursts of youthful spirits and energy occurred. We concluded from our daily experience that the classes were composed of a number of first class young men who were generally good students, of others who 'in their stars and in themselves were underlings,' and some who were just human animals. These last did not seem much in evidence till a certain Falstaff from some American school came among them and became their inspiration.

The better element seemed much in preponderance and, as straws show which way the wind blows, an incident is given as an indication. "One day some hilarious youth threw a stick across the class-room and it alighted, whether by design or accident, on the lap of one of the ladies. At once cries of 'Shame, Shame! Coward!' arose from the senior and better students."

Our demonstrators were always kind and capable, and, being good students themselves, they no doubt appreciated earnest work in others. Even the janitor, Tom, sometimes 'Tom Coffee,' more often 'Coffee,' seldom 'Mr. Coffee,' was our kind confederate. As we desired to be always in class and seated before the men students came in, the janitor would come to our waiting room and say, "Yez can be goin' in now, leddies," and he gave us a good start before the peals of his heavy bell rang out to call the 'bhoys' to class.

Meeting some of the students out of college bounds we were always pretty well in touch with their interests. We knew of their 'Courts' at times and their peculiar pledge of 'the truth and nothing but the truth' Holy Al Oliver. "We heard a great deal about some fiascos, such as the burning of the College sheds, etc., etc. There was an assembly room on the ground floor at the College called 'the den' and here the Medicals held what they called 're-unions.' Never in my waking or sleeping hours have I heard anything similar to the appalling sounds that disturbed the quiet of the early morning hours of that part of the city when they were dispersing." Another letter states, "You have no idea of the horrors possible in the Jurisprudence class, not Jurisprudence but the by-stories of the lecturer and the noisy applause of some of the class. It all depends on the lecturer. In obstetrics, which you would think had great possibilities of embarrassment, the students are quiet and attentive; the Professor (also Dean of the College) is a Christian gentleman, most kind, efficient and reliable. We take both of these classes in separate rooms."

We went regularly and quietly about our work and were after all well considered by the best of the College. We received invitations to the Annual Medical Dinner, which we of course declined in the same good feeling in which they were sent. At this era of the Royal there was a holiday after the dinner *which we enjoyed more than they did*. As we were there for a purpose, under effort of will and strain of feeling, we were naturally not fooling away our time and were generally able to answer questions when they were asked. This was brought to our attention one day, as perhaps not desirable, by a flattering but inelegant writing on the blackboard which said, "Bully for the women, they take the cake in answering." The lecturer in Anatomy further flattered us by asking one of us to be prosector for the class, which honor was too prominent for acceptance.

After the close of the session of '81-'82, not a word of complaint against the presence of ladies, or against any conditions in the College, was received....

At the beginning of the session '82-'83 there was a larger class of freshmen than usual, there being some twenty-five or thirty and three new lady students. We began under much the same conditions as when we left off, there were the usual varieties in a new class at College, perhaps more accentuated in a Medical College....

Before October had waned we felt there was a change in attitude in some of the classes. Two things contributed to produce this. (1) A class of seniors such as Garrett, Denike, Anglin, Jarvis and others had graduated and gone out and a not desirable element in one of the years had come nearer the lead in student ranks. (2) More menacing was the fact that the lecturer in Physiology, who had been so debonair and capable the previous year, had openly voiced his objections to women studying medicine. We found that this was due to the fact that he had come into opposition with the senior members of the Faculty because they would not agree with and approve of some plans of his ...

"He has not so far given us any personal evidence of his disaffection and we hope he will not for we love peace."

One of the events in November of this year was the return of Principal Grant from his trip around the world. At a Convocation to welcome him and install a new Professor, the galleries were crowded as well as the hall. In the midst of a sentence when the Principal began to speak, rose loud and clear a prolonged 'squack' of a goosequill. It was so sorrowful and sonorous that everyone laughed, even the speaker, but with that quick wit of his the Principal turned to the source of the sound and said, "I hope that gentleman was not speaking in his own vernacular." This settled his gooseship for a time, anyway.

In the classes with the Queen's Professors, in the senior classes with Drs. Lavell, Fowler and Sullivan, and others with Drs. Oliver and Dupuis, we were treated with much kindness and sympathy, but there were two classes where we were at times chilled and hurt by evidences of worse than levity. There was, however, much goodwill from the better class of students, such as was evidenced in Anatomy one day after one of the ladies had answered all the questions asked her. The lecturer turned to the students and said, "I will see if some of the men can answer," ending with some remark that he was proud of Miss.... "A murmur from the rear said, "So are we, so are we all." However the disaffection grew by encouragement, and when a first and second time the lecturer in Physiology by unnecessary stories, and a smiling appeal to the back benches, brought forth the appreciation invited, it became very hard to bear. Nov. 22nd: "No one knows or can know what a furnace we are passing through these days at College. We suffer torment, we shrink inwardly, we are hurt cruelly. Not by anything in the whole range of Medicine, the awe-inspiring wonders of the human being are of deepest interest—it is not that, it is the environment. It is that encouraged current through the class of whispers, innuendo, of derisive treading, the turning of what was never meant as unseemly into horrible meaning and the thousand and one ways that can be devised by evil minds to bring responsive smiles from their own kind. Day by day it seems harder to bear for we have borne so much.

Do we desire to be here? Do we like to live this way? God forbid! We are earnestly seeking to acquire the knowledge necessary to equip us to practice medicine, and separate classes in this men's College is the best available to that end. We wish with all our hearts, with all the power of wishing, for a separate College, but there is none. If 'because right is right, to follow right is wisdom, in the scorn of consequences,' then surely we deserve praise, not blame."

One day after one of these bad hours we consulted, and agreed that we could not, and would not, sit in the class and hear these objectionable stories. On December 9th the impending crisis came. The lecturer was on 'human speech and voice', and he took occasion to enlarge the subject by unnecessary side-issues and with a direct appeal by smile and inflection to call forth applause from the back benches. Not content with this he repeated, and added some possible social aspects of his statements which made such direct appeal to the worst elements of the class that the applause was uproarious. When he could be again heard he began, "This reminds me of an anecdote . . . " but with one accord we were on our feet and walked quietly from the class-room. We went to the Registrar and told him exactly what had occurred. He was indignant and said, "If mild measures did not mend the matter, severe measures would be resorted to." This was the natural attitude of the Registrar who had a chivalrous and kindly respect for women, but circumstances were more powerful than personal inclination; mild measures did not settle it and a meeting of the Faculty was called.

Our written statement of facts was sent in and it is recorded, "glad were we that every Professor was staunch to our position, except the rebellious lecturer concerned, and they assure us that we shall have our rights and all our lectures in separate class-rooms." Then some ill-advised person wrote a gross misstatement of facts to the papers and the trouble became public. We were informed by a leading Kingstonian that this lecturer had told him he meant to do the very thing he did, and could not be dissuaded from his purpose.

The ground taken by the lecturer as reason for his objecting to women in the College, was that he was under the necessity of garbling his lectures when giving them to mixed classes, though all the other Professors stated to the contrary. The students took this cue and made it the ground of their objection, stating they were therefore not getting a full 'quid pro quo' for their fees. That this argument was not necessarily true was evidenced by such outstanding men as Professor Simpson of Edinburgh, who, it was said, in lecturing on Obstetrics, never uttered anything in his teaching that a gentleman could not say or a lady listen to. As evidenced by the famous Dr. McLean of Ann Arbor who wrote his testimony to the papers at that time: "Permit me to draw attention to the fact that at the Medical College of Michigan, Ann Arbor, the clinical lectures are attended by some sixty ladies along with two or three hundred gentlemen, and that, as the Faculty has repeatedly testified, there has never been the slightest difficulty or unpleasantness, or any injurious consequences to the students or the institution." Also Dec. 13th, Dean Lavell added his testimony to his view of it. In part he said: "I have been lecturing on midwifery and diseases of women for twenty-two years, the past two years to the mixed classes. That is, the ladies occupy a room adjoining the large lecture room, in a position to hear the lecturer and see all appliances and diagrams used. Several of the male members of the present class have attended my lectures previous to the attendance of the ladies and they frankly state that the lectures are as full and complete in detail, omitting nothing, as when lecturing to them alone. The ladies as frankly state that nothing has been said or done by me in the lecture rooms to which they could take exception. I can state further that the male students while in my class-room have not by act or word given the least cause for complaint to the ladies, themselves so stating. Also, at the close of last session the class, male and female, congratulated all parties on the pleasant result of the experiment."

The men students sent a letter to the Faculty stating that they were not getting full lectures for causes stated, and asking them to close the doors of the College to the ladies. The tenor of this letter can be judged by the reply from the Registrar: "I have been instructed by the Medical Faculty to return to you the enclosed document as not being respectful. The Faculty also desire it to be distinctly understood that the government of the College belongs exclusively to the Professors, not to the students." The students sent another letter and a reply was sent asking for a clearer statement of what it meant. Then came the 'ultimatum' from the students to the Faculty, stating they ought to have a share in the management of the College to which they paid their fees, and if the ladies were to continue at College they would go in a body to Trinity.

The Faculty were much harassed. They had spent much labor for years on building up the College and their only salaries were derived from the fees paid by the students. Trinity, too, consented to take in the strikers. When things were at this deadlock a body of prominent citizens, Mayor Gaskin, Ex-Mayors McIntyre, Gildersleeves, and Pense offered their services as mediators, and after much talk and discussion succeeded in bringing about a compromise. The Faculty promised that they would give separate classes to the ladies in attendance and keep faith with them to their graduation, but they promised not to admit any new women students in future.

Some phases of the disturbance were interesting and instructive. The most objectionable type of medical men who apparently hated the idea of women practising medicine were eager for them to be nurses. They all knew that doctors in practice have few obnoxious things to do, and nurses have many, also that the income of practitioners exceeds that of nurses, and that nurses' fees do not in any sense affect theirs. Also, as some of the men students observed, it was generally and absurdly the man without fine feelings who expressed such concern at the imminent danger to a woman's fine feelings if she studied medicine. Another phase was the selfishness or want of view of those opposing the attendance of women in the Medical College for the purpose of acquiring the right to practice. For the College of Physicians and Surgeons of Ontario only admitted the right to registration (which empowered those registered to practice) to those who passed the examination of Medical Colleges of Ontario and Quebec. But to admit to examinations the law required attendance in some Ontario or Quebec Medical College, and how were women to do these things if no college would permit attendance?

Another striking phase was the unexpected endorsation and support of the ladies' cause, and of higher education of women generally, by the public and the press. The leading papers of Toronto and Montreal and others, wrote vivid editorials and published many letters. Possibly it was public opinion so freely expressed that encouraged the Ontario Legislature to lend kindly ears to the petition to open the doors of Toronto University to women, for it was at this time that their fiat went forth that pried open the doors of the Provincial University to women students.

Fortunately, the Christmas holidays gave time for repentance and better thoughts and when classes reassembled we began much as usual. Speaking generally, the classes went on satisfactorily in the separate room. It was no doubt hard for the objecting Professor to have to give us lectures without his supporting class of men. The first occasion was an event. He strangled, he raced, fell headlong over phrases, splashed, struggled, and away again, and was just sixteen minutes delivering this burst of science. We made futile attempts to put down notes, but our main energies were occupied in trying to maintain a dignified decorum under such ludicrous circumstances.

He endured his trial as little as possible for his lectures seldom exceeded twenty minutes and occurred sometimes only twice a week. His lectures of previous years and our textbooks were our sources of information.

There was still much opposition, some bitterness, and much talking. There were meetings in the 'den' and not a few resolutions made, discussed and passed at various times. Results of second thoughts by some of the students,—"If the Professors have left nothing out of their lectures then we have been working without grounds and have been made fools of before the public," and again, "What's the difference, if they won't allow women here they will only go somewhere else and we might as well have them here," and such like reached our ears. On only one further occasion that session, because of protest at our attending clinics, did they need to be pacified by the Faculty.

The seven or eight medicals who were really responsible for most of the trouble, apart from the would-be popular lecturer, had queer methods of reasoning. "They say that women attending here keep men away, but oddly enough there is the largest class of Freshmen this year in the history of the College." They say in their wisdom that women will lower the standard, "and yet the public and not a few of the Professors think that the fear of the ladies excelling them in the spring is one motive actuating some of the agitators. There was a funny incident indicative of this. At the most acute stage of the trouble, the list of students having passed the Botany exams appeared on the bulletin board with Miss R. next to the top. A youth looking for his own name and seeing this, flung himself away from the board, stamped and raged, went up and looked again, and went off muttering malevolent things at them for 'putting *her* there.'"

A paradox of reasoning was when the youngest of the lady students, after three months of this trouble, altercation and depression, fell ill for a short time, a yell of 'I told you so, women can't stand a college course,' reached the public ear! When one of the women students went home by way of Toronto, Stratford and St. Marys she was quite lionized and she heard in Toronto on her return that there was some talk of a possible future College for women students. We heard more of this from time to time, but on February 13th in a letter from Dr. Trout we were told it had fallen through. However, there was talk both in Toronto and Kingston of the desirability and possibility of a Women's Medical College. The *Canadian Practitioner*, Toronto, in April said, "The organization of a Medical School for women in Toronto is under consideration. Many of both sexes who have strong convictions on the question will give substantial assistance to form an endowment fund on a permanent basis and it is thought a commencement will be made in October. The Toronto *World* says "a number of the best doctors have expressed their willingness to lecture to the girl medicals." Dr. Jennie K. Trout offered, it was said, $10,000 toward such a College but with the stipulation that the 'chairs' should be open to women when, and if, fully qualified and competent, and that the Governing Board of Directors should include women.

"A letter from Dr. Trout dated May 12, 1883, informs me that Dr. Barrett called his prospective Faculty together and they concluded that they could not work under a Board composed partly of women nor were they willing to admit ladies to fill any of the chairs. (They had previously considered the demonstratorship). So those holding out against Dr.

Trout's conditions in Toronto concluded to go on alone. In the meantime Mr. A. P. Knight was trying to get together the interested friends in Kingston, in promoting a separate Medical College there for the women. This resulted in a great meeting on the evening of June 8th in the City Council Chamber. Mr. Knight opened the meeting by a good statement of the need of such an institution and moved "That in the opinion of this meeting facilities should be given to females for obtaining a thorough medical education similar to those provided for men, that Canadian women should not be obliged to go to Britain or the United States to obtain such education...."

There were no restrictive regulations debarring women from filling lectureships, if desirable and qualified; nor against a Directorate of both ladies and gentlemen. On June 11th the Toronto papers stated that Dr. Barrett and his coadjutors would withdraw their objections and accept Dr. Trout's conditions; and on June 13th there was an interesting meeting held in Toronto to further the establishment of a Medical School for women in Toronto. At this meeting Mr. Trout of the *Monetary Times* stated that he thought that "the calling of a meeting at this late date was an act of discourtesy toward the Kingston people. They had waited patiently until there seemed no prospect of the school in Toronto succeeding. Then they worked vigorously and established their College on a liberal basis," etc. Dr. Barrett then explained the liberal basis on which they were now willing to work, and Dr. Carlyle moved that this meeting recommend that steps be taken to give the project substantial aid. This was carried and a committee appointed to raise funds.

Although there were personal inclinations and disinclinations, little wheels within wheels, that complicated matters, still the fact that Dr. Trout's liberal view of women on the Directorate, and as possible occupants of professorial chairs, was *not* acceptable to the Toronto promoters of a Women's Medical College, *was the rock* that divided the forces which led to there being two such Colleges available in October, 1883....

4.   WORK

The doctrine of 'true womanhood' hardly acknowledged that women participated in the Canadian labour force. Women's place was in the home. If women worked they would lose their femininity; work would only coarsen them and they would lose their influence for moral good. Nevertheless even some advocates of women's sphere acknowledged that some women worked, but only as a result of a defective social system. If society functioned properly there would be no need for women workers since husbands and fathers would provide for them.

The prejudice against women working essentially pertained only to married women; it was permissible for single women to work, but only until marriage. Needless to say such convictions meant that employers looked upon women as temporary labour and treated them accordingly. Some Canadians thought women did not work; yet by 1901 just over 14 per cent did. This was, however, a far cry from the situation in Britain, where 28.9 per cent were in the labour force as early as 1851. But it is necessary to bear in mind that employment figures do not include the women who worked at home, either doing domestic chores or through the putting-out system. Neither do the statistics include the labour of farm women. What did the statistics represent then? Who were these women and what did they do?

For the most part Canadian women who worked were single. In fact as late as 1941 less than 4 per cent of married women were employed. Seemingly, then, women worked before marriage, the greatest proportion being in their late teens and early twenties. In a survey taken in 1912, the National Council of Women estimated that 35 per cent of women between the ages of 15 and 24 were employed. Thus the pattern of life for Canadian women was a relatively short period of work before marriage, at which time a woman would leave her job. Unlike today, when women bear fewer children and have a longer life expectancy, women did not re-enter the labour force in middle age when family responsibilities had lessened.

It is not surprising that more women did not work in Canada: most jobs open to them were menial. In 1901, for example, the largest percentage of women were employed either as domestic servants or as dressmakers or seamstresses. Life for a domestic servant was not enviable—hours were very long and, since most 'lived in', privacy was at a premium. Moreover social snobbery was rampant. It is no wonder that with the advances in technology and the rapid expansion of the factory system more and more girls flocked to jobs other than domestic service. By 1921 78,342 women were employed as clerical workers; the invention of the typewriter opened up a whole new field of work that women quickly made their own.

Although more and more women were entering the work force, the idea of a woman having a career was very slow to win widespread acceptance. For a woman deliberately to choose to work and work in a profession that would bring her prestige and financial independence appeared to be an attack on the sanctity of the home. It was not easy to choose a profession. Sometimes it was impossible. Not until 1879 were medical schools open to women. Not until the 1890s was a career in law open to them. As late as 1919 a woman could not be a chartered accountant. The one profession that women were permitted to enter was teaching, so much so that by the late nineteenth century women almost totally dominated primary school teaching. Women were hired because they could be paid less than men. Men were thus released to teach the higher grades. With such discrimination it is little wonder that few women were attracted by 'a career'.

WOMEN INVADE THE PROFESSIONS, 1892

'The Law and the Lady', *Grip*, September 1892, vol. XXXIX, 202.

> I think all lawyers must agree
> On keeping our profession free
> From females whose admission would
> Result in anything but good.
>
> Because it yet has to be shown
> That men are fit to hold their own.
> In such a contest, I've no doubt,
> We'd some of us be crowded out.
>
> In other spheres of business life
> Much discontent 'mong men is rife,
> For women quick, alert and deft
> Supplant their rivals right and left.

The salesmen, book-keepers and clerks
Can tell how competition works.
They can't against the women stand,
Or former salaries command.

As doctors, artists, and no less,
In writing for the public press,
The "weaker vessel" stands the brunt,
And looms up bravely to the front.

Soon the invading female ranks
Will fill the warehouses and banks;
The pulpit next, no doubt will fall
And men be driven to the wall.

Oh, say, my brethren! shall not then
One refuge be reserved for men,
One male monopoly where we
Can claim our old supremacy,

One relic of that good old day
When man held undisputed sway,
And women knew no more than crave
To be some husband's toy or slave?

Bethink ye, too, if females are
Freely admitted to the bar,
Could our profession long withstand
The ruthless, innovating hand?

The people have a shrewd misgiving
That law, by which we make our living,
Is an imposture in disguise,
A thing of quibbles, shams and lies.

That under words and loud pretence
It veils a lack of common sense
That oft an ass in ermine brays
With glib pomposity a phrase.

Now woman has perceptions bright,
And a keen sense of wrong and right
Her sympathies are deep and warm,
Impatient of red tape and form.

With her *esprit de corps* is lacking
Which gives the legal shyster backing.
Some day she'd turn, beyond doubt,
The legal system inside out,

And, as the vulgar sometimes say,
Completely give the snap away
And stripped of technical disguise,
Expose our refuge of lies.

Praise to the benchers who have stood
Against the innovating flood,
To save us and our ample fees
From tribulations such as these.

Ananias Limberjaw, Q.C..

EMPLOYMENT FOR WOMEN, 1876

'Employment for Women', *Christian Guardian*, 6 September 1876, p. 284.

The majority of women do not need any one to find work for them. But the question of how to find remunerative and suitable employment for single women, who are compelled to earn their own living, is one of great practical interest. In most countries, the female population is largely in excess of the masculine portion. A very considerable proportion of the males, from one cause or other, count for nothing as bread-winners and fathers of families. When the idle, the sickly, and the vicious are counted out, the number which may be reckoned upon as eligible material for husbands, is largely reduced. And even of these a considerable number obstinately refuse to wed. A considerable number of unmarried females, to say nothing of poor widows, must, therefore, exist in every country, who are without fortune or friends, or any means of support but their own industry. How can this class find healthy employment, that will enable them to provide for their own wants, and render them useful to society? The difficulty of the problem is increased by the hindrances which women find in pushing their way into any new sphere of industry, from which prejudice or social custom has previously excluded them. Yet the practical solution of this grave social problem is intimately connected with the welfare of an important section of society, and the utilization of powers of usefulness, which may be lost and wasted by not finding their proper sphere.

We say nothing here of factory-work, needle-work, or teaching. These are already full to overflowing. Neither need we speak of female clerks, telegraph-operators, and workers in the lighter forms of industry; as the tendency towards these departments of work is already sufficiently strong to supply the demand. Women should not be debarred from these forms of industry, nor from any artistic or professional work for which they are adapted, and which they may pursue without destroying the delicacy of womanhood. There is still room for extension in this direction, though beyond all doubt, women are, from several causes, at a great disadvantage in competing with men in the spheres of professional work. We wish here briefly to refer to three spheres of work for women.

1. *Domestic Service.* Several considerations invest this branch of female industry with importance. It is a department in which the demand is large, and not subject to fluctuation; as well as not likely to be invaded by modern inventions. So much has been done, that we must express our doubts modestly. Still, artificial substitutes for cooks and housemaids will not probably be perfected before the close of the next century. Household work is not only suited to the capacity of women; the ability to do such work well must always be of great use to those who have acquired this art. Some kinds of employment leave girls without either the taste or ability to keep their own houses properly, in case of their being married. But domestic service is, on the contrary, a suitable training or apprenticeship for girls, in the very things that, in case of marriage, they will need most to know. Domestic servants receive, on the average, a remuneration as nearly adequate to their wants as any class of workers. Their necessary expenses are small. A home and all the most numerous and essential wants of life are supplied, in addition to the stipulated wages, without costing them any anxiety. Where the family is in good circumstances, the domestic servants share to a considerable extent in the advantages of its position. The average servant in a good family works no harder than many a wealthy farmer's wife, and has generally much more of the comforts of life than the wife of a poor mechanic or laborer. There must, however, be some drawbacks, which cause most single women, who are permanently thrown upon their own resources, to prefer sewing or being saleswomen, or almost anything, to being a domestic servant. Domestic service is not socially respectable, and people place a high value upon anything that lifts them up in the scale of social respectability. Besides, the greater number of those who employ domestic servants, either from inability or indisposition, do not give their female servants a home so comfortable as to be attractive as a permanent residence. Mistresses greatly stand in their own light when they do not do all in their power to make the lives of those who live in their households pleasant and agreea-

ble. They should not be treated as mere working machines; but as fellow-beings, with social instincts and human feelings, similar to those of their employers.

2. *Skill in sick-nursing*. This is a sphere of useful and remunerative employment for women of a higher grade of intelligence than the ordinary domestic servant. It is recently attracting a good deal of attention in England, because in many diseases the recovery of patients depends much more upon intelligent nursing than upon the prescriptions of the physician. This is work that requires intelligence, firmness of purpose, and kindness of heart. It is employment for which the natural tenderness of women specially fits them. Miss Nightingale and her band of assistants, during the Crimean war, taught us what inestimable service women can render in the sick hospital. This lesson was also effectively illustrated by the heroic devotion of female nurses, during the American civil war. As long as there is so much sickness and physical suffering in the world, there must be a large demand for competent nurses; and only those who have been tossed upon the couch of pain can know what balm and blessing there is in the soft touch of a woman's gentle hand, and the kindly, hopeful words of a tender woman's voice. A recent article in *Chambers' Journal* presents some striking thoughts on this subject. Miss Florence Lees, the friend and assistant of Florence Nightingale, was the first student in the art of nursing at St. Thomas' Hospital, London. Since then she has had a great deal of experience in the hospitals of the continent. She is now superintendent of the Metropolitan Institution for providing trained nurses for the sick poor. In an address recently given before the National Health Society she strongly urged the importance of trained female nurses for the sick. She tells us that nursing the sick is by no means a cheerless or depressing employment. She is anxious to induce gentlewomen to join her staff of nurses, and to qualify themselves by the prescribed training for the work. One thing is certain, such work must develop the kindliest sympathies of those who engage in it.

3. *Missionary Work*. There are many foreign fields of labor, in which the employment of intelligent Christian ladies as teachers and workers is recommended, both on grounds of efficiency and economy. A great proportion of the missionary work of the different churches does not consist in eloquent sermons by popular preachers to large audiences. There is a great deal of slow, painstaking dealing with individuals. In countries like Turkey, India, and China, where social custom shuts up the females in seclusion, women have such access to the female portion of the population as men cannot have. In many of these fields a female missionary may be just as useful as a missionary of the sterner sex, especially where she can work in connection with an established mission. Such a laborer costs far less than what is necessary to support a married missionary and his family. We think in seeking out spheres of employment for intelligent

unmarried ladies, it is well to have regard to the peculiar fitness of women for such employment as demand sympathy, tact, delicacy, gentleness, and other qualities of womanhood. Some women may succeed as well as men in some masculine employments; but in selecting departments of labor they should choose those in which there is good reason to believe that they will succeed better than men.

CONDITIONS OF FEMALE LABOUR IN ONTARIO, 1889

Jean Scott Thomas, 'The Conditions of Female Labour in Ontario', *University of Toronto Studies in Political Science*, ed. W. J. Ashley, 1889, series III, pp. 18-25.

SECTION I.—WAGES IN EMPLOYMENTS EXCLUSIVELY FEMALE.

It may not be possible to draw an absolute line between what is skilled and what is unskilled labour, since all labour requires if not training at least aptitude; still it is evident that some employments are more easily entered than others because it is not necessary to have special training for them.

As might be expected the employments requiring comparatively unskilled labour cannot command such high wages *in the long run* as those demanding skilled labour, other things being equal.

The wages of skilled labour are subject to greater variation owing to the various degrees of proficiency from the apprentice to the finished workwoman; while the wages of unskilled labour are more uniform and do not rise much above what they were at starting, because such labour can easily be supplied when needed.

Even in different branches of the same employment some parts will require more special training than others. The very fact of there being a number of employments requiring unskilled labour has led, no doubt, to the increased employment of young girls and women. We shall first take up those employments demanding only unskilled labour and then consider those requiring more or less training.

The position of domestic servants, however, seems to fall under both heads and it will be considered first.

1. *Domestic Servants.*

In Canada the class of domestic servants most universally in demand is the *general*. Owing to the fact that there are but a few wealthy people, in the vast majority of cases where servants are kept only one is employed:

and the supply of specially trained servants is as limited as the demand for them. Girls who are able to live at home and earn enough to partially support themselves have no inducement to go into domestic service; and in cities the supply of domestics is kept up only be draining the surrounding country of girls who come to the cities for the higher wages and other advantages. In some cases too they are imported from Great Britain and Ireland. Of late years so many employments have opened up for women that the supply of domestic servants is rather short of the demand; and, as a consequence, their wages have risen considerably, so that many mistresses of households are obliged to do without or take incompetent servants. An inexperienced girl who goes "to assist in light housework," as the advertisements put it, will earn from $6 to $7 a month in a city. A good general servant can command from $8 to $14 a month, according to her work—"with or without washing." In some cases it really amounts to a cook's position, only it seems to be the custom to call it that of a "general" to avoid such disputes as might arise over questions of work.

Cooks are rewarded with from $12 to $20 a month, according to the amount and kind of work to be done. Cooks for hotels and restaurants are paid higher than those in private families; because as a rule the work is heavier and many girls object to the position. Housemaids are paid from $8 to $12 a month; and parlourmaids from $10 to $14. In many cases one girl does the work of both, as house and parlourmaid, where it is not convenient to keep the two. Nurses get from $8 to $12. Under nurses $5. Kitchen maids from $8 to $12. Laundresses get as high as $16 a month. Seamstresses $14. Another class of servant is called "lady's help"—whose duties seem to be rather indefinite. The women who seek such positions are those who from adverse circumstances are in need of a home and the remuneration is not the first consideration. The demand is perhaps less than the supply.

The general reluctance of girls to go into service in Canada has been much discussed. Many point out that they are really better off than girls working in factories or shops so far as wages and comfort are concerned. On the other hand the factory or shop girl has certain hours; and when her work is over her time is her own. Then, too, many prefer to work where there are a number of other girls employed; and as has been already stated, as long as a girl can live at home and earn a little money at some light employment there is no need for her to go into service. Moreover, there can be no doubt that the social barrier which exists between mistress and maid deters many from service in a new country where class distinctions are not as fixed and definite as in older countries.

The work of a girl in a factory or shop is definite and soon learned, while the work of a domestic, especially of a "general," is more indefinite and varied. This indefiniteness with regard to what a girl is expected to do, and what she is not expected to do, is one of the causes of disputes which often end in a notice to leave or a dismissal. The fact that some mistresses require their servants to do too much leads servants very often to try to do as little as possible. On the other hand mistresses who treat their servants kindly are sometimes taken advantage of. Girls are expected, in Toronto, to give at least two weeks notice to leave. Each girl expects one evening a week for herself at least, and often more are given. Part of Sunday also is given. Some mistresses only ask that a girl should get through her work, and impose no restrictions. It is next to impossible to generalize on the various privileges and requirements of general servants. Each household seems to be a law to itself.

The majority of servants do not stop long in one place. Of course there are many exceptions, but the fact that a girl knows that she can get a place at any time makes her more independent. In cities many families who go away for the summer dismiss the servants; and in the autumn there is a general readjusting of service everywhere. Many girls work in summer hotels for the season and return when it is over.

At present there does not seem to be any expectation of the supply of domestics being increased. Wages have risen, so that many families who formerly were able to keep a servant now do without, and those who kept two or three can only keep one or two. In Canada the majority of housekeepers are able to do their own work in an emergency; so that the interval between the leaving of one servant and the advent of another does not mean a complete interregnum in the work of the household. Owing to the invention of many modern conveniences it is possible to reduce the work to a minimum; and by getting partial assistance for the very heavy work many are able to do without house servants altogether.

2. Apprentices.

Apprentices in dressmaking, tailoring and millinery are not required to pay any premium, but are not, as a rule, paid for the first six months. At the end of that time they receive some small remuneration as improvers and assistants. Much depends on the special talent and adaptability of the worker. As improvers and assistants they may receive $1 or $2 a week. In stores, girls sometimes serve as saleswomen for a short time for nothing; but more often they are paid from the start, especially if it is known to the employer that they are dependent on themselves. Sometimes they start as check and parcel hands at $1.50 and $2.50 a week. In the large majority of employments there seems to be no definite regulations in regard to fixed increase of wages. Many employers, of course, try to keep them as low as possible, and this they can do when they know that there are always many who are willing to work for what they can get.

3. Miscellaneous Employments

In canning factories young girls are employed in preparing the fruit and vegetables for canning in the summer months for $1 and $2 a week.

In cigar and tobacco factories girls do the stripping, *i.e.* taking out the midrib of the leaf, receiving on an average about $2.50 a week.

In soap factories girls are employed in wrapping up toilet soap and packing it in boxes for $2 and $3 a week.

In seed factories girls empty and fill the seed packets. Those emptying receive ½ cent per hundred and those filling get 1¾ cents per hundred. At this they make from $2 to $3 a week and when particularly expert, even more.

In cotton, woollen and knitting mills there are various occupations, which are suited for girls, only requiring dexterity and nimbleness, such as tending the bobbins, for which they earn an average of $2 a week.

In biscuit factories girls sort and pack the biscuits in boxes and label them, starting at $2.50 a week. Those who are particularly skilful pack special grades, receiving as high as $5 a week.

Girls employed in colouring bamboo work with gas jets and pokers receive $2.50 a week.

In window shades factories girls tack on rollers, assist in decorating and sew in fringes and ornaments, starting on $2 and $3 a week.

Women employed in sorting rags for shoddy mills are paid by the bale. The work is not enticing, and young girls do not take it up. The only experience necessary is to be able to tell the difference between woollen, cotton and silk goods and those which are mixtures. Women get from $2 to $5 at it.

As waitresses in restaurants and coffee houses girls receive $2 and $3, and are given their meals besides, except on Sunday. Those employed from 11 a.m. to 3 p.m. receive $1.50 and their dinner. No special training is necessary, but a girl is required to be neat, quick and able to write a good hand to take down orders.

In bookbinderies girls do the folding and stitching. The wages run from $1.50 for beginners to $5. In one bindery the wages for one week were as follows:—One girl received $5, four girls received $4, sixteen received $3, and a few received less.

In a number of employments women are paid by the piece, and then of course the wages vary considerably. In some cases quite high wages are paid, but they must be regarded as exceptional. Wages in large towns and cities seem to average more than those in small towns, where the cost of living is not so high and rents are lower.

In knitting factories where women tend the machines, much depends on the kind of garment that is made, but $5 a week seems the limit, a forewoman getting about $6. In woollen mills the wages also vary, the weavers getting the best pay, but at most $5, the average being $3.50. In cotton mills the wages seem to be slightly higher on the average, weavers and web-drawers getting over $5 and $6.

In boot and shoe factories, on piece work, the women do the stitching, getting as much as $7. The men do the heaviest stitching and the soleing. Girls employed in the finishing room in putting in laces and buttons are paid about $3 a week.

In corset factories the women do the stitching and men do the cutting. The less experienced do the plain stitching and the best hands do the closing in, while others sew on trimmings: the wages vary from $1.50 up to $8 and $9, but $5 seems a good average.

In laundries, wash-house women get from $3 to $5. Starchers get from $4.75 to $5.50, and ironers get from $4 to $8 a week.

In tobacco factories women do the packing and men do the weighing and pressing. The women receive as high as $1 a day if good workers.

In cigar factories "bunch breakers" and "bookers" get from $4 to $5. Cigarmakers and rollers obtain higher wages. When very expert and experienced they have been known to make as high as $13 a week.

In glove factories men do the cutting out and girls do the stitching and embroidering, earning from $2 to $6, averaging between $4 and $5.

Capmakers employed in stitching soft caps together make on piece work from $4 to $8.

In candy works those packing and finishing start on $2.50 a week. Those working at chocolate candies and lozenges, paid by piece work get $5 and $6 a week.

Saleswomen in dry-goods stores get about $3 and $4 on the average. The heads of departments get from $6 to $15; but this only in the large stores. In small stores girls have no special department, but sell in all. In large stores millinery and mantel departments form a part of the establishment and are always in charge of women.

Dressmakers as waist and skirt hands rarely get over $5 a week; cutters and fitters, generally being forewomen, get from $6 to $20, the average perhaps being about $10.

Tailoresses doing wholesale work in shops are not often paid by the piece, and earn between $3 and $4 a week. Those working at home average about the same, but of course all depends on steady work. Those who do custom tailoring are paid better especially in busy seasons. Pant and vestmakers can make from $5 to $7 and coatmakers as high as $11 and $13 a week.

Bagmakers on piece work make from $6 to $9 during the busy season from October to March—these for special orders only; for the ordinary sizes of paper bags are made wholly by machinery.

In jewellery manufactories girls employed at burnishing start at $1.50 and earn as much as $4 and $5. Engravers and chainmakers get better wages on the average, but $5 seems the limit.

In tin and stamping works girls do the japanning and soldering. Girls are started on $2 and $2.50 a week; and when capable they are put on piece work. At soldering they can earn $4 and $5. Special hands earn as much as $1.50 a day.

In dyeing and cleaning works, feather curlers get $5 if expert. Ironers range from $3 for plain ironers to $7.50 and $8 for fancy ironers.

In paperbox factories wages run from $3 to $6.

Machine operators on women's and children's underwear are generally on piece work. The cutters get $6 and $5.50, and the machine workers get from $2.50 to $6.

Girls employed as book-keepers, assistant cashiers and in other office work get from $3 to $10; a good average being $6.

As type-setters girls begin at $2 and get about $4 when experienced; but there are not many women employed as compositors in Toronto.

Girls employed as telephone clerks in Toronto get nothing for the first few weeks till they are able to manage a switch alone. Then they get $15 a month; after the first three months they get $20 a month. The head operators get $25 and $30 a month. For each Sunday's work 75¢ is paid, and 25¢ for a dinner hour if a girl is then employed; 10¢ an hour being paid for work done after hours in the evening.

The free library assistants receive $300 for the first year and $400 for the second. The head assistant gets $450 a year.

Professional nurses with hospital training can command $14 a week for ordinary cases and $16 for infectious cases. Non-professional nurses ask from $5 to $10 a week.

Telegraphers generally start in large offices in Toronto as check girls getting $12 and $15 a month. As operators they get from $25 to $40 a month. In some offices, especially expert operators get $45 and $55 a month.

Typewriters and stenographers start at $3 and $4 when they have not much experience, and average from $6 to $8 as expert workers.

Public school teachers in towns and cities receive higher pay than those in villages and country districts. In Toronto the minimum salary for a public school teacher is $324 a year; which is raised annually, irrespective of the grades taught, by $24 a year till a maximum of $636 is reached. Head mistresses receive as much as $1,000; and in some cases increases are made on account of length of service.

The average salary for a woman teacher for the whole province is $296 a year.

In the High Schools and Collegiate Institutes the average salary of a woman assistant in general work is $575; and for those who act as specialists in any department, a position for which a university degree is necessary, the average salary is $875; the highest being $1,500 for a woman.

Women in the civil service, employed as clerks, average $536 a year. The lowest is $400, the highest $800. Women in Ontario have entered at least one of the learned professions, namely, medicine; the number of lady doctors is rapidly increasing. Some go away as medical missionaries, others remain as local practitioners.

SECTION II.—EFFECT ON WAGES OF COMPETITION WITH MEN.

"It is difficult," as was recently pointed out at the meeting of the British Association, "to find cases in which men and women are employed at precisely similar work. In the great majority of cases in which the hiring takes place by time the inferior physical strength of women of necessity almost always tells against them."

In a number of employments, however, where the work is not too difficult for women they are gradually displacing men.

1. *Cigarmaking.*

In the cigar manufacture in Ontario, in which formerly men were largely employed, the work is now almost entirely done by women and children.

In one factory of one hundred and fifty employés only thirteen were men. The object of this is of course to cheapen the cost of production. The preliminary parts of stripping the leaf and breaking the bunch can be done by children with little practice; and in the past it was the custom to employ them until they learned how to do it and wanted higher wages, and then a fresh supply was obtained. Women who make the cigars can generally earn good wages, but they do not get on an average as high wages as men even where they are paid the same rate for piece work.

In Toronto there are very few women employed in cigar-making. The reason being that all the employés belong to a union which insists on all workers being paid alike, and the employers prefer to employ men, because they are likely to remain longer in the business. One woman who was paid the same wages as men on piece work stated that she did not make as much on an average as the men, because she did not care to risk the loss of her health by too close application to work.

In the tobacco trade women and children are also largely employed. The girls do the stripping and the women make the plugs, the men now only doing the weighing and pressing. Some attempt has been made to supersede the work even of women in cigar-making by the use of machines for that purpose; but as yet machine made cigars are not in universal favour.

There is no doubt that if women were paid the same rates as the men they would not be so largely employed.

2. *Tailoring.*

In tailoring women and girls work largely for the wholesale trade in ready-made clothing; and the majority of the pant and vest makers doing custom work are women also. Coat-making for custom trade is done by both men and women, but women cannot command such high wages as men for the same work. For making a coat a woman will ask only two-thirds of what a man will: the probability being that if she asked the same she would not get the order. The question as to whether their work is as good is one on which a difference of opinion seems to exist. In some cases the men take the orders for custom work and employ girls to do the sewing on week work, which has the advantage of securing steady employment for them. Cutting the garments is seldom done by women, except in a small way for custom work in boy's clothing.

Comparisons are often drawn between the wages women receive for wholesale work and those they receive for custom work. A woman may receive only twenty-five cents for making a vest for the wholesale trade in ready-made clothing, while she will receive $1 and more for an ordered vest. But it must be remembered that the garments are made quite differently and four vests of the first kind might be made during the time occupied in making one of the second kind. Those who are paid by week work do not of course receive as good wages as those on piece work.

3. *Saleswomen.*

Where both men and women are employed in selling goods in dry-goods stores, the women have charge of the lighter departments, such as gloves, hosiery, laces, buttons, fancy goods, ribbons, etc., while the men take the heavier departments of dress goods, carpets and other house furnishings, so that it is not possible to compare the wages in such cases. The women of course invariably receive less, except perhaps when they are heads of departments and are entrusted with the buying in their special lines. In small stores girls are not given any particular department on account of the limited stock carried, but sell in all, even dress goods, so that in some cases the work proves too heavy. Some employers who do not carry a large stock of light articles prefer men altogether. Here as elsewhere in the employment of girls and women it is a question of cheaper labour; but in the large stores especially it seems that there is room for the employment of both men and women, the particular sphere of each being different. As in all other employments entered by women, the probability of marriage is a drawback to the permanency of their employment.

4. *Stenography, Typewriting, Book-keeping and other Office Work.*

It is in office work more particularly that women of late years have displaced men; and it is probably in part the result of this is that the standard of wages for men in this kind of work has been perceptibly lowered. Another reason, however, for the low wages is that the supply is becoming greater than the demand. Although it is true that really efficient and competent workers can get positions, the market is overstocked with inexperienced clerks, owing to the system adopted in some business colleges and schools of accepting as pupils any who offer themselves for instruction, whether they have sufficient education or not. This is particularly true of typewriting and amateur stenography. The larger business colleges, it is true, state in their circulars that they prefer those with a good common education, but as yet there is no standard absolutely required for those who wish to pursue a commercial education. In Ontario there is a commercial course in the high schools for which certificates are granted, but the instruction does not include all branches of a business education. If a check is to be placed on this overcrowding, the business colleges will have to insist on some standard of excellence in the branches of an ordinary English education before accepting a pupil, and positions should only be given to those who are known to be competent. Women seem as fitted for this work as men, and have proved as competent where the work was not too severe.

5. *Telegraphy.*

In telegraphy it is generally believed that women do not receive as good pay as the men. In Ontario men do all the night work; and where men and women are employed in the same office the men work the heavier lines. In this employment, as in others, one result of the competition of women is the lowering of salaries. In a few cases, it is true, women do as good work and receive as good pay as *some* men. In some cases girls, after learning the business in Canada, have found more lucrative positions in the States, where the salaries are as a rule much higher than here. That these higher salaries are to a large extent counterbalanced by the higher cost of living is usually not realized before migrating.

6. *Teaching in Public Schools.*

That the number of men in the teaching profession in Ontario is decreasing, and the number of women increasing is shown from the following figures:—In 1877 the number of men teaching in the public schools in Ontario was 3,020, and the number of women 3,448. In 1889 the number of men was 2,774, and of women, 5,193. Although the whole number of teachers had increased by 1,499 in twelve years, the number of men had decreased 226, and the number of women had increased 1,345. In 1889 the average salary for a male public school teacher was $421, the highest being $1,500 and the average salary for a woman was $296. This difference is partially explained by the fact that men hold the positions of head masters especially in the graded schools of the towns and cities, and as a consequence receive larger salaries. Still, in the small ungraded schools, where women have frequently charge of a whole school, their salaries are undoubtedly smaller than those of men in similar positions. The large increase of women teachers at low salaries has led to the abandonment of the profession by men in most cases, except as a stepping stone to some other work.

The objection generally urged that women do not take up work with the intention of remaining at it for any length of time applies equally to men as far as public school teaching is concerned, especially in the smaller schools. Women remain in this profession fully as long as, if not longer than, men do, and in some cases teach equally well if not better; so that there seems to be no reason why they should not be paid as well. Except in cases where the duties of a head master entail more labour there is no difference in the kind of work.

In the High Schools and Collegiate Institutes until within the last few years women only occupied the lower positions, at, of course, lower salaries; but since the advent of higher education for women they have been able to take their places beside the men in teaching the same work, and the tendency at present is to pay them well. So far only one woman has held the position of head master of a high school. In Toronto some of the smaller public schools have women as head mistresses, and recently an attempt was made to increase their number. It is to be hoped that the present tendency towards paying women teachers the same as the men will grow, so that it will be a question of getting the best teacher in each case and not the cheapest.

EMPLOYMENT OF MARRIED WOMEN.

The employment of married women in factories and stores in Ontario is not general. In a large number of factories and stores there are no married women at all; at most only one or two widows. Married women in Canada do not seem to go out to work as long as their husbands are at all able to support them. In canning factories, during the summer months, numbers of married women may be found; many work in laundries; and in a mill stock factory (preparing rags for shoddy mills) visited by the writer most of the women were married. Market gardening is a means of subsistence to some. Women whose husbands are dead or are not able to support them, will not go out as long as they have children at home to care for, but prefer, if they can, to engage in some work which will keep them at home. Women in poor circumstances go out washing and ironing to private houses or else take it home to do. In many cases they take in sewing or dressmaking, and do tailoring for the wholesale trade at their homes.

In Toronto during a greater part of the year there is a large student population gathered from all parts of the province, and accommodation for them needs to be ample, as well as for many other young men and women who find employment away from their homes; so that taking in boarders is a frequent resource for married women who have homes but need to increase their income.

As yet there seems no need for special legislation in the Factories' Act on behalf of married women as in more thickly populated countries.

UNEQUAL PAY FOR EQUAL WORK, 1890

Miss Minnie Phelps, 'Women as Wage-Earners', in Rev. B. F. Austin, *Woman: Her Character, Culture and Calling* (Brantford, 1890), pp. 51-5.

It is a geometrical axiom, "That things which are halves of the same thing are equal to one another." It follows then, that woman being the one-half of the human whole, is equal to the other half, the male fraction, and they being "one," have a common interest in all that relates to either sex—their mutual aspirations—spiritual advances and the struggles for existence.

Two-thirds of the human family are laborers, either of brain or muscle. One-half of the whole is woman, and the question presents itself, What is the per cent. of women as laborers, and as wage-earners, and what is the accredited value of that labor?

In 1840, that good and great woman, Harriet Martineau, visited America, and found seven employments open to women: teaching, sewing, keeping boarding-house, folding and stitching in binderies, work in factories, as compositors, or in domestic service. So great have been the changes since Miss Martineau's visit, that in the United States 300 doors are now open to women, and in our Canada, from the census of 1881, we find 227 occupations, where, in 1840, our mothers had but seven.

In the two main departments of manufacture in the United States, including boots and shoes, carpets, cotton goods, silks, woollen hats, there are employed 535,000, one-third of which are women, or about 180,000. In the Province of Ontario there are 18,650 women employed in the various trades and occupations, and in the Dominion of Canada there are 45,889. In the factories of our Province there are 7,594 women, 247 girls between the ages of 12 and 14 years; 1,588 between the ages of 14 and 18 years. These women, working side by side of the male laborers, battling with the same physical struggles, full of the same higher aspirations, the value of the world's market of exchange being equal, find they receive from one-third to one-half less wages, doing the same work with as much skill as their brother workers.

Let me give a few instances of the wages paid to women in the great industry of underwear for women. We hear now-a-days of the cheapness of these garments. "So much cheaper," you say, "than you could make them yourselves." You wonder at it. Here are the reasons, and the only reasons. For the underclothing that some of you are wearing at this very hour, some poor, needy sister has been paid the sum of 48 cents per dozen, or 4 cents a piece, for the manufacture of the same. She has been paid 40 cents per dozen for coarse drawers; night-dresses, tucked and trimmed, $1.30 per dozen; while for the white skirts, tucked ruffles, she gets $1.00 per dozen. This is not all. These women and girls must buy their own needles, thread, oil and soap; 20 cents for one spool of thread, 40 cents for another, which lasts two weeks. These women work nine and one-half hours per day, if late five minutes are fined five cents. These facts are from the City of Toronto,—"the city of churches," and while you are reading these things, the rush of the shuttle and the hurrying needle is being plied while some of us wear these garments which mean life and virtue to some poor girl.

Do you not catch the echo of Tom Hood's "stitch, stitch," and do you not see finally the picture of "one more unfortunate?" This is but one example of a class of women who, compelled by necessity, are slaving for the merest pittance. There is a terrible affinity between vice and hunger, between low wages and the eating cancer of our cities—the social evil.

Take again the profession of dressmaking as an industry, and compare its relative value to that of the brewers and distillers. In 1885 the returns from the census of 1881 were as follows:

	Brewers.	Distillers.	Dressmakers.
Capital	$4,592,990	$1,305,000	$1,601,209
Employ	4,129	285	7,838
Value of production	$4,766,449	$1,790,000	$4,926,811

Dressmaking is an industry of a class whose value by our returns is little better than that of the Mongolians, and of not as much value as that of our Indians. The productive value is greater than that of either the brewer or the distiller, and nearly equal to both. The employees outnumber both.

Take again another class, school teachers, both male and female, giving the same amount of time, their standard of excellence being equal. What do we find? That women do the work and men get the wages. In my own city, St. Catharines, I have gleaned these facts. There are two teachers in our central school, both doing entrance examination work; last year the woman promoted 14, the man 2; the woman gets $600 the man $900. Giving as is granted $100 for the responsibility of head master, why is it that the woman, whose work is superior to the man's, gets $200 less wages? Answer, sex. In 1880 there were 7,218 school teachers in the Province of Ontario. In ten years the increase has been 1,033, all females; there are 2,744 male teachers, and 4,474 female teachers.

Average salary for male teachers in cities $776
Average salary for female teachers in cities 358
Average salary for male teachers in country 427
Average salary for female teachers in country 287

These are facts, and they jostle theories.

In every line of occupation given, we have shown that woman is equal to man in the quality and quantity of work; the question naturally arises, if woman can do and does do the same kind of work as man, why should she not have the same wages, and along what lines can we remedy this inequality?

1st—By giving the same protection to woman as to man, by allowing woman a chance to enter any field of labor she may find open to her. The sphere of each man or of each woman is that which he or she can best fill with the highest exercise of their respective abilities; and all that I ask for woman is the same liberty of choice as that offered man, and the chance to prove by that liberty of choice her ability to do her chosen work. Has God equipped woman, physically, mentally and morally, as members of society, as the one-half of the human whole? Then what God made her able and capable to do, it is a strong argument He intended she should do. I do not plead the identity of the sexes. I plead their equality. I do not ask that woman plead protection from these glaring evils. I *do ask* that woman may have a chance to protect herself by the same lines as the other fraction of the human whole—man—because there are about as many women as men who have to rely upon their own energies for bread. Despite the fact that for every 100 females born, 106 males are given life, and strange as it may seem, in 16 of the States there is a majority of women, while the Canadian outlook is about the same. Rum, tobacco and vice have killed off man, while the "survival of the fittest" seems to be woman's lot.

Again, woman's wages are cheaper, because she labors too much in a few occupations. To-day, on this continent alone, there are more than 3,000,000 of women who have to rely solely upon their own energies and earnings for their support. 250,000 are the public school teachers, 500,000 are working with their needles for scanty wages, 500,000 more are in the factories of this continent, while more than 1,000,000 are in the kitchens of America. Throw open the doors of every profession, trade and occupation, so that if one line becomes a "glut on the market," she may, like her brother, look elsewhere.

2nd—Give woman the same preparation for her chosen calling as that of her brother—all sons are expected to learn some trade or profession, why not all daughters, so that when reverses come, and some rich man is not on hand to marry the girl, she may find herself in a position to earn a respectable living. This touches a very vital subject, viz.:—the Social

Purity work of the W.C.T.U. Hundreds of women, through reverses of fortune, have been compelled to go out into life's battle unequipped for its struggles and unprepared for its competitions. What do we find? They seek for some genteel employment, never having been taught that some time they would enter the ranks of the world's wage-earners to compete with equipped hands, and they go down in the awful sea of vice. Joseph Cook, of Boston, tells us that in that city alone, there are 18,000 young women keeping up their daily occupations and getting the remainder of their support from a life of sin. Many of these are clerks, who are obliged to keep up appearances for the sake of their position, whose salaries are too small. Give woman a thorough preparation for life, in some trade or profession, teach her to feel, whether she be a daughter of a millionaire or that of a mechanic, that God never intended that there should be drones in this moving, busy world, and that in any and every position of life, it is the duty of every person, man or woman, to be able to earn an honest penny, if the urgency of the case demands it.

3rd—Back of the two plans for the bettering of woman as wage-earners, is the foundation upon which both must build, e.g.—the ballot—for as Canon Kingsley once said, "Women will never have social equity, until she has legal equity." That which is true of women as wage-earners to-day, was true of the workingman in England fifty years ago, when during that great famine, mass meetings were held all over the country, and in Manchester the great and good John Bright, attempted to tell them the causes of their poverty, and to give as the remedy—the ballot. The great hungry audience in response shouted back, "We want no franchise, give us bread," and the meeting was broken up. These laboring men were at the mercy of capitalists, they organized trade unions and strikes, and by means of these extorted better wages. But after a time reformers like Cobden and Bright began to agitate for Household Suffrage. As soon as Household Suffrage became a law in England, a bill was introduced into Parliament asking for appropriations to build school houses for the education of the children of the laboring classes. Up to that time no politician had ever made a move in that direction, and every session of Parliament since, labor and laborers have received some attention.

I present these remedies to you from a trial and from experimental knowledge of the one-half of integral humanity—man. The steps by which man has developed and assumed his present position, are the steps that womanhood now and the womanhood of the future must tread. Some of you are fearful that if the ballot be given woman, and with that, the ever opening doors of commerce and of trade, the widening doors of the legal profession, the doctor's healing art, the editorial chair, the preacher's desk, and the various occupations and trades, as various as the talents of woman, that somewhere possibly woman may lose her womanliness and aspire to the other sex.

It is not occupation or work that makes noble womanhood. The noble qualities must be in the woman, and these qualities can be set forth if she be called to earn her living at the wash tub, or in the preacher's position.

True womanhood depends on the individual, not on the occupation.

Again, it is another law of geometry that the whole is greater than its parts. To develop the whole in the early history of the human family, God put forth this axiom in another way, when He said, "It is not good for man to be alone," so He created woman as a helpmeet, as the one-half of the whole, as man's equal, the complement and the supplement of each other, and the development of either one means the advance of the other.

EQUAL PAY FOR WOMEN TEACHERS, 1893

Miss E. Binmore, 'Financial Outlook of the Women Teachers of Montreal', *The Educational Record* (Quebec, March 1893), vol. XIII, no. 3, 70-4.

Perhaps no tendency of the age is more repulsive to the general public than that of women to claim their rights too independently. For this, we may blame those who seem to believe their right to be to take the best of everything to the entire exclusion of men. But such women, though often quoted, must be comparatively few. I never knew one. I know they must exist from reading the newspapers, but they must form a less per cent. of our number than the followers of Malthus among the men. I am afraid Lord Lytton's "Coming Race" and Rider Haggard's "She" are blamable to a certain extent for our disfavor. But, at least, equally repulsive is the opposite type given us in Anderson's "Patient Griselda." What is the just medium? This is essentially a century of change. Women are gradually declaring and proving their ability and willingness to bear the burden of their own support. It is no longer absolutely necessary that every woman in the family should be dependent upon the men—to be reduced to unknown straits and intolerable suffering on the death of the latter. Almost every day sees some new employment thrown open to women, though there are still many employments they can not enter. This causes an undue development of those accessible and calls into requisition the law of demand and supply. What is the result? Such a sweeping reform as making wage-earners of women, of course, cannot be accomplished in a moment. This affects their remuneration unfavourably, but can only do so temporarily. At first, woman works on sufferance for him who cannot afford to pay the usual amount of remuneration. But, as one position after another is tentatively thrown open to woman, her conscientious discharge of her work brings her into favor. The natural result cannot be long delayed. The days of sufferance are gradually forgotten, and she, like man, is paid according to her efficiency and success.

Nor is the teaching profession any exception to this general law. At first admitted to the most subordinate positions only, by degrees all positions have become accessible to her. For instance, the Superintendent of Schools in Pittsburg wrote me, "We have thirty-seven principals, twelve of whom are ladies. Of these, two ladies and one gentleman receive $2,000 and seven gentlemen and six ladies $1,800. We make no difference in salary, between those doing the same work, for sex." San Francisco, Boston and several other cities take a like view of the matter. Even where a distinction is made it is becoming daily less marked. In St. Louis, Mo., only women are admitted to the competitive examinations for principal-ship of primary schools. Many cities still make the old distinction. In Montreal the distinction is retained; but let us not, therefore, feel discour-aged. It can be only a question of time, when the difference shall be removed. All we can do to hasten it is to give to our teaching that energy and purpose, and devote to self-advance that time which shall enable us to win only by superiority. It would be false modesty or hypocrisy to pretend we do not do our best now. But let us bear in mind that with every advance in our position there will be a corresponding advance in general education. There is always room at the top of the ladder and we cannot strive too earnestly to advance our capabilities. Time will do the rest for us. Rome was not built in a day.

Those of our citizens whose generosity to the Art Gallery, Hospitals, McGill, etc., I mentioned above, evidently appreciate the importance of education, and I feel certain their feeling in that respect would be endorsed by the general mass of our citizens did they know the state of the case. Montreal supplies one-third the finances of the Province, and it stands to reason it would see that charity began at home. But, unfortun-ately for us, the city has not yet become imbued with a sense of the importance of its education, or else has misunderstood the matter. Less than a year ago the Board of School Commissioners here petitioned the City Council to grant them an increase of taxation. Only one-half of the amount asked was accorded, and the Board was thus handicapped. Now, the members of that Board have in several ways shown a desire to consult the interest of its teachers, but cannot spend what it has not got.

The women teachers of this city presented a petition that the scale of their salaries be increased, and especially that $245 ($250 less superannua-tion) is too little for anyone to live upon for twelve months. Let me prove this last statement. Board in this city is $3.50 to $4.50 per week, *i.e.*, $182 to $234 per annum, according to the locality of the school. For, when a teacher cannot afford to drive, she must live near her school. That is, the unfortunate teacher has $11 to $63 from which to pay annually for clothing, doctor's bills, books, church contributions, etc., and finally, though by no means least, take advantage of the educational advantages the city holds out to her so temptingly. Perhaps you believe I exaggerate or make an error in mathematical computation, because so many do come forward to receive this exceedingly small sum. On enquiry, you will find these live with their parents and are exempted from board, or pay a mere nominal amount, or else kind friends compassionate them and receive them into their homes during the summer months. Even at the best the majority of them cannot rise in salary beyond $392 ($400 less pension deduction). I do not believe that a teacher should necessarily be able to save the first year of her teaching, but after that she should be able to lay by in store for a rainy day and the old age, which comes none the less rapidly for the petty stings of insufficient means.

"Evil is wrought by want of thought far more than want of heart." I am positive our fellow-citizens do not recognize these facts or they would not suffer themselves to lie under this stigma. Do they wish their children educated at the expense of private individuals? If not, let them so raise their school tax as to pay their teachers a fair and just remuneration for labor conscientiously and successfully performed—so well done that our sons and daughters have almost universal success in competing with our neighbors across the line on their own ground. Why not vie with these neighbors in generosity to those who educate their children? Let me call your attention to statistics concerning several of the largest cities in the United States. They are furnished in answer to a letter asking for them, by the Superintendents of the various cities included in the table, and are furnished with a view to aiding our demand for higher salaries. I cannot too warmly thank these gentlemen for acceding, in many instances by return of mail, to my request for information. Their kindness was uniform; not one failed to reply, busy though they must unavoidably be.

While on the subject of thanks, let me also thank the fellow-teacher who both suggested to me the title of this paper and the best means of procuring information. I would thank him, if for no other reason, for the insight I have hereby gained into our Brother Jonathan's educational system, and I hope this injustice will ultimately be reformed in our own city.

In placing the balance on the right hand side, I have always taken the least favorable number mentioned and obtained the minimum result. Where the salary has been given as an average in both grammar and common schools, I choose the common school sum. Where women are not separately mentioned, as well as men, I have hunted down the scale of salaries till the former are distinctly mentioned, though in several instances there seems reason to believe some receive higher salaries. In Philadelphia, three ladies receive $2,015, but, as their position lapses with the cessation of their occupancy, I call the next lower amount the maximum. Otherwise, the order of the schools would be considerably altered,

City.	Grammar Schools Max.	Min.	Maj.	Common Schools Max.	Min.	Maj.	Per Week Board.	Balance.
New Orleans	$1,600	$ 750	....	$1,000	$350	$750	$6.00	$438
San Francisco	1,680	1,200	$1,500	960	600	800	6.00–$8.00	385
Philadelphia	1,550	800	....	1,400	450	700	4.50– 6.50	360
Brooklyn	1,750	1,250	....	700	400	600	6.00	288
Buffalo	1,400	400	800	1,200	400	600	6.00	288
Chicago	2,500	450	1,375	800	400	600	6.00	288
Pittsburg	2,500	600	1,193	600	350	500	3.50– 5.00	240
New York	1,900	740	1,170	1,015	504	643	6.00– 8.00	227
St. Louis	2,000	650	....	850	450	560	6.00– 7.00	195
			456	816	432	....	5.00– 8.00	185
Boston	1,080	456	754	650	450	580	7.00	180
Cleveland	1,600	800	....	700	400	550	6.00– 8.00	130
Cincinnati	1,200	600	....	500	250	343(?)	3.50– 5.00	83
Montreal	1,500	....	....					

City.	Max.	Min.	City.	Max.	Min.
Lowell	$ 450	$ 600	Detroit	$ 350	$ 600
Springfield	400	600	Indianapolis	500	650
Milwaukee	400	600	Kansas City	650	....
St. Paul	400	600	Providence	350	600
Baltimore	408	696	Worcester	450	600

San Francisco *claiming* to stand first (in the Superintendent's report which he sent me), and Boston second. San Francisco's Superintendent also sent me statistics of maximum and minimum salaries in ten other cities, which follow below the table. I have the papers from which these statistics are drawn and shall be happy to give any additional information in my power.

DOMESTIC LABOUR AND CONDITIONS OF WORK, 1910

'Good Cooking', *The Grain Growers' Guide*, 6 April 1910, vol. 4, 28.

Every here and there in the newspapers one sees little protests made against the disposition of the feminine youth of the land toward every line of trade and industry—factory work, what not—rather than toward that most needful of all works, the proper cooking of good foods. The protests are ineffective, however, and a remedy is sought, but, of course, never in the direction of the cause of girls' avoidance of housework and cooking as a means of livelihood. Yet there is a cause, a good cause, why girls seek every other avenue of labor rather than domestic labor.

In the first place, consider the people who employ labor in other lines. For the greater part they are merchants, professional men, factory owners, business men in a liberal interpretation of that term; men whose ideas have been broadened by contact and conflict with their fellows and have gotten past the narrow, meagre trifles that still cause so much friction to those who persist in seeing only those.

Now consider the employers in domestic service. They are, for the most part, women whose mental horizon is bounded by the walls of their own home, whose sympathies are all expended upon their own families; who have never tried to view life even theoretically from the angles of vision that is necessarily that of the domestic employee.

When a man goes out to farm labor he has regular hours for work. When a woman goes to farm labor, she works all the time, for no farmer will pay a woman wages unless he has work enough to keep her all the long day, and paying work at that, such as butter-making, for her to do. Now, the quality of the labor or its profit or otherwise to the farmer ought not to govern the hours of labor for the domestic. She should not be compelled to work longer than the man. She should be allowed some waking hours of every day for recreation, for her own pursuits, whatever they may be. It is the confining and endless supervised long, drawn out working day that makes the lot of the average domestic intolerable. Since it is a necessity to work late in the evenings and early in the mornings on the farm, surely compensations could be worked in in the afternoons were the employers willing and humane.

In cities a domestic has one afternoon a week out, and perhaps a chance to attend church service once a Sabbath. Every other hour of the waking week is her employers'. What unnecessary restraint—what needless servitude. There must be many an hour in the week of every servant which could be more profitably spent in a walk in the park, a visit to a friend, a call at the public library, than dawdling over work with no incentive to speed or efficiency which the promise of a short outing would bring about, to say nothing of improved health and spirits, and consequently more carefully prepared foods and more cheerful work in every department. Why surround the lives of our fellow creatures with greater restrictions than are necessary for our profit or for their comfort or well-being? It seems quite reasonable to aver that the healthful, fairly remunerative occupation of domestic service would gain a large army—of most desirable recruits from the ranks of the underpaid, underfed, unhealthful sewing room, store and office workers who at present prefer to half-starve that "they may call their souls their own" for a brief hour each day, and for the opportunity of association with their kind, for the isolation of the domestic is one of her standing grievances and a very just one. Pity it is that conditions affecting the labor of the paid house worker were not less irksome and lonely, so that many of our finest young women would seek this means of maintenance and endeavor to acquire a proficiency in the noble art of preparing food in a wholesome manner in order that mankind may benefit from the stimulus that well-cooked food gives.

It will, no doubt, appear "a far cry" to lay crime at the door of evil cooking, yet that is the indisputable conclusion arrived at after years of exhaustive inquiry by philanthropic Christian men, whose life work was to trace crime to its source, in order to remove its cause. A professor of a German criminological society reports that a private confidential questioning of some 1,500 prisoners held in five prisons, 300 in each, one in England, one in France, one in the United States and two in Germany, revealed the evidence that 305, or over twenty per cent, of these criminals, were led to crime through bad food. This is a terrible arraignment, and what is more it is claimed that more than half of them were reared in the country. Can it be possible that country cooking is so much worse than that in town or city—in the country where the freshest and best foods may be had.

Apart from the criminiality that seems beyond question to attend upon bad cooking, it seems most culpable that women will be content with anything short of the very best in such multitudes of cases where good food is furnished to work with.

Good cooking should be extolled as a fine art and the artists should have their place (other things being equal) in a world of recreation and recuperation, and then this almost abandoned field of labor will be re-organized and girls return to grace the occupation which they from choice would seek were it not interdicted by unfortunate prejudice.

MODERN CONVENIENCES FOR THE FARM, 1910

'Keeping the Girls on the Farm', *The Grain Growers' Guide*, 9 March 1910, vol. 4, 28.

...It may be thought that the preference of many country girls for city life is the fault of the farm boys. In the majority of cases, however, this is untrue. As a rule the country boy dresses as well, is as agreeable company, and can 'show a girl as good a time' as his city rival.

Neither is the migration of the girls to the city the result of the 'glamour' of city life, as we are often told. The first thought that a country girl has when she finds herself in a great city is, 'how dirty,' or 'how awfully crowded.' But, notwithstanding the dirt and the crowds she remains in the city. She would much prefer the blue grass sod and the back pasture to the cement sidewalks of the noisy streets, but she knows too well that if she were to become a farmer's wife she would have not time to take early morning walks in the sparkling dew, nor to spend the afternoons picking wild flowers and hunting for strawberries.

The girl has seen her mother give the best years of her life to rearing a large family of children, while running at the same time a boarding house and laundry for her husband and two or three hired men. The girl has been to visit friends in the city perhaps. She has opened her eyes in astonishment at the many labor-saving conveniences with which the house was supplied. The hot and cold water system, bathroom, gas range, refrigerator, furnace, and other such accessories that seem so much of a necessity in town, and yet are almost wholly lacking in the majority of country homes, fill her with a longing to live in a place where such devices are obtainable. When she goes home again 'the old oaken bucket' seems doubly heavy, and the work of picking up cobs to start a fire in the smoky stove doubly tedious. It is these simple conveniences, and not the brightly lighted streets, the theatre, nor the dance hall that constitute the so-called 'glamor' of city life.

We need the girls on the farm. We need them in the church and in the social life of the community. We need them to get up picnics once in a while, to pull us up out of the ruts that we are likely to sink into when we have nothing to think of but our work. We need them as an incentive for us to slick up once in a while, put on a clean collar and a happy smile, and spend Sunday afternoon in polishing up our neglected social qualities. But we do not need them to do the work of windmills, gasoline engines and steam laundries. There are too many things that only a girl or a woman can do to ask or even allow them to spend their life in a round of drudgery that can be largely eliminated by the use of a few modern conveniences.

AN IMMIGRANT'S EXPERIENCE, 1912

PAC, Department of the Interior, Immigration Files.

Mr. J. S. Graham   005305
                                                66 Arlington Avenue
                                                       ˙Westmount
                                                         Montreal
                                                      Oct. 22/1912

To the Superintendant of Immigration   (Stamped Immigration
                                                        Oct. 24 1912
Dear Sir: Received)
    In reply to your letter which I received on or about the twelfth of this month; I may say I have had nothing to regret since my arrival in Canada. I have been in Canada two years and three months, and I have got along very well. I have had very nice places, and have been treated very well indeed by my mistress. I like the country and since I have lived

in Canada I have had better health, than I ever did have in England. I find that if you are honest and straightforward you need have no fear of getting on; and if you leave one place you can soon find another. I would advise girls coming to Canada, to try and do just what the Canadians wants you to do; (I mean with reason) and don't try and tell them what we do in England; for their ways are not like the English ways, and of course we have to learn; and they will soon tell you, that you are not in England but Canada. I sincerely trust that, all girls who are thinking of coming to Canada, will get along alright, and that they may all be very happy; and above all don't forget you are English, and try and keep our standard up. I know lots of girls who thought that in Canada, they had to do no work, but they soon found out their mistake, for you have to work in Canada as you have elsewhere; and I find that you need a great deal of patience out here too. But if every girl does as well as I have done in the two situations I have been in; I feel sure they will not have anything to regret.

I arrived in Canada on July the second 1910; and obtained employment with Mrs. J. McLaren, Buckingham; and stayed with her about thirteen months. The wages I received during my stay there; were fourteen dollars monthly. I left of my own accord and came to stay with friends in Montreal. I have been in my present situation since June of this year, and I now receive fifteen dollars monthly; but I am happy and have got a nice situation.

In regard to advantages for domestics in England and Canada, I don't know for England, as all the girls I know, speak very highly of their English mistress and their situations; but I think Canada could be greatly improved for girls coming out from the Old Country.

I don't know if this is intended for the "Women's Domestic Guild" but it was under the auspices of the "Guild" that I came to Canada.

Of course the "Guild" has a great many advantages, but it has also its dis-advantages.

I would like to know why the girls are treated as they are on arrival in Canada? At the time I came, we all wondered if we were coming to a civilized country; for we were brought from the ship as though we were prisoners, and had to sit in a room, and hardly dare move, let alone speak. We were not allowed to bid good-bye to our friends we had made during the voyage, and in fact, I think they thought we were heathens. Several passengers passed the remark as we were driven as cattle. I have met several "Guild girls", since I have been in Montreal, and they all say the same; that we don't get a very good impression of Canada or her people on our arrival here. Now I would like to know the reason, why the "Guild girls" are treated like that? Of course the "Guild" does it self a lot of harm by such treatment; for no girls is going to ask her friends to come, when she knows how they will be treated; we all have feelings for others, and would not bring them from home and loved ones, to be broken-hearted on their arrival in Canada. If you could give me a good reason for such treatment I would be very glad. And again how is it that all the fares are not the same? Why has some girls, even if they pay their fare to Liverpool have just as much to pay as those who don't? And why have some to place a deposit in England and others have not?

And why does it say the girls have twenty four hours rest on arrival, when some of them are sent out to places as soon as they can, after arrival in Montreal? And why are the girls not told about vaccination in England? I did not know so I was vaccinated on board the ship; a week later I was taken ill; and the Dr. said I had got inflamation in my ankles, and blood-poisoning, all through my system; very encouraging for a young emigrant, and all caused through vaccination.

Now I think the most important question that we girls have to ask is:— Why is there not a proper "Guild" room or some Home for the many girls that come out under their care? We all have to pay ten shillings as member-ship fee, but what benefit do we derive from the "Guild"? none at all. I am sure that what the girls pay to the "Guild", a proper place could be built for the benefit of the same; and where the girls could always find a shelter. How many girls are there in Montreal who have no friends and no where to go? Can you wonder at girls who are not strong-willed going astray? I have met at least six girls from the Guild, who have no friends or no where to go in Montreal; they have to spend their evenings and Sundays in the house; or go straight to Church and come back; or they roam the streets, and of course we know, that it is not a very good idea, but can you wonder? a girl in the house all week wants a little change.

I think, and I am not the only one, that a place could be built out of the money the girls pay, where they could go and spend their evenings and Sundays; and stay when they leave one situation; and of course renew the member-ship fee each year, or to suit the girls best; and why not have different classes each evening; in fact I think it could be carried on the same principle as the Y.W.C.A. and other Institutions; and have it under the supervision of a good Christian Matron; and then it would be a "Home from Home"; and I feel sure much appreciated by the majority of the girls.

Miss Mary Thompson
c/o Mrs. H. B. Young
   66 Arlington Avenue
     Westmount
      Montreal,
       P.Q.

Yours in Anticipation
Mary Thompson

A SURVEY OF WOMAN'S WORK, 1919

Marjory MacMurchy, *The Canadian Girl at Work* (Ontario, Ministry of Education, 1919), preface, iii-vi.

The life of the average woman is divided, generally, into two periods of work, that of paid employment and that of home-making. No adequate scheme of training for girls can fail to take account of this fact. They should be equipped with knowledge and skill for home-making, and assisted in making the best use of their years in paid work. Happily, it appears from an investigation of the conditions affecting girls as wage-earners that the knowledge which helps them to be good home-makers is necessary to their well-being in paid employment. Technical training and skill are not more helpful to a girl at work than specialized knowledge in matters of food, clothing, health, and daily regimen. Lack of training in home-making is probably the greatest drawback which a girl in paid employment can have. Her business during her first years of paid employment may not require much skill or experience, but her living conditions require all the specialized woman's knowledge that training can give her. . . .

When considering the employments of to-day as part of their own lives, girls of the twentieth century may well look back through the long ages to women's work in the past. The study of anthropology appears to indicate that in primeval ages women began the textile industry and, possibly, agriculture. There seems to be no doubt that they were primitive architects, and that they tamed some of the smaller domestic animals. They had most to do with the preparation of food and may have introduced the use of herbs and medicines. They were spinners, weavers, upholsterers, and sail-makers. Most of these employments were taken up by men and specialized and developed almost past imagination. It is evident that women have always worked, and worked hard. If they had not done so, the race would not have reached its present position, and women themselves would have remained undeveloped, without a realization of their own possibilities.

The history of Anglo-Saxon times shows women engaged in spinning, weaving, dyeing, and embroidering, carrying on these industrial arts in the home, side by side with the work of the house. The work of women in home manufactures was a by-industry, not occupying the worker's whole time, but nevertheless an important occupation. Later, women were employed in many kinds of industrial work as assistants to their husbands and fathers. It is doubtful if wages were paid for such work. Employment of this kind is not to be thought of merely as a romantic or picturesque accompaniment of home life. Houses and comforts centuries back were not such as they are to-day; and the work of women was toil, side by side with men who toiled also.

The modern factory did not originate industrial work. The factory carried many industries away from the home where they had originated; and women followed their work to large establishments where they were trained to work collectively. The statement can be made with truth that machinery has made it possible for women to perform work for which their strength would otherwise have been insufficient. Through the industrial revolution brought about by factory work, the general body of women workers became wage-earners, rather than unpaid workers who contributed to the financial earnings of their fathers and husbands.

In Canada, the process of development of women's work in the past fifty years has been rapid. The grandmothers of the women of this generation carded wool and used spinning wheels within the memory of workers of less than middle age. One old woman who died not many years ago told how she used to bake in an oven out-of-doors and had dyed homespun with butternut. The soap cauldron stood on the levelled stump of what had been once a forest tree. Candles were moulded in iron moulds. Household industries were carried on expertly in the homes of pioneers by the women of the family.

When these days had gone, there followed other days in which the children of the pioneers devoted themselves to the schooling so highly esteemed but rarely enjoyed by their parents. The boys, after school life, turned to business, railway employments, teaching, banking, farming, became ministers, lawyers, doctors, or gave their thoughts to politics. The girls taught school, were milliners or dressmakers, went into shops, or became the wives of nation builders in every walk of life. A few were nurses, journalists, doctors, or missionaries.

The work of that generation has been followed by a century in which Canadian girls are invited to share in nearly every form of activity. This great freedom with its many opportunities has come for noble ends. What the girls of to-day must strive to do is to take up their work with a vision of what it may be made to mean—men and women in co-partnership laying the foundations of a new earth.

It is probable that the social and domestic conditions of the earliest workers were far below those of the average worker of to-day. But, although present conditions are better than those of the past, the process of amelioration should be greatly advanced by this generation. The increasing opportunities of girls, both in home-making and paid employment, are likely to become a contributing factor in the humanizing of every form of industry. We have learned to realize the possibilities of machinery. What we must do now is to imagine and realize the possibilities of the individual worker. This can be done only through study, experience, and actual work in industrial occupations which offer employment to women.

The woman of the home has work of unrivalled value. She has to study new standards of living, to help to control the food supply, to improve the health of children, and to lower the rate of infant mortality. A standard of living in each community might be tabulated by women home-makers. Such information should be available in each locality and should be accessible to all classes in the community. How are workers—girls, boys, men, or women—to know on what sums individuals and families can live and maintain health and efficiency in one district or another, if these matters are not studied, determined, and published for their use?

5. ORGANIZATIONS

Many aspects of Canadian society placed women at a disadvantage—in law, in economics, and in education. There were also many features of that society that needed reforming—poverty, crime, and intemperance. If women were going to make any impact upon that society in order to better their own position in it and help to solve some of its problems, they would have to group together. Many women's clubs were formed for social and cultural purposes, but some of the most interesting ones were organized to exert moral pressure on those people and institutions that could change society.

By the end of the nineteenth century women's clubs and organizations had begun to proliferate. But banding together was hardly a new phenomenon. At a very early stage in the history of Canada—first in New France and later in the English-speaking parts of the country—women had organized to provide education, hospitals, and orphanages. Sometimes these were women in religious orders, at others they were pioneer women responding to the immediate needs of a new community. As the society moved beyond the pioneering stage women continued to organize for philanthropic, educational, and religious purposes. The leading women in a community could often afford some domestic help, and this allowed them time to engage in activities outside the home.

As the century progressed technology and labour-saving devices lessened the household burdens of more and more women. Increasing amounts of leisure time could now be devoted to fulfilling those social responsibilities that the Christian consciences of many Canadian women urged them to take up. In early twentieth-century society positive approaches appeared to be necessary to combat disease, unsanitary living and working conditions, delinquency, and prostitution. These were problems that struck at the very centre of the home, for disease recognized no economic barriers. Consequently some of the earliest women's organizations—the Woman's Christian Temperance Union, and the Young Women's Christian Association, to take two obvious examples—directed the energies of Canadian women towards those problems that seemed to threaten family and home life. Who were better qualified to devise responses to these social problems than other women?

With the expansion of Canadian cities and towns women became aware that local charity organizations were no longer sufficient to meet the needs of an increasingly mobile society. Organizations with provincial, national, and even international connections gradually sprang into existence. The following is only a partial list of women's clubs formed in late nineteenth and early twentieth century: the Woman's Christian Temperance Union, 1883; the National Council of Women of Canada, 1893; the Young Women's Christian Association, 1893; the Imperial Order of the Daughters of the Empire, 1900; the Women's Institutes, 1897; the National Council of Jewish Women, 1894; International Order of King's Daughters and Sons, 1886; Aberdeen Association, 1897; the Girls' Friendly Society of Canada, 1882; the Victorian Order of Nurses, 1897; the Dominion Women's Enfranchisement Association, 1889; the Catholic Women's League, 1920; the Canadian Federation of University Women, 1919. To these could be added a plethora of musical, historical, literary, charitable, and athletic societies. Initially almost all these clubs organized for one specific purpose, but in most cases one interest led to many others. For example the W.C.T.U. was originally established to combat intemperance. Yet by the turn of the century it had twenty-six departments covering such diverse subjects as dress reform, the conservation of certain endangered species of birds, and the teaching of domestic science in schools.

What was the attraction of these clubs? For one thing they did not absorb a lot of a woman's time and thus did not interfere with normal domestic duties. To those stepping outside the home for the first time they provided the security that went with being associated with like-minded women. And of course they gave these women a sense of doing something useful and humanitarian, a sense of importance at a time when the demands of domestic life were growing less exacting. Through these clubs many Canadian women learned the skills of organization, public speaking, and social investigation, and this may have been of more importance than the aims for which the women had allegedly come together.

Perhaps most significant, these were *women*'s organizations, founded, organized, and run by and for women. Men were excluded. In these clubs women could create and enjoy their own social values, free from those of the normally male-dominated society in which they lived. They did, however, accept for the most part the predominant view that women's primary role was played out in the home. Indeed most of the club activities were designed to ensure that the home remained the fundamental unit of Canadian society. That belief ensured that club women would extol the virtues of domesticity even when their participation in these organizations revealed that women were gradually discovering new roles for themselves outside the home.

THE NATIONAL COUNCIL OF WOMEN, 1894

Women Workers of Canada, National Council of Women of Canada
(Ottawa, 1894), pp. 10-13.

The First Annual Meeting of Conference of the National Council of
Women of Canada opened in the Convocation Hall at the Normal
School, at 10 o'clock, Wednesday Morning, April the 11th.

THE PRESIDENT [Lady Aberdeen].—Ladies, it is with feelings of the
greatest responsibility that I take the chair this morning as the first President of the first National Council of Women of Canada. When this movement was set on foot I think we could scarcely have hoped that at our first
annual meeting we should be able to come together representing so many
different districts of the country, and with the hope of including yet many
more. But we do come here to-day feeling that we can truly say that we
represent women of all the different races, sections, classes and churches
that go to make up Canada. We come together as women who are more or
less alive to the high duties and opportunities which are ours in virtue of
our womanhood, but who are at the same time earnestly desirous to make
their work more effective for the common good by taking counsel with one
another as to the carrying on of our grand women's mission. Some seem
inclined to regret that this organization was not formed on lines which
would have included all workers without respect to sex; but I think we feel
that we can probably do best, at least for a time, by keeping by ourselves,
and that we need to go through an apprenticeship. Perhaps if we show what
we can do, and how we can be successful on these lines, others may follow.

But in the meantime, how can be best describe this woman's mission in
a word? Can we not best describe it as "mothering" in one sense or
another? We are not all called upon to be mothers of little children, but
every woman is called upon to "mother" in some way or another; and it
is impossible to be in this country, even for a little while, and not be
impressed with a sense of what a great work of "mothering" is in a special
sense committed to the women of Canada.

It is one of the great glories of this country that almost all its people are
workers, and that there are very few drones. Its sons are all engrossed in
the battle of life, striving for a sufficiency for themselves and their dear
ones; and therefore on the women, hard-worked though they often are
with domestic duties, must devolve the duty of building up the homes of
the nation in the truest sense. And what sort of homes? Homes where the
love of all that is beautiful and artistic and cultured is natural; where the
true dignity of labour of every kind is recognized and acted upon; where
a spirit of patriotism inspires young men and maidens to count it a high

privilege to serve their country with single-minded disinterestedness, in however humble a way; where mutual love, consideration, forbearance, are the common rule, and the spirit of self-sacrifice is accounted the first necessity in the glorious work of helping others.

Are these homes common, either in this or in any land? And if not, if we find the majority of children going out into the world from homes where the custom has been to look upon life not as a high mission and duty, but rather as a search for happiness, a study of their own well-being, must we not admit that the women have failed in their first duty, that they have not known how rightly to reign in that kingdom where none dispute their sway? (Applause.) They may have made their homes healthy and comfortable; they may have provided good and wholesome dinners, and seen that the babies were properly clothed and fed—and far indeed be it from any of us to minimize these the very foundations of home life! Well indeed were it for every home if it were built on these foundations. But the house needs more than foundations. The woman who aspires to make home a place for rest after work and for strengthening before labor, a centre of holy associations and inspiring memories, has need herself to be in touch with every side of our manifold life. She must realize that no walls can shelter her dear ones from the temptations, the sorrows, the discouragements of life. She must needs arm then with armour suited for the fray. She must learn that if the poor around her doors are not cared for, the orphans not housed, the erring not reclaimed, because she was too much engrossed in her own house to lend a helping hand, the results of her self-absorption may be in the future to provide pitfalls for her own children, whom she so desires to cherish. If she is to be truly her husband's companion, her children's friend and guide, the maker of a home that will shed light and blessing, not only on its own inmates, but on the strangers who pass from time to time within her gates, she must needs understand the changes that are taking place in social conditions, the progress of thought in all directions.

For this also is a special and peculiar feature of woman's work in Canada. Day by day strangers come into this beautiful land, young men and maidens, on whom the future of this country depends. What is Canada, which has had so fair a beginning, to become? We indulge in golden dreams of a free, prosperous, law-abiding, God-fearing people, making use of their prosperity for the good of the community, and bringing up a race who will be a blessing to the world. But what guarantee have we for the realization of these dreams? We may indeed point to the past, of which every Canadian has reason to be proud; we may point to the educational system of this country, to our churches, to the manifold organizations which are being carried on for the good of the people; but what of those strangers whom we are hoping to see come in ever-increasing numbers to take up their homes amongst us? Are they to be a source of strength or of weakness? We recognize that these strangers need binding together with ourselves by a power far stronger than can be supplied by laws or government, and is not that power largely in the hands of women? Do not the destinies of the country depend very much upon how they are moulded through the influences which are brought to bear upon them in the homes which open kindly doors of welcome, and which keep alive within them that high ideal of a pure and holy family life which is the chief strength of all nations? I trust and pray that this Council, which is now assembled for the first time, may be able to forge a mighty bond of union between us all in arousing us to realize the full scope and glory of our vocation as home-makers and home-builders, and to understand all that that involves.

I think we have good reason not only to hope but to believe that this will be the case, as we look at the programme which is before us today. Whether in the resolutions or in the sections for conference, we see the idea of this "mothering" of which I spoke running through all. Whether it be the providing of police matrons or of women inspectors for introducing industrial training into our schools; or the encouragement of unity of purpose and work; or the cultivation of art, and music, and literary effort, and the love of all that is beautiful; or the caring for the fatherless and motherless, the sick and the fallen; or the examination into the science of motherhood and the problem of domestic service, we see the same thought running through all—the caring for others, the striving to act towards all who come within our influence in the spirit of our Father, who thinks for all, cares for all, has patience for all, whose "loving kindness is over all His works". It is to further the application of His golden rule that this Council has been formed, and I am very sure that we meet together this morning with our hearts full of thankfulness to Him for the way by which He has led us so far, for the fellow-workers whom He has given us in this Council, for the guidance and the blessing which He has vouchsafed during the perilous and difficult times of organization, and for this new opportunity which he affords us of being fellow-workers with Him for all that makes for righteousness.

We are bound to meet with difficulties; we are sure to buy our experience by mistakes; we are very human, and in coming into close contact one with another in handling subjects which touch very nearly our hearts and lives, perhaps that frail humanity of ours will be sorely tried at times. But do not let us be afraid of or shirk these difficulties; let us only hold fast that golden rule which is the basis of our Council, and then let us meet difficulties bravely, let us grasp our nettle firmly, believing that by these means we shall surely win our way along the road of progress to the goal which we have in view. . . .

ACHIEVEMENTS OF THE NATIONAL COUNCIL OF WOMEN,
1898

Lady Aberdeen, "Address', in *Women Workers of Canada*, National
Council of Women of Canada (Ottawa, 1898), pp. 362-4.

It would ... be a useful piece of work to have ... a history [of the Council]
written, and as I like to get my work done for me, I am going to offer two
prizes for the two best essays on the history and work of the Council since
its institution and two other prizes for the best essays on the aims and future
ideal for the Council. These prizes are open to all who care to compete for
them, but, of course, are especially offered to the members of the Council,
who have the best oportunity of understanding the subject. I should like
these essays to be sent in to me at Government House by October 1st, and I
am hopeful that the successful papers may prove of great assistance to our
Councils and to our workers generally.

They will have plenty of material to deal with in the past achievements
of the Council both from national and social points of view

Let me give a rough outline of these for the benefit of those here who
are unacquainted with our work and who have an idea we only meet
together to talk.

1. It obtained the endorsation of the Educational Department to the
introduction of Manual Training and the instruction in Domestic Science
in the public schools of Ontario, and the training of teachers so that they
may be able to give instruction in these arts. It has also given an impetus
to the same movement in other Provinces.

2. It has obtained the appointment of Women Factory Inspectors for
factories and workshops where women are employed in the Provinces of
Quebec and Ontario.

3. It has obtained the extension of the provisions of the Factory Act in
Ontario as regards the supervision of women workers.

4. It has obtained the appointment of women on the Boards of School
Trustees in New Brunswick, and the amendment of the School Act so that
they may be elected in British Columbia.

5. It has brought about very desirable changes in the arrangements for
women prisoners in various places, notably in the City of Quebec, where
matrons are now in charge of the women, and young girls are now sent to
a separate institution.

6. It has organized in various centres Boards of Associated Charities or
other systems of co-operation in the relief of distress, and is still working
in this direction wherever it has opportunity so to do, and is this year
circulating a valuable paper or study on the problem of the unemployed.

7. It has established hospitals in some of its smaller centres.

8. It originated the Victorian Order of Nurses and has taken a leading part in its establishment in various centres.

9. It has organized Cooking Schools, Cooking Classes and at Quebec is helping in the formation of a Training School for Domestic Service.

10. It has spread sanitary knowledge, especially by means of Health Talks for Mothers given by physicians. This has been specially successful in Montreal, both amongst the French and English mothers.

11. It has held an enquiry all over the country into the circulation of Impure Literature, and has been able to do something, as well as to warn parents and teachers as to the very real danger that exists in this direction. It hopes to be able to do more both by legislation and by circulation of healthy and interesting literature. It also inaugurated the Home Reading Union to promote habits of good and systematic reading.

12. It instituted enquiries into the conditions surrounding working women in various centres, and urges on its members various methods whereby they may work for their amelioration.

13. It conducted an enquiry into the laws for the Protection of Women and Children, and has laid certain recommendations before the Minister of Justice which it earnestly hopes he will adopt when amending the Criminal Law.

14. It is at the present moment earnestly concerning itself in the Care and Treatment of the Aged Poor, so many of whom now find their only refuge in the jails for want of any other provision for them. On the authority of the Chief Inspector of Prisons for Ontario, some 60 per cent of the jail population of that Province belong to the infirm, aged, destitute, feeble-minded class.

15. It is now calling on all its members to unite in efforts for the Protection of Animal or Bird Life from useless destruction in the interests of fashion.

16. Through one of its affiliated societies it is endeavoring a plan for the Better Care and Wiser Distribution of Women Immigrants than has hitherto been possible.

17. It is pledged to co-operate with Dr. Bryce and other medical authorities, in urging immediate measures to be taken to check the ever-increasing ravages of consumptive diseases in this country, to spread knowledge on the subject, and to press responsibility home on individuals.

18. It will endeavour to promote the Systematic Instruction in Art Design, adaptable to industries and manufactures, as opening up a field full of opportunities for women.

I might largely increase this list if I were to describe various other useful efforts instituted by our Local Councils, but I forbear.

Perhaps you think that "these are mere deeds on paper," but I assure you that this is not the case, and that all this has been brought about by earnest, devoted work, which must bear fruit apart from its immediate results. The results which we can thus report are a surprise to ourselves, I know, as we see them gathered together, and they rebuke us for our want of faith. It is a constant source of delight and astonishment to see how elastic and adaptable our Constitution has shown itself, and how it can develop just to suit the needs of each place but possessing everywhere *one great distinguishing characteristic—that it brings together and blends for common work the most earnest women of every place, irrespective of creed, class, political party or race.* That is the great achievement of the Council.

THE W.C.T.U. AND TEMPERANCE FOR SEAMEN, 1897

Woman's Christian Temperance Union (Nova Scotia, 1897), pp. 21-2.

REFORMS FOR SEAMEN

In view of the fact that sailors and fishermen, owing to long absences from land, are specially liable to be the victims of the saloon when on shore, and in view of the promised plebiscite in the near future, we suggest, that our provincial and local superintendents of this department, pay marked attention to the distribution of suitable prohibition literature, as a means of improving the minds, and influencing the votes, of these classes.

We further strongly suggest that when possible, personal canvass be made among these classes, and that the literature distributed be backed up by personal appeal on behalf of prohibition.

BECAUSE

1. It is right;
2. It will reduce criminals;
3. It will exterminate pauperism;
4. It will cut down the cost of penitentiaries, jails, poor houses and asylums;
5. All license systems have proven a failure;
6. The money employed in liquor, if invested in other industries, would employ more men;
7. It would promote thrift, and general business prosperity;
8. It will put more money circulating in legitimate channels;
9. It will provide better homes, better clothes, and better food, for the people;
10. It can be enforced as well as any criminal law;

11. It will make the sailor as happy and as safe on land as he is on sea;

12. It will give the sailor's wife and children continual joy, peace, prosperity and love.

We suggest that in our department we begin work now; that every union be responsible for the work just at hand, at home first, other places next, if possible.

We suggest that other lines of work, leaflets issued by the Dominion alliance for the suppression of the liquor traffic be distributed very largely among our sailors and fishermen. See to it now.

Notably among these leaflets we would suggest "Thy Bottle," "What it Costs," "Beer-drinking and Business."

We suggest that other lines of work, as sailors' rooms, gospel temperance services, comfort bags and literature distribution, Christmas letters be not forgotten.

We would also suggest to the consideration of our unions the mission to deep sea fishermen, which on this side of the Atlantic finds an outlet at Labrador.

I would suggest to superintendents that they subscribe for "Toilers of the Deep," a monthly record of mission work amongst them. Frequently in this magazine may be found an account of the work done at Labrador. This magazine will tell us much that we need to know about the mission. While we commence work at home, let us broaden out with true missionary spirit.

Let our motto for this year in our department be: Our department for Jesus.

Respectfully submitted,
O.C. WHITMAN.

THE CHURCH WORK OF PROTESTANT WOMEN IN CANADA, 1900

Frances Elizabeth Murray, 'The Church Work of Protestant Women in Canada' (Other than Roman Catholic), in *Women of Canada: Their Life and Work*, compiled by The National Council of Women of Canada (Ottawa, 1900), pp. 296-302.

The Church work of Protestant women in Canada began when the first British Colonists came to the country, and like all permanent and effective work in this progressive world, it has proceeded along the lines of evolution and gradual development. It has had its initial stages, its periods of growth, and it can also show the promise of unknown future possibilities.

As the statistics of the work are to be dealt with elsewhere, the effort in this Essay will be to give word-pictures or short accounts of the different stages through which, since its beginning, the Church work of Protestant women has passed, and to outline its present state of development.

The initial stage in years gone by was often to be seen in the depths of a Canadian forest. A log-house, the new home of the immigrant and his family, stands in the middle of a "clearing." The week has been a hard struggle with the giants of the forest, but now it is Sunday, the husband is restfully smoking as he sits on one of the huge stumps, and the wife, who has toiled through the week from early morning until late at night to make her husband and children comfortable, has now gathered the little ones round her under the shade of the maples and the sweet-scented spruce. They are far away from their old home, which may have been within the sound of Cathedral chimes, or near some "auld Kirk" of bonnie Scotland, or they may have been members of some fervent warm-hearted Methodist or Baptist congregation. All is now changed, but the children are in their "Sunday best," they are repeating their Bible verses, their hymns or their catechism, they are learning a lesson of Sunday observance and worship, and Protestant women's Church work in Canada has begun. Thus here and there in many a lonely spot, the roots of religion were quietly planted in Eastern Canada by women's hands, and now in the far North-West of our wide Dominion, the same work is being initiated in the same unobtrusive way.

Years passed on—the immigrant's log-cabin has given place to the colonist's neat cottage. The clearing has grown wider; the sky is no longer hemmed in by the pointed tops of fir and spruce trees. Neighbours are not far distant, and a schoolhouse stands near the centre of the settlement. There, Sunday after Sunday, women's work is again in evidence. It is possible that the superintendent may be one of the principal men of the village, but at the head of each class sits a woman and in the arrangement of classes, in the preparation for Sunday School treats, in the discussion of plans for raising money to build a place of worship, the Church work of Protestant women in Canada shows its first rudimentary signs of organization.

As the century grows older, Canadians are linked more closely together, and their life, both secular and religious, runs with a fuller, deeper current. Settlements and villages develop into thriving towns from each of which more than one spire ascends; every spire indicating a radiating centre of woman's active religious work, which is now more prominent than before. Sunday schools increase in number and importance. The village "Sewing Circle" which had for its object the raising of money for Church purposes is divided into several societies, each with its special Missionary or Church work. Presidents, vice-presidents, secretaries, are chosen by ballot, committees are formed, reports of the proceedings appear in print and thus even the most conservative are prepared to enter the wider and more varied field of Church work which is opening before women at the present day. This work may be classified thus: (1) Work in connection with the Church edifice and with the Church services. (2) Sunday School work. (3) Work among the poor of the parish or congregation. As regards the first division, it may be said that Protestant women in Canada have contributed largely to the funds raised during the last fifty years for the building and adornment of churches. Many wealthy women have presented windows, organs, pulpits and large sums of money as individual gifts, but a great deal of money for church purposes has also been obtained in a more laborious way by bazaars, or sales of fancy work. These may be condemned, criticized, tolerated or praised, but they are too prominent a part of woman's work to be ignored. It might seem at first sight that these occasions are but frivolous, self-indulgent plans for raising money, which ought to be given in a more earnest fashion. But those who look below the surface know how much self-denying toil, how much anxious thought, are called out in the preparation and organization of these affairs, which, while obtaining money, serve at the same time to draw the members of Churches closer together in the bond of a common aim and common work, an important object in these days of disintegration among Church members not equally endowed with this world's goods. Thus it is that almost every church has its annual sale; earnest thoughtful women, giving their sanction and aid to proceedings that they evidently consider both legitimate and beneficial.

Also in the services of the Church, women do much to increase the interest by a full and regular attendance. In Episcopal liturgical churches, there are altar guilds and chancel guilds, the duties being to attend to the vestments of the clergy and choirs, to provide flowers and other chancel decorations. Most exquisite embroidery is done for stoles, altar cloths and chalice veils; time and money being as lavishly given as was the spikenard ointment in olden times by Mary of Bethany. In non-liturgical churches such work is not needed, but they have their Ladies' Aid societies which attend to the decorations of the church and other accessories of worship. Also in these churches, which as a rule have no boy choristers, women assist in the musical part of the services, forming an important portion of mixed choirs. Even in liturgical churches, women are often needed to support the boys' voices, and lately in several Canadian churches women wearing the usual vestments have altogether replaced the boy choristers.

The second and most important work done by women for the Church is in Sunday Schools. It must be acknowledged with regret that owing to various causes, such as the divided state of our religious opinions, the pressure of study, the rush of home life, our children get but little systematic religious instruction either at home, or at the day schools. Thus the Sunday School is absolutely necessary to make our young people acquainted with the contents of our sacred book, the Bible; to teach the fundamental truths of Christianity and their application to daily life, and at the same time to foster a thoughtful realization of the unseen, a devotional spirit of worship. This Sunday School work has passed largely into the hands of women. The pastor often acts as superintendent, or one of the prominent members of the church is elected to the office. Young men act as librarians. Perhaps one or two boys' classes have male teachers, but it may be safely affirmed that, throughout Canada, Sunday School teachers are very generally women. This is not surprising. Child-teaching and child-training are familiar duties to a woman, but men after being absorbed in business during the week find themselves unfitted on Sunday for such unaccustomed work. Our Canadian women feel the weight of this responsibility, and although they lead busy lives, they fit themselves for their Sunday School duties by study, by attending Teachers' conferences and by passing Teachers' examinations. Many papers also on Sunday School subjects are written by women and read before conferences. These papers have been published and one or two have appeared in a well-known English Sunday School magazine. The latest development of Sunday School work must not be omitted—work among the Chinese; these foreigners are knocking at the doors of our Sunday Schools. We should be hardly worthy of our Christian name did we refuse them admittance. They are quiet, attentive pupils, eager to learn English and very grateful to their teachers.

We now mention thirdly the charitable Church work done by women among the poor. This is very diversified. In small churches much friendly intercourse takes place and kindly help is given in a quiet, individual way; but large churches have their district visitors, their Bible women, their deaconesses and a few have "sisters," distinguished by their peculiar dress. These make regular visits to the poor. They find and report those who need and deserve help. When possible they give a word of advice, and are aiding to bridge over the chasm which is widening between "the classes and masses." Then there are Mothers' meetings where hard-working women spend a couple of hours together one afternoon in the week. They sew while ladies read to them or give them a little music; after that comes the cup of tea. Also, about sixteen years ago, a Canadian Branch of the Girls' Friendly Society was started by members of the Church of England to hold out a helping hand to working girls of any denomination and to provide a pleasant place for evening meetings and recreation. Besides all this, there are connected with every Church, Bands and Associations of willing helpers, who, under various names, are doing their share of Church work. They get up musical and literary entertainments to create social intercourse among Church members and to procure money for Church purposes, they prepare Christmas presents for their Sunday School tree, or send gifts to far-off Missions.

Having thus far watched the Church work of Protestant women through .

its earlier stages, we now come to its latest, its highest, its most unselfish development, in the great organizations formed to carry on Missionary work among the Red Indians of our North-West Territory and among the heathen of China, Japan, India and the islands of the sea. For some time we, in the colonies, considered ourselves in the position of those who needed help rather than of those whose aid was called for in Missionary work. Collections, it is true, were made from time to time for Missions, but no systematized work was done. To the Baptist denomination belongs the credit of the first Missionary movement among Protestant women in the Maritime Provinces. In 1870, an enthusiastic girl, Miss Norris, of Canso, Nova Scotia, travelled through her Province arousing the interest of women in their sisters in heathen lands. She formed thirty-three Mission Bands, and then went herself as a Missionary to Burmah. In 1876 the Presbyterian women of Canada were organized into two large Missionary Boards or Auxiliaries, one for Eastern, one for Western Canada, in connection with the Eastern and Western sections of their Foreign Missionary Committee. In 1881, at the Ladies' College, Hamilton, a Society was inaugurated under the title of "The Woman's Missionary Society of the Methodist Church in Canada." And in 1886, at a meeting of representative women of the Church of England in Montreal, a Woman's Auxiliary to the Church of England Board of Missions was formed, which has increased very rapidly in numbers and contributions. Thousands of women are enrolled in these large societies and similar smaller ones, all of which are organized on much the same plan. The Central Society is composed of many affiliated Societies which have numerous Branches. The Branches make their collections, and send in their reports to the larger Societies, these again send in collections and reports to the Central Society, which meets annually in some large city.

The great object of all this work of Protestant women is to extend the knowledge of Christian truth, and the benefits of Christian education and civilization to their sisters deprived of these blessings, by sending out Missionaries and school teachers, and by building and supporting churches, schools and hospitals. The statistics will show the large sums of money which are collected and disbursed yearly by Protestant women in Canada for these purposes. This expenditure is most carefully regulated, each Board having several secretaries (generally unpaid) who are in correspondence with the Missionaries and are intimately acquainted with the needs of the Mission field. To fully estimate the extent of this Mission work, it is necessary to attend one of the annual meetings of a large society. Representative women come from a distance as delegates and are hospitably entertained. Three or four days are devoted to business. Reports are presented from different parts of the Mission field, appeals for help are received and considered, appropriations are judiciously granted, and woman's work receives an impulse and impetus nowhere else to be felt, until of late years "The National Council of Canada" was formed.

There is one more feature to note in the Church work of Protestant women—and that the most pathetic and interesting—the lives of hardship and danger so cheerfully endured by women who go out from our societies as Missionaries in foreign lands, or in our Northern regions. Each Society has its own tale of suffering and privation through which its Missionaries are passing, or have passed. Want of space forbids the mention of more than two instances. A Canadian woman in Japan, Mrs. Large, of the Methodist Society, went through the terrible experience of seeing her husband murdered before her eyes, she barely escaping with her own life. Another Canadian woman has accompanied her husband to the far North, where, within the Arctic circle, they are working as Missionaries of the Church of England among the poor Eskimos. The self-sacrifice and privations of such a life can be but faintly realized, yet the Rev. Mr. Stringer and his devoted wife are braving all difficulties, and have so endeared themselves by teaching the children and caring for the sick during an epidemic that they have been named the "Father" and "Mother" of the tribe.

We have described the development of the Church work of Protestant women in Canada up to the present day, the future is beyond our ken, but through the veil of mist which hides the distant prospect may be read in letters of living light,

"That which they have done but earnest of the things which they shall do."

FRANCES ELIZABETH MURRAY.

St. John, N.B.

THE W.C.T.U. IN B.C., 1912

Woman's Christian Temperance Union, British Columbia, *Report*, 1912, pp. 79-82.

RESOLUTIONS

1. Resolved, that we, the White Ribboners of British Columbia return thanks to the Heavenly Father for His loving care and protection dur'ng the twenty-eight years we have been organized, and that we take fresh courage and continue vigorously to work for the overthrow of every legalized vice, and the elevation of the standard of citizenship of our well-favored province.

2. Resolved, that we place on record our hearty appreciation of the

untiring efforts of our provincial officers, the work accomplished through their efforts, and pray that God's blessing may rest upon them.

3. Resolved, that we place on record our appreciation of the aggressive efforts of the Ministerial Associations and individual clergymen, and Good Government Leagues throughout the province on behalf of moral reform.

4. Resolved, that we convey to the Attorney-General the appreciation of the W.C.T.U. of the province of the more stringent enforcement of the liquor license laws, and for a measure of the observance of the Lord's Day Act.

5. Resolved, that as an organization we lend our energies to combat the evils of children attending questionable places of amusement, inasmuch as this tends to a low conception of life, and that we endeavor to secure censorship for theatres and moving picture shows.

5.[sic] Resolved, that we heartily commend and urge the support of the Victoria News for the splendid assistance it has given the work of moral reform, and that we urge upon White Ribboners that they stand loyally by those who give space in their papers to the interests of temperance and reform work.

6. Whereas, there is no restriction as to the hours of sale of liquor in unorganized districts, and the moral conditions, and the peace of said districts are greatly disturbed thereby.

Resolved, that the Attorney-General be approached to ascertain if there cannot be restriction of the hours of sale of liquor in these, as in organized districts.

7. Whereas, we deplore the fact that the Criminal Code of Canada as it applies to segregated districts of vice is not enforced;

Resolved, that the unions in the cities and towns throughout the province urge upon the authorities their responsibility in this regard, and suggest that frequenters, equally with inmates, be punished, and if possible that the names of owners of property used for purposes of vice be published.

8. Whereas, more than one-half the pupils in the public schools are girls, and four-fifths of the teachers are women, and whereas women are more definitely connected with the education of the children, and experience has taught that the influence of boards of school trustees has been most helpful;

Resolved, that we urge the W.C.T.U. in every municipality to endeavor to get capable and properly qualified women to offer themselves as candidates at the election for school trustees, and further that the W.C.T.U. pledge their heartiest support to secure the election of said candidates.

9. Realizing that many girls are led into vice because they are not given a decent living wage,

Resolved, that we express our appreciation of the action of the Trades and Labor Council in asking that a commission be appointed to look into this matter.

10. Whereas, the proper instruction and the care of the youth of the country is of vital importance, since in its children lies its future hope;

Resolved, that we urge all unions to arrange for a series of meetings during the year whereby young mothers may be aided in training their children to purity of thought and action, and instructing them in the mysteries of birth and of sex, which is so strongly emphasized by all purity workers.

11. Resolved, that we place on record our appreciation of the action of Vancouver City Council in erecting ten drinking fountains throughout the city, trusting that this example in a forward step may emulate other cities to similar action.

12. Whereas, the importance of foreign work is emphasized by reason of the large influx of foreigners to Canada, especially the Western Provinces;

Resolved, that we ask the Dominion W.C.T.U. to create the department of foreign work and to furnish literature suitable for the needs of the department through the Dominion W.C.T.U. Depository.

13. Believing that some persons err through ignorance of the law in selling cigarettes to boys;

Resolved, that we urge the local unions to continue the work of placing copies of the Act forbidding the same in all stores where cigarettes and tobacco are sold, thus drawing attention to the penalities for the violation of the Act.

14. Whereas, we believe that the present laws of this province are unjust to the wives and mothers in the control of children, and as they relate to property, therefore

Resolved, that we continue to urge upon the government the importance of amending the present laws, that fathers and mothers may be made joint owners of their children, and husbands and wives of their property.

16. Resolved, that we urge women to use the limited franchise which they now possess, and that we continue our efforts for the full enfranchisement of our sex, realizing that the ballot is a strong weapon in the advocacy of the principles for which we stand.

17. Resolved, that superintendents whose department requires more than the nominal allowance of $2.50 shall make application for increase to the convention, submitting their plans and stating the amount required.

18. Resolved, that the W.C.T.U. of British Columbia hereby place on record its regret at, and disapproval of the undignified use of the title and portraits of our late most gracious Sovereign, King Edward VIII, and of His Majesty George v on brands of intoxicating liquors, as being unworthy the illustrious monarchs.

WOMEN AND THE GRAIN GROWERS' ASSOCIATION, 1913

Saskatchewan Grain Growers' Association, *Year Book 1916* (Regina, 1916), pp. 24-6.

CONSTITUTION

Constitution of the Grain Growers' Association adopted in 1913 at Convention of women in Saskatoon.

Section 14—Women's Section
1. Women shall have the same standing in the Association as men.

2. It shall be competent for any five or more women who are members of a Local to form themselves into a Women's Section of the Local for the purpose of discussing ways and means for dealing with women's questions and work. Such section when formed shall be termed the Women's Section and shall be governed by this (Grain Growers) Constitution and By-laws.

3. At the annual Convention the women delegates may meet in the general meeting or separately as they see fit. In separate meetings they may discuss any question or matter not inconsistent with the objects of the Association, as set forth in Section 3 hereof, but it shall not be competent for them to petition Parliament or the Legislature on any matter independently of the Central.

4. Such separate meeting may be called the Women's Section and it shall have power to elect a Board composed of such officers as it may see fit. This Board shall have especial charge of such branches of the Association's work as relate especially to women and children.

* * * * * *

Section 12—Local Associations
1. Any five or more members residing in the same locality may request the Central Executive to create a Local Association for the said locality, and the Executive on such request—or without request—may establish a local for any locality.

2. A membership fee of one dollar per annum shall be paid by each member to the Secretary of the Local to which such member belongs. The local shall for each of its members pay to the Central annually a membership fee of 50¢. It shall not be required to pay to the Central anything for such of its members as are life members of the Association. A life member may become a member of the Local by paying 50¢ per annum to the Local secretary.

3. The Local shall make payment of all membership fees owing to the Central promptly and at least once every three months.

If women do not wish voting privileges of the men's local they may form their own Local. See Sec. 12, G.G. Constitution.

* * * * * *

Objects of Women's Section

The objects of the Women's Section of the Association shall be:

To establish libraries, literary societies, reading rooms, arrange lectures and to further extend the knowledge of the members and their families along social and economic lines, with a view of elevating the standard of living in the rural communities.

To encourage members to provide suitable halls and meeting places and properly equip and furnish same for the social and educational benefits of the members.

To foster and encourage the co-operative method of distribution of farm products, and the supplying of staple commodities.

To make farm life more attractive thereby keeping the young people on the farm.

To beautify the home, the home surroundings and the school.

To increase the efficiency of the homekeeper and raise the ideal of home life and work.

To work for better school boards with women among the trustees.

To ascertain the views of the members of the Provincial Legislature on questions directly affecting farm women.

To foster and develop local taste for literature, music and the finer things of life.

In addition see Plan of Work adopted by Convention at Regina in 1915.

* * * * * *

Platform of the Women's Section

The Women Grain Growers advocate the following causes and install them as planks in their platform: Banish the Bar; Woman's Franchise; Policy of Peace; Co-operation; Rural Education; Establishment of Social Centers; Just Dower Law; Help and Strengthen the Association as a whole.

* * * * * *

Government of Women's Sections

Each Women's Section of a Local may hold meetings at the call of the president or the secretary-treasurer and shall hold an annual meeting of the members not later than January 15th. This meeting shall elect a president, a vice-president, a secretary-treasurer and three or more directors, who shall hold office until their successors are appointed.

To become members of the local with full voting privileges women must pay full membership fee into local treasury. They must become members of the Women's Section through the Local.

They may keep in their own treasury any funds that they may accumulate beside membership fees.

Women's Sections may work on same basis as Provincial Women's Section by obtaining grant from Local to supplement their funds.

* * * * * *

Convention Delegates

In order to have full standing in main body of the Annual Convention, delegates must be elected from the full Local meetings, or members of the Women's Section may confer with men members of the Local and arrange to send delegates in proportion to numbers, with the authority of the Local.

* * * * * *

Method of Organizing

The work of the Women Grain Growers may be carried on in the manner best suited to the various conditions of the different communities. In some cases it will be more expedient to meet with the men members of the Local and co-operate in their work in as many ways as possible.

Women members when desiring to hold meetings of their own may organize a women's Section of the Local.

In case there is no Local existing they may form a Local of their own. See Section numbered 12 under heading Constitution.

At any meeting of at least five women who have become members of the Local, a Women's Section can be organized.

Upon assembling a Chairman and Secretary shall be appointed to take temporary charge of the meeting, until officers are elected.

First motion in order is that a Women's Section of the Local Grain Growers' Association shall be organized.

Next in order is election of officers, when more than one name is to be voted upon decision should be made by ballot.

A Women's Grain Growers' Club or Women's Section of the Grain Growers is then in readiness for work, the first step of which should be the arranging of a time and place for the following meeting and the planning of a program for a few succeeding meetings.

WOMEN'S ORGANIZATIONS, 1916

M. MacMurchy, *The Woman—Bless Her* (Toronto, 1916), pp. 9-33.

Woman's organisations offer a promising starting point for a study of the Canadian woman. Supposed to be efficient and progressive, they are often spoken of as representative of the best work of women in Canada. An analysis of their characteristics and the actual work which they have accomplished cannot fail to produce interesting results.

According to a careful estimate, two hundred and fifty thousand women belong to national organisations in Canada. But so far no question has been asked as to the influence these associations exert on the development of Canadian women. Many of the most thoughtful among this membership already must be considering if their work is producing any appreciable effect in higher standards of living. But it is necessary to discover first if they have decided what these higher standards ought to be.

Broadly speaking, women's organisations in Canada may be divided into two, or even three, groups.

The first group consists of such large bodies as the National Council of the Women of Canada, the Imperial Order of the Daughters of the Empire, Women's Institutes, the Young Women's Christian Association, the Women's Christian Temperance Union and Women's Canadian Clubs. The National Council, with its affiliated societies, is estimated to have a membership of 150,000. The Daughters of the Empire, an affiliated society, has a membership of 30,000. Women's Institutes have a membership of 30,000 in Ontario alone. These Institutes and Home Makers' Clubs, comprising the most remarkable body of women in Canada, are organised in all the provinces and must number from 80,000 to 100,000.

The second group includes clubs for the study of literature, travel, social science, art, music; clubs in occupations such as associations of nurses, women journalists, teachers and business women; political organisations both Conservative and Liberal; suffrage societies; and women's trade unions. Organisations in this second group are comparatively small; they deal more or less with the work of occupations, and have definite or restricted ends.

The third remarkable group consists of missionary societies in the various religious denominations, and has a membership of not under 200,000. These missionary societies are not affiliated with any other body and are not included as societies in the Women's Council group. They were the first great national organisations to develop among women in Canada and have retained a special character. The income which this third group collected, managed and designated in an average year before the war was between $400,000 and $500,000. No other women's organisation raises money of any large amount altogether for altruistic purposes. During the war, however, all the women of Canada, in local and national organisations and as individuals, are earning and collecting hundreds of thousands of dollars for Red Cross, patriotic and relief work.

With membership statistics such as these, why is the estimate of the total membership placed as low as 250,000? It is not unusual for a woman to belong to four or five different organisations. She may be a member of a missionary society, the W.C.T.U., a Women's Canadian Club, a Chapter of the I.O.D.E., and if she has joined these four, she probably will not escape joining one or two more. It is literally impossible to tell how many women are actually represented in national organisations. Two hundred and fifty thousand is a conservative estimate. But, important as such a membership is, it is well to remember that the Census of 1911 places the number of women in Canada between fifteen and eighty years of age at 2,186,000. For one woman who belongs to a national association eight do not.

Canadian women have a genius for organisation. The national character of their associations must be regarded as an achievement of real social value. It is considered by them as a matter of course for a single association to have branches in Halifax, St. John, Charlottetown, Quebec, Ottawa, Montreal, Toronto, Winnipeg, Regina, Calgary, Edmonton, Vancouver and Victoria. To have succeeded again and again in establishing and maintaining this intercommunication between province and province is a genuine contribution to national life.

These organisations, however, with the exception of the missionary societies, are claiming largely to speak for the women of Canada; their leaders are being put forward as the leaders of all Canadian women. This statement is specially true of the 150,000 group. It is necessary to distinguish clearly, therefore, between the first and third groups in women's organisations.

The national missionary societies, broadly speaking, are wholly devoted to missionary work, and have consistently refused to express an opinion on public or social questions. They began to organise thirty or forty years ago, convinced that their work could be best accomplished by keeping to a single purpose.

We have then two great groups of women's associations in Canada, both highly and efficiently organised, the one with a more or less definite purpose to be heard in public affairs and to represent Canadian women; the other, with a single purpose for missionary work and an extraordinary business development, publishing magazines, books and leaflets, supporting and managing hospitals, employing, educating and supporting missionaries and deaconesses, collecting and designating an income of somewhat under half a million. This business is carried on almost altogether by voluntary effort. The only charge for management is less than three per cent.

The typical member of these associations in both groups is married, not single. She is middle-aged. She is a woman with household occupations and yet with some leisure. Her children are wholly or half-way grown up and she is able to undertake some work outside. *As the employment of home-making is at present understood,* a woman in charge of a house, whose children are not in need of constant attention, has time for other employment. She also has sufficient initiative and energy to make other occupation necessary. She must have social intercourse. Few things are more unhealthy mentally than for a woman whose work is keeping house to remain indoors alone, all day, every day. The need of this middle-aged, married woman for work and social co-operation, her impulse to help others and accomplish something worth doing in the world outside, are the forces which have created women's organisations.

These associations undoubtedly have developed sympathetic understanding amongst their membership and have helped to broaden the interests of women.

What else are they developing? To arrive at the correct answer to this question a number of points should be considered: The autocratic or democratic character of the organisation; the distribution of authority throughout the country; the type of officer; the type of member; and the efficiency of any work actually accomplished.

In the early days of what are now national associations the movement began in a single meeting in one city. It has spread gradually over thousands of miles and multiplied into hundreds of meetings. The simple procedure and work have grown extremely complex. One of the greatest dangers which has threatened, and still threatens, women's national organizations is the tendency to keep all the business and all the authority in one city. During the last two or three years provincial councils or boards have been developed to take over a good deal of the work and some of the authority of the central board. But discontent with the policy of keeping the management in one city has been unmistakable in different parts of the country, particularly in the west. The peculiar difficulty and temptation of Ontario is that the central board in many cases originated and has remained in Ontario.

If leaders are competent they must learn that all business and authority which can be distributed amongst provincial boards must be so distributed. Details of reform may be difficult, but they must be arranged. In this way Canadian women can actually work powerfully and immediately for national unity. No one can possess sufficient vision, imagination and knowledge to decide details of management for the whole of this country in any one city.

Is any one unwise enough to think that the management of women's organisations is unimportant? On the contrary, it is a question of real statesmanship. Every woman who is a member of a national association should test the character of her association by the degree in which it distributes business and authority. These women, whether they are aware of it or not, are to some extent responsible for strengthening or weakening Canadian unity.

Few people outside the management have any adequate idea of the exacting duties of a typical officer in a national organisation. Suppose this middle-aged, married, home-making woman is the president of a central board. In this case she takes charge regularly of as complicated a business meeting as any business man would care to handle. She is a member of fifteen or twenty committees, each responsible for a section of work, neglect of which would mean a breakdown in somewhat important affairs. Her work involves endless conferences, consultations, planning and thought. It is as hard work as the paid skilled occupation of an average man or woman. Women who are officers of national organisations in reality have developed an occupation of their own. Their home circumstances must be such as to allow them to give the time. The circumstances of the president must be exceptional. Surely, the uninformed citizen will say, there are practically no Canadian women who follow this occupation. On the contrary, there must be four or five hundred women in Canada who are making an occupation of being an officer in a national association. The occupation is having a decided effect on the character of Canadian women. Some idea can be formed now as to the importance of whether the management of these associations is autocratic or democratic. There is always, of course, the additional consideration that so much organisation, procedure and machinery of work tend to destroy equality in social co-operation and make the business of running an association an end in itself.

And now, dear madam, do you enjoy making a pedestal with the president on its summit out of the officers of your association; or do you favour a plain democracy, each woman's word and brains as good as another's, with due use of talents possessed by officers and members alike? Is a president a presiding officer, a woman like the rest of you, or do you feel that she is a member of a royal family, a reigning president as it were, and you instinctively speak lower in her presence? The reflection is somewhat comic, but the democratic and the ruling ideals both exist in Canada. It is not certain that the ruling ideal is not more prevalent than it used to be in women's organisations.

There are two clear conceptions of the nature of officers. One is that the officers are there because they work harder than the rest of the membership. It is their task to discover the prevailing views of majorities and minorities, to reconcile and compromise, to bind together the different sections of the organisation. Such officers rarely have their own way; they have to devise plans which meet with the approval of every one, or at least a large majority. Above all, they must have intimate friendly relations with as large a number of members as possible. The strength of a democratic organisation is great; but it can only be obtained through the self-denying labours of officers who serve the membership regardless of self-interest, while the membership must co-operate actively and sympathetically.

The other conception of leadership is that the officers are superior to the membership. They have authority, and the members wait to be told what is to be done. The etiquette of approaching and addressing the president of this kind of society is considerable and it is rigorously enforced. Men have foibles as well as women. And something about the autocratic organisation reminds one irresistibly of politics. Certainly, there are women politicians as well as men politicians. But the women's organisation, unless it is democratic, offers a field for the development of a type of official lady whose authority, it is true, is derived only from the membership, although the onlooker would never believe such to be the case, so remote seems to be her responsibility to those who have elected her. In this class of organisation decisions are arrived at in a hidden way. A few elected leaders, and a few others who establish an unexplained influence, decide what is to be done. A plain member may be on a committee and may wait to be summoned to a meeting which will frame a decision or a policy to be submitted to the association. Instead of being called to a meeting she will be told that it is all arranged already. "So much less trouble and so much better done if a few talk over things amongst themselves!"

When an organisation of this kind holds an annual meeting the business is arranged beforehand and goes through with a skilful management which one is persuaded no meeting of men, bank directors or other, could emulate. Such an organisation is constituted of members who know nothing and see the wheels go round, never understanding what makes them go round at all.

Which is to be your choice, dear madam, the democratic women's organisation or the autocratic? Remember, if you refuse to continue in its membership the autocratic organisation ceases to exist. Only the silent membership, who do what they are told, without exerting an intelligent co-operation in work, make it possible for officers to be autocratic. There is no real power, except in the membership, and no real authority, except what is given by you and your equals.

These exact types of women's associations may not be found in Canada. But organisations with a tendency to be autocratic and those with a tendency to be democratic do exist in this country. The first are harmful. The second, the democratic, promote a social co-operation which is of great benefit to our citizenship.

What is the degree of efficiency in the work actually carried on by women's organisations in Canada? Not what kind of work do they do, but in what way is their work done? As far as the missionary societies are concerned, the question may be put to one side. They have shown that the givings of women—generally savings—are of economic importance. What effect the placing of responsibility for missionary giving on women rather than on men and women together has had on church and social life would be a difficult question to determine. Perhaps any effect this may have had is now largely ended, having been met by the Laymen's Missionary work and the Young Men's Christian Association. Whether or not the business management of the missionary societies is saving of labour could only be determined by a special study. Their contribution of voluntary work is so great, and has been so beneficial to the contributors, that the question may not be a pressing one. In the same way the work of Women's Institutes and Home Makers' Clubs may be exempted from discussion. Their organisation is comparatively recent, and the work of the association is practically identical with the occupation of its members, which is home-making. The management also is directly under the governments of the provinces.

The harshest criticisms brought against women's organisations are that the result of their work is inefficient rather than efficient, and that there is too prevalent a tendency to emphasise the importance of receiving credit for work accomplished.

Only prolonged discipline teaches women or men how to work well. It is just this discipline of work which the average member and officer of women's organisations have not experienced. Partly as a consequence of this, women's associations, or rather some of them, attach too great importance to having placed on record, especially in the public press, that they were the first to begin the movement for some remarkable reform, that they bore the heat and labour of the day and that in fact no one else is entitled to any credit. What difference does it make who does the work if the work is done? It is seldom a useful business, this determining of credit. The great opportunity of women's associations in Canada is to grow more efficient and thorough in their work, to raise their standards so that what they do, no matter how small in quantity, in quality will rank with professional work anywhere.

Women's organisations have helped to develop social feeling and friendliness, mutual understanding and sympathy amongst women. They will continue to do so if they resolutely determine to remain democratic and promote democracy. If they are inefficient in work and undemocratic in management, they will fail in leadership. They may not fail with the few, the 250,000; but they will do so with the many, the 3,000,000 women of Canada.

Are women's associations, especially national organisations, likely to be permanent characteristics of modern society, or will they disappear, be merged in something better? Lastly, have they helped, and are they helping now, to promote comradeship between men and women? Is the type of woman developed by women's associations—if there is such a type—

better fitted to work in partnership with men as well as with other women?

It would take much knowledge and courage—perhaps useless courage—to answer these questions fairly.

Women should ask themselves, however, why their organisations have not made a particular study of the special business of women, for this special business merges into national questions to solve which every effort must be made by the men and women of Canada. Why have not these associations studied thoroughly and scientifically the subject of infant mortality, collected money to employ experts if necessary, but made the saving of infant life and the health of children their special care? The reply will be made that they have done so. The answer to this assertion is, Where are your statistics, and where is the improvement which would have taken place, as sure as sunrise, if women's organisations had done this work? The rate can be reduced to 50 in 1,000; it is double this in Canada.

Why have not women's organisations studied the food supply of Canada; why have they not issued food bulletins? Ten million dollars was spent last year in Canada, practically by women, in buying imported fresh fruits and vegetables. Do any of the women's organisations know this? Will not Canadian women take the trouble to work out a diet as interesting, as palatable and as wholesome, using our own food? At the same time, if they so desire, they should press for the growing of fruit and vegetables under glass in Canada.

The economic welfare of the country is a question which men and women must solve together. It cannot be solved unless women who buy co-operate with men who produce, manufacture, export and import. The experience of the business women of Canada is that men welcome co-operation, whenever the co-operation is skilled and efficient. There are not enough of us to do the work of Canada in any case. The co-operation of women cannot be lacking. It is particularly the work of women's associations to help in the solution of these questions and others, such as public health, sympathetic unity between the east and west of Canada, the education of boys and girls, employments of women, immigration, and the effect on social well-being of a more economical, more elevated standard of living.

To introduce a finer standard of living can be accomplished only by women, middle-aged married women with time to give, such as make the membership of women's associations. But it means economic study and consecutive thinking. Will they undertake it?

6.   ⴒORⴒLITY

The proper sphere of women was not politics or economics, it was the home, the nurturing of family life and values. The formation of the National Council of Women in 1893, with its aim of 'mothering', indicated that even the more reform-oriented women's clubs were not going to upset the established system. There was, however, one area in which women felt they should become involved and should change the system, and that was in the area of morality. Women had been told they were more moral than men, in fact, that they were the keepers of morality for society.

It is not surprising that women felt that, as the keepers of society's virtues and finer attributes, they should do more than simply preserve them. They should actively defend them. This was particularly important in the increasingly materialistic years of expansion after 1900. Certainly young girls in the work force were faced with temptations that not all could resist. Some women, such as those in the Young Women's Christian Association, believed that assistance should be given to these girls in order to prevent their fall from virtue. But more significantly women felt a positive relationship with all women. They felt obliged to be the protectors of women whether they were the heathen in foreign lands or the women within their own community.

The one aspect of society that they focused upon was the double standard of morality for men and women. This is not too surprising. More and more women were becoming involved in society, whether through increased educational opportunities, increased work opportunities, or the desire to protect their own homes by combatting social problems that could so easily harm or tempt their own families. Certainly many of the problems that society seemed to be facing were 'male' problems. It was relatively easy to surmise then that if only men would adopt the values and behaviour of women, society would be cleansed. One illustration of the double moral standard was the sexual one. Women were considered more passive than men. Because this was so it was more serious for a woman to break the sexual code than a man, for in a woman this transgression went against her very nature. What many women wanted was not a recognition of woman's ability to feel sexual passion but rather restrictions upon male behaviour. These women were not prudish in stating what they wanted. The Woman's Christian Temperance Union felt that it was unjust to publish only the names of the prostitutes when a house of ill-repute was raided. They wanted the names of their male customers made public too, so that virtuous women would know which men to shun. The N.C.W. wanted adultery declared a crime.

This concern about man's sexual purity was part of a larger concern that in turn centred on the well-being of the family, that gauge of society's health. By the late nineteenth century in Canada interest had developed in the new science of eugenics with its stress upon the importance of heredity in ensuring not only the physical health of children but their moral health too. Men and women were urged to pick their respective spouses wisely, with an eye to the future. Man's purity was just as significant in determining the characteristics of his children as the woman's. Each must guard against any profane action that would subsequently hurt the well-being of the race.

In the last analysis what women desired was a society in which they felt comfortable, a society that practised virtue, purity, and morality. They wanted a society in which the aggressiveness in man could not reach its ultimate culmination—war.

MAKING THE NATION PURE, 1890

Mrs Dr Parker, 'Woman in Nation-Building', in Rev. B. F. Austin, *Woman: Her Character, Culture and Calling* (Brantford, 1890), pp. 462-6.

There are two features in nation-building which are peculiarly the work of woman, but which we are convinced have never yet received their just meed of recognition, viz., the physical and the social. What is to be the physical character of the nation? Shall our sons and daughters be weak and nervous and puny of constitution, or, shall they have strength of bone and muscle and sinew, and vigor of brain? For answer we must look chiefly to the mothers. Whether we shall be a strong, pure, intellectual people depends most of all upon our women, and their just apprehension of all the possibilities attaching to the holy office of motherhood. As this subject is closely allied to "The Physical Culture of Women," which is to be treated in another chapter, we pass on to notice what we may designate the social upbuilding of the nation. The savage nations give no evidence of culture, refinement or education. Their policy or custom of retaining their women in a state of degradation has re-acted upon them with a fearful retribution. They are themselves degraded, and exert no influence on the great stage of the world. They have no social life. Christianity which elevated woman is the force which has given to the world the measure of social organization we now possess, and it is safe to say, when the world reinstates woman, in the place which God originally assigned her as the equal of man, the first step will be taken to introduce the millenium. What we understand by the term society in its broadest sense, is no doubt under the domain of woman, and to her we must look for its maintenance in purity and its advances to the truest standard embodied in the teachings of God's word. A modern writer gives the following pen-picture of society: "The rich eating up the poor; the poor stabbing at the rich; fashion playing in the halls of gilded sensualism; folly dancing to the tune of ignorant mirth; intemperance gloating over its roast beef, or whiskey-jug, brandy-punch, champagne-bottle, bearing thousands upon thousands down to the grave of ignominy, sensualism and drunkenness." Does this picture portray a phase of Canadian society? We cannot say nay. Where is the remedy? Not in increasing wealth, for we have all seen wealth prostituted to just such uses. Not in education, for some of the best educated men are victims of drink and licentiousness. Not in culture or refinement, for these have been known to be handmaidens of debauchery. Where then? The remedy is in the hands of Christian womanhood, through the application to society's laws and customs, of that cleansing element, the Gospel of our Lord Jesus Christ, which, as a personal force regenerates the individual. This is the key to the solution of all our social problems. To our bright young Canadian women, just stepping on the sphere of life's possibilities, we appeal. Give your allegiance to reconstructing the social life of the nation, on the line of one standard of virtue for the sexes, that you may command the purity that is exacted of you; the entire abolition of every form of alcoholic beverage, that the fathers of your children may be sober men; the substitution of amusements requiring the exercise of brains instead of heels; the recognition of true worth wherever found, though it walk in fustian; and the knowing of God, His Sabbath, and His teaching. Surely here are aims worthy your best endeavor. . . .

It has been said by some distinguished writer that people carry their minds, much as they do their watches, content that they go, but indifferent as to the plan or quality of their mechanism. Just so, many people live from day to day and year to year accepting conditions as they find them, receiving standards as they are, without any thought of the why or how, the causes or effects, the good or evil. It is however well for the world, that there are also many who are possessed with the spirit of questioning; of reforming, or reconstructing; of righting old wrongs; and exploding old theories; leaving the old narrow trail, and hewing out a broader pathway for the march of human progress. The women of to-day have left the narrow trail. It was so narrow they had not room to grow. They have been toiling for ages in the great work of nation-building. In the home, the school, the great field of philanthropy, in social, moral and religious effort; in art, literature, commerce, medicine, missions: indeed in all departments of the nation's activities, with energy, fidelity, and success. And surely have earned a just title to rank as citizens, and be no longer classed by law with *infants* and *idiots*. Every advance of the cause of woman has been made through opposition; but in common with every righteous cause advances have been made, and the result has been fraught with abounding good to the nation. As reforms never go backward, the greatest reform, that which contains the germs of all true reforms, the political equality of women with men, will we trust at no very distant day be accomplished. But to this hour the boasted enlightenment of the nineteenth century takes us no further in the work of nation-building. It is ours only to deal with conditions resulting from certain evil legislation without power to improve it, though in every sense our "qualification" meet the standard which gives to men the voting power. Women may not protect themselves. Every intelligent person to-day knows that the ballot is the standard of value to the legislator. Electors secure their ends by the ballot. But not all the logic, for which the male sex are so wonderfully distinguished above the female, can convince our legislators that the woman who has trained a band of boys up to honorable citizenship; who has led them from the cradle to the polls, and who moreover pays taxes in her own right; has as much interest in her country as the bloated whiskey sot who sells his franchise for fifty cents!

We read that the fundamental idea of the State is justice. "For what is the State," says Cicero, "if not a Society of Justice?" More pithily, Cousin says, "Justice personified—that is the State." But the State has reversed the plan of God. God made man and woman equal. "He said unto *them"*— "have dominion." The State has made woman inferior. As a flash of light in darkness, and even as a sure word of prophecy, it is borne in upon us: "How apt the personification of justice!" A WOMAN blindfolded holding balances, and a sword, denoting that she is no respecter of persons, but weighs and decides according to law; and impartially executes its decisions! Passing through that wonderful structure known as Brooklyn bridge, which a woman's brain so helped to construct, we look upon the figure of "Liberty enlightening the world." Is it not an impressive fact, that it is a woman's hand that holds the light? Liberty and justice! The battle-cry of ages, personified by woman! May we not accept this fact as emblematic of the future, when both Liberty and Justice shall be given to woman?

The question is often asked, Why do women desire political equality? We may say, first, as a matter of simple justice, that they may have the right to defend themselves, and secondly, because the ballot is the point at which public opinion takes hold on public action. It is the point where sentiment crystallizes into law. It is the instrument by which we may infuse into the corporate body of the State that Christianity which, as a personal force in the individual, renews the nature, and puts him in harmony with the designs and will of God. Though, as we have seen, women are neither idlers nor a burden to the State, but perform all the functions of useful citizens, they are yet debarred from impressing their God-given characteristics upon the nation, by the very power that admits to the full franchise, the vicious, the drunken and the illiterate.

It is therefore little wonder that politics, the science of government, highest of all sciences, has degenerated into that "soiled thing," our virtuous statesmen "fear to have women touch." But, as Henry Ward Beecher said, "Woman dawned into literature and changed the spirit of letters. When she became a reader, men no longer wrote as if for men. She enforced purity and higher decorum." It is not then, that woman will sink to the "low level of politics," but rather that she will lift politics to their proper sphere.

The "womanizing of society," or the reconstruction of the State upon the broader basis involving the principle of political equality, means the introduction of elements that in their very nature tend to consolidate and perpetuate the nation.

The qualities in womanhood which revere purity and chastity, embodied in the national laws, would rid us of evils under which we groan; and snap the fetters these evils are now forging, with which to bind the yet unborn. That quality of womanhood which shrinks from the spilling of blood, woven into national law, will make for that triumph of conscience, intellect and humanity, over the mere brute force which men call war, and hasten the day when "swords shall be beaten into plough-shares and spears into pruning-hooks." That quality of womanhood which instinctively guards the innocence and purity of youth, woven into national law, will accord to the young of the State the highest protection from destruction; and licensed sins, either of liquor selling or prostitution, will be blotted from the Nation's Statute Books. To the mind of woman the presence of an evil demands a wherefore. It demands also a removal. And the problem "how to do it?" is sure to be demonstrated. "Ah" said that school janitor, "they have put women on our school board, and for the first time in my life, I'm ordered to clean and air the cellar."

In every true Canadian woman's heart there is a strong aspiration after the ideal nation, built on the best foundation: God, Freedom, Righteousness, Love. Canada, our beloved land, favored of God in her broad rivers, immense lakes, exhaustless fisheries, illimitable forests and mineral wealth, of boundless extent; with a territory large enough for the homes of 40,-000,000; free from the blighting evils that afflict and torment older lands; with the opportunity to graft upon our young national stock the best elements of the four or five nationalities that claim kinship with us; why should not Canada lead the world to-day, in all that makes for human progress? May we not hope in shaping our national life to avoid the mistakes of older nations? Is it too much to expect, that with the records of all peoples open before us, we may learn lessons of wisdom and dealing with our problems, make precedents to suit ourselves?

Is this fair land to be cursed with the vile and degrading liquor traffic, whose destructive influences flow on from generation to generation?

Is our country to lift up its voice against the command of the God of Heaven, and secularise His holy day?

Are we Canadians to yield ourselves and our children's children to be yoked in the bondage of priestcraft and Romish oppression?

Shall we ever, in servile truculence to partizanship, forgetting our manhood, and our God-given convictions, compromise with unrighteousness? We trust not! Great is our heritage of light and liberty and Christian teaching! Great things will God require of us!

What if we have no landed aristocracy, if every man and woman bears the stamp of Nature's nobility, honest industry?

What if we have no great tenanted estates, if every man be his own landlord? What if we have no princely palaces absorbing treasure, if the riches of the nation flow out to bless all the people? What if we have no inherited royalty, if we are the children and servants of the King of kings?

Women of Canada, around whose board sit the statesmen of the future, the lawyers, judges, physicians, the legislators, ministers, mechanics, and perchance the inventors of the next generation, how important is our work! "No man liveth to himself!" The principles of righteousness must be implanted by us. It must be "precept upon precept, line upon line, here a little and there a little." We want to grow a patriotism of that holy type which shall harmonize with all the claims the God of nations makes! We want every man and woman, every boy and girl, inspired with the ambition to do their best for their country.

Let Canadians respect themselves! Let us respect our laws and institutions! Let us speak proudly of *our* country, and God grant that Canada, under His divine guidance, may yet give the world the highest ideal it has ever known.

"And it shall be to me a name of joy, a praise and an honor before all the nations of the earth, which shall hear all the good that I do unto them: and they shall fear and tremble for all the goodness and for all the prosperity that I procure unto it."

SOCIAL PURITY, 1898

Jessie C. Smith, 'Social Purity', Woman's Christian Temperance Union, (Nova Scotia, 1898), pp. 58-63.

"A nation rises no higher than its mothers."

Would that these words might be printed indelibly on the mind of every woman, and burn like fire in her heart, giving her no rest day nor night, until she should recognize her own little individual responsibility before God as a factor in His work for the elevation of humanity, aye and in united work with her sisters, His most powerful agent on this earth.

Let the few of us assembled here this afternoon bring home to ourselves our responsibility as co-workers with God—and I make no apology for the use of the word "us," when addressing wives and mothers, for the painful solicitude of the old maid, for the proper bringing up of her children has become a matter of proverb and notoriety and, since the partial emancipation of woman through their admission to education and a consequent participation in a more active and public life than was formerly possible to them, the children of the desolate have become more than of her that is a married wife. So let us all, mother creatures endeavoring to realize our responsibility toward the rising generations, consider in what ways and by what means we may help to cleanse away the sins that are a shame unto this people, and how we may help to bring in, working with God, the righteousness that healeth a nation. Here we are from many parts of Nova Scotia, every one of us, disclaim the burden as we may, distinctly conscious that, each in her own community is, must be, an influence for or against progress, a worker with or against God—and inaction counts with God for opposition. With this admission of our responsibility let us further admit that there are everywhere, many women like-minded with ourselves, and many more who would gladly join in our interest and help in our work if we wisely and lovingly tried to win them over. So enlarging our circle and extending our influence, let us look forward twenty years and say whether or not we may, by earnest loving service, help the generation that is now rising around us to a higher plane of life than is the lot of days in which we live. A very awful thought it is that

"A partnership with God is motherhood,"

and well may we continue,

"What strength, what purity, what self-control,
What love, what wisdom should belong to her
Who helps God fashion an immortal soul."

That is the burden that rests on Christian Mothers, helping God fashion immortal souls, and our W.C.T.U. true to God, and Home, and Native land, sets itself to help Mothers, and Fathers too, in laying, as the hearth-stone of every home, the foundation of Social Purity in Canada, let us, then, like charity, begin at home. In this department we lay hands first on the little child that is born,—for the little unborn child, with its heritage as it may be, of pure or of sinful tendencies, of weakness or of strength of body and mind, is the charge, in our work, of the Department of Health and Heredity.

What can Mothers do? What can they not do! "give me the first five years of a child's life," says a wise man, and you may do what you like with him afterwards; he is always mine. The wise man does not mean by this a child who only plays about his house for the first five years of its life, perhaps getting a good-night or a good morning kiss six days a week, and a loafing time with the over tired father on the Sabbath day. No, he means a child who is his constant companion, modelling its early deportment on that of the admired "big man," and so growing into habits of rudeness or of courtesy; imitating his speech, refined or vulgar, foul or clean; absorbing his ideas on every subject; knowing only the books that he reads,—and the Bible *may* be among them,—on every side of his nature, while mind and heart are yet as "wax to receive, and marble to retain," receiving those impressions which will *never* pass away, because at this stage of life they form habit, and, in weaker and slower minds, even character. We sadly admit, that many Mothers do not sufficiently estimate the importance of the earliest days and years of a child's life. If they did, and in the fear of God, with sense of responsibility for immortal souls committed to their charge, how soon, oh! how soon, would this sad world change into a great house of purity and peace, and, generation by generation grow again into the lost likeness of sons of God, dwellers on earth on that great day when angels stood in multitudinous ranks to see God's wonders in creation.

"When up against the white shore of their feet,
The depths of creation swelled and brake,
And the new worlds, the beaded foam and flower
Of all that coil, roared outward into space."

When the morning stars sang together, and all the sons of God shouted for joy. Oh! let us, my sisters, bear witness continually, at every opportunity, in every home that we enter, to mothers and to fathers, of the eternal importance of the first five years of a child's life, and of their awful responsibility in regard thereto.

We are not sufficiently informed on these matters, some of you will say. Well *be* informed. Pray God to give you deep convictions in this line of W.C.T.U. work, and, take my word for it, by this time next year you will be informed, for we know that if we ask according to His will He heareth us. You will observe, you will read, you will act, for God uses not the wilfully ignorant, nor the idler. The better informed we are the more respect will our work receive from those whom we approach and the more valuable will be our help.

We will suppose that, by day and by night, while the little child has been wholly under the influence and tuition of father and mother, it has been carefully watched and guarded from every impurity of thought or of act, taught cleanliness and modesty, and most of all, has learned to *pray* to God—not merely to say its prayers. Now comes the launch into life, entrance into school, and companionship with the vile. This cannot be avoided. At this time there is circulating in Ontario schools, and God knows in how many other places, an abominable doggerel verse, set to a familiar air which gives with obscene wit the whole story of ante-natal life of a child, and of its birth, and we know that there are everywhere circulating filthy slang expressions which fasten as burrs in the minds of children and cannot be got rid of. What shall we do about this? Get the help of the teachers. Ask them and they are already interested in great part, and the unawakened teachers will be stirred and helped by your interest—ask them to keep sharp ears for foul language and writings on walls of outhouses and elsewhere, keep sharp ears yourselves for what children bring home in their hitherto clean little mouths. Look out for nasty pictures that are often circulated in schools by those debased creatures whose business in life it is, for trade purposes to create a taste for filthy literature and illustrations in young minds. Look after the outhouses in connection with your schools, and, if your own schools are well provided, take the country schools to your heart. We all know what the country school house outhouse is like,—if there happens to be one. A little box of a place with one door half off its hinges, and no decencies. Boys and girls have to dodge each other, and modesty is in danger of strangulation. Here you have to confer with school commissioners. Get up a sentiment among the women—(and their husbands), before you move in this matter, then move, and your sentiment will find itself a power. Next thing, if you go so far, you will see the necessity for women being members of school boards. There are many things in school management on which young women teachers feel themselves unable to talk with men —strangers to them. A pure minded, earnest, intelligent woman on a school board would be a greater power for purity among school children than any three men have ever been,—and this not by way of disparagement of our brothers, but merely as a statement of fact which they will be the last to question—for by their works, particularly in the line of outhouses for schools, do we know them.

Still your boys and girls are growing. Are they questioning? They have heard things of curious import, and a sense of shame and indecency becomes connected with what is a pure ordinance of God. "Where did I come from?" asks the child, and if Mother or Father has not already prepared the way, by suitable, delicate, loving instruction in regard to the bodies in which we live, the child is not apt to ask that question of those who have the responsibility of helping at that time. What the parent does not tell cleanly, and make sacred, as belonging to Father-hood, to Mother-hood, some one else will tell foully. Henceforth it is more than difficult to keep the heart pure,—and out of it are the issues of life. Ignorance is not purity, nor ever can be,—nor is it a friend of purity, nor helpful to the cause.

I have lately received a letter from a lady interested in this subject, in which she tells me that last winter, in one place an infamous scoundrel, a music teacher, ruined the lives of thirteen young girls. Probably the great majority of these girls were absolutely ignorant of what, as women, they should have known. They were ignorant, but the world will never again call them innocent. For youth or for maiden properly instructed in regard to their bodies as temples of God, in every function, sacred to Him, I believe that knowledge concerning all functions is the safeguard of purity, health and happiness which it is the duty of every Christian parent to impart.

Now look out for the Press. Watch for objectionable stories, for smart reports of questionable plays, and for nasty advertisements, and help your Press Superintendent in her work for the suppression of all these features in your local as well as in our Provincial news-papers. She cannot do it all alone, but if all the women in your district would combine to protest against the publication of advertisements which tell of crime and disease, and, among women lead to further sin. Your local Press Superintendent would find her hands strengthened and her work accomplished. Help her also, to watch the post office. She will or should have, a list of prohibited magazines and papers, get a copy, and if you see one of the number in possession of any one notify her of your discovery and the postmaster will, if requested at once suppress that evil.

Now your boys and girls are forming friendships, going into society, and they are yet in danger. You know of some whom they must meet socially, and you advise and warn. Do more than this investigate the record of every man or woman your children may meet. They are not, I hope, many of those utterly abandoned men who use drugged sweets to accomplish their purposes, but I have known of two cases myself in one of which a young married man attempted unsuccessfully, the ruin of a girl of sixteen, his own cousin at that, a stranger in this country, whom he was taking home in his carriage to visit in his family. Another case I know, most pitiful, in which a young girl innocent, sweet, religious, was ruined by her lover, and quite without her knowledge or even a suspicion. Her anguish was terrible. Her family forced a marriage but the poor girl has never lived with the man who served her so, and now, with her little child, lives worse than widowed.

You are aware that, up to the age of sixteen years only our girls are protected by law against seductions. Here is a field for work in Social Purity. A girl ruined early becomes a seduction, a ruin to the young men. For the sake of the boys, if not for the sake of the girls even, let us endeavor to influence legislation to help keep our girls pure until they have reached an age at which the great majority of them at least do know the consequences of error or sin on their part.

But above all, let us constantly endeavor to elevate the standard of Social Purity among men. Mr. Stead says that the English have taught the men to be brave, and women to be chaste. Let us go farther, teaching men to be chaste and women to be brave. Let us insist on a white life for two, holding the boy's chastity of as vital importance as the girl's, and let our own girls be brave in choosing only pure companionship among young men. It has been said that society's public opinion has been, and is, the safeguard of women. Why should not this be so of men. What we expect of obedience from a child we get. What we expect from courtesy of friends we get. What we expect from purity in women we get. Why not expect purity of young men? Of all men? Let us not shrink from the battle, but be vigilant watching the cradle, the home, the school, the press, our legislative bodies, ever endeavoring with the Purity Alliance, "to secure the repression of vice, the better protection of the young, the rescue of the fallen, the extension of the white cross work among men, the maintenance of the law of purity as equally binding on men and women."

Let us be practical, beginning work in our own neighbourhood. Let us find out where are the disreputable houses, and get the names of the frequenters and their inmates, and let us, as Christians, do personal work with both classes as we may get to know them. Christ when on earth must needs go through Samaria. His great heart sorrowed for the woman who was a sinner, and He sought her out, and got her on His side and she worked with Him and for Him, and does yet, in the story of her change of heart and life under the power of Love incarnate.

What did Christ see in this lost woman? He saw great spiritual nature which time nor sin can destroy. He saw a heart burdened with sin, longing for purity, He saw a life held down to the ruin of others; He lifted it up for the help of others. No heart is fully evil. Every soul hears the divine message and honors it. Every soul may be saved—Shall we let the women of the city go down to death and lead the young after them, when we may, like Christ, approach them in some humane office, win their confidence, awaken interest, love, and bring them, by the grace of God, again to the purity and peace that is ever for women.

THE NEED FOR SEX EDUCATION, 1907

Mrs Spofford, 'Address', *Yearbook*, compiled by The National Council of Women of Canada (Ottawa, 1907), pp. 85-91.

It is with a great degree of hesitancy that I presume to introduce to a body of women such as the National Council of Women, the question we are now about to consider, and one of so great moment in our individual, our social and our national life, that of Purity. A question the underlying principles of which are the vital principles on which depends the successful building of the individual's or the nation's life. A question tremendous in its importance, and which on the surface appears not only most difficult of solution, but of presentation, but which in the light of God's truth as it is made known to us, ought to be very simply, very directly and very practically dealt with. And in view of the grave importance of the subject and the apparent difficulty in adequately presenting it, my only apology in attempting to do so is the earnest desire on the part of my Council for a helpful discussion, from which we may gather from those of larger knowledge and wider experience than we ourselves possess, how best to deal with this burning question of an infamous evil. Throughout the ages which have come and gone, during which nations have arisen, reached the zenith of their glory and passed away, their experience and history have proven the statement, "Righteousness exalteth a nation, but sin is a reproach unto any people."

There have been national sins from the time Israel wedded itself to idolatry and paid the penalty through captivity until our present day, the result to the nation being in accord to the extent to which that sin has degraded the manhood of the nation. That "the fountain cannot rise higher than its source" decrees that as the individual is, the people will be. The individual sows to the flesh and the nation reaps corruption; and to the mind, and we reap the whirlwind of destruction. No scourge of sin is more universal, more deadly in effect, more sure of a harvest one hundredfold increased, than is the sin of sensuality.

We read that God made man in His own image, spiritually constituted that he may continue to live through all eternity. A partaker of an inheritance incorruptible, abiding for ever; intellectually qualified to cope with the conditions of his environment, subduing the natural forces and making them subservant [sic] to his needs, physically endowed to beget the race; and in no respect is man more Godlike than in his creative capacity, and from the time when God saw the need of and gave to man the moral law, we find Him through that law protecting and safeguarding that Godlike creative power, and to that end enjoining upon man purity, cleanness, chastity. Through the written as well as the unwritten law, we read His emphatic "Thou shalt not" to the prostitution of this wondrous power. But so perverse is the human heart, that in defiance of God's expressed fiat, man has declared this prostitution a necessity to his well-being—nay, more unrighteous still, he has decreed that for one-half the race unchastity is virtue, while for the other half through whom this virtuous necessity is accomplished, it is impure, unclean, unchaste, the sin from which there is redemption neither in this life nor in that to come.

How it comes that between God's standard of morality for man and man's standard so great a gulf is fixed, it is not necessary that we take time to discuss, further than to know the cause, that we may seek the remedy. We *do* know that God most emphatically declares, and His laws prove to us, that chastity and purity are *essential* to the highest well-being of the race. And we also know that in the past there has, and to-day there does exist, a moral ethical code decreed by man and assented to by woman, which declares unchastity a "necessity," the result being a national evil so widespread, so pernicious, so deadly in effect, that to-day the race is groaning under a burden of disability, moral and physical, a comprehensive knowledge even of which causes us humiliation and sadness unspeakable.

What is the cause, and where the remedy? Ah! that is the question which in view of the heinousness of the offence, the magnitude of the evil, we to-day are asking. I shall touch only on what we consider some essential points, leaving them to be developed through the discussion which will follow.

As to the cause, let me suggest first a false conception as to sex and sex relationship, which false conception is apparent through the almost universal association of impurity and shame which is connected with our thoughts of sex, of self-hood, of parentage. I shall not dwell on this point, but go on to consider that the foundation principle being false, what more likely than that the further building shall be untrue? This false idea leads on to that which has ever been a potent factor in the propagation of evil—*ignorance*. The parents who know themselves and their sacred functions only with a sense of impurity or shame—for these are one and the same thing—cannot instruct the child they have called into being in the holy purpose of its being, and *evasion* presents itself as duty to the most earnest, most sincere parent. Consequently ignorance of self, ignorance of the holy purpose of sexhood, has led to a perversion of these sacred functions into unholy channels, which step by step has led to the false, pernicious doctrine of a double standard of morality, a doctrine well designated "the Devil's doctrine," "the heathenish doctrine of a 'necessary evil,'" the doctrine which has lowered the standard of morality to the lowest level, poisoning the very fountain of life, polluting our manhood and defiling our womanhood. These we believe to be the real causes of the great evil of impurity. As to the remedy, what have we to offer? As for every known physical disease there is provided by nature an antidote, so for every moral disease we believe there is a remedy, which, faithfully applied, will give relief. Truth has ever been the most effective remedy for error, and if we would eradicate this loathsome social evil we must be willing that the searchlight of knowledge and truth be turned on at whatever cost before cleansing and healing will come to this running sore of the human family. We must be willing to know somewhat of the effects of the physical ills which are the result of this evil. To speak of it in my own words, I dare not attempt to describe it adequately—it would be an impossibility—so I quote to you from an eminent scientist, who, describing the fearful evil, says: "It is a plague spot which in spite of all that science can do, remains to fester, to kill, to maim, to disfigure, to sap the health of millions, deserving and undeserving alike; the great curse of humanity, the foul stream meandering whither it will through the world of life." By medical authority this disease incident to the evil is declared to be an ineradicable poison—the most terrible of all maladies, from which there is no absolute cleansing, though men seek it with repentance and tears; pure women are polluted by it, and to innocent offspring it is transmitted in many unrecognized forms. Of the thousands committed to insane asylums and languishing in hospitals, a large percentage are the deserving or undeserving victims of this disease. If such be the results physically, what must they be morally? Need they be depicted? We thank God that in this day of pressing forward, men and women are ceasing to confound ignorance with innocence, but rather are learning that ignorance may be *culpable guilt*.

During this meeting it has been said, "It is wiser and more economical to save the child than to reform the criminal." Women! Is there in regard to the salvation of the child any sense in which this statement applies more forcibly than in this? If we would save the child, we must teach him naturally, and as his development requires, to know himself and the purpose of his being, inspiring him with a due respect for God's intention in creating him. And let us not longer presume in this day of enlightened Christianity, to continue to think ourselves, or teach to others, that the plans and purposes of a holy Creator can be associated with thoughts otherwise than those which are pure, dignified, sacred.

But before we can thus teach the child, we must first instruct the mother. An eminent physician said the childhood of to-day is crying out, "Educate my mother." There the work must begin. We are bound to assume that the true mother instinct desires for her offspring the highest and best in life: let us set before the motherhood of the world the truer and better way—God's way—and she will walk in it. Then will be issued the death proclamation of what Mrs. Josephine Butler designated "the old world wicked doctrine, the ancient chartered lie, that man may and must be impure, and that a whole class for whom Christ died may and must be devoted to minister to this impudently and impiously proclaimed necessity to sin in man." Then will womanhood no longer speak lightly of impurity in men, and permit their daughters to marry men of profligate habits, while they denounce the woman; for we shall realize that when from Sinai God declared "thou shalt not commit adultery," the command was given man and woman alike, and that when Christ said the pure in heart shall see God, it applied to man and woman equally. When we set up the standard of a "white life for two," and demand of men the same blameless life we require of woman, then, and not till then, will the race be freed from its bondage of sensuality. It can never be done through the law. Attempts have been made for legal restriction as a partial remedy, but usually such have been severe repressive measures directed chiefly against the women, and calculated to diminish, not the sin itself, but the physical ills which attend the evil. Not the law, but knowledge and truth, must be the means applied. If the truth shall make you free, then are you free indeed.

MRS. THOMPSON, who followed, said:

Generally when we speak or think upon the subject of Purity, our first thought is the "Social Evil," or the White Slave Traffic. In this Province there are about 3,000 *known* fallen women, and to one fallen woman there are ten fallen men at the very least. What about the manhood of our country? We may say this will not affect us, our children are pure; but how do we know whether one of our daughters may not marry one of these men! Inpurity has become a disease, fastening upon our manhood, and unless we wake up and do something to remedy it, our future generation will be, at the least, a race of weaklings and imbeciles. The social evil is so entrenched between the saloon on one side and the dance hall and low theatre on the other, that it is almost impossible to touch it. This is a terrible part of the question, but to-day we will go back and think of the cause of these conditions, rather than the consequences. Impurity is the cause of nine-tenths of our divorces and our domestic troubles to-day. Sometimes it is wickedness, but generally, I believe, igno-rance is at the back of it all.

Purity means cleanness; it means right living. Ignorance of danger is not safety. He alone is safe who, knowing the dangers that beset him, guards against them, resists evil and recognizes and lives the truth. The time has come when we believe the truth must be made known. Ignorance has had its day. No false modesty or foolish sentimentality must now prevent us from giving the truth as we understand it, for we know that there is no security in ignorance that parades as false modesty. The first element of safety is a knowledge of actual danger. We believe that igno-rance has been the curse of the past, and that knowledge of the truth is to be the salvation of the future. We do not think our young people should be kept in ignorance. It is better that their modesty should be shocked, if by so doing their virtue can be saved. We know that the sexual instinct is not low or vile, but the expression of Divine law, which demands the perpetuation of the race. Therefore it is our chief duty to teach the truth regarding this forceful impulse of every human being, and to find the best way to teach the first principles of the hygiene of the sexual instinct. Dr. Lewis says: "The study of psychology and physiology—we mean physiol-ogy of the whole body, and not a part—shows us that next in importance to the preservation of the individual is the instinct that determines the perpetuation of the species." There is nothing low in this statement. The sexual instinct predominates, because of chief importance is the perpetua-tion of the species. The need of the species is greater than the need of the individual. How shall we teach these truths and first principles? First, I would teach the truth to everybody at the earliest possible moment. When the child begins to ask questions is the time for the mother to begin. First principles in reproduction should be taught in the kindergarten by telling about the dandelion and downy yellow chicken. Of course you could not explain in detail, but the truth could be taught in a general way, rather than fairy tales about the stork and cabbage, etc., etc., which are false, or allow the child to receive absurd explanations from schoolmates and others. At a very early age attention is directed to the sexual organs, and if the parent does not tell the truth, the child has not the proper incentive for right living. This awakened force will make itself known, and if parents do not give their children the right and best thoughts about it, others may and probably will give them thoughts and information which often lead to harmful and indiscreet practices. This does not mean that the child is bad or depraved, but that generally he is misled and unfortun-ate. In the past, and to a great extent at the present time, nothing is said to our children regarding this force of nature. It is considered immodest; it is said only children who are "not nice" think of these things. The father engrossed in business forgets about the perils of his childhood. The mother remembers no one told her when she was a girl; she sends her children to the best schools, where they only associate with other nice children; she dislikes to speak of these "nasty things." She is positive her child has never had an impure thought. I have seen much of the misery of life. I have known of young children infected with incurable disease. These and other unfortunate conditions are becoming all too common, and the saddest fact we must admit in regard to them is that the most favoured child may be the next victim. We are thankful that our child is not like the others. I tell you candidly that what has been the fate of one ignorant child may be the fate of another, not because they are depraved or wicked, but because of the demand of the sexual instinct for expression. Culture, refinement, even religion, offer no protection unless the child knows of the danger that menaces, and is told how to guard against it. We must not allow a false modesty to make us shrink from all reference to the most important of all functions; we must realize our duty to the child and not shirk. This imperious force needs direction. Is it not folly to talk to the child of purity when he does not know even the meaning of the word? We are frauds and hypocrites if we do not try to tell the child regarding conditions that may cause him ruin. We warn against the motor car and teach the child to be careful in crossing the street, but never tell him a word about the dreadful shame and disease which may be his unless he has been taught the perils that confront him. We teach our children everything except to be fathers and mothers. We allow our boys to grow up and be married; they know next thing to nothing about sexual hygiene; they are not able to take care of themselves, much less care for a wife. The consequence is that children are born with the sexual instinct abnormally developed, and we wonder why they go astray so easily. They are cursed before they are born, and in the majority of cases it is owing to ignorance, thinking that the marriage certificate gives them free license to their passions. Parents should tell the truth. Dr. Lewis says: "I recently had a patient who has a boy eight years of age. He had been told to expect a little brother or sister, and had been told how the little one was developing under mother's protection. His loving care of his mother was beautiful. He had learned a lesson in life processes which he will not forget. He has had demonstrated to him an example of purity, for his mother has fulfilled her highest destiny. With the knowledge that this boy has acquired regarding the reproduction of life, it will be a simple matter, as he gets older to tell him the new sensations he experiences indicate that he is becoming a man, and that in due time under the necessary restrictions of civilization and religion he in turn will be privileged to do his share towards perpetuating the species. It should be explained to him that this new feeling asserts itself with force not because it is vile, but because it is preeminently an expression of God's will to secure the continuance of the human race. He should know that the sexual instinct exists for this purpose and not primarily for self-gratification. He should be taught the advisability and healthfulness of continence, the dignity of virility and the sentiment of honour and chivalry toward the young girl. He should also know of the danger of premature indulgence, both as regards venereal infection and the consequences to the girl. He learns in this way the worth of honour and the beauty of purity. He repudiates impure advances, for his common sense instruction in matters pertaining to sex relationship has become part of his nature, that as a man of honour there are things that he can not do. A knowledge of the laws of health is necessary if children are to develop into perfect manhood and womanhood and maintain that purity of life which alone secures the greatest happiness. For that reason hygiene and physiology should be the chief study in every curriculum from kindergarten to university the truth should be made manifest. The medical profession in every community can supply special teachers, whose statements will be accepted as authoritative. Medical men realize as never before the great necessity of an exposition of the truth. Their efforts to warn off danger, to fortify against disaster, and to save from disgrace, should be understood, appreciated and encouraged. Their endeavour must be supplemented by an enlightened public opinion which gives moral support to strengthen the earnest worker when his efforts are misunderstood, misrepresented or ridiculed. Let every woman go forth from this convention with the conviction that the most effective method of warfare against impurity is in effect the equipment of the soldier with the whole armour of God. "The breast-plate of righteousness, the shield of faith, the helmet of salvation and the sword of the Spirit." But let us not forget that we are also told to have the "loins girt about with *truth*." Let education, civilization and religion do everything possible in the cause of purity. Let us make a combined effort; let each one do what he can fearlessly, confidently, resolutely; let us bear the great Light of Truth into the world . . .

PROSTITUTION IN TORONTO, 1911

Lucy W. Brooking, 'Conditions in Toronto', in *Canada's War on the White Slave Trade* (London, 1911), pp. 364-80.

While this traffic in young girls is not perhaps so thoroughly organized in Toronto, as it is in some cities, quite enough proof of its existence comes to every rescue worker in this city. That there is a tremendous, and to those not thrown into immediate touch with the underworld, unsuspected, amount of immorality, both professional and unprofessional, is also most certain.

That there are in Toronto scores of attractive houses for professional immorality, is a well known fact to workers, and that there are also scores of dens and dives carried on by those who have sunk too low, or become too unattractive for the higher (save the mark) grade houses, is even more widely known for these last are continually brought to the notice of officials, and the occupants divide their time between the jail and Reformatories. My personal knowledge of these conditions has been gathered during nearly four years' experience as Superintendent of Toronto Haven. One of the departments of this Mission being the rescue of young girls who have fallen, and another the care and uplift of chronic female inebriates, and women just out of jail or Reformatory. While in the first line of work we do not come very frequently into touch with those who have led a professionally immoral life, we come upon enough proof that it is there and shamelessly there, and in the Prison Gate side of our work we have the care of many who have been frequenters of the lowest dens of the underworld.

In one case known to me, a widowed mother struggled to bring up two little daughters in at least decency. One of them married a man apparently above her in station, who soon compelled her to support him by going to the streets and the old mother told me herself that the daughter was often driven out at night for the purpose of capturing men.

The other daughter was enticed away by a young man also much above her in station, and the last news was that she was out in Winnipeg living the unspeakable life and supporting the wretch who misled her.

A young West Indian girl with her little child was brought to us from the jail where she had served a term for attacking a man with a revolver. The truth lying behind the story was, that she had come to the country on the promise of well paid work, and under the protection (?) of a male relative. This man took her to his "home," soon found to be of a very questionable character. There she lived and sank. When she found that not only was the promised marriage refused her, but even worse degradtion was in store, her fiery tropical temper overcame everything and with a revolver she threatened the man who had led her into this pitfall. Then the law stepped in, and she was sent to jail for merely threatening the life of the man who had without interference wrought her ruin both soul and body. We kept her in charge for some time, but when finally she was placed in a situation this man tracked her up again and she was soon lost in the quagmire of the underworld.

A young woman of respectable family recently came to me, in sad trouble. Had been keeping company with an apparently respectable young man. After some months friendship, she was invited to spend the evening at the home of a "married sister" living on a respectable street.

Shortly after arriving there the sister put on her outdoor clothing and left the house, then the girl's ruin was accomplished. This house is thought to be a house of assignation.

A young servant girl, innocent enough, but somewhat simple-minded, was walking with a companion down on Yonge street in the early evening. The companion, joined by a young man, went off and left her alone. She was presently accosted by a well dressed young man whom she had never seen before. He was evidently sharp enough to recognize easy prey, and offered to see her home. He invited her to go with him to a friend's house; but she held to her purpose of going home. So she was just dragged into an alley-way between two houses and the evil purpose accomplished, without money and without price, except to the poor feeble-minded girl whose life was ruined.

A young girl coming into the city to attend school took a room in an apparently respectable house on an apparently respectable street. The first evening she was invited to join the "boarders" in the parlor. Having some unpacking to do, she excused herself. The prolongation of this "social time" and the amount of coming up and down stairs all through the evening rather surprised her, but she was too ignorantly innocent to be really suspicious. The next evening she was pressed to come down and even told by the house mistress that it was expected of all the boarders that they should make themselves agreeable during the evening. But this evening she had studies to prepare and again retired to her room. Becoming a little nervous she pulled some furniture against the door, as well as locking it. Late that night her door was tried with a duplicate key, and she was plainly told where she was, and that resistance was useless. Having more of resource and courage than the average country girl she opened her window and screamed for the police and so was saved.

Another girl in almost the same circumstances had accepted the invitation to spend the evening down stairs where there was quite a large and well-dressed mixed company, but she retired earlier than the others. When partly undressed she heard some one at her door and innocently opened it to find one of the men to whom she had been introduced down stairs. Although a frequenter of this place he was touched by her innocence, told her where she was, took her away under his protection, and placed her in a respectable boarding house.

A friend of my own, a beautiful and attractive young married woman, both very young and very innocent of the world, was boarding with her husband in a first-class boarding house. Another boarder was an attractive young widow who paid considerable attention to my young friend, who coming from the country was rather lonely in the city. Her husband being away on business for a few days, this lady invited her to spend the evening with her at the house of a friend. The unsuspecting girl went and all looked well, though she was somewhat surprised at the size and brilliancy of the company assembled; she saw nothing to alarm her, but the false note was struck when the widow lady requested her to accompany her again and to say nothing of their little amusement to her husband, who might not wish her to enjoy herself without him. She refused the second invitation and told her husband the whole thing immediately on his return. He found the place to be one noted in its character and the next morning the interesting widow was missing.

A young married couple just out from the Old Country came under my notice. The little wife was in the Hospital with newborn twin babies and the boy husband out of work. So we took the wife and babies into the shelter of the Haven. Months passed, the husband just managing to eke out a living by odd jobs, and the wife in the Haven, learning to care for her babies, and also something about housekeeping. They were devoted to each other and to the babies, and eagerly looking for some situation that would provide a home for them. One night the young fellow came in radiant, such a fine situation offered, care-taker of a boarding house, none but married couple need apply, babies no drawback, indeed an ASSET, young children adored. Three rooms for their little home, light and fuel and food provided and good wages given besides. The owners resided in Hamilton, but a branch was to be kept in Toronto, and managed by a sister of the Hamilton people, with the assitance of a SPECIALLY respectable young married couple. For the first week or two they brought glowing accounts of the beautiful and convenient furnishings being put into this house, and the kindness with which they were treated. In fact almost too much consideration shown, every desire granted. The only boarders yet arrived were some young ladies, and several transient gentlemen, but they would probably fill up shortly. One evening the young husband was accosted by a detective, who told him that as he and his wife were evidently innocent and respectable and probably employed as a blind, they were advised to leave their situation immediately as a raid was on the programme. The wife and babies again slept at the Haven that night, the branch house in Toronto and the headquarters in Hamilton both being broken up.

I was told by an officer of the Traveler's Aid Society of the case of a young girl coming into Toronto to visit a brother, who was to meet her at the Union Station. She got into conversation with some apparently friendly people on the train, who told her it was much more direct for her to leave the train with them at the Riverdale Station, which she did, and at the time I was told the story, some weeks after it happened, her relatives had not been able to find trace of her.

We come into frequent touch with the occupants of the dens and dives of Slumdom, as one or another of these women comes to us for shelter after coming in from jail or Police Court. The conditions are simply unthinkable, as to physical filth and moral degradation. Of course, the life is just as horribly immoral in the gilded halls, but in them the girl occupants have still some remnants of shame and of love for the beautiful and good. A forced slavery is something above a willing slavery, though the last state is the child of the first. The willing slaves in the dens of the Slums often began their career in the Palaces, though often again, the love of intoxicants or drugs has led to their fall. There are dens in Toronto where amid intolerable filth, the master of the house keeps different women (generally middle-aged confirmed drunkards). These women are in turn his favorites, and while living under his favor and protection are expected to bring him in at least a dollar a night. If careless or rebellious there are tales rife in these circles, of his strapping them down, and bringing in his own clients. If growing too troublesome, there often ensues a free fight, when the rebellious woman is kicked and beaten nearly to death. The police step in, the man is sent to jail for one, two, three or six months, and the woman goes either to the Hospital or Haven, to be nursed back to health. Sometimes this is followed by apparently renewed desires for decency of life, generally to be dissipated the moment the lord and master gets out of jail, and takes a room in some other part of Slumdom. In one case this was repeated, the woman being cared for and nursed back to health, until some day when the man's term of imprisonment would be up, there would be a sound of whistling in the back lane, and the next morning the woman would be missing. This was kept up until, finding the Haven being used as a convenience only, the woman was barred out. (This also goes to show the efficacy(?) of the short term.)

In another case the woman, who had in her youth been respectably married, and had two nice daughters, became so lost to all decency and natural feeling, that she wrote to her two young daughters to come up to the city from the small country town where they were living, and herself met and took them to the vile and filthy den where she was the willing slave of a brutal and degraded man. Even this wretch had more conscience than the woman, for he refused to admit her with the girls.

So much for professional vice, either gilded over, or in its naked ugliness. The work of the Haven apart from the department for chronic inebriates, really shows one more of unprofessional immorality, the general conditions of life in the underworld and from our experiences there, we would gather the desperate need for two distinct lines of work, i. e., the protective care of friendless girls and women, and the permanent custodial care of the feeble-minded.

During the past three years more than 200 cases of illegitimate motherhood have come under our care. About one-half of these cases were recently from the Old World, therefore, my observations are two-edged, dealing about equally with the problems of immigration, and with the conditions of Canadian life. Of these 200 illegitimate children fully 190 were defective or diseased. Of the mothers nearly three-fourths were feeble-minded and about the same proportion were absolutely alone and friendless. A few were hopelessly immoral, and a few were not bad, but led away by their affections. Nearly all were either friendless or feeble-minded, so it is the general makeup of these two classes we will study. And in studying them, let us remember we are all of pretty much the same human nature. These poor souls are where we would be in the same circumstances and under the same influences. The Colonel's lady and Biddy O'Grady are sisters under their skins. I often say in my heart, "But for the grace of God" (which includes good heredity and environment) "but for the grace of God, there goes_____ _____." On the other hand, I have seen gleams of the Divine in a poor soul, whose life had been, beyond expression, immoral. And, referring to the Temptations and pitfalls waiting for the ignorant and friendless, let us remember that anybody's daughter may be placed in any one of the sets of circumstances with which I illustrate.

Take girls of normal intelligence, but homeless, unrestrained, in the case of emigrants, unaccustomed to the freedom of a new country, it goes like wine to their heads, and they lose all sense of propriety or safety. Therefore, we frequently see girls, who, in the old country, have lived virtuous and respected lives, often bringing over with them the best of references, coming out here and falling during the first few months. All alone and unprotected, unwarned and unarmed, with no idea of the dangers in the way, they become an easy prey, often to some one "from home." One good and true-hearted English girl came out here to be married to her lover, to whom she had been engaged for some time. She had with her her wedding clothing and her wedding presents. She went to live for a few days in a boarding house, until arrangements could be completed for their wedding. She had no friends, and only her bedroom in which to receive her lover's visits. He being a scoundrel and she being weak the usual thing happened. He deserted her forthwith, later she came to us, she struggled along for months with her poor little diseased baby in her arms. Another English girl, a "Home Girl," without friends or relatives, not one of the brightest, but quite capable of earning her own living if sheltered, was only fitted for work in a fifth-class restaurant when left to herself, came under the notice of one of those fiends in human form, who make a living out of the bodies and souls of friendless girls. This woman was more than kind to the girl, invited her for tea on her lonely "days out" and finally persuaded her to go and make her a little visit. In one week the poor simple child had enough sense to run away from the unspeakable life and drifted into the Haven, where she is now with her poor little baby boy.

Another case where the ruse was the old one of the mock marriage. A young woman of education and refinement came to this country as a governess. She met a man of education and culture who posed as a professional man from New York. They became engaged and were finally married by a personal friend of the "Professor," a Presbyterian minister. After two or three months of married life, the professor was obliged to go west on some scientific expedition, and has never been heard of since. Neither has the most painstaking search been successful in locating the minister. Some months later, this poor girl crawled over from the Hospital to ask if we would help her. In order to give the necessary care to her fragile little child, this educated and refined girl came into the Haven, and fell into line with the others for some months. The child developed splendidly, and the mother is now an honored member of the staff on one of our charitable institutions.

One night a boarding-house keeper, a kindly Christian woman, came to me with a tale of sorrow and suffering. An elderly man, with his young wife and child, had taken lodgings with her some months previously. The husband seemed all affection, but after a time paid a week's board in advance, went away on business, and failed to come back. Hearing the poor girl weeping at night and knowing that she was soon again to become a mother, this good woman persuaded her to tell her trouble. She had been the faithful, helpful daughter of a widowed mother in an Ontario village, all the family, down to the small errand-boy brother, working together to help pay for their little cottage home. The same elderly man frequently came to the village on business, noticed her in a fatherly way, and told her she might do much better for herself in the city where he himself would get her a good situation. He finally persuaded both the mother and girl. He met her at Toronto Union Station, and took her to her situation. All looked well. About twelve o'clock that night he entered her room and locking the door, disclosed the nature of the "situation," telling her that her character was forever gone, that no one would ever believe her story, but that if she gave no trouble he would ultimately marry her. The last act in the tragedy came after she had been with us for some time with her two lovely babies, when the poor old mother, to whom we had at last written the whole sad story, came to bring the lost daughter home with her little ones. I had a letter from her the other day. The whole family are living together bearing their added burdens, doing well and bringing up these little children in the fear and love of the Lord.

These are only a few instances out of many, differing widely as to class, capability and circumstance, but all showing the awful need of protection for even the capable friendless.

How much more may be said of those of limited capacity, thrown out upon a world of temptation and danger; two-thirds of our maternity cases are decidedly feeble-minded. Physically they are women, mentally they are children, morally they are degenerates. For their shelter and protection and defense I would plead. An American authority has said, "In the feeble-minded person the animal passions are usually present, and are often abnormally developed, while will and reason, which should control and repress them, are absent. The feeble-minded woman thus lacking the protection which should be her birthright, falls easily into vice."

In very few cases are relatives able adequately to protect these poor unfortunates. The community owes them care and protection, and it is a debt which if not paid, will some day be exacted in tears and blood, for if left at large they are an ever increasing menace to the community. Plague spots spread, and oftentimes spread upward. No one can say "My family will be safe from this taint." Somebody was calculating recently the length of time to be hoped for, before, at the present rate, all the world would go mad. At the present rate of increase the time is surely within easy calculation when we shall all be feeble-minded. Some few years ago the community was horrified at the case of a young girl taking the life of a baby who had been left outside one of our large stores. The story of that family has been under my immediate notice for some time and is an illustration of the desperate need of some control over the increase of degenerates. Shortly after that tragedy, this home, if it could be called a home, was broken up, this girl being sent to Kingston. The other two elder children of the first marriage were taken charge of by the Children's Aid Society, as was also the wife's illegitimate child. The husband, a confirmed inebriate, and the wife, a moral degenerate and the victim of an insane temper, separated. The wife with the two infant children came to us. After some months she decided to hand these little children also over to the Children's Aid Society, and to go into service. One child was adopted, and one died at the Haven. As he was the inheritor of various family traits, notably the mother's insane temper, we were thankful that he was safely folded while innocent. The mother now being unencumbered, went into a situation in the country, and as soon as possible, was back as a maternity case. In time the husband turned up again, they mutually forgave each other, and having successfully turned six children, all more or less degenerate, over to the care of the Province, have set up shop again, and will no doubt shortly be replenishing hospitals, institutions and jails.

One poor girl, upon the death of her parents, was placed in an easy situation in the country, fell a victim to her employer, who threatened to "kill her if she told." Some two years later one Easter time we laid them both away in safety at last, her little tubercular feeble-minded babe in her arms.

Another girl, the youngest child in a poor but cultured home, was watched like a baby, first by her mother, then by a devoted elder sister, yet became a victim while on a short visit to a relative. Still another, watched for twenty-nine years by mother and sister in turn, was found to be pregnant. Nothing was ever known of the circumstances, but the poor soul was safe and happy with us till she died, and an almost intolerable burden was lifted from the family life. These things coming before me

MORALITY 249

from day to day make me long to cry. "How long, O Lord, how long shall these things be?"

"How long before our legislature rouses to the duty of protecting these poor weak ones from the horrors to which they are exposed in this Christian Canada, and of protecting the country from the horrible danger of such an increase? . . .

WOMEN AGAINST WAR, 1914

Flora MacDonald Denison, *War and Women* (Canadian Suffrage Association, 1914), pp. 2-7.

In recent years it has dawned on the consciousness of all well-meaning people that war is not only Hell, kept alive and burning by hatred and malice, but that as malice and hatred can be evolved out of human beings by love and common sense, so war can be evolved out of nations by the same method.

In a few short years so rapidly did this peace idea grow that in 1913 a palace of peace was actually dedicated to mankind in the city of The Hague in the quaint little country of Holland.

Representative delegates congregated in that charming city and not only "Peace on Earth, Goodwill to Men" was shouted through the length and breadth of the land but also the cry for general disarmament.

To-day the United States and Canada are celebrating a hundred years of peace.

Three thousand miles of frontier stretches between two young nations without a fort or gun or ship to guard or menace.

A gigantic river flows peacefully to the ocean, great lakes wash peaceful shores, tremendous sweep of prairies having homesteads on the boundary line are peace blessed, and the wonderland of Giant Mountains war only with the thunder clouds that burst and kiss their snowcapped summits.

The peace idea has been tried out and not found wanting, and with this splendid New World revelation and celebration which was going to culminate with a great world exhibition to celebrate all commerce joined in peace by the completion of the Panama Canal—just as the world seemed ready for a step up the ladder of progress—behold a war cloud bursts, and eight nations—five of which are major powers, are involved in war.

The poor little white Dove of Peace fluttered and fell at the first cruel scratch from the talons of the Eagle of War, and the world is wondering and suffering and gasping with horror and terror.

The peace conference even laid down rules and regulations for "civilized warfare", and the cannon and the bomb, the rifle and the bayonet have hissed back their cruel laugh and shown us all that there is no such a thing as "civilized warfare".

And what does it all mean?

Have the Altruists all lived and worked and thought for nothing?

Have women come into the game of life in the past generation with their wondrous power of organization as shown at their world's represented congresses and passed resolutions of peace and arbitration to be absolutely ignored by the sons to whom they have given birth?

Has Democracy appeared on the stage only to have the curtain rung down at the beginning of the first act and slapped in the face by autocracy?

Is there any meaning to the great platitudes about the "Brotherhood of Man" and "Love your Neighbor as Yourself", and "We're all one human family".

Is Nietzsche right and will war eternally return to tell its gruesome story?

Faith has been wrested from the faithful.

Hope has been buried by the hopeful.

Ambition no longer builds and aspiration receives no inspiring help.

But—It is only yesterday that a social conscience was born.

It is only yesterday since a gleam of light entered the human brain relative to the meaning of psychology and suggestion—of heredity and environment, and the evolutionary theory is still in its infancy.

A barbarian race of human beings evolved through stress and strain of the necessities of existence, has carried the attributes of combat continuously because it meant primarily self protection and self preservation.

The human, and especially the male, has thought in terms of combat and of dominance through force.

But through it all the better and greatest thinkers have been planning a wiser way.

When the brain of man was able to conceive and materialize a great Ocean Liner, it was not expressly to carry guns with which to destroy life and property.

When the brain of man invented a heavier-than-air ship to sail above the clouds it was not simply to carry bombs to drop and destroy life and property.

Steel was not tempered to unheard of hardness to pierce through an army of human flesh.

But the male through centuries upon centuries has been combative and war has resulted and how quickly this dominant note took advantage of the inventions of the keenest brains and utilized them to the killing industry.

To-day we do know something of psychology and the subtle telepathy which reaches mind after mind tuned to the same key, and we can explain scientifically the mob spirit and the war spirit.

Tribes grew into greater tribes through dominance and conquest, nations grew into greater nations by the same methods, and ever and ever the worshipped hero was the warrior.

Travel over Europe and who are the heroes flaunted in the face of the people.

Look at Wellington and Nelson in Great Britain. In Germany Frederick the Great is heralded in statue and story the length and breadth of the land, and Napoleon's tomb in Paris is awe inspiring beyond description.

When we studied history, what was the keynote of it all? Battles, battles, battles.

A reign was of importance or not according to the degree and length of the wars.

If we cultivate a piece of land and sow it with thistles and nettles we cannot expect to reap a crop of roses and lilies.

If we cultivate race hatred and militarism we will get war.

No one nation is to blame, it is the outcome of the custom of generations, the outcome of false and cruel standards.

That this war is so much more deadly than all previous wars is that the world has reached the maximum degree of efficiency in warfare.

In its deadliness lies our hope, and when it is all over a new standard of values will have to be written.

In writing this another pen than that held by Mars will have to be used.

Venus must be the star in the ascendant and the mothers of the race must assist in tracing out a new code of ethics.

Woman's thought and action have always been constructive.

They have made the homes in which all sons are born, and they know the cost of life.

Every man who went to battle meant that some woman had gone down into the valley of suffering to give him birth.

Women paid the first great price and at last women are demanding that she have some say as to how her property and her sons shall be treated.

Woman demands a say in the social scheme which has cost her so much.

She demands not only protection for her young but the conservation of human life by a more human civilization.

The women of England have no quarrel with the women of Germany.

Both were standing together like sisters asking, pleading, and petitioning that International Arbitration keep peace between nations and that women be given the power of the ballot to assist in protecting their homes and making their laws.

The world howled and shrieked in derision at a little property being destroyed in order to awaken it to the existence of unjust conditions, but now, with whole cities being destroyed and lives swept away by the thousands, women can only bear the burden of slaughtered sons and husbands and ruined homes.

Their voices were not yet strong enough to make a dent in the murderous giant of militarism.

What now of woman's place being in the home, and what will home be with the darling boy rotting in the trench, the devoted husband crippled for life and the brother diseased and ruined.

For every man killed there is also killed a wife—a mother and a family of children.

Dead men will make no homes, and widows and childless women will take little heart in just houses.

Many women are now filled with the spirit of patriotism, and the primal instinct to conserve and help is meritoriously showing itself in the work being done, but let not the glamor of victory nor the sorrow of defeat blind women to the real important issue.

The important issue before, during, and after the war is Democratic Freedom, and there is no freedom and no democracy while women are a disfranchised class.

Had women stood shoulder to shoulder with men in thinking out world problems this war would never have been.

This war is the most conclusive argument that has ever blazed its electric message across the sky of human consciousness in favor of political equality.

"Prevention is better than cure." We are learning to apply this great truism, and besides, war never cured.

The conquered Napoleon left behind a legacy of hate which is bearing fruit to-day.

The battle of Waterloo was not decisive and the only decisive battle will be a bloodless one, fought out by representatives from nations who will be elected by the whole people.

In that court of arbitration great men and great women will discuss side by side what is best for their children—best for the human race.

WOMEN'S VIEW OF CONSCRIPTION, 1917

Francis Marion Beynon, 'Conscription', *The Grain Growers' Guide*, 30 May 1917, vol. X, 934.

There are four objections to the government's announced intention of forcing conscription upon the people of Canada, the first and greatest being that the people have not been consulted about it, the second that it should include married as well as single men; third, that it should be accompanied by conscription of all wealth and all moneys invested in the war loans, and fourth, that the government of Great Britain no longer ago than last week closed out a motion saying that they were not fighting for imperialistic conquest or aggrandisement.

Before men are arbitrarily taken from their homes and put through the military machine, they and their mothers and fathers have a right to say that they are willing it should be done. More particularly is this the case since the killing or physical maiming of them is among the lesser evils that have befallen many of the Canadian boys who have gone to serve in the army. It was admitted in the British House of Commons the other day that in one Canadian camp alone there were seven thousand men suffering from venereal disease, and medical reports in Great Britain show that ten per cent of the forces are affected.

Of these thousands of men who have been ruined there are numbers who would not in any case have led a blameless life, but there are also thousands of clean-minded innocent young boys who would otherwise have been decent upright citizens who will now be nothing but a scourge to their country when they return and whose lives have been completely ruined. Their chances of marrying and having a happy home and healthy children have been taken away from them. Before any mother sees her son forcibly exposed to these temptations she has a right to say whether or not she is willing to have it so. When Everywoman's World took a vote of its women readers on the question of conscription recently it was defeated six to one. If this is any indication of public opinion it is certainly a minority decision the government has arrived at. If you feel at all strongly on this question, bombard Premier Borden with letters demanding a referendum, and write at once.

Although the government doubtless intends to follow the example of Great Britain of taking first the single men and then extending the principle to apply to the married men, as the demand increases, it seems fairer to make it apply to both from the outset. If the good of the individual is to be set aside at the demands of the country, then the rights of the individual ought to be completely disregarded, and those men, married or single, left at home who are most useful to the country. There is nothing to be gained by deceiving ourselves, it means conscription for married men also, sooner or later, if the war goes on, as it seems likely to do, indefinitely. The Canadian government has followed so far, exactly the system that was followed in England at the beginning of the war, and it is likely that they will continue to follow it in every particular.

Then as regards the conscription of wealth. It has been said over and over again that this war will be won by the silver bullet, but instead of the government getting this silver bullet through war loans at five per cent and forever exempt from income tax, let them conscript the city houses and the bank accounts and the railways and the munition plants and the farms, and let all the citizens pay rent to the government. Then with this income pay a generous separation allowance to the wives of married men, and a liberal pension to their widows, and above all an especially generous pension to returned soldiers who are partially or completely disabled, so that these men who have faced death for their country may not need to be the objects of charity from people who have gotten rich out of war profits. Moreover it is obviously unjust to conscript the life of the poor working man, which is all that stands between his family and destitution, while another man can go to the front knowing that in the event of his complete disablement, neither he nor his family will have to eke out a miserable existence for years and years to come.

Finally, before men are compelled to go against their will to serve in the army they have a right to know what they are fighting for, whether it is indeed the principle of democracy, which they were assured at the beginning of the war it was, or whether it is for territory, the acquisition of which will lead to the shedding of the blood of hundreds of thousands of other men at a later date, as territory snatching almost invariably does. . . .

Now as has been pointed out in this column over and over again there is no territory in the world that is worth the slaughter of human beings, and, moreover, this snatching of territory is a positively bad and wicked thing, sowing the seeds of other wars for other men to be slaughtered in. It is utterly opposed to the principle of democracy for which the British Empire is supposed to stand and for which men believe they are dying in this war. No group of people have a right to be transferred from one government to another without their own consent, in a fair referendum, and they ought not so to be transferred at any time, whether in war time or peace. Therefore before conscription comes into force in Canada the British government should be compelled to repudiate any desire for territorial aggrandisement. Men have no right to be forcibly killed and maimed to acquire a few acres of land.

7. SUFFRAGE

The struggle for the vote by Canadian women was influenced by similar movements in the United States and Great Britain. The form in which it developed was, however, a response to Canadian conditions. Compared to the movement in the United States, the Canadian one was perhaps lacklustre and slow. But if so, there were reasons for it. The early beginnings of the American struggle resulted from its association with the abolitionist movement. American women's participation in the anti-slavery campaign had introduced them to public debate and perhaps more significantly had forced the American public to acknowledge that women could speak rationally and intelligently. But the abolitionist movement not only taught women about the power of organizing, it also familiarized them with the political precepts of their country—that all men were created equal and that the vote was not a privilege but an inalienable right. It was not a tremendous leap of imagination to take these two precepts and apply them to the condition of women. Thus not only were all men created equal but all men *and women*, and thus women had an equal right to the vote.

In Canada women did not have that tradition. The vote was not the right of all men but neither was it a privilege of only a few as in Britain. It was, however, the prerogative of those who had a stake in the country, those men who owned property. Because land was more available than in Britain this meant that a large number of Canadian men voted, but it did not mean a universal franchise. This association of the vote with property accounts for the municipal vote being the first franchise to be extended to women in the 1880s; it was not a recognition of a woman's right to vote but an acknowledgement that her property had a right to be represented.

The suffrage movement certainly got off to a slow start. Although a small cadre of women in Toronto had formed a suffrage club under the ostensible name of the Toronto Women's Literary Club in 1877, not until 1910 did there appear a popular following for the movement. When it came the initiative passed out of the hands of the women in the east, who had for many years struggled to keep the question before an uninterested public, and into the hands of women in the west.

There were several reasons why the west responded in a more positive way to the demands of the ladies. For one there was a scarcity of women in the western provinces and thus women were appreciated more. The women who led the advance guard of the suffrage movement were largely Ontario born and bred. They had given up comfortable homes to become pioneers out west with their husbands, brothers, and fathers. Their sacrifices and contributions to building up a new life were obvious. When the years of hardship had somewhat abated and these women had a bit more time to become involved in activities outside the home, many became attracted to the suffrage movement. They certainly saw no reason why they should not have the vote. They did not feel inferior to men and had proven by their fortitude that they were not inferior. Obviously their menfolk agreed. In 1916, four years after the Political Equality League was formed in Winnipeg, Manitoba granted women the vote, the first province to do so.

THE VOTE TO DO AWAY WITH DRINK, 1888

Mrs Gordon Grant, 'Franchise', address to the 5th convention, Woman's Christian Temperance Union, British Columbia, 1888.

MRS. PRESIDENT AND FRIENDS.—A subject has been assigned to me this evening which I cannot begin to do justice to, but as no one else has undertaken it I could not let it pass over unnoticed for it is a subject of great importance, which lies very near to my heart, as I see in its proper use, the downfall of the strongholds of Satan, the overthrow of the liquor traffic and the purifying of the moral atmosphere of every hamlet, province and country where it has free exercise. It is the subject of the franchise, or in other words it is the laws which govern us, it is the protection of our homes. A great deal is being said at the present time about protection: citizens are crying out for protection for their businesses, manufacturerers want protection for their industries, farmers want protection for their produce, fishermen want protection for their fish, sealers want protection for their schooners and mothers want protection for their boys. The question with each class who is seeking protection is, what is the quickest and easiest way to accomplish the desired end, and it is the same problem which we mothers are trying to solve. Our little ones come to us and by their very helplessness appeal to all that is pure and holy, all that is tender and loving in our natures and as we carefully watch over them, nourishing their bodies that they may become strong and vigorous, educating their minds that they may be intelligent and enterprising, inculcating right principles and pure thoughts in their hearts, that they may become a light in society, a blessing to their fellowmen, and promoters of all that is noble and good in the different spheres to which they are called, yet as they pass out of the gates of their homes, we tremble for them, surrounded as they are by houses of vice and dens of iniquity, which infest our towns and cities, many of them being sustained by a law which licenses them, and makes their murderous business legitimate and respectable. Oh how our mother-heart aches for our youth. We have prayed and prayed that God would watch over their footsteps, but we know that while we pray we must also work, and realizing that the power next to prayer is the franchise, we come before you to-night and plead for your influence in favor of its being extended to women. We plead for it first, because it is our right, and second, because it is our duty. We are as deeply interested in our country's welfare and in our country's laws, as our gentlemen friends, we have as much refinement, education and wealth, as many of the sterner sex and though perhaps many of us have never studied political economy, we understand that bad laws compel us to practice too much household economy, for our rightful living oftentimes sustains the saloon keeper, and yet we are placed below all men, no matter how ignorant or wicked they may be, even the foreigner, who perhaps can neither read or write, but who by residing on Canadian soil one year and taking the oath of allegiance, though he may know nothing of our laws, nothing of the men who aspire to office, perhaps he cannot speak one word of English, and yet he can say, who shall be our legislators, while we women are placed side by side with idiots, lunatics, and children. Oh brothers and husbands think of the humiliating position of your mothers, sisters and wives. Shall she have no voice as to what sort of laws shall govern her children and demand their and her obedience, while a man too ignorant to read, and therefore incapable of forming an intelligent opinion, has the legal right to assist in forming our laws by his vote. Shall this age progress in all things save that which pertains to woman's highest destiny. To the praise of British Columbia let me say, we enjoy the municipal franchise here—we enjoy the privilege of voting for school trustees, but why stop there? Have we not cast our votes in these two instances in a womanly, intelligent manner; has it resulted in bickering and quarrelling in the home; has it caused a disturbance at the polls, if not then, wherein is the objection to increasing our privilege. Woman's work is to cleanse, beautify and restore the broken harmony of the home, and has, or will the franchise interfere with the work, will it not rather make her work more effectual. But perhaps some of you feel as Mrs. Beacher's colored man Cato did, she said to him. Now that you are free and can vote, Cato, I hope you will use your influence with the colored people to get me the ballot. "Lor, Miss Beacher," said Cato, rolling up his eyes while an incredulous smile broadened his kind-hearted, honest face—"dus you rely belebe dat wimmen is got sense enough to know how to vote." The argument of woman's intellectual inequality with man's has been so thoroughly disproved that it has been given up. The argument that because she cannot fight with musket has given way, because she can do so much better warfare with her own peculiar weapon, than her stronger brother can, even tho' it be small and sometimes unruly. Women themselves need education on this subject, they have been taught that it was their's to pray and suffer, and man's to work and fight. We have not realized the power of the ballot. We have prayed and worked for prohibition, but now we see the need of adding to our other efforts the ballot, for "While prohibition is the nail, woman's ballot is the hammer that must drive it home." Francis E. Willard says "What if on 364 days women wrought patiently to build defences around their homes with their moral suasion weapons, do not the voters carry them away as with a flood upon election day, entrenching the triumphant dram shop behind the sheltering of the commonwealth. Oh, our friends, we have awakened from a delusion. It is a duty we owe our homes, our children and our country, to use every effort to gain the power which will enable us to unite our votes to those of our worthy fathers, husbands and brothers to place in positions of trust and in the halls of legislation, men who are not only intellectually, but morally capable to fill their office. Men whose principles are pure, whose lives are upright and whose word is sacred. Men who will not flinch in putting down the wrong with a strong hand. Men who will clear from our midst the gins, the traps and snares, laid for unwary feet. And let it not be said of us dear sisters, that by our silence on this question we consent to the great impurities around us.

Consent? "Yes, the consent of the lamb to the hand that is poising the knife;"
Consent? "Yes, the consent of the worm to the foot that is crushing its life;"
"Dumb like the lamb and the worm, denied any voice of her own;
Told that no argument lies in her heart-broken moan.
Over a half-orphaned land how the mother-heart yearns;
Over its wrongs and its shames how the mother-heart burns.
Yet she is gagged by the law, has no vote, has no voice;
Others make laws for her children and she has no choice.
Place the white vote in her hand, it shall never be bartered nor lent;
No one shall dare to affirm, that this crime has a 'woman's consent.'"

A WOMAN IS A CITIZEN, 1904

Dr Stowe-Gullen, 'Woman as Citizen', paper read at the Eleventh Annual Meeting of the National Council of Women of Canada, Winnipeg, 1904, in *National Council of Women of Canada* (London, 1904), pp. 155-61.

In studying any question there are always certain underlying principles and truths to be determined, and there is probably no better method of arriving at a true estimate of the question under discussion than can be obtained by studying the requirements, necessities and particular phase of development of the individual unit, for what is determined or required for one is necessary and true for all. Spencer has aptly said, "The principles for the right ruling of humanity in its state of multitude are to be found in humanity in its state of unitude."

To understand humanity, it is necessary therefore to analyze and study the individual integer man and his needs, status and relationship to all other members of the social organism. Society is but an aggregation of individual units, these units constituting the nation.

Now, a law in ethics enunciates that every individual has the inherent right to all the freedom that any one else has, provided he infringes not the freedom of another, therefore the law of equal freedom applies to the whole community, all citizens of a state or community possessing equal claims to the exercise of all natural rights and privileges, and any infringement being contrary to ethical law.

Now, we further ascertain that all persons born within a country or state, irrespective of sex, are designated citizens of that state or country, all others being citizens by adoption, and yet for many centuries the world has witnessed an anomalous perversion of this natural basis for national life.

There have existed two classes of individual units or citizens—those who have participated in the judicial legislative and municipal authority of the state and who possessed the right to vote for public officers; in fact, those who have been permitted to partake in all that makes for good citizenship, and another equally as important class who have been denied the exercise of all natural and inherent privileges.

Such inequalities and perversions of natural law is [sic] all the more remarkable when we recollect that each unit of society possesses the same needs and requirements, each having inherently equal claim to all natural rights and opportunities.

Any country, government, any law which gives power to one class over another is iniquitous and unjust; pernicious in precept and disastrous to the happiness and well-being of the whole.

Equity knows no sex, no class, no color. Invidious distinctions held and perpetuated, whether between man and woman, or one class of society over another, are not in accordance with basic principles, and the country, race and civilization, which is unmindful of the true spirit of ethics—will ultimately sink into oblivion. As civilization advanced, men became more and more imbued with the importance of their status as citizens vigorously resenting any infringement of their liberties, wielding sword and pen in defense of their natural and inherent rights, and the world has ever awarded ample recognition for this defense. Every age, country and nation has enrolled among its illustrious the defenders of human liberties and paid homage to the lovers of freedom.

Those who are thoroughly imbued with a love of country and state, those who are in short, ideally patriotic—such souls love freedom better than a miser loves his gold—love liberty in its most ennobling sense—for its own sake, irrespective of its apparent advantages, and they estimate good citizenship at its true value. A country's greatness does not depend on its monetary wealth, its natural resources, the strength of its armies, nor individual nor isolated instances of genius, but is measured by the degree of universal intelligence and moral characteristics of its citizens.

Character building is the true test of individual or national greatness. So that country, that nation, is worthiest of recognition which comprises the greatest number of highly intelligent, justice-loving citizens.

If education be commendable or necessary for man it is equally so for woman, if a love of home and country be ennobling for man, it cannot be less so for a woman. If a highly developed moral sense be requisite or desirable for man, it is equally essential for woman, if the promulgation and practice of the highest idealism be contributory to man's evolvement, it is of equal value for woman's; what is true of one holds good for the other. One is but the complement of the other. Nature is dual, and in all departments of life men and women are intended to be co-mates and co-equals.

Man or woman alone cannot be a success; they must stand side by side, and work hand in hand, not because of their identity, but because of their diversity. Woman has all the interests on earth that man has, and the hope for the future that man possesses.

Now, as our freedom from existing disabilities is largely dependent upon our own efforts, it behooves us to awaken from our apathy, and to rightfully understand our assigned and actual position in the body politic, and to accord to these questions careful and unprejudiced consideration, for individually and collectively, we work out our own salvation. Nature is never vicarious. Each is responsible in life and death. The supreme law does not consider whether the individual is ignorant or wise, whether masculine or feminine. Results are unerring and inevitable to all transgressors of laws. As we sow, so must we reap. Each must endure the consequence of his or her own acts, however great the moral cowardice that incites to postponement or evades results. Each has special duties to perform, difficulties to encounter and surmount, responsibilities to bear and the future evolutionary progress and happiness and well-being of the race depends upon the right performance of our own duties and the assumption of our own responsibilities. Each possesses the same faculties, the same potentialities—the difference being in degree, not kind.

All evolution proceeds through the individual, and the evolution of the individual is ultimately the perfection of the whole.

Some of the existing impediments to woman's progress towards the complete establishment of her recognition by the state have been her own primitive perception of just principles—the excessive development of the maternal love nature, her willingness to be led, to be utilized, and quietly submit to the appropriation of her labors without due recognition and recompensation. Woman has laid herself upon the altar of self-sacrifice, and the results are disastrously self-evident. If we weakly submit to wrong or injustice, we are individually and collectively morally responsible.

Habits of submission make both men and women servile-minded and every human being suffers in their highest nature by disregrading the sacredness of human liberties.

The entire world has and does still suffer because women through their subjection have transmitted servile dispositions, a smallness of soul and mental calibre—direct evidence of bondage—which under just and equitable conditions would have been impossible.

If it be our duty to respect the claims of others, it is likewise a duty to maintain our own; ours are no less sacred than those of others, and we may not carelessly ignore or abandon our dues for the sake of peace.

While the social thought continues to regard the mental, legal, economic and political claims of woman as unworthy of attention, woman's happiness, work and worth will be lightly estimated, and inasmuch as woman has failed in her first duty, a proper and just appreciation of self— has woman been the culpable co-partner of man.

All these varying factors have been contributory elements in assigning woman's position as the unrecognized, unremunerated member of society.

Suppose we contemplate briefly woman's so-called economic dependence in the marriage relation. Think of the injustice of denying to the wife and mother any legal share in the family income. What man in his sane mind would expect to form a business partnership, one of the members of that firm to receive no monetary compensation outside of board and clothing (and these not always cheerfully awarded), although previously promised an equal financial standing for services rendered —how long, think you, before that firm would be dissolved? Yet most wives and mothers toil day and night in the interests of their homes and families, seldom feeling entitled to any money in payment for their important and all-absorbing duties. Whatever they possess the husbands are said to have given them. And women are adjudged pensioners upon the bounty of another. Neither the law nor society regards them as rightful sharers and earners of the combined income, and yet these same women are the mothers of the race, performing the most important service that can be rendered by any citizen to the nation.

What is the work of the merchant, farmer, or laborer, compared to the tasks of the mothers who bear and rear the coming generation? Just how detrimental this condition of affairs has been, never can be rightly determined, but every man is the child of his mother, and whatever injustice, whatever loss of respect, whatever degradation she has endured is reflected and transmitted to her offspring.

Half a century ago the legal, educational and political position of woman was that of bond slave, in accordance with the old common law of England. Rights of person and property were completely under the absolute control of fathers and husbands. Women were excluded from universities, colleges or schools, professions and trades, with the small exception of teaching, sewing, cooking and factory work—their remuneration likewise limited, and all avenues for the highest development denied them.

From such conditions women have emerged, until at the present moment almost every industry and profession has been opened at their insistent demand.

Women are creditably filling all positions of trust; they are lawyers, doctors, ministers, teachers, authors, architects, chemists and inventors; in fact, women are not only assisting in the world's work, but are doing it.

Concerning the avocation of inventors, we frequently hear the statement, "women are not inventors," yet what are the facts?

By a careful study of the records of the patent offices, the knowledge is elicited that women are numerous among this class of the world's workers.

(Dr. Gullen here gave a long list of valuable and varied inventions by women, and of numerous and responsible positions of public trust held by women.)

Now, from our brief analysis of woman's status in the immediate past and present, there was ground for the supposition that these flagrant injustices would be corrected in elective governments, governments which claim to be "elected for and by the people," deriving their just powers from consent of the governed and not from less than half the governed, the male portion only.

Again, we further hear, "Taxation without representation, is tyranny." "Political power inheres in the people," and we know that women are taxed, and women are the people. Yet we find no better conditions in elective governments save in a few notable and worthy instances.

Disfranchisement is not alone political, but educational, legal and social degradation.

Woman's enfranchisement means expanded and idealistic conditions for home and nation; therefore, woman's enfranchisement is man's enfranchisement from existing evils and disabilities.

The ballot symbolizes freedom, is the external manifestation of the right and need of every member of the social organism for self-protection. The farmer, manufacturer, lawyer, doctor, all need the ballot that the agricultural, manufacturing, legal and medical interests of a community be regarded and protected; and if these different and varying elements of society deem the ballot essential for the furtherance of their welfare (which are mainly materialistic), how much more necessary is the ballot to the homemaker of society, for the home is the corner stone of the nation, which in its last analysis is but an aggregation of homes.

When every prayer and tear represents a ballot, the mothers of the race will no longer weep in vain, but seeing, act. One vote is a good preventive, and as some one aptly said, worth tons of unclinched influence; and experience long ago demonstrated that sympathy as a governing agent was vague and powerless. It is much more scientific to deal with causes than effects; infinitely less destructive to society to prevent crime, than to cure the criminal; wiser to protect the youth of our country by effective legislation than to regret and deplore their ruin and loss to home and nation.

It is no more unwomanly to express an opinion by dropping a slip of paper into a box than it is to voice an opinion in conversation. A vote is merely a printed opinion.

Nature can generally be trusted to take care of itself, and in the historic words of Samantha Allen:

"Men and women voting side by side would no more alter their natural disposition than singing Watt's hymns—one would sing bass and the other air as long as the world will stand."

Womanly character is broadened and ennobled by patriotism and an intelligent interest in all public questions, so let us hasten the glad time when every human being will occupy the common platform of an equality of interests and opportunities, and good government is the natural sequence.

Again it is said, "Women are too good and pure to enter politics"; they must not be contaminated. To these objections we would reply women are associated with these same men in all the relationships of life. Women are their mothers; women are their sisters, sweethearts and their wives, and it is radically impossible to have impurity in one class of society without disastrously affecting all. Humanity is a unit and its oneness must ever be remembered.

Then again, it is not our intention to leave politics as we find them, for there is much injustice to be remedied, many wrongs to be righted, and burning question that will demand our highest, most idealistic thought crystallized into effort.

We thoroughly appreciate the fact that great privileges bring in their train great responsibilities. They who overlook their fellows have the responsibility of that overlooking. We hope to be able to fill all obligations.

We claim, and not without reason, that among all the English-speaking nations at least, woman, by the force of her character, active, intelligent interest in all the reforms and issues of the day, contribution and participation in the world's work, has abundantly established her status as citizen and demonstrated her claim to the full exercise of the important duties of citizenship.

Though all asked for by woman has not been secured, still, considering the strength and obstinacy of inherent and acquired prejudices, the advances made in the past fifty years are perhaps on the whole phenomenal. Wider educational and practical experience of the great advantages to be derived through equal suffrage are destined to consummate the political emancipation of women.

In looking over the world there is undoubted evidence of the growth of this important movement. In England women may vote in the school, parish, district and council elections, but are debarred from the parliamentary franchise. With our sister neighbors over the way, nearly all the states have school suffrage, and four states full suffrage. In the State of Kansas, municipal suffrage for all women is on the same basis as men. Louisiana extends to women voting privileges on all tax and bond questions.

Canadian, municipal suffrage to spinsters and widows; thus putting a premium on these one-sided conditions; school suffrage to married women who pay taxes in their own right; though this privilege is almost rendered null and void through the difficulty of securing the addition of the women's names to the existing voters' list. Full suffrage is established in New Zealand, Australia and the Isle of Man.

(An interesting account of the success of the Suffrage Movement in New Zealand here followed, which has to be omitted for lack of space.)

Experience in New Zealand, Australia, the Western States and the Isle of Man, unites in proving that if women possess the suffrage, they will exercise the privilege, that there is no disorder in consequence, nor rudeness to the women voters; that they are not afraid to go to the polls, nor do the men of any class endeavor to discourage them from doing so, and household duties are not neglected, no sign of family discord, disdain for marriage, no revolution in dress or manners.

Enfranchisement has led neither to divided households nor divided skirts. On the contrary, family life has been strengthened with a new sympathy. Politics gained a new influence, full of high motives, and comparatively free from commercialism; the home has gained additional force in political life; character, more weight in elections, party and money loss. Temperance, morality, justice and high principles, more influence and the passage and enforcement of humanitarian laws is more vigorously demanded and jealously watched, the prophecies of evil have not been fulfilled, nor the millennium been attained.

A people's civilization may be judged by the position and advantages enjoyed by its women, so that country and civilization, which fully recognizes woman's claim to all natural rights and opportunities, will be the country and possess the civilization that will withstand the onslaught of ages.

Justice is symbolized by woman holding the balance. Truth by women holding on high the torchlight, both significant emblems of this the women's era.

The torch already in woman's hand will never be extinguished until the ancient barriers of long established custom have disappeared and the path illuminated for that new and better day that must come for mankind.

As the sun rises in the east and sinks in the west so shall human thought generated in the east evolve to its highest culmination in the western world—unfolding and disclosing the full destiny of mankind.

DEMANDS FOR MUNICIPAL FRANCHISE, 1909

Woman's Christian Temperance Union, *Report of the Sixth Annual Convention*, Medicine Hat, 1-4 October 1909, pp. 48-9.

REPORT OF WOMAN'S FRANCHISE AND
CHRISTIAN CITIZENSHIP

In the beginning of the year all the Unions in Alberta and Saskatchewan were corresponded with in regard to Municipal Franchise for married women owning property, asking if the Unions were willing to circulate a petition on this question.

Later the form of the petition was submitted to the executive for approval which was given. The following forms were printed:

THE PETITION
OF THE
WOMEN'S CHRISTIAN TEMPERANCE UNION FOR MUNICI-
PAL FRANCHISE FOR MARRIED WOMEN OWNING
PROPERTY

To the Honourable the Legislative Assembly of Alberta.

The petition of the undersigned humbly sheweth

WHEREAS, the principle that there should be no taxation without representation is one of the foundation stones of British Responsible Government;

AND, WHEREAS, the married women of Alberta are separate as to property and those owning property are taxed for it without representation;

AND, WHEREAS, it is not true that the husband represents his wife's property as he has not two votes, but one, which represents his own property;

AND, WHEREAS, your Government has, by granting municipal franchise to widows and spinsters, acknowledged the ability of a woman to cast a municipal vote;

AND, WHEREAS, the fact that many of these widows and spinsters who have the municipal franchise, do not exercise it, is no argument that married women would not;

AND, WHEREAS, married women who have children growing up in the community have more vital interest in the management of that community than spinsters and elderly widows;

WHEREFORE, your petitioners humbly pray that your honourable house will enact during the present session a law granting to the married women of Alberta, who own property, the same municipal franchise as has been given to the women of Manitoba;

And your petitioners as in duty bound will ever pray.

These forms will be sent out immediately after Convention, as it was thought more intelligent interest would be taken in the petition after it had been discussed at Convention.

The following correspondence between the Attorney General and myself is appended to this report.

Notices were sent out in September to the different Unions asking for reports of work done for Franchise and Christian Citizenship. Many of the Unions have not replied so a full report cannot be given, but it is encouraging to find in the replies which have come, a willingness to work and some work accomplished.

Respectfully submitted,
HENRIETTA MUIR EDWARDS,
Sept. 26th, 1909.   Prov. Supt. of Franchise and
Macleod, Alta.   Christian Citizenship.

EQUAL SUFFRAGE, 1910

James L. Hughes, *Equal Suffrage* (Toronto, 1910), pp. 25-68.

1. *"It is unwomanly to vote."* Why? By whose standard? By what authority is this statement made? There is no reason, there never has been a reason, there can be no reason for saying so. The prejudices of mankind and the conventionalities of society: these are the foundations on which the statements rest. Woman does a great many things now, with the approval of all right thinking people, that conventionalities once declared to be improper. Nothing is unwomanly that is in harmony with a true

woman's conscientious sense of her duty. It cannot be unwomanly to perform the highest functions of Christian citizenship.

2. *"Woman suffrage is a revolutionary measure."* This is an age of evolution, not of revolution. In the suffrage question, for instance, no one proposes to disfranchise man, and enfranchise woman in his stead. That would be revolutionary. The proposal of this era is to recognize the duty of voting, and extend the right of voting to interested, intelligent and responsible human beings who are not now enfranchised. This is just and reasonable evolution, not "revolution."

3. *"Women would not vote if they had the opportunity."* Women do vote when they get the opportunity to do so. In all countries where they have the parliamentary franchise they vote quite as well as men. In some countries even a larger percentage of women vote than of men.

There is no use in theorizing about the question. Men proved conclusively that locomotives could not run on smooth rails, but they ran, and that settled the discussion. Women do vote in Church matters, in school elections, in municipal elections and in parliamentary elections wherever they have the legal right to do so. If women would not vote, no harm could come from making the experiment of granting woman suffrage.

4. *"All women do not wish to vote."* True. Neither do all men. It would, therefore, be as logical to refuse to let men vote because some men do not care to vote as to refuse to let women vote because some of them do not yet wish to vote. Less than half the men vote at ordinary municipal elections in many places. It would be utterly unjust on this account to disfranchise those who wish to vote. If only one hundred women in Canada believed it to be their right and duty to vote, there is no spirit of justice, human or divine, that would prevent their voting merely because other women do not wish to vote. Not one woman in a hundred wishes to teach school. The same argument would prohibit all women from teaching because all women do not wish to teach. The logical outcome of this argument allows no woman to do anything unless all women desire to do it. Many women do vote in municipal matters, and desire the right to vote on other questions. The indifference of women not yet aroused cannot affect the rights of those who are awake. The ballot was given to the negroes not because all negroes wanted it, but because it was right that they should have it. Duty is the broad ground on which the question rests. Thousands of true, pure, home-loving women sincerely believe it to be their duty to vote in order to help to decide great social and national questions that affect the well-being of their country and their homes. They surely have as well-defined a right to desire to vote as other women have to oppose woman's enfranchisement. The women who wish to vote do not try to compel those women to vote who oppose woman suffrage. This is an age of individual liberty. Right and duty and conscience should guide us. Each woman should be at liberty to decide for herself.

5. *"The number of women who have spontaneously asked for the change appears to be small."* Every extension of the franchise from the time of Simon de Montfort to the present might at first have been objected to on the same ground. No other unenfranchised body ever awakened to a sense of the injustice of being refused the ballot so rapidly as women have during the past ten years. If this argument had force it might have been used to prevent every progressive movement in the development of civilization. Even Christianity itself must have been condemned if it had been tested by the number who "spontaneously" asked for it.

6. *"Most good women, intelligent, domestic, godly mothers are opposed to the suffrage for women."* Most of such women opposed allowing girls to go to colleges and universities. The same classes of women at first objected to women as teachers, or doctors, or lawyers, or lecturers, or preachers, or anything else but what very proper conventionalities made them. When Elizabeth Blackwell began the study of medicine the women in the same boarding house would not speak to her, and even on the streets women would turn aside and look scornfully at her to show their condemnation of her unwomanliness.

It would be marvellous if the majority were at once progressively radical.

Good women in India threaten to drown themselves if a Hindu proposes to educate his daughter.

7. *"The basal conviction of our best manhood is against it."* Not so! The majority of the members of the British House of Commons voted to give all women, married and single, the right to vote and be elected in all school and municipal elections. Bishop Simpson, Bishop Bowman, Bishop Hurst, Bishop Gilbert Haven, Longfellow, Whittier, Wendell Phillips, George William Curtis, Emerson, Abraham Lincoln and Charles Sumner labored earnestly for it. The majority of Protestant ministers are in favor of it. The great Prohibition Conventions have passed strong resolutions in favor of it. The National Grange of the United States did the same thing. Patrons of Industry and labor associations are almost universally in favor of it. It is stupendously impudent for an occasional man of ability to assume that because his prejudices will not let him see the light, therefore all good men are blind. One thing is certain, however; most bad men are against it. Lewd men and liquor organizations will oppose it to the last.

8. *"Bad women will vote."* Do not bad men vote? Is there any greater danger in allowing bad women to vote than in allowing bad men to vote? If a moral standard could be fixed and a moral test practically applied, it would be wise to exclude both bad men and bad women. In any case, they should be treated alike. To allow bad men to vote, and at the same time experience a shock at the thought of allowing bad women to vote, is illogical and ridiculously inconsistent.

9. *"Women cannot claim the suffrage as a class, since they are not a*

class, but a sex." The injustice of refusing the suffrage to a sex is much greater than refusing it to a race or a class. No race or class includes half the people in the world. But women do not claim the suffrage either as a class or a sex. They claim it as individuals, as beings created by God, and held responsible for their acts quite as much as men are. They realize their power to think, and they ask the right to crystallize their thoughts into effective agencies against evil. They deny that the fact of being women destroys their individuality or relieves them of responsibility. Women do not think it right to give the suffrage to any class, as a class, but to all honest individuals capable of using it intelligently.

10. *"Woman's mental nature is different from man's."* However it may be expressed, this is precisely the strongest reason why they should vote. God made man and woman different in characteristics, but He made the one the complement of the other. Perfect unity is wrought out of different but harmonious elements. Legislation will be essentially one-sided until man's ideals are balanced by woman's. Woman's individuality does differ from man's, and her individuality is necessary to perfect justice and harmony in the senate as well as in the home.

Woman's different mental attitude makes her vote valuable. She is the complement of man in the divine conception of humanity. Her vote should therefore be the complement of man's vote. The unity of related diversity produces harmony. The male and female elements of intellect and character when balanced produce the grandest unities of human intelligence. The enfranchisement of a sex means more than the liberation of a class chiefly because it brings a distinct and hitherto unrepresented element into the voting power of the world. There would be only a partial hope in securing woman suffrage if it would simply increase the number of voters. It will do much more than this. It will not only enlarge the voting power; it will enrich it.

11. *"Politics will degrade women."* *"It is because women have kept out of politics and generally out of the contentious arena, that they have remained gentle, tender and delicate women."* Politics should not be degrading. It is discreditable to men that the sacred duty of statecraft should be associated with any processes or experiences of a debasing character. But the presence of woman purifies politics. The women of Wyoming are as womanly and as gentle as those in the neighboring States where women do not vote. The women who lead in municipal reforms in England, or who champion the cause of woman's enfranchisement there, are as true and pure and sweet-voiced as those who are conventional models. Politics should mean high thinking on social and national questions, and the carrying out of calm decisions by voting for right measures. Thinking about her country's history and present condition and hopes and relationships to other countries, need not destroy a woman's gentleness. Strength of character does not rob woman of her witching charm. The

condition of politics, as admitted by this objection, indicates the need of woman's elevating, purifying influence.

Wendell Phillips crystallized the reply to this argument when he said, "Women will make the polling booth as pure as the parlor," and there is every reason to believe with Mr. Phillips that instead of politics degrading women, women would elevate politics. Why should it degrade a woman to do her part in making the laws of her country harmonize with her purest feelings and her highest thought? It is impossible to believe that such a result could follow such action. Character is not ennobled by thinking good thoughts, but by executing them. History proves conclusively that men have always risen to a higher dignity of manhood after being entrusted with the ballot. The result would inevitably be the same in the case of woman. The sense of responsibility would define and strengthen her character.

If politics are really degrading in themselves, men should be prohibited from taking part in them as well as women, but they are not necessarily degrading either to men or women. It is not necessary to theorize about this question, however. The test has been made for nearly forty years in Wyoming, and there has been no degradation of the women there, no unsexing, no loss of the sweetness and tenderness of woman's character. Rev. Dr. Crary, presiding elder in the Methodist Episcopal Church in Wyoming, writes: "The women of Wyoming are an honor to their sex, and deserve the respect of all who wish good government." Hon. Senator Carey, of Wyoming, said: "I know women who have exercised the fullest political rights for more than twenty years. Neither in their homes nor in public places have they lost one womanly quality." He says further: "In over twenty years I have never known a woman insulted or affronted in any way when exercising the privilege of citizenship." The *Daily Sentinel*, Laramie City, says: "We do not know of a decent man in Wyoming who wishes woman suffrage abolished."

12. *"When party lays its hand on the home, those who care for the home more than for party receive a warning to be on their guard."* The home should be a vital element in national life. Whoever brings the home element to bear more directly on politics is a benefactor to his race. The larger the voting power of a home, the greater its influence becomes in moulding the laws by which homes are to be governed. Woman should lay her hand on parties.

13. *"Hitherto the family has been a unit, represented in the State by its head; a change that throws the family into the political caldron surely calls for special consideration."* Hitherto the family has not been represented at all as a unity. One unit in the family has represented himself and assumed to represent others. The man who gathers the adult members of his family together to consult them with a view of representing the opinion of the majority of them by his vote, would be a curiosity. No man can, with any

sense of fairness, be said to represent his family unless he does this. The family has not always been a unit, because in many cases the father and several adult sons in the same family have votes. This fact has not disrupted the peace of reasonable families.

14. *"Wives might vote against their own husbands, and thus destroy the harmony of the home."* It is a strange conception of family harmony that husband and wife must think alike in regard to all subjects. This would not be true harmony, it would be mere sameness; and it is only logically conceivable on the surrender of the individuality of one to that of the other. This can never be done without degradation to the one who has to submit. Woman has had too much of such degradation. Why should two reasonable beings cease to recognize each other's right to independent judgment because they are married to each other? Woman suffrage will elevate the condition of both husband and wife. The wife will be emancipated from a subjection pronouned by God to be a curse, and the husband will be saved from the debasing selfishness of believing himself to be the only member of his household worthy of being entrusted with the dignity of voting.

It would be a great advantage if the drunkard's wife and the moderate drinker's wife could vote in opposition to their husbands. Such opposition would result in ultimate peace and not discord.

15. *"Wives would usually vote as their husbands wished, so the result would not be materially changed."* Wives would not always vote in accord with their husbands, but even if they felt disposed to do so in every case, they would do so only on condition that their husband's parties brought out clean candidates. This would mean a great deal, and would justify the admission of woman to the political arena, if no other argument could be advanced in favor of it.

It should be remembered that there are many unmarried women and widows who will have votes when woman suffrage is granted, so that it will not do to consider wives alone.

The hopeful answer to this objection lies in the fact that the wives and daughters of good men would be more likely than the wives and daughters of bad men to vote in harmony with their husbands.

16. *"Women are fairly represented by men. Their fathers and brothers vote."* They have never been fairly represented. There is no country in the world where the laws are fair to women. Since women began to take an interest in public affairs great changes have been made to improve the laws so as to make them fair to women, but the laws are still unjust to women. This is the natural result of having laws made by men alone. Buckle says: "There is no instance on record in the history of England of any class possessing power without abusing it." From the first establishment of representative government the class that held the franchise has always claimed that it represented all other classes, and that, therefore,

the other classes did not need to vote. The same claim is now made on behalf of the men. "Our class represents your class, men represent women, why are you not satisfied?" This is exactly what the hereditary aristocrat once said to all others, and it took centuries to induce the people of England to allow workingmen to vote. There should be no class legislation, but all classes must be allowed the right to vote or there can be no true representation of the people. When did woman surrender to man the right to represent her? No such surrender was ever made. Man arrogantly assumed the function of lawmaker, and now claims it as a right. George William Curtis forcibly said: "There is no audacity so insolent, no tyranny so wanton, no inhumanity so revolting as the spirit which says to any human being, or to a class of human beings, 'you shall be developed just as far as we choose, and as fast as we choose, and your mental and moral life shall be subject to our pleasure,' and this is what men have always said to women." If men are to represent women, women have at least the right to help to choose the men who are to represent them.

17. "*Women as a sex have no wrongs which male legislators cannot be expected to redress.*" The question is not whether male legislatures are qualified to redress wrongs or not. Women do not ask the right to vote merely to redress their wrongs. They ask the franchise because they believe themselves to be important elements in the national life of the country in which they live. They seek to vote and claim the right to be elected to positions on school boards, municipal councils, and even in legislatures, parliaments and congresses, in order that they may elevate the tone of public morals, and aid in securing laws for the protection of their brothers, sisters, sons and daughters. They do not wish to vote only for women, or on questions relating to women. They know that "unconsciousness of sex is essential to the best work of either sex." They wish to stand side by side with men in working out the grandest destiny of the race. It may not be out of place to say, however, that male legislatures never can represent women fully. No legislature composed of one class or sex ever has or ever can represent another class or sex. Again, until women are allowed to vote no legislature of any kind can possibly represent them. Representation necessitates voluntary choice on the part of those represented. Unless a parliament is elected by women as well as men it cannot claim to represent women in any accurate sense.

18. "*Male legislatures have already gone far in giving women statutory protection.*" Women do not ask protection. They ask justice. They ask recognition of their powers, and of their rights to use them. They ask freedom to perform their duty as they conceive it. True women resent man's idea that they are weak and delicate beings to be protected. From what are they to be protected? The only protection they need is from man himself in his assumption of their just rights and privileges. Woman

claims liberty, not protection. She is not content with barbaric or oriental subordination, nor with the equally degrading ideal of an extravagant chivalry. She asks recognition as a good, sensible human being, with powers as distinct and as essential as man's, which she purposes to use in co-operation with man in working out human destiny.

19. *"Women should have confidence in men."* Women have confidence in the justice of enlightened and unprejudiced men, and they are now engaged in enlightening man, and freeing him from his dwarfing prejudices. The fact that the ablest modern theologians and social scientists and many of the greatest statesmen are in favor of woman suffrage, gives woman confidence in man's justice. Woman asks man to undo a great wrong, and she believes he will be wise enough to recognize woman's responsible individuality, and just enough to free her from the restrictions of a primitive civilization. The fact that woman appeals to man for justice does not prove that women should be satisfied to allow man alone to continue to make laws, but the reverse. She appeals to man because at present he holds the power in his own hands, so that her appeal cannot logically be used as the basis of an argument against woman suffrage.

Men should trust women as much as they expect women to trust them. Women love and respect men quite as much as men love and respect women. Women would be as fair to men as men could be to women, but none of the men who urge women to be satisfied to allow male parliaments, responsible to men alone, to make laws for them, would themselves be willing to be governed by female parliaments responsible to women only. One case is as reasonable as the other.

20. *"There remain few bars to the competition of women with men in the professions and trades."* Why should there be any artificial barriers in woman's way to prevent her doing any honest work for which she has a taste, and for which she deems herself fitted? What right has a man to raise any barriers against woman? What right have women, even, to bar any pathway against an individual woman who wishes to walk therein? Liberal men and women are rapidly sweeping away the conventionalities that have crippled the efforts of women and circumscribed their spheres and dwarfed their very souls; but every step towards the light has been taken in opposition to unprogressive men and conventional women who vainly tried to check enlightening truth.

21. *"The transfer of power from the military to the unmilitary sex involves a change in the character of a nation. It involves, in short, national emasculation."* Again it is assumed that woman suffrage means woman's rule and man's dethronement. Again it must be stated that unity of rule, not woman's rule, is the aim of all reputable advocates of woman's enfranchisement. It is probable this would result in "a change in the character of the nation," but not such a change as that dreaded by its opponents.

The "war" argument is a very old one often answered. Women suffer as much as men from war. Their hardships at home are often equal, and their anxieties greater than those of the soldiers on the field or in the camp. Those soldiers are husbands, sons, brothers or lovers of sorrowing women. Many women labor in hospitals and various other ways for the soldiers. Woman's work is not man's work, nor man's work woman's, in war or in peace; but her work is quite as needful to the world's advancement, both in peace and war, as man's is. The time cometh, too, when "war shall be no more," and however man may sneer at woman suffrage, woman's work will aid in the fulfilment of this prophecy.

Then, too, very few men ever really fight for their country. The "war argument" would, therefore, disqualify most of the very men who use it from voting, and, carried to its logical limit, it would confine suffrage to soldiers alone. If the function of the State be only to raise armies and build court-houses and jails, woman may safely be refused the ballot; but if the State should deal with education, with moral, social, and industrial evolution, with art, science, charity, justice, manufactures and commerce, woman is entitled to her share in guiding the affairs of State.

22. *"Man alone can uphold government and enforce the law. Let the edifice of law be as moral as you will, its foundation is the force of the community, and the force of the community is male. Laws passed by the woman's vote will be felt to have no force behind them. Would the stronger sex obey any laws manifestly carried by the female vote in the interests of woman against man? Man would be tempted to resist woman's government when it galled him."* Women have made no proposal to establish a government by women. They strongly object to government by one sex, either male or female. It is not possible to have all the men voting on one side, and all the women on the other. All women do not think alike, nor will they ever vote unanimously any more than do the men. It is purely imaginary to speak of woman's government. Government will always be maintained by a majority composed of the united votes of men and women. Moreover votes are now cast in the ballot box, and it will not be possible to find out whether the majority consists chiefly of men or of women. Therefore it is clear that the question of force cannot be brought into the suffrage discussion. The force of a nation must remain on the side of the majority. But modern governments do not rely on force for their existence or for the execution of their laws. The edicts of despots had to be forced on unwilling people. Rebels to-day know that their rebellion is not against kings or governments, but against the will of the people. Men submit to laws because they have shared in making them.

23. *"The elevation of woman is a different thing from assimilation to man."* Woman does not ask assimilation to man. She could not be assimilated if she wished such a change. God made her woman, and she cannot make herself man. Her mental and moral nature is as distinctive as her

physical nature. Just why some people imagine that the suffrage would assimilate her to man is not clear. Woman has now the right to think, and to express her thoughts in books or on the platform. These things do not assimilate her to man; neither would the marking of a ballot paper.

24. *"Woman, if she becomes a man, will be a weaker man."* This statement rests upon a misconception. Women do not wish to be virified. Women are not virified by public work. Women write learnedly on public questions without loss of womanly tenderness or grace. Surely voting once in four or five years, or even once a year, will not make a woman virile. Lucy Stone could quell riotous mobs at anti-slavery meetings, but she was always a sweet-voiced, modest little woman, and she loved her husband and babe as well as any wife or mother ever did. Women cannot be transformed into men. If they could be, there would be less hope in their enfranchisement. Woman suffrage will not merely increase votes, it will bring a new element into the voting power of the world. Women are essentially different from men, and they cannot become like men. The unity of the woman element with the man element in character is as essential to true harmony and true progress in the State as in the home.

> "Everywhere
> Two heads in council, two beside the hearth,
> Two in the tangled business of the world,
> Two in the liberal offices of life,
> Two plummets, dropt for one, to sound the abyss
> Of science, and the secrets of the mind."
>
> —*Tennyson.*

25. *"If woman becomes a man she must be prepared to resign her privilege as a woman. She cannot expect to have both privilege and equality."* Thoughtful women demand no privileges because they are women. They would be satisfied if they could stand beside their brothers on a perfectly equal footing. They reject subordination, and they resent the patronizing gallantry which assumes their inferiority or their vanity. They see that their sex has been weakened both by subjection and by sentimental gallantry. It is not complimentary to men to assume that they are courteous to women because they believe them to be inferior or weaker, or that men would be less polite to women if women had the privilege of living up to their highest ideals of duty by taking part in the development of their country. Neither is it complimentary to womanhood to tell women that they have special privileges because they are effeminate, and that they will lose these privileges unless they respectfully keep their places in the sphere assigned to them by men. Even the most exquisite language fails to give dignity to this old "Then you may stand in the street car" argument.

If women had votes, politicians at any rate would be much more deferential to them. When workingmen got votes, the politicians began to take off their hats to them, never before. Give women more power, and you necessarily increase their dignity, not only in the eyes of others, but in their own estimation. The latter result is of even more importance than the former. The consciousness of added dignity and higher duties is a mighty, uplifting force. True gentlemen do not lift their hats to women because women are weak and pretty, but because they are true. Lifting the hat should be an act of reverence, not of mere gallantry. The courage of conviction that leads a woman to do her duty to her country does not make her less truly modest.

26. *"Woman never painted a transfiguration or wrote a great epic."* If there is any reasonable foundation in such an argument, it may be answered by saying, "Do not allow women to vote in regard to great epics, or great paintings." But the argument is irrelevant. It is not necessary for women to write epics or paint transfigurations in order to be qualified to vote. If this test were applied to men, there would not be an average of one male voter for each great nation in the world.

27. *"Woman is weaker than man physically."* Has she strength enough to go to the polls and vote? If she has, the question of strength has nothing more to do with deciding the question of suffrage.

Men are allowed to vote who are carried in bed to the polls, so that by man's own physical standard set for himself, woman is competent to vote. No physical test has been adopted for men; none must be fixed for women. The strength test, and the sex test cannot be the same.

28. *"Woman's brain is not so large as man's, therefore she should not vote."* Size of brain has never been made a test in deciding man's right to vote, so this objection is irrelevant. No one ever saw an official at a polling booth with a tape-line to measure men's heads to decide whether they should vote or not. It is therefore perfectly illogical to raise the question of the size of woman's head in discussing her right to vote. If a standard could be fixed for the size of a voter's head, and applied in the case of men as well as women, there would be justice in the rule, but little sense. Only small-headed men, with their largest development in the back of their heads near the top, could be illogical enough to propose such a test. Quality of brain is more important than size of brain. Thousands of men vote in every country who are not equal in intelligence to the average woman. The great body of men most uniformly opposed to equal suffrage are not only small-headed, but small-hearted.

29. *"Brain work is more exhaustive to woman than to man."* What has this statement of an assumed fact to do with suffrage? The only logical relationship it can have in deciding the question is in deciding whether a woman can vote without becoming a mental wreck. There is no more mental exhaustion in going out to vote than in going out to buy a yard of

ribbon. The necessary reading and thought to enable women to vote intelligently will be stimulating, not exhausting. "What! Stimulating to the laboring woman?" Yes; stimulating most of all to her, because it will bring most variety, most new intellectual life to her.

30. *"Women are more nervous than men, and the excitement of elections would undermine their constitutions and tend to unbalance them."* Thousands of men vote whose nervous systems are in a worse condition than the nervous system of the average woman. Men indulge in smoking, in the drink habit and in other habits exhaustive to the nervous system more than women do, so men should take care lest, by suggesting a nervous test, they may be establishing a principle that will disfranchise the male sex at no distant date. If humanity demands that woman should be prohibited from voting in order to prevent her physical deterioration in consequence of her present weakness, surely the same principle would prohibit those men from voting who are weaker than women, in order to prevent the further deterioration of their already enfeebled bodies.

It is very satisfactory to note that men as well as women are becoming aroused in regard to the physical deterioration of women under false conditions, and that widespread efforts are being made to improve the conditions of training and living so that woman may have the opportunity to develop vigor and endurance as freely as man.

Woman has been restricted in her physical development by conventionalities and erroneous notions that proscribed outdoor games as improper for her. She has, by custom, been confined to the house. Men have made it popular with women to be somewhat delicate, because they have too often shown a decided tendency to admire the frail, timid, dependent, "clinging little creatures." Robustness was really a disadvantage to a woman, and was likely to gain for her a reputation for masculinity. Dr. Gregory, in his "Legacy to My Daughters," recommended girls who were so unfortunate as to be robust by nature, to constantly simulate a sickly delicacy, so that they might have the necessary feminine charm.

Sensible men and women have ceased to regard weakness as an essential characteristic of true womanhood. Women are freeing themselves from the tyranny of social customs which injure their health, and they are rapidly regaining the individuality which enables them to discard modes of dress that prevent the full and natural growth of their vital organs. Popular opinion and popular sentiment are removing the ban from girls and young women which made it immodest for them to play at outdoor sports, and so the women of the future are likely to get a fair chance to have better bodies. They need boating, the ball games, the running games and all sports that make energetic physical effort an essential to success quite as much as boys do; they need them more, indeed, to help to overcome the false training of centuries.

31. *"There appears to be a tendency among the leaders of the revolt of*

woman to disparage matrimony as a bondage, and the rearing of children as an aim too low for an intellectual being." It is natural to suppose that this general statement is limited to the female leaders of the so-called revolt. No one would charge such men as Wendell Phillips, George William Curtis, Phillips Brooks, Joseph Cook, T. W. Higginson, Emerson, Longfellow, Whittier, Bishop Simpson, Charles Sumner, Chief Justice Chase, Charles Kingsley, Professor Huxley, or more than half the members of the British Parliament with such a tendency. The statement is equally foundationless in regard to the women among the leaders. All distinguished women do not marry. Neither do all distinguished men.

32. *"Women must bear and nurse children, and if they do this, it is impossible that they should compete with men in occupations which demand complete devotion as well as superior strength of muscle or brain."* This argument might fairly be ruled out of a discussion on woman suffrage, but it may be answered in several ways. Women do not wish to compete with men in all occupations. They are the best judges of what they should or should not do, and every rule of fair play demands that they be allowed to decide for themselves. All women do not get the opportunity of marrying. Voting is not a laborious occupation "requiring complete devotion as well as superior strength." It means but a pleasant walk and a few minutes time. Canvassing will not always be an important factor in elections, and so long as it has to be done, married women with young families can be spared from taking part in it. There are plenty of men, and unmarried women, and widows, and married women with grown-up children, to do all the essential work of electioneering. Voting would waste none of woman's strength, and not so much of her time as is needed to make a fashionable call. But many married women have to bear and raise their children, and earn most of the money for their support, too. There are too many cases in cities where women support drunken husbands in addition to their children, yet on election day the husband may vote for the politicians who license the drink traffic, while the suffering wife has no right to vote for the protection of herself and her children.

33. *"The strain of political life would disqualify women for motherhood."* This would be a fatal objection if it had either a sound, practical or physiological basis. It has neither. The argument is foundationless, practically, because there are plenty of widows, of mothers, whose families are grown up, and of elderly unmarried women to do all the necessary active political work of organization and canvassing that should properly be done by women. The great mass of women would simply have to decide how to vote, and then vote. The intellectual effort of decision in regard to public questions would be no more exhaustive than the intellectual effort to decide many other questions that women have to decide at present. The vast majority of women do all the thinking and feeling now that is

necessary to enable them to vote intelligently. They hear public questions discussed in their own homes, at social gatherings, at Christian Endeavor meetings, at Epworth League meetings, at temperance meetings, at lectures and even at political meetings. Women generally have already arrived at clear decisions in regard to many social reforms, and are quite ready to vote now without any mental exhaustion whatever.

This argument is equally foundationless from the physiological standpoint. Of course, Herbert Spencer is quoted as saying that "a deficiency of reproductive power in women results from overtaxing their brains." But no one can truthfully assert that to allow women to vote will "overtax their brains." Neither can anyone reasonably claim that woman has not as much right to think and as much need to think as man has. Even if it be granted that Mr. Spencer's statement be quite correct, it does not prove that energetic and sustained mental effort by women is essentially an evil, but it does prove that to direct the whole of the forces of our being to one department of our power to the neglect of other departments, is necessarily evil. Mr. Spencer himself evidently holds this view, because he asserts that "physical labor makes woman less fertile," although he thinks more evidence is needed to prove this fully. Clearly his opinion is, that the intensification of intellectual effort to the neglect of physical training, must lead to the deterioration of physical energy, the weakening of the vital organism, and, therefore, to a "deficiency of reproductive power." This statement is also true if the physical powers be overstrained and the intellectual powers neglected. The destruction of the natural and essential harmony between the physical, intellectual and spiritual powers by overtraining, or overexerting any department of human power at the expense of the others, is inevitably evil in its effects. Mr. Spencer was narrow in looking among women only for loss of reproductive power, as a result of overtaxing the brain. Mr. Galton found a similar result among men under similar conditions. There is no question of sex involved in the facts. It is as true of man as of woman, that overtaxing one department of power inevitably entails loss of power in others; and the danger of loss increases as the overtaxing is prolonged. No sane person will claim, however, that because this is true, therefore men or women should stop either intellectual or physical effort.

Even if the loss of power described was confined to women, there is no reasonable man , however prejudiced he may be against woman suffrage, who will claim that the Creator intended women to do no thinking. It would be equally unreasonable to allow women to think without giving them perfect freedom in applying their thought. Freedom of thought is a myth, unless the right to think is accompanied by the right to execute thought within the recognized limits fixed by the rights of others. Overexertion of the brain is an evil for either man or woman; but a proper amount of intellectual effort is essential to the best development of both sexes. The intellectual effort that is most productive of good to both men and women, is that which does not die as mere thought, but which lives in executed purpose for the good of humanity. To think is good, but it is still better for the thinker as well as the world to crystallize the thought into a vote. Nothing stimulates new thought so much as executing the thought we already have. Nothing has a more paralyzing effect on the moral force of the race than to train it to think without performing the results of its thinking.

Voting will ennoble womanhood, and qualify woman for truer mother-hood. Henry Ward Beecher truly said: "In the augmentation of her liberty and the enlargement of her sphere, she has forsaken no duty of home, and lost no grace of tenderness and love. She has become a better mother, a better wife, daughter, sister, friend, by just that enlargement which it was predicted would unsex her. A woman is better fitted for home, who is also fit for something else."

34. *"If women were allowed to vote there would be too many voters."* This is a last refuge for men without argument. It has always been the cry of the voting class when an extension of the franchise was proposed. It is now the cry of the voting sex.

Even if the statement were reasonable, sex is neither a logical nor a practical basis for the suffrage. If it was suggested that a certain amount of intelligence and experience should be the basis for the right to vote, there would be some force in the argument of the restrictionists. It cannot be denied that thousands of women have intelligence enough to vote and wish to vote, that thousands of women pay taxes, and that all women have to submit to the laws. Sex is an absurd basis for suffrage. All just men would see that it is so, if some of them were not still blinded by prejudice.

35. *"Women would quarrel with each other if they had to conduct public business."* Women even with a very limited experience now conduct large meetings, conventions, congresses, etc., as quietly and in as business-like a manner as men.

It must be remembered, too, that no one proposes to have women alone in Parliament.

It is possible that women might sometimes get angry, but so do men. Unfortunately, there have been disgraceful scenes in the highest representative bodies of men in the parliaments of such Christian nations as Canada, United States, France, Germany and England, even during recent years. It is a recognized fact that when the two sexes are present each one acts as a restraining and an elevating power on the other. God made the one sex the helpful complement of the other. Political meetings have lost their bitterness and rowdyism since women began to attend them. Parliamentary procedure will be more dignified and polished as soon as women sit in Parliament.

36. *"To withhold a vote is not essentially an interference with liberty. A man may have liberty without a vote, and a vote without liberty."* This statement is more epigrammatic than accurate. No man is free, in the true sense of the word, unless he has the fullest rights of citizenship, independent of all limitations. The right to vote is the highest test of liberty.

37. *"For an abstract claim of right there appears to be no foundation. Power which is natural carries with it right, though it is subject to the restraint of conscience."* This is simply a beautifully masked assertion of the horrible doctrine that "might is right." It ignores the fact, too, that intellectual and spiritual powers are the highest powers, and that they are "natural powers" quite as much as physical force is. Nothing but the inherited tendency to assume superiority for the male sex could lead any liberal or cultured man to state that man has any abstract right to vote that does not equally belong to woman. Woman is governed by law as man is; woman may own property and pay taxes as man does; woman is interested in the home and in the State as fully as man is; woman is as much interested in her children as man is; woman is a responsible individual quite as much as man is. It is utterly unjust to say that every abstract claim of right that can be established in favor of man's voting does not belong equally to woman.

38. *"What leaders of the women's rights movement practically seek is for the woman power without reponsibility, for the man responsibility without power."* Both these statements misrepresent the men and women who advocate woman suffrage. Women recognize their responsibility; at least, those who ask enfranchisement do so. Experience would deepen this sense of responsibility. Some women do not ask the right to vote simply because they do not recognize their responsibility. Those who clearly see their responsibility merely ask the right to do their duty. Women do not seek to take the power out of men's hands. They wish to share power as well as responsibility with them.

39. *"Man's life is more or less public, while that of woman is in the home."* Granting the correctness of this statement, does it not prove the need of woman suffrage in order that the home may be represented in the body politic? Is the home of so little consequence to the State that it needs no direct representation? The home element is the most important in the State, and the fact that "the life of the woman is in the home," proves beyond a doubt that woman is naturally intended to speak and vote for the home.

40. *"Men feel, as a sex, the full measure of responsibility in public action. This is not felt as strongly by their partners."* It would be a great blessing if by a stroke of his magic wand some magician could make men live up to the first of these statements. Comparatively few men realize the sacred responsibility of public action, even in voting. It may be true that men feel public responsibility more than women. There is only one way in

which responsibility can become clear to the minds either of men or women, and that is by doing duty. Self-activity is an absolute essential in revealing thought, feeling or responsibility. Woman will feel the responsibilities of public duties when she is allowed to perform them.

41. *"The woman of the political platform does not limit her ambition to a vote. She wants to sit in Parliament or in Congress."* Why not? Many of the men in any Parliament or in Congress could easily be replaced by women of larger intelligence, greater breadth of view and better education. There are plenty of women of leisure whose duties would permit them to assume the responsibilities of representing their fellow-citizens in Parliament. There is no new principle in this idea. Women have long been elected to positions on school boards and municipal councils. It might shock the prejudices of some conventional people at first to see women in Parliament, but prejudices have a habit of being shocked by the practical developments of our progressive age. The best thing to do with prejudices is to shock them. Prejudices must always yield to common-sense and justice, and each successive generation becomes freer from the bondage of prejudices. There is no danger that women will turn all the men out of Parliament. It would be as unjust and as unwise to have the men ruled by women alone as it now is to have women ruled by men alone.

What right has man to draw lines to debar women from the fullest growth possible? Gibbon properly named man "the usurping sex." He has usurped the right to circumscribe woman in regard to her education, her sphere, her privileges and her duties for centuries; but women, conscious of their own individuality and their own responsibilities, have gone bravely on and ignoring the lines so arrogantly drawn by man, have assumed many duties formerly reserved for men, and have forced the world to acknowledge their fitness for any sphere of honorable labor to which they have aspired. Men may as well learn once for all that man has no divine commission to "draw lines" for women. The genius of the age is in favor of removing the barriers from the paths of both men and women, instead of placing restrictions in their way. Why should not women be elected to any positions if the people deem them qualified to fill them? All women are not qualified to be members of Parliament. All men are not so qualified. It is a difficult matter to get one well-qualified man in each municipality to represent it in Parliament. When women are permitted to sit in Parliament there will be more good candidates to choose from. Unless men deteriorate, the sexes in the ideal condition should be represented equally, or nearly so. At first only a very small proportion of women would be elected, because women, so far, have not been allowed to receive the necessary training to qualify them for parliamentary duties. Twenty-five years will make a great change in this respect, however.

42. *"If the Creator had intended woman to be man's equal in every respect He would have made her man instead of woman."* Women do not

claim to be equal to man in every respect. Man is not equal to woman in every respect. The question of equality of the sexes does not logically enter into the discussion of the right and duty of woman suffrage. Henry Ward Beecher's answer to this objection is probably the best ever written. He says: "It will scarcely be denied that men are superior to women—as men; and that women are immeasurably superior to men—as women; while both of them together are more than a match for either of them separately."

SUMMARY OF REASONS IN FAVOR OF EQUAL SUFFRAGE.

1. Men and women were created equal in rights and responsibility. The more unequal they are in powers and qualities, the greater the need for women to vote.

2. Subordination to man was pronounced by God as a curse, a part of Eve's curse for her sin. Christ made it possible to overcome all the effects of this curse. Failure to overcome is sinful.

3. Women were chosen by God for the highest official positions in the State during the theocracy, when He directed the appointment of the rulers of His people.

4. Women were distinctly recognized by Christ as important workers in His cause.

5. Women held official positions in the early Christian Church.

6. Woman's freedom marks the distinction between Christian and pagan nations more definitely than anything else.

7. Individual liberty and individual responsibility were the greatest lessons taught by Christ.

8. Woman is a responsible individual; and the fact of being a woman does not destroy her individuality or lesson her responsibility.

9. Women vote in church meetings by consent of the most advanced Christian opinion. This being granted, there is no logical ground for denying their right to vote in the State. Christians at any rate cannot claim that the work of the State is more important than the work of the Church.

10. Woman's vote would speedily settle the saloon question, and many other moral and social questions.

11. Even if all married women remained faithful to their husbands' political opinions, parties would be compelled to choose pure, honest men with clean records as candidates.

12. Women have as much right as men to have their opinion crystallized into law.

13. Woman represents the home, and the home should be represented in the State. The fiends who ruin the sons and daughters of the home may vote. The mothers of those sons and daughters should help to make laws to protect the home.

14. Woman represents an idea of God, evidenced by her being created with feelings and powers different from man's. The development and influence of the woman ideal is essential to the true progress of humanity.

15. The unity of manhood and womanhood in the State is as important as their unity in the home. God made each the necessary complement of the other.

16. Woman represents the moral force of the community more fully than man. There are ten times as many men as women in the penitentiaries of the world.

17. Woman, like man, is a creature in whom progressive civilizations develop higher capacities and new aptitudes. Man has no right to limit growth that God meant to be infinite.

18. Women love their husbands, fathers, brothers and sons quite as much as men love their wives, mothers, sisters and daughters; therefore, no class is in danger from woman suffrage.

19. From the home with seven sons, eight votes go out on election day, however ignorant or wicked father and sons may be. From the neighboring home, in which the family consists of seven daughters, only one vote may be cast, however cultured and pure the daughters of the second home may be.

20. Women may hold property and pay taxes; therefore, so long as property-holding and tax-paying are elements in qualifying for the suffrage, women should be entitled to vote.

21. If the standard for voting be intelligence and education, women who pass the required tests should have votes. Imbecile males and all females are now prohibited from voting.

22. If morality and conformity to law be the basis of voting rights, then women who are moral and law-abiding should have the right to vote. Criminal men and all women are now prohibited from voting.

23. Women who violate the law of their country must submit to its penalties. It is cowardly and unjust to refuse women the right to assist in making the laws by which they have to be governed.

24. Woman's voting would purify elections, and make the polling booth as refining as the parlor.

25. Woman's voting would help to do away with the double standard of morality for men and women.

26. Equal suffrage would be a stimulus to woman's culture, an agency in her development, and the most direct and effective process by which she could perform her duty, as she conceives it, towards God and humanity.

27. Woman's voting in school, municipal and Parliamentary elections has proved a perfect success and shown the fallacy of all theoretical objections to it.

SKETCHES WITH MORALS.

Mr. Jones and Mr. Smith are neighbors. Mr. Jones is an educated gentleman, and his wife is a woman of broad culture. Both have generous, altruistic purposes and high national and social ideals. They have seven daughters, who have all grown to maturity. None of them are married. They have all received a liberal education. They have read widely in regard to social questions and political economy. They are exemplary women, who are active in devotion to religious and philanthropic duties. They have clear and definite views on public questions.

Mr. Smith is an ignorant, dissipated man, and his wife is an ignorant, dispirited woman. They have seven sons, whose education is of the most meagre character. Their moral training has been very defective. They have been allowed to grow up in idleness, without learning any trade or following any regular means of earning a living. Three of them have been fined for breaches of the peace while under the influence of liquor, and two of them served short terms in prison for stealing.

On election day the Jones family counts one, and the Smith family counts eight. The family that is a burden to the State and a menace to civilization has eight times as much influence as the family that is self-respecting, self-supporting and co-operative in all that tends to uplift society. The family that respects and obeys law counts one; the family that despises and defies law counts eight. The family whose votes may be bought by any evil system or immoral institution or corrupt party, votes eight times; the family that is incorruptible votes but once, and even its poor solitary vote is dependent on the short life of a delicate old man. A March wind, a November rain, or an accident may rob the entire Jones family of its franchise. Seven males in the Smith family may be carried to the grave, and still the Smith family will have as much ballot power as the Jones family.

Clearly sex is not a true basis for suffrage either logically or practically.

Mr. and Mrs. Thompson live on a poor street in a large city. They have five children, all boys. They were born in a rural district, but came to live in the city eight years after they were married. Mr. Thompson is a plasterer, and for about two years after they came to live in the city he worked regularly at his trade. During the winter season, while out of work he fell in with bad company and learned to drink. He is now a confirmed drunkard. He rarely does a day's work. His wife supports the family by washing, and is assisted by kind friends connected with the church which she attends with her children. She pays the rent of the home. She provides the food for her children and her husband. She works at night making over gifts of old clothing so that her family may be kept respectable. She gives every power of her life willingly to the man who once loved her, and to her boys. Her greatest hope is that her boys may become honest, sober,

Christian men and good citizens. She looks with a heavy heart at her youngest, bright little Sam, with the fearful consciousness that he will probably have an inherited taste for liquor, a willpower weakened by the dissipation of his father, and a nervous system enfeebled by the anxiety, the hopeless waiting, and the overwork of his mother before he was born. She knows that the saloon wrecked her happy home, and she fears that it may destroy her hopes of brighter days in future when her sons grow up. She longs for the time when her country shall stop licensing men to rob women and children. She has been told that the laws of a nation are made by the votes of the people in it. She reasons that as she is one of the people she is entitled to help to make the laws by which she has to be governed, and that is is her duty to do so. She resolves to vote on election day for the man who promises to work for closing the saloons. She goes to the polling booth and asks for her ballot paper. She is told she has no vote. Coarse men jeer at her, and despairingly she turns to go home. As she turns she sees her husband in a state of intoxicated stupor, led in to vote by a ruffian hired by the saloon party. The representative of the State gives him a ballot, which he proceeds to mark as he has been instructed by the enemies of home, and womanhood, and childhood.

The man was allowed by the laws of a Christian nation to vote for the perpetuation of a traffic that is the greatest enemy to Christian civilization; the woman who supports him and his family, and pays taxes in the same Christian nation was not permitted to vote against a system that has blighted her life and threatens to curse the five boys who are now the sources of her only earthly hope. The man's motive in voting was solely to pay for the free whiskey given him that morning: the woman's motive was to save her husband and her sons, and to aid in the propagation of truth and justice.

Sex is clearly not a true basis for suffrage, either logically or practically.

Yonder is an immense host of negroes, a great army of men marching to the ballot-box to help to make their country's laws. Through no fault of theirs, they are nearly all ignorant, uncultured men. They have had no training in political economy. They know nothing of the historical development of nations. They are allowed to vote, however, because they were born males. Here is a larger army who are educated in the fundamental laws of human progress and the development of civil institutions. Their whole experience has given them an intimate practical acquaintance with the best results of modern civilization. They are of mature years, sound judgment and strict morals. They are deeply interested in all social and economic questions, but they cannot aid in making the laws of their country. They happened to be born girls instead of boys. They must "keep their places," "remain in their proper spheres," fixed by men, and submit to the laws which the most ignorant males in their country help to make.

Sex is clearly not a true basis for suffrage, either logically or practically.

James Johnson was twenty-one yesterday. Mrs. Brown is the lecturer on History and Ethics in the university from which James has just graduated. James votes today. Mrs. Brown is not allowed to vote.

Sex is clearly not a true basis for suffrage, either logically or practically.

Here is a long line of foreigners who are waiting their turn to vote. They are in Ontario. They cannot speak the English language. They have lived in Canada but a short time. They know nothing of the issues to be decided by the election. They are guided in their voting by paid agents of a party or of parties. They are encouraged to vote because they were not born women. In the same city in which they live are thousands of intelligent, cultured women, authors, lecturers, teachers, managers of departments in large institutions, who have studied the great public questions of their country, but they are not permitted to vote.

Sex is clearly not a true basis for suffrage, either logically or practically.

'ANSWERS TO AN ANTI-SUFFRAGIST', 1913

Francis Marion Beynon, 'Answers to an Anti-suffragist', *The Grain Growers' Guide*, 1 October 1913, vol. X, 1010.

... The theory that a woman should appeal to a man through her basest qualities—her vanity, her weakness, for which a more honest word is incompetence; her mental dependence, which is either ignorance or stupidity, revolts me, more especially as these attributes appeal to the basest side of man's nature—his vanity, his sensual passions and his arrogance. I refuse to believe that such a low appeal is necessary to the perpetuation of the human race....

We have too long been contented with the kind of motherhood that can look out of the window and see little children toiling incredible hours in factories or canning sheds over the way, until their small heads grow dizzy and their little fingers are bruised and bleeding, and say calmly, "Thank God, it isn't my children," or who can see the poor wayward girl being driven into a life of disgrace and shame by economic conditions and turn coolly away, content that her own daughter is chaste; with the sort of motherhood that can know that in the poor districts of our cities tiny babies are dying like flies and yet feel no responsibility for the conditions that cause their death.

I tell you, sisters, this kind of motherhood isn't good enough for the present day. We want a new spirit of national motherhood—mothers whose love for their own children teaches them love for all children;

mothers who will not boast of their weakness but seek for strength to fight the battle for their own and their neighbors' children; mothers who are more concerned with raising the moral and intellectual standards of the community and country in which they live than in applying the latest suggestions of the beauty doctor.

WOMEN ARE DISCONTENTED

Nellie L. McClung, *The New Citizenship* (Political Equality League of Manitoba, n.d.), pp. 2-8. Reprinted by permission to the Estate of Nellie McClung.

Ideas are contagious and epidemic. They break out unexpectedly and without warning. Thought without expression is dynamic and gathers volume by repression. Evolution, when blocked and suppressed, becomes revolution.

At the present time there are many people seriously alarmed by the discontent among women. They say women are no longer contented with woman's work and woman's sphere. Women no longer find their highest joy in plain sewing and working in wool. The washboard has lost its charm and the days of the hair wreath are ended. Many people view this condition with alarm and believe that women are deserting the sacred sphere of home-making and the rearing of children; in short, that women are losing their usefulness. We may as well face the facts. We cannot drive women back to the spinning wheel and the mat hook. We do hear more of discontent among women than we once did. Labor saving devices have entered the home and women are saved the endless labor of days gone by, when a woman's hours of labor were: 5 a.m. to 5 a.m. The reason we hear of more discontent than formerly is that women have more time to be discontented. The horse on the treadmill may be discontented, but he has to keep on going, he has no time to tell his troubles to the horse near him.

But discontent is not necessarily wicked. There is such a thing as criminal contentment and there is such a thing as divine discontent. Discontent means the stirring of ambition, the desire to spread out, to improve, to grow. Discontent is a sign of life corresponding to growing pains in a healthy child. The poor woman who is making a brave struggle for existence, whose every energy is bent to the task of making a living, is not saying much. She has not time. The women who are making the disturbance are women who have time of their own, who have time for observation. Women have more leisure than men now and the question is what are they going to do with it. Custom and conventionality recommends amusements, social functions intermixed with kindly deeds of charity, the making of strong and durable garments for the poor, visiting the sick, comforting the sad, advising the erring, all of which women are doing, but the trouble arises here,—is this, while women do these things they are thinking, they wonder about the causes, the underlying conditions,—must they always be.

Women have never yet lived in their own world. Man has assigned woman her sphere. Woman's sphere is anything a man does not wish to do himself. This is a simple distribution of labor and easily understood and very satisfactory to half the population. Men have given a great deal of attention to women. They have told us exactly what we are like. They have declared us to be illogical, hysterical, impulsive, loving, patient, forgiving, malicious, vindictive, bitter, not any too honest, not very reliable. They have given us credit for all the good in the world and yet blamed us for all the evil. They are very prone to speak of women, as a class, of women—women in bulk, making each individual woman responsible for the sins of all.

Recently when members of the W.C.T.U. went before our law makers in Ottawa, pleading for a much needed reform, the prohibition of cigarettes, pleading in the name of our boys, who are every day being ruined in body and soul, one of the members of Parliament rose in his place and told these women to go home and reform their own sex before they came looking for any reforms from men. He said women were the slaves of fashion and should not look for any measure of reform from men until their own sex was emancipated. No one would have dared to speak so illogically to men. Think of telling half-a-dozen men to go home and reform all mankind! Quite a large order, too,—yet women have constantly to listen to such unjust and unreasonable criticism. This insult to womanhood passes unchallenged! The fault is not with the individual, but with the race. Our earliest writers spoke of women always in the mass. St. Augustine, one of the early writers of the Christian Church, described women as "a household menace, a daily peril, a necessary evil." St. Paul made his contribution, too, and although he was careful to say that in this matter he spoke on his own authority, yet this has not in any way obscured the faith of those who wish to believe as he did. "Wives obey your husbands." A woman must not speak in the Church but ask her husband quietly at home. St. Paul has made his commentary on the marriage question too, and advises all Christian workers to remain single "even as I am," but he goes on, "Marry if you must, only do not say 'I did not warn you.'"

No wonder women have had a hard time living down these things. In our own day we have historians who undertake to state what we are like and just where we stand. Sir Almoth Wright has recently written a book which no doubt will be popular in some circles. He says there are no good women, though there are some women who have come under the influence of good men. Women have never yet lived in their own world. Our world has been made for us; even the fashions for which we receive so much criticism are made by men. The feet of little girls in China are bound by the mother and the nurse, but it is not for their pleasure that this torture is practised, but that the little girl may be pleasing in the eyes of her father and in the eyes of a possible future husband. Missionaries tell us of the mother's grief and compassion for the little sufferer, yet the cruel fashion goes on. In our own civilization women have been taught that they must attract men. The attractive girl is the successful girl in the judgment of the world, and there is a deeper reason for this than appears, for the attractiveness of a girl often determines her social standing. A pretty girl marries a millionaire, is presented at court and travels in Europe; her plainer sister, though perhaps more intelligent and more unselfish, marries a boy from home, lives on a farm and works out in the harvest time. I am not comparing the two destinies as to which holds the greatest chances for usefulness or happiness, but merely showing how widely divergent two lives may be. A woman's social standing largely depends upon her ability to attract men and her chances of marriage are so directly in proportion to her personal charm that our girls have one definite problem which excludes all others. For this reason beauty parlors flourish and University extension lectures languish.

We blame girls for dressing foolishly, boldly and immodestly, yet we who uphold this system of women's economic and social dependence are responsible for it. It is perfectly true that men are attracted by the bold, foolish and frivolous girls, and that the girl who is quite independent and strong minded is matrimonially disqualified. My little boy, in giving me directions one time as to what he wanted his birthday present to be, told me he wanted "something foolish"—thereby expressing a truly masculine wish.

Under our present social conditions many a woman has found that it pays to be foolish. Men like frivolity before marriage and yet all the sterner virtues after marriage. Men like frivolity and women have taken them at their word and given them too much of it.

The economic dependence of women, making it necessary that women must attract for a living, is one of the greatest injustices that has been done us.

Women are naturally the guardians of the race. Women know the cost of human life as no man can ever know it. Women learned to cook so that her children might be fed, learned to sew that her children might be clothed, learned to think that her children might be guided. Women no longer can be flattered or threatened into silence. For long years the old iniquitous lie has been told us that the hand that rocks the cradle rules the world, but it is no longer believed by thinking women. It is intended more as a bouquet than as a straight statement of facts. It is given as a sedative to soothe us if we grow restless. When driving with a small child we often let the little fellow hold the end of the reins, and if the child really believes he is driving we consider the game successful, but we cannot deceive the average child very long. So, too, the average woman refuses to be deceived when she is praised like an angel and treated like an idiot. The hand that rocks the cradle does not rule the world or the liquor traffic would have been outlawed many years ago. Would any mother accept money in return for her boy's soul, the purity of his mind and the health of his body? Would any liquor dealer dare to offer you money for the privilege of corrupting your son? "May your money perish with you!" you would cry in scorn, yet our Province does this, our Government does this and glorifies and justifies its action. If it is wrong for the individual to accept blood money, why is it not wrong for a State? The liquor traffic and the white slave traffic are kept up by men for men, women are the victims, women pay the price. Oh no, when the hand that rocks the cradle gets its chance at ruling the world, it will be a safer, sweeter, cleaner world for the occupant of the cradle. Women have kept silence a long time. They have religiously believed it their duty like charity to bear all things, believe all things, endure all things. Now a change has come. Women are awakening to a sense of citizenship. No longer is the ideal woman the one who never lifts her eyes higher than the top pantry shelf nor allows her sympathy to extend past her own family. Women who believed they must sit down and be resigned are now rising up and being indignant. The new womanhood is the new citizenship. Women are asking why should property be held more sacred than human life, why is a man punished more severely for stealing a fur coat or a gold watch than he is for stealing a woman's virtue, her happiness and her good name? Why is it that in the law of this Province a woman has no legal claim on either her home or her child? Why is a man liable to five years' imprisonment for stealing a young girl and fourteen years' imprisonment for stealing cattle? Why is a woman's virtue valued at only $25.00 in this Province? Why is not a woman factory inspector in this city, where there are so many more women employees than men? Why are women's petitions so regularly and systematically ignored? Why are women not given equal pay for equal work? Why are women debarred from taking up homesteads? Why are women, physically weaker than men, further handicapped in the race of life by political nonentity? Why are women on election day classed with idiots, lunatics and criminals? These are some of the questions women are asking in this Province and the wise politician is the one who listens. It is no use to try to hush us up, we refuse to be hushed. These questions cannot be smoothed over, they must be settled.

Politicians tell us it would never do to give women equal pay with men or let them take up homesteads, for that would make women even more independent of marriage than they are at the present time, and it is not independent women we want—it is population.

Granting that population is very desirable, would it not be a wise plan to try to save what we have? Six thousand boys are needed in Canada every year to take the place of the six thousand drunkards who drop out of the race. How would it be to save them? Thousands of babies die every year from preventable causes. Would it not be a good plan to try to save them? In the far West where women are beyond the reach of nurses and doctors, many mothers and babies die every year from lack of medical skill. How would it be to save them? Public spirited women, but alas, without votes, have interviewed august bodies on the subject of sending Government nurses to these brave women who pay the toll of colonization. These delegates have always been courteously received and complimented on their work, but up to date not one dollar of government money has been spent, notwithstanding the fact that when a prince or a duke comes to our country to visit, we can pour out money like water.

Women are beginning to think of these things and to talk of them, and the argument which is so often put forth—it would suit women better to go home and darn their children's stockings—does not exactly relieve the difficulty. It does not take all of woman's energy or brains to keep the stockings darned or the meals cooked. Women are cooks and housemaids and home makers and dressmakers and nurses, but they are something more, they are citizens. Already women have attained citizenship in ten states of the Union and Alaska, and instead of disaster to the homes, it has brought happiness and prosperity.

Last month when the strikers' war in Colorado had culminated in dreadful loss of life and still greater loss was imminent; when the Colorado Government sat dazed and helpless; in the face of these appalling disasters the women of Denver, one thousand of them, marched to the capital and demanded that an appeal be sent to the President for Federal troops to put an end to the trouble. The Governor haughtily refused, but the thousand women had a thousand votes and so their words were words of power. They assured the Governor that five thousand women instead of one thousand would be on his door step in another twelve hours if he did not do as he was told, so the haughtiness of his manner disappeared. He did their bidding promptly and without delay. There were many technicalities in the way, but the women were conscious of only one thing, men were being shot down like dogs, women and children too, and they demanded that this should cease. The newspapers are loud in their praise of the women's interference. It may not have been regular, may not have happened according to parliamentary procedure, but it was effective. Only one journal raised its puny wail and asks who was minding these women's children while they were interviewing the Governor. People are slow to forgive women for believing that they have social as well as private duties.

But the dawn is breaking and the darkness flees away. Women who long have sat in their boudoirs like the Lady of Shallot, looking at life in a mirror, are now throwing the glass aside and coming down into the conflict. The awakened womanhood, the aroused motherhood is the New Citizenship.

VOTES FOR WOMEN–AN ARGUMENT IN FAVOUR, 1913

Sonia Leathes, 'Votes for Women', speech given to National Council of Women of Canada, Montreal, 1913, in *University Magazine*, Feb. 1914, vol. XIII, 68-78.

A high authority on constitutional law says that it requires a great deal of time to have opinions. The object of every reformer is, therefore, not so much to convert people to any particular way of thinking, as to make them realize that in the vast mass of ready made statements–many of them handed down from generation to generation for centuries–there is a great deal which, in the light of an advanced or altered social and spiritual condition of society, no longer applies. In other words, the reformer's object is to make people realize that there is a problem, that there is something to think about with reference to matters which the average man and woman have taken for granted.

The question of women's suffrage falls into this category. Some centuries ago it was the question whether the individual was to possess the liberty of holding, and of professing, the religious faith which answered to his individual spiritual needs. Luther's claim that the masses should have the right and the opportunity to read the Bible met with the most ardent opposition, not only on account of heresy but because of the sincere conviction in the minds of many that it would not "be safe to trust the common people with the word of God." For many centuries religious liberty for the individual had been held as utterly incompatible with the keeping up of any established social order and government of a state.

Far more recently the political privilege which from times immemorial had been held by the aristocracy of all nations, the privilege to make and to administer the laws and to exercise control over conditions by which unrepresented classes were to be governed was questioned, denied, and abolished by the common people.

The right of a dominant race to exercise absolute proprietary powers over other subject races, the right to buy, and to sell human beings at will, a right which the strong exercised over the weak ever since the remotest days of which historical records have reached us, which the Bible even seems to accept without comment, this immemorial right was challenged and finally abolished less than fifty years ago. Antiquity is not a proof of finality.

The problem of women suffrage which, though only a part of a general movement, is its culminating point, has its roots in, and grows directly out of these problems. It is indeed but a further, perhaps the last, chapter in the great history of the emancipation of the individual, black or white, rich or poor, male or female, from social and political disability imposed upon him or her on account of birth alone. This is the true meaning of democracy. It is not that all persons shall, or indeed ever can, be abso-lutely equal in intellect, moral power, influence, and wealth, and in the position among their fellows which is determined by the possession of these qualities. Democracy does not imply identity or equality in social status. The essence of democracy is the removal of all artificial restrictions which bar the way to the progress, development, and advancement, be it economic, social, or political, of any individual or of any class on account of birth, colour, religious creed, or sex alone. Democracy does not deal with people in herds or in sections. It says to each individual: "The road is clear. Go forth, and in your struggle onwards no one shall have the right to say to you, these are the limits of your sphere," or, "a further advance will injure your peculiar disposition and qualities, and I shall therefore take it upon myself to prevent your exceeding what I consider to be your limits." As one of the most eloquent preachers asked half a century ago: "Has God made woman capable, morally, physically, intel-lectually, of taking part in all human affairs? Then what God made her able to do, there is strong argument that He intended her to do. Our divine sense of justice tells us that the being who is to be governed by laws should first assent to them, that the being who is taxed shall have a voice in fixing the character and amount of the financial burden which it is to bear. Then, if woman is made responsible before the law, if she is admitted to the gallows, to the gaol, and to the tax lists, we have no right to debar her from the ballot box."

Practically all the arguments against women's suffrage fall under three categories: Some people say that they do not believe in women's suffrage, when really what they do not believe in is representative government. They observe the deficiencies created by our system of party government; they watch the abuse of electoral privileges; the comparative civil incom-petency of a considerable portion of the existing electorate, the periodical occurrence of unseemly proceedings in the various parliaments, and they are disgusted. These persons will do well to study the probable conditions under which they themselves and the class to which they belong would have to live to-day if the three Reform Bills and the British North

America Act had never been passed, and were the whole population of Great Britain, Ireland, and the Colonies still governed exclusively by the privileged class of land-owners of Great Britain, who until then controlled the election of the House of Commons, whilst they themselves then, as to-day, occupied a majority of the seats in the House of Lords.

The British Constitution allowed this state of things, but the people arose and claimed that the spirit of the British tradition of fair play, justice, and liberty was against it. They claimed that every class should have the right to protect its own interests directly instead of having to depend upon the sense of justice, generosity, or protection of another class. And they won on all points—where men were concerned. Women to-day still continue to live under conditions denounced as "a stigma" by Mr. Gladstone, when speaking of the then unenfranchised status of the agricultural labourer. "It is an intolerable injustice to inflict the stigma of electoral disfranchisement on any man," he exclaimed in 1884, yet, on the same occasion, he caused his supporters to abandon an amendment to the Bill which was to enfranchise women.

This brings us to the second category of the anti-suffrage arguments. Some people think that they do not believe in women's suffrage, when really what they do not believe is that women are persons. They have thought of women as "wives," "mothers," "daughters"; and though they have been obliged to admit the existence of the female stenographer, shop assistant, clerk, physician, even of the female mayor and city councillor, they cannot as yet fully grasp the fact that in addition to her private relationship to some man, a woman is still a social unit, a citizen, a subject, a person. The fact of her being somebody's wife, or daughter, or sister, has nothing to do with her being a tax-payer. She remains personally responsible for her observance or non-observance of the law of the land. She is equally affected by war, conditions of climate, finance, industry, national prosperity or adversity. All these matters affect women as well as men, and women should have the right to help decide all questions of policy for precisely the same reason that men possess this right. Yet how deeply rooted this androcentric view of society still is was illustrated again on the occasion when the Naval Bill was before the House of Commons. "Shall it be," said the premier on that occasion, "that we, contributing to that defence of the whole Empire, shall have absolutely, as citizens of this country, no voice whatever in the councils of the Empire? I do not think that such would be a tolerable condition." Unless the premier contemplated a measure for the enfranchisement of all the adult women of the Dominion, it is perfectly evident that he had, as many others had before him, entirely forgotten at the time, that women in Canada are one-half of the people and that the condition which he describes as "not tolerable" for the male half of the population of Canada is one under which the other, the female half, habitually has to live. "To exclude all women, a whole sex, from representative government," said John Stuart Mill, "is tantamount to saying that women are not called upon to take an interest in the affairs of the nation." Yet, what nation can hope to possess public spirited men as long as it discourages its mothers from taking that interest in its collective concerns which only direct responsibility can create and keep up?

But, comes the great objection, woman must remain within her sphere, which is the home. If, by one's sphere is meant the place where one's daily occupation lies, then the place of those women who are wives and mothers, and have husbands who can, and will, support them and their children, will certainly be within the four walls of their home. In this same sense a man's place is the office or work-shop or farm or pulpit. Nobody's place is the polling booth. To be a voter does not mean sitting in parliament. Only a small number of voters are able or willing to stand for election to that august body and, if duly elected, parliament becomes their proper sphere. For the rest of the electors the recording of their ballots once every few years represents not so much the power to govern as the power to indict, to call to account those who govern them. This power to call the government to account, if it should fail to pursue a policy acceptable to a majority of its electors, an unenfranchised portion of the population does not possess. Where women are not electors, parliament is not responsible to women, and their interests and wishes are not directly represented. Even when legislation is passed affecting the special interests of women,—for instance, the hours and time of work in factories, their admission to, or exclusion from, certain trades and professions, and the minimum wage,—such laws are dealt with entirely as seems best to the representatives of the male electorate, and in no case are the women themselves consulted. This inability to control legislation brings with it hardships which increase with the advent of every newly enfranchised male section of the population. It becomes increasingly hard since, during this last century, the introduction of power-driven machinery has forced the woman of the working classes to the factory, in order to continue to do that share of her economically productive work which she used a century ago to do at home, by which she then, as now, contributed her share towards the support of herself and of the household to which she belongs, as wife, mother, or daughter. She has, thus, reluctantly in many cases, become the competitor and the rival of the working man.

And this brings us to the third category of arguments, which assumes that there is such a thing as a dividing line between the sphere properly belonging to men and the sphere belonging to women. There is no such thing in modern days. And if we make it our business to inquire into the exact circumstances relating to the obliteration of this dividing line, we cannot but come to the conclusion that the invasion of men into what was properly considered to be "woman's sphere" not only preceded but overwhelmingly exceeds the invasion of women into "man's sphere." It is, in fact, not too much to say that the former resulted in the latter.

A hundred years ago the home was not only a family but also an industrial unit. Woman was the spinner, the weaver, the provider of the food and of the clothing for the household; and the impelling motive behind these home industries was love and service. The linen that was "homespun," the cloth that was "home woven," the stockings which were "home knitted," were produced as strongly and as well made as it was possible to make them, in order that they might be of service as long as possible. The milk was pure and the butter sweet, for this was most profitable to the health of the household. There were no other profits to be considered.

Then it gradually began to dawn upon humanity,—and to be just, almost entirely upon its male half,—that it would be profitable to extend the principle of collective enterprise, a principle which had already been applied in matters of state and city defence and in the rudiments of public means of communication, to the feeding and to the clothing of society. Whilst the invention of power-driven machinery led to a rapid application of the principle to the latter needs, an improved system of the means of communication and transport soon revolutionized the principle of the former. Food, from being a thing to eat, became a thing to sell. It became more profitable to sell dirty and watered milk, cleanliness being a costly matter. It became profitable to sell adulterated food and adulterated cloth and shoddy articles of clothing, deliberately manufactured so as not to last and in order that the consumer might have to purchase again. It became profitable to carry on these collective industries by the sweated labour of men, and especially of women and children, and the most profitable forms of collective industrial enterprise left, and still leave, behind them a trail of broken health and broken lives and broken morals as inevitable by-products. "Let women attend to the work which still remains within their home-sphere," says the opponent, and leaves thereby entirely out of account that the remaining home industries of cooking and cleaning and washing to which he or she presumably alludes are already in the significant transition stage between individual, or private, and collective, or social, enterprise. "Laundry interests," and "baking interests," "canning interests," "jam and preserving interests," "dairy interests," have invaded the individual housewife's immemorial "sphere," and have wrenched from her hands her exclusive control and responsibility for the health and for the well-being of the household. And in all cases the "socializing" of a home industry meant the employment of many men where women used before to be exclusively employed. To sit at the domestic spinning wheel, to stand at the domestic wash tub or at the domestic kitchen-range was esteemed to be an exclusively female privilege and esteemed to be degrading to a man. To attend the powerdriven washing machines, spindles, and weaving loom, and bakeries is now not only "man's work," but the presence of female labour in this socialized form of female industries is condemned, in many cases successfully abolished, and in almost all cases discouraged by an arbitrary payment of a lower wage for an equivalent amount of work. Recently the London County Council established training classes for boys who wish to become cooks and waiters. To these classes no girls are admitted, the training which is offered to girls being of a "domestic" nature, for their own husbands and children, whilst the boys are trained to be specialists and social servants.

On all sides we hear this outcry that the inevitable advent of women into the socialized work of the world will react injuriously on the home. If the adaptation of the home to a new stage of social development is to be branded as injurious, it is the inoffensive looking baker's, dairy or laundry man's or department stores' delivery cart, stationed at our back door, that is the real offender against which the wrath should be directed with presumably as happy results. And let us remember that there is another side to the whole question. For centuries the home was almost the only humanizing centre where the spiritual ideals of love and service were kept alive and handed down from generation to generation. It was the inevitable result of the entrance of women into all the departments where the public business of the nation is carried on that there should steadily manifest itself a new but ever growing desire, peculiar to woman's nature, a desire to assist the weak, to make dirty places clean and crooked places straight. Those who attack this new phase of social development seem to be unable to comprehend that women will remain women whatever their occupation, and that if a woman's delicate feelings and susceptibilities have survived the realities and trials of a weekly "wash" for a family of six, they are likely to triumph in the face of her direct contact with any of the duties of her occupation in office, store, or factory. Women, instead of becoming unsexed, have a way of infusing their own home view into business, industry, and politics. Imperceptible at first, but increasing by degrees, this "indirect influence," though it cannot take the place of the direct power of the ballot, has yet placed its unmistakeable stamp on all the departments of social work to which it has been admitted. Hence the wave of reforms and enquiries into conditions which had previously been accepted with unquestioning acquiescence. It is this home-side, this human side, which has, wherever women have been granted the ballot, at once come to the forefront of politics.

The world is in a transition stage. Everywhere private and amateur service is being replaced by social and specialized service. We have discovered that it is more profitable and less wasteful for social purposes if the man who makes boots does not also kill pigs or build his own house. We have realized that, because a man is a good father or a woman is a good mother, they are neither of them necessarily able to instruct their children in mathematics, Latin, or art, or to remove their adenoids; and the employment of specialists to instruct their children and to treat their ailments is no longer a matter of privilege for the few but open to all classes. Our railways and mail service, our lighting and drainage, our press, our art collections, are for general use, and they are the results of collective enterprise and could never have existed but for it.

Our failure lies not in the replacement of private enterprise by collective and social enterprise, but in our slowness to grasp that just as private control and responsibility accompanied the former, collective control and collective responsibility must accompany the latter. And collective control is exercised through legislation, through the administration of laws, and through the control of public funds. From this collective control, in countries which do not possess women suffrage, women are completely excluded. They have no voice in the councils of the nation which decide whether a "pure milk bill" or a "housing bill" or a "mental deficiency bill" shall save the lives of millions of babies born and unborn, and mercifully protect the feeble-minded from society and society from the feeble-minded. They have not at their disposal the only effectual means of persuading a government that to offend the "dairy interests" or "the canning interests" will not mean disaster to the party in power. They have not the means of stamping upon the statutes and regulations referring to the meat trade the uncompromising point of view of all mothers and housekeepers, that meat which is not good enough for export purposes is not good enough for home consumption. At present the Canadian and American householder consumes, as is known to those familiar with blue books, a large proportion of the meat classified as "unfit for export." Unenfranchised women cannot effectually say to unscrupulous employers and slum landlords: you can make money, but you shall not make it at the expense of the physical, mental, and moral welfare of our children, or by excluding light and air and breathing space, and by causing the deadly perils of overcrowding. "The average man," as an eminent professor of political economy said, "thinks in terms of dollars, the average woman in terms of home, husband, and unborn babies." With the average man property interests come first. Man is the restless explorer, inventor, and conqueror. He roams the seas and the air. He bridles the forces of nature to do his bidding. He orders Niagara to grind his corn and to milk his cows, and he chains the lightning to his desk and to his toast rack. But there is just one industry from which he is forever excluded: it is the women who hold the monopoly of producing the people who are to benefit by all these great achievements, and without which the world within one generation would become a desert.

To be able to adequately protect human life from the onslaught of property interests, women must to-day have the ballot. The individual interests of yesterday have become collective interests to-day. The individual responsibilities of the home-maker of yesterday have become the collective interests of the home-maker of to-day. And collective interests are controlled by parliament, by legislation, and by the expenditure of public funds which are all in turn controlled by the elector's ballot.

It is on this account that women to-day say to the governments of all the world: You have usurped what used to be our authority, what used to be our responsibility. It is you who determine to-day the nature of the air which we breathe, of the food which we eat, of the clothing which we wear. It is you who determine when, and how long, and what our children are to be taught and what their prospects as future wage-earners are to be. It is you who can condone or stamp out the white slave traffic and the starvation wage. It is you who by granting or by refusing pensions to the mothers of young children can preserve or destroy the fatherless home. It is you who decide what action shall be considered a crime and how the offender, man, woman, or child, shall be dealt with. It is you who decide whether cannons and torpedoes are to blow to pieces the bodies of the sons which we bore. And since all these matters strike at the very heartstrings of the mothers of all nations, we shall not rest until we have secured the power vested in the ballot: to give or to withhold our consent, to encourage or to forbid any policy or course of action which concerns the people—our children every one.

VOTES FOR WOMEN—AN ARGUMENT AGAINST, 1914

Andrew Macphail, 'On certain Aspects of Feminism', *University Magazine*, Feb. 1914, vol. XIII, 79-91.

Every generation has its own problems, and each generation creates problems which it leaves to a succeeding generation to solve. The fathers eat the bitter fruit: it is the children whose teeth are set on edge.

The nineteenth century was rich in experiment; and the people who lived in those ancient days have left to us the task of reaping as they sowed and gathering up what they strawed so recklessly. They tried everything. They invented machinery to free the world from labour, and we are bound in a hard mechanical routine. They gave liberty to the people, and a new slavery has arisen on the ruins of the old. They freed men from superstition, and we are left without religion, according to the degree of their success. They enfranchised adult males, and we vote wrongly or corruptly, or will not vote at all. They introduced free education, and now the educated ones bewilder their minds by reading not the best, but the worst. They emancipated women, and the women avenge themselves by brawling in public places. They opened every trade and every profession to women; yet women will persist in marrying and giving in marriage, and encumbering the earth with their progeny.

From the beginning of time men have done their best in their poor, blind way to make the world a better place for themselves and their womenkind to live in; yet they hear on every hand that the first misfortune for a woman is to be born, the second to be married, and the last to become a mother. Everything in these days seems to turn out wrong. If a law is made that women shall be paid the same wages as men for doing work which seems to be the same, it quickly follows that the women are driven out of that field of employment entirely. We insure workers against sickness, and sickness increases in duration and intensity. The aged receive pensions, and in the time of youth they make no provision for themselves. In pursuit of the excellent ideal of pure food it is soon discovered that impure food is better than no food at all, except in the estimation of utterly cynical minds.

At this worst moment of scepticism, when men are assailed by the conviction of failure, they are met with the temptation of help of a new kind from a quarter to which they have always looked for consolation, and rarely failed to find it. Women are offering assistance of a less passive nature. Instead of contenting themselves with binding up the wounds of those who fight, they are demanding that they be given a place in the forefront of the fray.

The first equipment they demand is the right to vote. On the part of the gentler it is an appeal rather than a demand. They ask that they be allowed,—if one may be permitted for the time being, without offence even to the most petulant, to interpret their mind by the employment of a term which is hortative rather than mandatory,—to assume the privilege and undertake the duty of casting the ballot, so that they may work side by side with men, as comrades in social service for the uplift of humanity, if one may be permitted again to employ those flamboyant terms with which constant iteration has made us all so familiar. There is something pathetic in the appeal, and none but the most hardened can be insensible to it.

If men have shown little alacrity in welcoming these volunteers to their ranks, it is because they are not convinced of the value of the "work" which is proposed to be done. Enough committee meetings have been held, enough reports discussed, enough public assemblages where the converted have been preached to and the righteous called to repentance. If women choose to walk in the slums doing social work rather than in the parks to make themselves healthy and beautiful, if they elect to visit the vicious poor rather than the vicious rich, and offer unsolicited and ill-considered advice to those who are too humble to resent it openly as an impertinence, the result of their enquiry may be a revelation to themselves. It will present nothing new to the world at large. It will only be new to them by reason of their inexperience.

The whole controversy turns on the meaning of this word, "work." Voting only occupies a few moments each year. Law-making is an employment for the very few. The world of work is free to all who show desire and capacity to undertake it. No profession or trade is closed to women. They may be sea-captains, farmers, or plumbers. They have proved their capacity as physicians, lawyers, and ministers of at least one form of religion. One woman is now at the head of the prison system, and another at the head of a department of hygiene in New York. Still another has so completely mastered the practice of law that she has been indicted on the charge of taking a false affidavit and of altering a complaint in an action. In the same city, and elsewhere, too, women monopolize entirely the business of singing certain operatic rôles. All these have succeeded by sheer capacity and by long years of industrious preparation. Such women are everywhere received as comrades. It is the incapable, idle women who, neglecting the work which lies ready, come forth with wild cries, and seek sanctuary as soon as they are opposed—it is these who are received, first with anger and then with open contempt. The women who really work are solving the problem for themselves. They are freeing themselves from conventions which grew up in a different environment, and are creating an atmosphere in which they can move more freely. They only require to be left alone by the professional agitators, the show-women, the "m'as-tu vus," since there is a limit to the patience of men, when they have serious business in hand.

Certain conventions have grown up in the world. It is agreed that a gulf shall be fixed between the abattoir and the dinner table. One who visits an abattoir for the first time is likely to come away wide-eyed with horror. If the visitor is a woman, and especially if she be surfeited with food, one of two things will happen. Either she will forswear the use of meat and condemn herself to a diet of acorns and cold water, or she will ease her conscience at a well-spread table by talking of the dreadful things which she has seen. A woman who has made an experiment of hunger and heard her children crying for food will contemplate the death of an animal with glee. She will have little patience with the well-fed woman, and will advise her to keep away from the slaughter-house if the spectacle which she witnesses is so harrowing to her soul.

It is conceivable, of course, that under the influence of emotion "a movement" might be commenced to make an abattoir where a butcher destroys animal life as dainty a place as an operating room where a surgeon destroys human life; but the main result would be that the poor would be reduced from a condition of hunger to a condition of starvation. Men are nervous about the incursion of women into the affairs of the world because they know how complicated those affairs really are, and they dread the result of inexperience, coupled with emotions which are uncontrolled by reality. They have schooled themselves into a suppression of wrath against things as they are, because they are fully aware that a wrath which is righteous is even more destructive than the *saeva indignatio* which is inspired by malignity. It is the untempered enthusiasm of women which alarms them. They are afraid, too, of the reformer's zeal. Whilst they are aware that many reforms and many changes masquerading as reforms have been accomplished in the face of opposition, they do not forget that opposition has put an end to much foolishness as well. Faddists and cranks are reformers in their own eyes. If they were suffered gladly, all civilization would long since have come to an end. At the moment the world is suffering from too much reformation. When a ship is labouring in a heavy sea, that is no time for increasing the top-hamper; nor does a man choose the occasion of a hurricane for repairing his house.

All the world is a stage. The men and women play their respective parts; but even on the circus stage the performance is a very complicated affair. The function of the clown is to demonstrate the embarrassment which is caused to the players by the intrusion of good-natured, enthusiastic inexperience. Occasionally, however, it turns out that this foolish person discloses himself as a most finished performer; but he must first strip himself of his queer clothes, his foolishness, and his intention to please by antics alone. The world is a more serious affair than the comic stage. It is very old and very wise. No legislative expedient has gone untried. It may well be excused for doubting that these new volunteers are in possession of a magical remedy for things as they are, which will be put into operation so soon as they attain to a political vantage. It is easy to mistake for a panacea an old fallacy in a new guise.

The great problem of the world has always been poverty. It is the mother of all social evils excepting those which arise from wealth. The cry of women is that there is a mystical efficacy in the legislation which they will devise in which the material resources of the rich will be made to play a part. The real remedy is in the moral resources of the poor, and that is not governed by any parliament which has yet been assembled. Money may save the poor: it gives longer life to pauperism.

There is something pathetic in this appeal by emancipated women to men for comradeship. They have so little in common with normal women that they are condemned to solitude or to the company of each other; and they are not sufficiently like men to make them preferable to a man itself. The more they strive to become so, the less likely are they to succeed; and, besides, a man's own immediate womenkind always have something to say on the subject of his choice of friends. A man and a woman must be something more or something less than friends. The poor man cannot be a friend of the rich man, so long as the rich man does not share his possessions; and when he does the two are friends no longer. That brilliant Frenchwoman whose achievement in the world of science has made her an everlasting argument for the enfranchisement of all females, failed in the relation of friendship with her fellow laboratory-worker. At least that was the opinion of the man's wife, and it was endorsed by the judge who awarded her a bill of divorcement.

Women as well as men demand an outlet for their energy. Idleness is the worst form of misery, but relief of the idlers is purchased too dearly when freedom to make mischief is the price. By the shifting of economic conditions whole classes of men as well as of women find themselves in the backwater of life, but the first lesson in wisdom is to make the best of things as they are. This desire on the part of the few women, who are otherwise unoccupied, to share in the work of government arises from sheer conscientiousness. They honestly wish to atone for their failure, through no fault of their own, to perform that function which is exclusively theirs. The failure of a man in life is covered up by various little activities. The failure of a woman is there for all the world to see. She magnifies its importance: he deprecates his futility by ironical laughter at himself. These women with their fine natures, approaching the masculine type, are deficient in the instinct for husband-getting. They are obliged to turn to other avocations, and they find them already preempted by men. Coarse women always marry.

What complicates the situation is that the persons who are appealing for the votes are of higher intelligence, but with shallower instincts, than the average of the sex to which they apparently belong. They are not typical. They belong to a higher, a more masculine, type. Their fate is a tragical one. The heart of all tragedy lies in this—even the tragedy of Shakespeare's kings—that all those are destined to perish who do not conform with a type that is lower than themselves. The Falstaffs are of the earth earthy, and they come to their end babbling of green fields. The exceptionally kingly perish on the scaffold or in the dungeon.

It is due to no preconceived plan that so little attention is being paid by men to the performance of those ardent spirits even in England where they are the most ardent. This neglect is based upon the profound belief that the type itself will in due time deal with the aberrants who have risen above the line, by reason of superior intelligence and lessened instincts, as faithfully, as it has dealt with the aberrants who have sunk below the line on account of diminished intelligence and too grossly animal passion. The cruelty of the female is wisely ordained, and may be trusted to award impartial justice to excess, no matter upon which side of the line it is to be found.

And this hesitancy to sanction or advocate so revolutionary a measure is increased by the lack of agreement amongst women themselves. It is a matter of common knowledge that the feminist propaganda is confined to a small number of persons. Indeed it is their continual complaint that they cannot arouse their married sisters to a sense of the enormity which they endure. The average woman goes upon her way unmoved, loving and capable of being loved, now as beforetime, the subject of all verse, strong because she is weak, secure in the ideal, content to leave undisturbed that high, pure atmosphere in which men have decreed for themselves that she shall live and move and have her being. The explanation which is offered of this anomaly is that slaves grow to love their chains, and the necessity is all the greater for enlightening their minds and strengthening their wills. If all women were anxious to have the franchise, and were willing to exercise it, they could have it to-morrow. Even the bachelor would not oppose the measure, although he was fully aware that a man who had a wife and daughter would then have three votes, whilst he himself would continue to have only one.

It is not from mere prejudice or from any frivolous reasons that men display so little alacrity in undertaking the large experiment of enfranchising women. There are, of course, prejudices and reasons against such a measure, but the underlying one—it may be reason or prejudice—is fear that they would attempt to achieve by force what can only be effected by persuasion or, failing that, cannot be achieved at all. Their militancy in the one cause is proof that it would be employed in others; and if a woman should begin to starve herself when she is contradicted, what is a man to do? Political perfection or progress is never attained by force. It was not by pulling down the palings in Hyde Park that the franchise for men was enlarged. It came about because men were persuaded and convinced by the peaceful labours of John Bright and his fellow Quakers.

There is a field of social service into which the originators of this new movement believe that it will project itself with peculiar force, because it is a field which another class of women has made inevitably its own. They profess that they will exercise a new skill in the harrying of the harlot, a task for which men have always proved themselves unfitted because they would persist in remembering that a woman is a woman after all.

Without claiming any superiority for either sex it may be affirmed that the pleasures of the world appeal to the one and to the other with different force. The effort to be certain on this point would be hopeless, since at times women are found indulging in such masculine pleasures as playing golf, drinking alcohol, and smoking tobacco, whilst men sit idly by taking tea and contemplating the beauty of their apparel. From pleasure to vice and from vice to crime is an easy descent; but to maintain a just attitude towards a diversion which one does not enjoy, towards a vice which does not allure, or a crime which does not tempt, is difficult for women or for men either. When a pleasure or a vice is classified as a crime the way to all public corruption is straightway opened. This explains the curious phenomenon that it is in communities where this puritanical confusion of thought prevails that the worst municipal government is witnessed.

There is a state of affairs specifically known as the social evil. Where it is treated as a crime, the briber and the black-mailer flourish. The officials entrusted with the prevention of a factitious crime are corrupted, and they quickly learn to accept bribes from criminals who are so in reality. Gambling is always a pleasure: it may become a vice. When it is treated as a crime, both gamblers and police are turned into murderers, and a community where murderers are in control of the execution of the laws is not a good place to live in. This social evil is in the same category. The recent history of New York substantiates the fact and proves the inference.

Women do well to be angry over this evil. They have a just and instinctive dread of the competition which is offered by the members of that ancient and dishonourable profession, those women who toil not nor spin, especially at a time when the desuetude into which these occupations have fallen leaves so many other women also in a condition of idleness. But there is always a danger in allowing any one class to execute its own private vengeance. As these outcasts are pushed further down into the underworld they descend into real criminality and lure their followers after them. The lower strata of humanity are always supplied from above. It is difficult to apportion the blame justly between the man and the woman. The mother of the man entertains one opinion. The mother of the woman entertains another. Probably the truth is that in every case of misfortune the woman is chargeable with contributory negligence at least.

It is hard for these intelligent super-women to understand in the first flush of their enthusiastic ignorance that there are some evils which cannot be cured, and are made worse by talking about them, especially when the talk must of necessity be a mere repetition of hearsay. The rescue work which they describe is not very encouraging. It is hard to rescue those who do not desire to be saved. Saved to what?—they may well ask in their own ribald way, as they behold a band of those saviours of society on the rampage through the streets of a great city.

How little they know of the subject is well illustrated by the word which is in the mouth of every earnest woman whose life work is social service for the uplift of that portion of humanity which they describe as white slaves. The harm they do is irreparable when they proclaim that women fall overcome by superior force and not by the voluntary betrayal of their own nature. If a woman is justified in yielding because her lot is hard, then is the soldier justified for his cowardice in deserting his post because it is a place of danger, or the renegade monk because his life is tiresome, or the bank clerk because his salary is small. What hope is there for the girl condemned to work for hire when other good, but idle, women proclaim that virtue is merely an affair of wages? Her hope lies in this, that her own heart tells her that the thing is false. A life of virtue may be lived in the slums as easily as on the castellated heights. And even for these slaves the only remedies suggested are, first, talking to them, and then putting them in gaol. If life were made easier for these women in their chosen profession they would all the sooner be enabled to abandon it.

Forty years ago there was a somewhat similar controversy over the system of education which, up to that time, had been prescribed for women. A sudden demand arose for the same kind of education which was ordained for men, not on the ground that it was best for the women, or for the men either, but on the ground that it should be the same for both.

As if this were not enough, the further demand was made that the system should be administered to both at the same time and in the same place. The one institution in Montreal at least, which complied most completely, closed its doors within the next few years; and the promiscuous public schools of Montreal are now avoided by boys and girls alike, whose parents can afford to send their children each to its own place. The institutions for the advancement, amongst women exclusively, of the higher learning are falling into a fresh danger. As they become centres for propaganda they lose their value for the general purpose of education.

The professor in a university who introduces his personal politics or theology into his class-room is in danger of his professorial life. A professor may be a politician, as Woodrow Wilson was, but he can only perform the functions proper to each sphere if he performs them in different places at different times. There are schools and colleges, of course, which have certain political and theological predilections; and they are favoured by certain parties and certain sects, but for so long only as education is merely tinctured and not replaced by propaganda. The supply of young Tories, or young Liberals, or young Presbyterians is practically inexhaustible. At least there is nothing implicit in the doctrines of those parties to prevent their production. But there is a natural decree against the reproduction of young suffragettes; and schools and colleges for women must close soon after they come to depend upon the children of childless women to fill their class-rooms.

The first requisite of a school is that it shall be a place of calm for the senses, and the beast which is so subtly blended with the angel be allowed to lie in its lair. It is only aroused by hearing the truth about itself. But the cry amongst women who fill the rôle of public educators now is to tell the truth even about those matters of which the truth cannot be told. Talk about a thing is not necessarily the truth of it. The truth of any serious matter lies too deep for words. The truth about a vicious, sleeping dog is not to trace his ancestry and describe his habits, or to compare him with the lilies of the field, and visualize his functions in biological terms, but to let him lie. Women of shallow instincts who have learned from books and lectures all they know of nature are under the delusion that knowledge can be acquired in no other way.

It is this little knowledge which is a dangerous thing. It creates an itching, a desire, a craving. It begets a curiosity, a lascivious uneasiness, a sensuality of mind which finds fulfilment in the very end which it was designed to postpone. There has always been a kind of hypocrite who was never effectually exposed for want of a phrase which was exactly descriptive until Charles Reade supplied the defect in our language and introduced to mankind the term, "prurient prude." The woman who has loved much and, therefore, is much forgiven is a better instructor in a school for girls, that is, if upon these matters any instruction whatever is required. Sexology, according to Judge Garvin, is merely "smut."

Persons newly emancipated find a difficulty in comporting themselves in harmony with their new surroundings. A man who has just begun to take his luncheon at the club at one o'clock, instead of his dinner on the work-bench at twelve o'clock, often makes the attempt to reassure himself by loud talk. A woman who has just come into the world of men is very apt to put herself and her hearers at ease by a freedom of speech which is very embarrassing. She is new to the conventions, and it takes a long time for a lady to learn to behave like a gentleman. Nothing is so difficult even for a man to acquire as the knowledge of those things which must not be spoken of amongst men. In Sweden it is considered a mark of gross ill-breeding to mention one's female relatives. The Germans are free-spoken on the subject. The reticence of the Turk is notorious. In England as far as they will go is to remark how bad the weather is and how well the Queen was looking. The nuances in conversation are very fine. The penalty for failure to observe them is also fine, though fatal. A lifted eyebrow may signify that an offender henceforward is marked with the mark of the beast.

And in truth, the main distinction between humanity and the beast is this habit of reticence. Accordingly, the most obscene novels are written by women and by the least highly specialized males. It is difficult to restore the mind of a man to its primitive gross condition. It is easy to brutalize the mind of a child, especially the mind of a girl, and to destroy that lovely strangeness which is best defined by that other lovely word, modesty, whose spirit is innocence and thrives best in an atmosphere of neutral ignorance.

Experience has decreed for women a decent reticence about things of which they have knowledge. Indeed it is knowledge which breeds reticence, and that in turn accounts for the reticence of men about matters which very young children and idiots speak of with the utmost freedom. In older persons such behaviour appears to be salacious and obscene; and it is the more revolting when it is covered by the thin guise of abstraction, since prurience and hypocrisy disclose their ugly features under the mask. The more sincere such loose talkers are the more they resemble impostors. Loose talk on the part of women is worse than loose conduct, since it would make a virtue out of cowardice and award to madness the place of courage. It is not given to every woman to be wise, but a woman who is femininely foolish is rarely disagreeable.

The possession by a woman of the great virtue, in which only one person in the world is really interested, does not compensate for the lack of all those lesser virtues which make life tolerable and pleasant for the large number of persons who come in contact with her. Its absence is rarely observed. The absence of the lesser virtues of reticence, gentleness, quietness, beauty, is there for all the world to notice and to lament.

VOTES FOR WOMEN—A FRENCH CANADIAN SAYS NO, 1913

Henri Bourassa, 'Le Suffragisme féminin, son efficacité, sa légitimité', *Le Devoir*, 24 avril 1913.

... Mais où nous ne sommes plus d'accord avec les apôtres du suffragisme, c'est dans la conception étroite et particulière que les suffragettes se font de la manière dont la femme peut et doit exercer cette collaboration et manifester son influence.

Que dans les civilisations anglo-saxonnes,—où la femme, longtemps déparée de ses charmes propres et de ses moyens naturels d'influence, n'a pas pu exercer son emprise sur la société, où par ailleurs l'on a fait des prérogatives politiques individuelles la source principale des initiatives sociales,—la femme cherche à exercer son influence par les mêmes moyens que l'homme, à jouer un rôle politique identique à celui de l'homme, on se l'explique, tout en restant sceptique à l'endroit des résultats. C'est en Angleterre que s'est dite cette parole brutale mais vraie: "Le parlement peut tout faire ... sauf changer une femme en homme".

Mais dans les pays de formation française et catholique, où l'influence prépondérante de la femme s'exerce depuis des siècles dans toutes les sphères de la pensée, du coeur et de l'action, où l'on a pu rendre banale cette parole: *"En toute chose, cherchez la femme"*, cette fausse conception du rôle social de la femme ne peut prévaloir contre les traditions, contre la mentalité générale, contre l'instinct de la nature. La très grande majorité des femmes la repousseraient, et elles auraient raison. Obéissant d'instinct à cette loi suprême, que chaque force s'accroît dans la proportion de sa concordance avec les lois propres à sa nature, elles sentent que le jour où elles exerceraient les mêmes moyens d'influence que l'homme, elles cesseraient de profiter de ceux qui leur sont propres, ou du moins que l'efficacité de ces moyens diminuerait sensiblement.

*   *   *   *

Les exemples concrets que les suffragettes peuvent donner à l'appui de leur thèse ne prouvent rien à l'encontre de cette loi générale.

Qu'en Australie ou ailleurs, les femmes électeurs aient réussi à accomplir telle ou telle réforme, ceci ne prouve nullement que sans être électeurs, les mêmes femmes n'eussent pu, par d'autres méthodes, obtenir les mêmes réformes et d'autres encore. Et surtout, cela prouve encore moins, qu'en d'autres pays, la femme obtiendrait comme électeur une influence qu'elle peut exercer plus efficacement par son influence personnelle ou sociale. sociale.

Qu'à Montréal, la mortalité infantile, l'alcoolisme, la tuberculose, le matérialisme vécu, et maintes autres plaies sociales,—physiques ou morales—appellent le dévouement et l'action individuelle et collective des femmes, c'est certain. Mais que ce dévouement et cette action aient besoin, pour agir sur la société, sur les lois et sur les pouvoirs publics, du droit de vote et de la participation aux luttes électorales, c'est beaucoup moins sûr. Avec notre mentalité française, c'est le contraire qui arriverait.

Que les femmes les plus intelligentes et les plus dévouées coordonnent leurs efforts et les fassent porter sur tous les points où leur infleunce de femmes peut s'exercer par des méthodes féminines avec des arguments que seuls le coeur et le charme de la femme peuvent trouver, et elles atteindront beaucoup plus sûrement leur but que par des conférences, des meetings, et des comités électoraux. Le travail considérable et discret accompli par un grand nombre de Canadiennes-françaises, réligieuses ou laïques,—qui du reste ignorent totalement la science des réclames tapageuses—prouve qu'elles sont capables de toutes les initiatives, de tous les dévouements feconds. Il suffirait d'élargir le cadre de leur action et de leur fournir les données nécessaires à la solution des problèmes nouveaux et grandissants qui s'imposent.

Si, par malheur, ce dévouement venait à tarir, ce n'est sûrement pas l'action politique et l'exercice du droit de suffrage qui y suppléeraient.

*   *   *   *

Je ne toucherai qu'en passant à la question du suffrage féminin envisagée comme droit absolu de la femme.

Avec cette faculté qui est propre aux femmes, et qui les rend aussi aptes à l'accomplissement des oeuvres particulières qu'incapables d'envisager les questions d'ensemble, les suffragettes voient dans le droit de vote un droit concret, absolu, une sorte d'alpha et d'omega du code de l'égalité des sexes.

Elles semblent ignorer que le droit de suffrage n'est que le corollaire de l'ensemble des devoirs et des fonctions nécessaires au gouvernement et à la défense de la société.

Le droit de suffrage comporte, en puissance au moins, l'éligibilité à toutes les fonctions administratives et législatives, et l'obligation de pourvoir à toutes les charges civiles ou militaires.

Jusqu'à ce que les suffragettes aient prouvé l'aptitude des femmes à remplir ces diverses fonctions et leur propre volonté d'assumer toutes ces charges, elles ne méritent aucune attention lorsqu'elles parlent de "droits", d'"égalité", "d'affranchissement".

Si elles objectent que la conformation physique de la femme et les exigences de la maternité lui interdisent la plupart de ces fonctions et de ces charges, elles fournissent elles-mêmes l'argument de fond qui ruine toute leur théorie: c'est que la différence des sexes entraine, non pas l'inégalité des conditions, mais le partage des fonctions et des charges sociales, et aussi le partage des droits que répondent à ces charges et à ces fonctions. Ce que les féministes et les suffragistes dénoncent comme une privation de droit, comme une marque de servitude, n'est en réalité que l'affranchissement de maintes obligations incompatibles avec les fonctions d'épouse et de mère, qui restent, en dépit du féminisme, les fonctions normales de la plupart des femmes.

* * * *

Quant sux suffragettes qui se bornent à réclamer le droit de vote sans prétendre à l'éligibilité aux fonctions d'Etat, elles sont encore moins conséquentes que les autres et ne voient pas plus clair, ni plus large.

Elles ignorent cette autre vérité élémentaire que le droit de suffrage n'est que la faculté donnée a ceux qui ont pour mission de protéger la société, de déléguer leurs pouvoirs à un certain nombre d'entre eux.

Sans doute, cette faculté est censée comporter chez ceux qui l'exercent la volonté et l'intelligence nécessaires pour faire un choix judicieux et, au besoin, pour accomplir eux-mêmes les fonctions qu'ils confient à leurs représentants. Et les féministes n'ont nulle peine à démontrer qu'un très grand nombre d'électeurs et d'élus sont fort peu propres à exercer leurs fonctions et leurs devoirs respectifs. On peut tirer de là d'excellents arguments contre le suffrage universel et contre le régime représentatif— comme les abus de tous les régimes politiques ont fourni des arguments fort probants contre chacun de ces régimes.

Mais du fait que les hommes remplissent mal les fonctions qui leur incombent, et même que beaucoup de femmes accompliraient ce devoir mieux que nombre d'hommes, il ne résulte nullement que ces fonctions devraient être confiées aux femmes—pas plus que le nombre considérable d'épouses infidèles et de mauvaises mères, de femmes dépravées, cruelles, stupides, légères ou dépensières ne prouve qu'il faudrait leur substituer des hommes-incubateurs, des hommes-nourrices, des hommes bonnes-d'enfant, des hommes-ménagères.

Il y a encore beaucoup à faire pour la réforme des moeurs, des lois et de la société, au Canada comme ailleurs;—mais ces réformes seront d'autant plus fécondes et durables qu'elles se feront d'accord avec les lois de la nature et les prescriptions de l'ordre providentiel.

VOTES FOR WOMEN—A FRENCH CANADIAN SAYS YES, 1913

Olivar Asselin, Montreal *Daily Herald*, 26 November 1913.

When government's sole purpose was to hold people and provinces together by means of a common system of defence, common highways, a common coinage, and the like, government was naturally man's business, and woman's claim to suffrage rights were weaker because women seemed less useful to the state.

With the prevailing world-wide tendency to Socialism, woman's kingdom, the home, is, for weal or for woe, more and more affected by legislation. The minimum wage, school attendance, factory inspection, child labor, are only a few of the subjects which have lately come under the supervision of the state and in which woman is just as much concerned as man, if not more so. War itself is no longer man's exclusive concern, since militarism in its present acute form, has a direct bearing on the welfare of the income.

Of course, if the family be looked upon as the basic unit of the state, the head of the family, man, is the natural spokesman of the family in the public councils. For myself, I am inclined to think that conception the wiser in principle. But then, the logical consequence would be the barring of unmarried men from suffrage. Since the family unit has, the world over, been given up for the man unit, and since woman has a far greater interest in government than unmarried men, there is no reason why women should not be allowed to share the right of government.

So much for the rights.

When public business was managed from the Forum, women could not have shared in its management without neglecting their household duties, and at the same time incurring physical hardship above the strength of their sex.

In modern communities, woman, through the press, has just as effective means of apprising herself of the needs of the commonwealth without injuring the home, as man without injuring his private business. So much for the practicability of woman suffrage.

The rise of labor's influence in politics, whatever its consequence in other respects, has had much to do with warning governments against increased armaments and unnecessary wars. Woman suffrage would likely have an identical effect. However patriotic in great national crises, women, as a rule, hate war, because they are bound to be in the end the greatest sufferers from war.

Education, liquor selling, city and town planning, public health and police, child labor, public charities, and dozens of other pithy questions would be nearer a proper solution if woman had the vote.

That sentiment, more than sober thought, might guide women in the exercise of the suffrage right is no argument at all. Any student of democratic government knows that the masses, as they are called, are saved—when saved—from the wiles of politicians, not by reason, but by instinct. In social legislation, at least, who would not trust a woman's instinct rather than man's?

The fear has been expressed that the atmosphere of the polling booth might deny the character of our women. I would rather expect woman's presence to purify the atmosphere of the polling booth. There are of course bad women, and plenty of them, but woman has a native moral cleanliness which men lack, and the chances are that her entrance into the political field would be something like her sudden advent into a circle of "gentlemen" while the later are engaged in telling nasty stories.

So much for the probable effects of woman suffrage.

I favor woman suffrage not so much out of a belief in equal rights as because I am convinced that woman suffrage would help to lift politics out of the slush into which personal appetites and capital's corporate greed have caused them to sink.

VOTES FOR WOMEN—A SUFFRAGIST SPEAKS, 1916

Nellie L. McClung, 'Speaking of Women', *MacLean's Magazine*, May 1916, pp. 25-6, 96-7. Reprinted by permission of the Estate of Nellie Mc-Clung.

The cave dweller, long ago, realizing that the food supply was limited and hard to obtain, was disposed to look upon every other man as a possible rival; and considered it good policy to kill at sight in order that the crowd around the Neolithic lunch counter might be lessened. The reasoning was economically sound, too. If the divisor is lessened, the quotient is correspondingly increased!

Life was simple then. Every man was his own lawyer, butcher, barber, drycleaner; he settled his own quarrels, without lawyers' fees or "notes";

there were no apartment houses, tax-notices, rural mail delivery, water rates, subscription lists, or any other complication.

But it was not long before men began to plan greater tasks than could be accomplished by individual effort, and the idea slowly grew that the other man might be a real help at times and perhaps it was a mistake always to kill him. Co-operation began when one man chased the bear out of the cave and another man killed him when he ran past the gap!

Since then the idea of co-operation has steadily grown. Now we are so utterly dependent upon the other man—or woman—that we cannot live a day without them. But the primitive instincts die hard! Men are still haunted by the ghost of that old fear that there may not be enough of some things to go around if too many people have the same chance of obtaining a share. They join in the thanksgiving of the old blessing:

"Six potatoes among the four of us;
Thank the Lord there ain't any more of us."

This deep-rooted fear, that any change may bring personal inconvenience, lies at the root of much of the opposition to all reform.

Men held to slavery for long years, condoning and justifying it, because they were afraid that without slave labor life would not be comfortable. Certain men have opposed the advancement of women for the same reason; their hearts have been beset with the old black fear that, if women were allowed equal rights with men, some day some man would go home and find the dinner not ready, and the potatoes not even peeled! But not many give expression to this fear, as a reason for their opposition. They say they oppose the enfranchisement of women because they are too frail, weak and sweet to mingle in the hurly-burly of life; that women have far more influence now than if they could vote, and besides, God never intended them to vote, and it would break up the home, and make life a howling wilderness; the world would be full of neglected children (or none at all) and the homely joys of the fireside would vanish from the earth.

I remember once hearing an eloquent speaker cry out in alarm, "If women ever get the vote, who will teach us to say our prayers?"

Surely his experience of the franchised class had been an unfortunate one when he could not believe that anyone could both vote and pray!

That women are physically inferior to men is a strange reason for placing them under a further handicap, and we are surprised to find it advanced in all seriousness as an argument against woman suffrage. The exercising of the ballot does not require physical strength or endurance. Surely the opponents of woman suffrage do not mean to advocate that a strong fist should rule; just now we are a bit sensitive about this, and such doctrine is not popular. Might is not right; with our heart's blood we declare it is not!

No man has the right to citizenship on his weight, height, or lifting power; he exercises this right because he is a human being, with hands to work, brain to think, and a life to live.

It is to save women from toil and fatigue and all unpleasantness that the chivalrous ones would deny her the right of exercising the privileges of citizenship; though just how this could be brought about is not stated. Women are already in the battle of life; thirty per cent of the adult women of Canada and the United States are wage earners, and the percentage grows every day. How does the lack of the ballot help them? Is it any comfort to the woman who feels the sting of social injustice to reflect that she, at least, had no part in making such a law? Or do the poor women who go through the deserted streets in the grey dawn to their homes, alone and unprotected after their hard night's work at office-cleaning, ever proudly reflect that at least they have never had to drag their skirts in the mire of the polls, or be stared at by rude men as they approach the ballot box?

The physical disability of women is an additional reason for their having the franchise. The ballot is such a simple, easy way of expressing a preference or wish so "genteel", ladylike and dignified.

Now even in the matter of homesteads women are not allowed free land unless they are widows with the care of minor children; although any man who is of the age of eighteen may have one hundred and sixty acres on payment of ten dollars, and the performance of certain duties. The alleged reason for this discrimination is that women cannot perform the required duties and so, to save them from the temptation of trying, the Government in its fatherly wisdom denies them the chance.

But women are doing homestead duties wherever homestead duties are being done. Women suffer the hardships—cold, hunger, loneliness—against which there is no law; and, when the homestead is "proved", all the scrub cleared, and the land broken, the husband may sell the whole thing without his wife's knowledge, and he can take the money and depart, without a word. Against this there is no law either!

No person objects to the homesteader's wife having to get out wood, or break up scrub land, or drive oxen, so long as she is not doing these things for herself and has no legal claim on the result of her labor. Working for someone else is very sweet and womanly, and most commendable. What a neat blending there is of kindness and cruelty in the complacent utterances of the armchair philosophers who tell us that women have not the physical strength to do the hard tasks of life, and therefore should not be allowed to vote! Kindness and cruelty have never blended well, though clever people have tried to bring it about.

Little Harry had a birthday party one day, and as part of the entertainment he proudly exhibited a fine family of young puppies, who occupied a corner of the barn. One of his little guests seemed to be greatly attracted by the smallest puppy. He carried it about in his arms and appeared to lavish great affection on it! At last, he took it into the house, and inter-viewed Harry's mother. "Oh, Mrs. Brown," he said, "this little puppy is smaller than any of the others—and Harry says it will never grow to be a fine big dog—and maybe it is sick—and it is a dear sweet pet—and please may we drown it!"

I saw a letter last week which was written to the Sunshine Editor of one of our papers, from a woman on the homestead. She asked if a pair of boots could be sent to her, for she had to get out all the wood from the bush. Her husband had gone to work in the mines in B.C. She expressed her gratitude for the help she had received from Sunshine before, and voiced the hope that when "she got things going" she would be able to show her gratitude by helping someone else. There was no word of complaint. And this brave woman is typical of many. Whether able or not able, women are out in the world, meeting its conditions, bearing its conditions, fighting their own battles, and always under a handicap.

Now the question is, what are we going to do about it?

One way, pursued by many, is to turn blind eyes to conditions as they are, and "haver" away about how frail and sweet women are; and that what they need is greater dependence. This babble of marriage and home for every woman sounds soothing, but does not seem to lead anywhere. Before the war, there were a million and a half more women than men in the Old Country alone—what will the proportion be when the war, with its fearful destruction of men, is over? One would think, to read the vaporings which pass as articles on the suffrage question, that good relia-ble husbands will be supplied upon request, if you would only write your name and address plainly and enclose a stamped envelope.

It is certainly true that the old avenues of labor have been closed to women. The introduction of machinery has done this, for now the work is done in factories, which formerly was done by hand labor. Women have not deserted their work, but the work has been taken from them. Some-times it is said that women are trying to usurp men's place in the world; and if they were, it would be merely an act of retaliation, for men have already usurped women's sphere. We have men cooks, milliners, hairdres-sers, dressmakers, laundrymen—yes, men have invaded women's sphere. It is inevitable and cannot be changed by words of protest. People do well to accept the inevitable.

Men and women have two distinct spheres, when considered as men and women, but as human beings there is a great field of activity which they may—and do occupy in common. Now it is in this common field of activity that women are asking for equal privileges. There is not really much argument in pointing out that women cannot lay bricks, nor string electric wire, and therefore can never be regarded as man's equal in the matter of citizenship. Man cannot live by bricks alone! And we might with equal foolishness declare that because a man (as a rule) cannot thread a needle, or "turn a heel", therefore he should not ever be allowed to vote. Life is more than laying bricks or threading needles, for we have diverse gifts given to us by an all-wise Creator!

The exceptional woman can do many things, and these exceptions simply prove that there is no rule. There is a woman in the Qu'Appelle Valley who runs a big wheat farm and makes money. The Agricultural Editor of the *Manitoba Free Press* is a woman who is acknowledged to be one of the best crop experts in Canada. Figures do not confuse her! Even if the average woman is not always sure of the binominal theorem, that does not prove that she is incapable of saying who shall make the laws under which she shall live.

But when all other arguments fail, the anti-suffragist can always go back to the 'saintly motherhood' one, and 'the hand that rocks'. There is the perennial bloom that flourishes in all climates. Women are the mothers of the race—therefore they can be nothing else. When once a woman has a child, they argue, she must stay right on the job of raising it. Children have been blamed for many things very unjustly, and one of the most outstanding of these is that they take up all their mother's time, and are never able to care for themselves; that no one can do anything for the child but the mother; not even caring for it once every four years. From observation and experience, I wish to state positively that children do grow up—indeed they do—far too soon. The delightful days of babyhood and childhood are all too short, and they grow independent of us; and in a little while the day comes, no matter how hard we try to delay it, when they go out from us, to make their own way in the world, and we realize, with a queer stabbing at our hearts, that in the going of our first-born, our own youthfulness has gone too! And it seems such a cruel short time since he was born!

Yes, it is true. Children do grow up. And when they have gone from their mother, she still has her life to live.

The strong, active, virile woman of fifty, with twenty good years ahead of her, with a wealth of experience and wisdom, with a heart mellowed by time and filled with that large charity which only comes by knowledge—is a force to be reckoned with in the uplift of the world.

But if a woman has had the narrow outlook on life all the way along—if her efforts have been all made on behalf of her own family, she cannot quickly adjust herself to anything else, even when her family no longer need her. There is no sadder sight than the middle-aged woman left alone and purposeless when her family have gone. "I am a woman of fifty, strong, healthy—a college graduate," I once heard a woman say. "My children no longer need me—my attentions embarrass them—I gave them all my thought, all my time—I stifled every ambition to serve them. Now I am too old to gain new interests. I am a woman without a job."

Yet this type of woman, who had no thought beyond her own family circle, has been exalted greatly as the perfect mother, the "living sacrifice", the "perfect slave" of her children.

It was a daring woman who claimed that she had a life of her own; and a perfect right to her own ambitions, hopes, interests, and desires.

But time goes on, and the world moves; and the ways of the world are growing kinder to women. Here and there in a sheltered eddy in the stream of life, where the big currents never are felt, you will find the old mossy arguments that women are intended to be wageless servants dependent upon man's bounty, with no life or hopes of their own. But the currents of life grow stronger and stronger in these terrible days, and the moss is being broken up, and driven out into the turbulent water.

On March 1st, at 3 o'clock in the afternoon, the Woman Suffrage Bill was given its second reading in the Legislature of Alberta, and the women of the Province gathered in large numbers to hear the debate. For over an hour before the galleries were opened; women waited at the foot of the stairs; white-haired women, women with little children by the hand, women with babies in their arms, smartly-dressed women, alert, tailor-made business women; quiet, dignified and earnest; they were all there, they filled the galleries; they packed every available space. Many were unable to find a place in the gallery, and stood outside in the corridors.

"I consider it an honor to stand anywhere in the building", one bright-eyed old lady said when someone expressed their regret at not having a seat for her, "and I can read the speeches to-morrow, and imagine that I heard them."

When the Premier rose to move the second reading of the Bill the silence of the legislative chamber was tense, and the great mass of humanity in the galleries did not appear to breathe. The Premier, in a straightforward way, outlined the reasons for the granting of the franchise; he did not speak of it as a favor, a boon, a gift, or a privilege, but a right, and declared that the extension of the franchise was an act of justice; he did not once refer to us as the "fair sex", or assure us of his deep respect for us. The Leader of the Opposition, whose advocacy of woman franchise dates back many years, seconded the reading of the Bill; and short speeches were made by other members. There was only one who opposed it; one timorous brother declared it would break up the home.

On the same day that the Bill got its second reading, and at the same hour, the women of Calgary met together to discuss what women should do with the vote; and they drafted a platform, which must commend itself to all thinking people. Each subject discussed was for human betterment, and social welfare.

Women will make mistakes, of course, — and pay for them. That will be nothing new — they have always paid for men's mistakes. It will be a change to pay for their own. Democracy has its failures — it falls down utterly sometimes, we know, but not so often, or so hopelessly, as any other form of government. There have been beneficent despotisms, when a good king ruled absolutely. But unfortunately the next king was not good, and he drove the country to ruin. "King Jehoash did that which was right in the sight of the Lord, but Amaziah, his son, did that which was evil."

Too much depended upon the man!

Democracy has its faults; the people may run the country to the dogs, but they will run it back again. People, including women, will make mistakes, but in paying for them they will learn wisdom.

WHAT WOMEN WILL DO WITH THE VOTE, 1916

Nellie L. McClung, 'What Will They Do With It?', *MacLean's Magazine*, July 1916, pp. 36-8. Reprinted by permission of the Estate of Nellie Mc-Clung.

In the good old days of chivalry, when a lady received a proposal of marriage, the proper thing for her to do was to blush a rosy blush, and tremulously say: "This is so sudden!" But in these hurried, matter-of-fact times, when so much of the color and romance has gone from life, it is said that young ladies receive proposals without the slightest agitation, and have been known to remark: "Well, I think it is about time!"

The women in the West, to whom the franchise has been extended, have received it in somewhat this fashion, not ungratefully, or ungraciously, but quite as a matter of course. Indeed, to some of them, who have long worked for it, it seemed to be long in coming!

And now the question naturally arises, "What will they do with it?" There are still some who fear that the franchise, for all its innocent looks, is an insidious evil, which will undermine and warp a woman's nature, and cause her to lose all interest in husband, home and children. There are some who say it will make no difference. There are others who look now for the beginning of better things. Every one is more or less interested; some are a bit frightened.

There has been very little spoken opposition. One timid brother did say that just as soon as any women got a seat in Parliament he would resign his; but this terrible threat did not stagger the community as much as he had hoped and the woman to whom he made it only said that to her this was another proof of the purifying effect that women would have on politics.

The vital point seems to be whether or not women will wish to sit in

Parliament. If they would only be content to be pound-keepers and draymen, it would not be so bad.

Dr. Anna Shaw was asked one time whether women would like to sit in Parliament and she said that she had no desire to do so, but that, of course, she could not speak for all women. She thought that the women who had stood behind counters, and stooped over wash tubs for so long would be very glad to sit anywhere! Sitting in Parliament does not seem like such a hard job to those of us who have sat in the Ladies' Gallery and observed the ways of members of Parliament. There is such wonderful unanimity among Government members. Such unquestioning faith!

In one of the Governments of the West, there sat for fifteen years an honored member, who never but once in all that time broke the clammy silence of the back bench except to say "Aye" when told to say "Aye". But on toward the end of his fifteenth year of public service he gave unmistakable signs of life. A window had been opened behind where he sat and, when the draft blew over him, he sneezed! Shortly after he got up and shut the window thereby putting to shame and silence the scoffers who had said he was dead!

Looking down upon such tranquil scenes as this there are women who have said in their boastful way that they thought they could do as well— with a little practice.

Women have not tried to get into Parliament in the countries where they have the franchise and I venture the prediction that it will be many years before there are women legislators in Canada. And when they are elected it will be by sheer force of merit; for there will be a heavy weight of prejudice against women which only patient years can dispel!

The first work undertaken by women will be to give help to other women, particularly mothers of families. The women of New Zealand did this; and, as a result of their activity, the infant mortality of that country was reduced from the highest rate in the world to the lowest. The Government of Manitoba at its last session passed an act for the paying of mothers' pensions, recognizing that the bearing and rearing of children is a service to the state, and should have, if necessary, state recognition. This act provides that a sum of money be paid to mothers of small children, who are left dependent upon their own efforts. The object is to hold families together, instead of letting them be scattered, by the mother having to go out to work. The old way, the stupid way, was to take the children from the mother and put them in a state institution where they were maintained at a public expense which far exceeded the miserable wages the mother was able to earn, and also was in excess of what would have been required to keep them in their own homes. The greatest wrong that can be done a child is to deprive him of his mother's love. A hundred excellent institutions cannot give a child the care, the love, the touch of one mother. Even a poor mother is better than a good institution....

The great objection urged against state aid for mothers, is that the women who are thus helped will lose their sense of independence, and become, perhaps too frivolous on their twenty-five dollars a month, and take to going to picture shows, forgetting the serious business of life. It was to allay these fears that the women of Winnipeg tried out the experiment; and they say that such has not been the case in the three families that they have helped. They claim that, after the women have fed and clothed their families and themselves on their slender allowance, they are fairly immune from all danger of frivolity. The Mother's Association of Winnipeg has been instrumental in having various women take a real personal interest in the families thus helped. "Family Friend" is the way they describe the relationship.

It seems a fitting thing that women should use their new political power to make motherhood easier, to rob colonization of its fears and dangers, to give the lonely woman on the outposts of civilization the assurance that she is part of a great sisterhood and is not left alone to struggle with conditions which may prove too hard for her!

When the fire broke out in the Parliament Buildings of Ottawa and the lights went off accidentally, darkness added greatly to the horror and danger. It becomes necessary for some one to reach the switch, but no one could make way through the choking, blinding smoke with any hope of return. So they formed a chain—a human chain, by clasping hands. The man who went first was sustained by the warm handclasp of the man behind him. In this way, the switch was reached in safety and many lives were, no doubt, saved. Women are going to form a chain, a greater sisterhood than the world has ever known.

As it is now, the pioneer woman, who goes bravely out with her husband to make a home for themselves beyond the reach of neighbors, or nurses or doctors, actually takes her life in her hands. Many children have been born in the far away places where skilled help was impossible to obtain and both mother and child have lived. But again, many a mother and child have died for the lack of proper nursing.

The attitude of the world has ever been one of great admiration for these women. Indeed, a few years ago there was an agitation to build a monument, or maybe two, to the memory of the pioneer women of the west. Money was subscribed and the plans were in progress. Fortunately, most people have a sense of the fitness of things; and there came a vision of the great absurdity of building a monument to those who are dead and gone while we, through our carelessness and lack of thought, let other women, just as brave and heroic, die before their time. The pioneer women deserve a monument. They are worthy of the highest tribute we can give them, but let it not be a bare pillar of marble, which brings no shelter, or warmth, or comfort to man or beast; in which no little bird can build its nest; no tired dog rest in its shade. The best monument we can build to the pioneer women is to institute a system of rural nursing, which will bring help and companionship to these women in their hour of need. The men and women who go to the far places and cultivate the land there, make wealth for all of us. Why should Governments hesitate to spend money to make their conditions tolerable, and their lives secure?

Already the women of Alberta are working out some such plan. One woman has offered her own home, and her services for a training school for rural nurses, and several women have asked that special training be given them in nursing, so that they may be able to help the women in the country. This would not seriously interfere with the work of the trained nurse, for only in rare cases are they employed in maternity cases in the far away places. Twenty-five dollars a week is a prohibitive price to many people for skilled nursing. The rural nurse would have to be a combination of house-keeper and nurse, and would take the place of the kind neighbor, and her wages would be about twenty-five or thirty dollars a month.

There is another plan applicable to the more populated districts which is being worked out by two of Calgary's progressive women. It is to establish in Alberta a system of nursing as free and accessible as education in the public schools, and to do this by building Provincial hospitals, staffed by trained nurses of the highest qualifications, and maintained by a land tax on the municipalities which they serve. At the town of Lloydminster, situated on the Alberta-Saskatchewan boundary, there is such a hospital, and it is on a paying basis. It is maintained by a tax of eleven cents on each acre, and those who require nursing receive it free. It seems quite fitting that the well and strong should help to pay the expenses of those who are sick. It works so satisfactorily in this instance that other municipalities are endeavoring to follow the example.

The whole scheme involves an insignificant outlay of money compared with what the rural population pay for medical care, and inefficient nursing.

Our whole attitude toward the bringing of children into the world has been vague and dreamy. We have left everything to all-wise Providence, shirking our own responsibility in that way. If everything went right and the woman was able to battle successfully with unfavorable conditions we joyously said: "God bless her!" But if something went wrong, and she fought a losing battle, we piously said: "Thy will be done—the Lord gave and the Lord hath taken away!" . . .

More and more the idea is growing upon us that certain services are best rendered by the state, and not left to depend on the caprice, inclination, or inability of the individual. If a man's house catches on fire, the fire department come and put it out, and the city pays the bill cheerfully. No one complains about the expense of keeping up a fire department. If a row breaks out in a back lane the police come and settle it and the city pays again. The salary of the police officials does not depend on the number of "cases" they attend to and, as a result, the policeman's chief business is to prevent trouble—not to make it. It may not be too ideal, or Utopian to look forward to a day when there will be in every city a Medical Board, whose business it will be to keep people well; whose work will be to teach people to do without them, but who will attend to every case which occurs, as the fireman puts out the fire, or the policeman settles the row.

As it is now many a man, woman, and child, suffers agony, or perhaps becomes a menace to their family, because medical aid cannot be afforded. Why should a child suffer from adenoids, which make him stupid and dull in school, and give him a tendency to tubercular trouble, just because his father cannot afford to pay the doctor's fee, or maybe does not know the danger?

The free school clinic is a beginning, and has been so successful it has opened the way for greater reforms along this line.

Women all over the West are thinking along such lines as these. They are interested in the questions of agricultural credit, consolidation of schools, proportional representation, and the abolition of capital punishment. Books are being read eagerly, and meetings are held, where the matters are thoroughly threshed out. Above all things the women are anxious to avoid asking for freakish, or ill-judged legislation. They want to go slow and sure, realizing that as they have waited long, they can always wait a little longer.

One of the most hopeful signs of the advent of the woman voter is the quiet determination to stay out of party politics. Party lines are not so tightly drawn in the West. Great issues have been decided by the people outside of politics. The temperance fight in Alberta and Manitoba obliterated the lines of party, and when that once happens they can never be quite so strong again. It is no uncommon thing to hear public men say: "I have voted both ways, and will change my politics any time I want to." The women have no intention of forming a woman's party. They see no future for such a movement. But they do see that a great body of intelligent women, who study public questions, fairly and honestly, uncontaminated by party hypothesis, not trying to fit their opinion to the platform of any political leader, may become a powerful influence in forming the policy of a Government, or perhaps in making the platform of an opposition. They will cautiously and seriously decide upon what legislation they want and then they will ask for it. If their legislation is fair and reasonable, it will be supported by a large body of the men voters; and governments, who are wise, will give it gladly. It is easy to get legislation when public sentiment demands it. The impact of public opinion is the still small voice of the politician's conscience. Or, if they are not identical, they are at least co-incident. When woman suffrage became popular in the

West, many a man *suddenly* remembered that he had been in favor of it for years!

Most governments are possessed of political sagacity, which is to say the "ability to tell the band wagon from the hearse!"

THE NATIONAL COUNCIL OF WOMEN AND THE VOTE

Public Archives of Canada, National Council of Women of Canada, *Papers*, vol. 117.

REPORT OF PLATFORM COMMITTEE
WOMEN OF CANADA

You are now citizens!

You have the privilege and the opportunity of expressing yourselves— indirectly—by your own vote!

You have a duty and an obligation to so express yourselves!

If the women voters of Canada should merely fall into line behind two political parties, their partisan vote would not help the country. Indeed, it would be but an added burden—by necessitating an extension of the machinery for voting and increasing the money cost of the same. On the other hand, while it is not desirable to form a woman's party, it is obvious that there are certain principles which should demand the support of the women of both parties.

This was in brief the conclusion of the Executive of the National Council of Women at its March meeting, where members from various Provinces & of all shades of politics were present.

It was therefore agreed to give an opportunity to the women of Canada to express themselves as to what, in their opinions were the most urgent and fundamental of these principles or objects and then sum them up in what might be called a Canadian Women's Platform—

A committee was arranged with representatives from each Province with sub-committee of the whole at Ottawa to carry out this plan.

MEMBERS OF PLATFORM COMMITTEE

Mrs. Adam Shortt (convener) 5 Marlborough Avenue, Ottawa.
Mrs. Vincent Massey Sub-committee
Mrs. Chas. Robson with convener
Mrs. Willoughby Cummings, D.C.L.
Miss Constance Boulton, Toronto.

Mrs. Arthur Murphy, Edmonton.
Miss A. M. Murray, East Picton.
Mrs. E. Atherton Smith, St. John.
Miss Margaret Brown, Halifax.
Mrs. Wm. C. Hawkins, Hamilton.
Miss Kennethe Haig, Winnipeg.
Mrs. O. C. Edwards, Alberta.
Mrs. R. S. Day, Victoria.
Miss Tatley, Montreal.
Mrs. S. E. Clement, Brandon.
Mrs. R. R. Jamieson, Calgary.
Mrs. Parlby, Alix, Man.
Mrs. McNaughtan, Sask.
Mrs. Gordon Wright, London.
Mrs. L. A. Hamilton, Toronto.
Mrs. B. C. Borden, Sackville.
Mrs. Stanfield, Truro.

In submitting this Report of a possible Women's Platform we wish to say that women in general express the desire that truth, honesty, purity, justice, and righteousness be the basis of any such platform.

Built on this foundation their idea of a Platform is to provide a rallying ground from which by their united votes they may more rapidly bring about the solution of those social problems for which tens of thousands of Canadian women have been giving their energy, time, and money during the last half century.

Replies came from ocean to ocean to a circular letter sent out. There is no poverty of expressed opinion as to wrongs that should be righted, or legislation needed to improve the condition of women and children.

It is impossible with such a long list of desired improvements to incorporate them all in any one platform that would be acceptable. Indeed—if all suggestions were used the platform would be so broad as to include everybody and we should end just where we began.

We have endeavoured to sum up the most urgent and fundamental reforms in as brief a way as possible in the hope of bringing at least some few things to fruition.

There are many live issues and reforms which have been submitted to us and which we in the main endorse—but which we consider inadvisable to add to our platform at the present time. We would like to express here our thanks and appreciation to all those who contributed their opinions, singly or in groups, as time would not permit us to do it personally.

After the experience of last spring in gathering so many desired opinions for the Women's Platform it has been of great interest to observe the great Liberal Convention which gathered in Ottawa in August. It was stated one day "that the Convention Committee was devoted to the digestion of a part of the scores of resolutions and proposals as to the form of the party platform and if all be adopted the declaration of faith will be as long as the moral code." Later, in the House of Commons, a leader said that it was not desirable for a political party to promise details of reform and that it was safer to stick to general principles, because he could not see the sense, of the party risking defeat at the next election by promising to do specific things which if they did not do would invite defeat. Just here is the big difference between the women standing by their reforms—their ideals—with their votes, irrespective of party affiliation, and being a political party whose first aim is to stay in, or get in, to power. Women must put their united strength behind the man or woman in the House or in the Legislature who carried their banner of reforms whether they were Conservative or Liberal, and that just by so much politically as they did or did not do this, would they be a lever to raise the standards of Canadian life and living.

WOMEN'S PLATFORM

As adopted by the N.C.W. at St. John, June 1920. for the consideration of Canadian Women—

Basis: TRUTH, JUSTICE, RIGHTEOUSNESS, LOYALTY

FEDERAL

1. Political Standards
   (a) Equal moral standards in public and private life.
   (b) Abolition of patronage.
   (c) Publication of amounts subscribed to party funds.
   (d) Open nomination of political candidates.
   (e) Political equality for men and women.
   (f) A speaking knowledge of either the English or French language for men and women before receiving the franchise.
   (g) The naturalization of women independent of the nationality of husband.
   (h) The practice of thrift in administration of public and private affairs.

SOCIAL STANDARDS

(a) That necessary legislation be enacted to permit of uniform marriage laws.
(b) That there be equality of cause for divorce in all divorce courts—and that there be no financial barrier.

(c) Prohibition of the sale of intoxicants.
(d) Raising the age of consent to 18 years.

INDUSTRIAL STANDARDS

(a) Equal pay for work of equal value in quantity and quality.
(b) The basis of employment to be physical and mental fitness without regard to sex.
(c) The *principle* of co-operation between employer and employed.
(d) The *principle* of collective bargaining as defined by the Federal Department of Labour.

PROVINCIAL

Political Standards:
  same as Federal.
SOCIAL STANDARDS
(a) A Child Welfare Section in all Departments of Health—Provincial and Municipal.
(b) Support of every effort made by Dominion and Provincial Governments in combatting Venereal Disease, and endorsation of establishment of free clinics.
(c) Segregation and care of the feebleminded.
(d) Prohibition of the sale of intoxicants.
(e) Adequate Mothers' Pensions or "Allowances".
(f) Equal guardianship of Children.
(g) Legal recognition of woman's share in husband's property and income during life.
(h) Free and compulsory education in all Provinces.
(i) Physical training of boys and girls in all schools.
(j) Medical inspection of all schools—with dental clinics where this is possible.
(k) Adequate salaries for School teachers.
(l) Equality of opportunity without regard to sex in all technical training; manual training in all school grades for boys and girls.
INDUSTRIAL STANDARDS
a-b-c-d-e-the same as Federal
f. Minimum wage for women.

All of which is respectfully submitted—
Convener.

THIRTY YEARS LATER AND WHAT THEY HAVE DONE, 1946

Charlotte Whitton, 'Is the Canadian Woman a Flop in Politics?', *Saturday Night*, 26 Jan. 1946. Reprinted by permission of the Estate of Charlotte Whitton.

Thursday, January 27, 1916, was a hysterically happy day in Manitoba. The galleries of the new and lavish Legislative Chamber were crowded, every seat on the floor taken but the premier's. The Hon. T. C. Norris, now more responsible than any one person for this happy issue from the affliction of woman's aggression, was in Chicago. The gallant Norseman "Tom" (Hon. T. H.) Johnston was leading the House. He moved it into Committee of the Whole. Not five minutes elapsed until, seconded by Col. Cringan, M.L.A. for Virden, he enthusiastically declared, "The bill is reported without amendment, Mr. Speaker. God save the King." (None apparently inferred that this patriotic fervor might portend a warning prayer!)

In tumultuous smashing of precedent, cheers rang from floor and gallery where the serried women sang "For they are jolly good fellows." The "fellows" jumped to their feet, started "O Canada" (how honest! they *were* going to *stand on guard*, just wait and see!) The executive of the Women's Political Equality League were invited to the floor. Speeches knew no limits of ardent adulation. Said J. W. Wilton of Assiniboia: "Today we complete the perfect democracy by extending to all the people the right to govern themselves." J. W. Hamelin, of Ste. Rose, doggedly dissented—family life would be disrupted, homes broken, children neglected as husbands tried to hush heart-broken children, their mothers absent in the violent controversies of political meetings.

But such a wisp of straw twirled away on the floods of advocacy. No other measure of the session, wrote one Winnipeg dispatch was likely to compare with one of such fundamental reform and potential force as this. "Women's mentality" should now "modify, moderate, temper, supplement and complement the mentality of man" with the "action of this day" translating itself into a more tolerable existence for the humblest inhabitant of the province. It will mean the establishment of higher values of life and living." . . .

Thirty years later, and in the New Year of man's hope of a new era, the women of Canada report a sorry stewardship to the surviving of those who purchased their electoral freedom. From the Atlantic seaboard to the western plains, not one woman sits from a Dominion or provincial riding. At Ottawa, Mrs. Gladys Strum, C.C.F. victor over General McNaughton, promises to revive the tradition of effectiveness of that first lone pioneer, Agnes MacPhail. She is the sole survivor of the seventeen women starters in a field of 1000 candidates in the Dominion contest of 1945. In the

Upper Chamber, there are, of course, our two women senators, appointed, like their colleagues, for life and good behaviour in the past and to come. They represent the maximum capitulation of two gallant bachelor prime ministers to woman's influence in the last quarter century. . . .

Why this sorry record?—the poorest in any enfranchised western democracy in a country whose women do compare favorably in education, opportunity, intelligence, energy and enterprise with those of the United Kingdom, the other Dominions, the United States and Scandinavia. Or does one hear a snort and sniff from certain quarters: "Do they?"

First, possibly, is the fact that the women of this country, like the Canadian democracy as a whole, are but half-appreciative beneficiaries of rich legacies of freedoms, rights and privileges, many of which have been bequeathed by greater, earlier crusaders in the two lands to which we are most closely allied—the United Kingdom and the United States. Of course, certain Canadian women were valiant warriors for the vote for over a quarter of a century (and another generation in Quebec.) The more vigorous fighters were western women. The women leaders, however, were in most cases primarily sworn to some other cause in the furtherance of which they found the ballot essential. . . .

Canadian women got the vote as a gift rather than a reward.

Moreover it was granted not as a conviction so much as a concession on the part of the major technicians within the parties. Even today, among those thinking—or presumably so—on policy, and those realistically operating the mechanics of election, there is not, at heart, any earnest and forthright desire to imperil the delicately temporizing procedures which have so long taken the place of any consistent or systematic political philosophy in Canada.

Another potent factor is the almost complete economic dependence of women in Canada. This is peculiar in a country where women actually hold, by inheritance or purchase, a large portion of invested capital, insurance payments, have enormous bank deposits and enjoy—albeit often for their males' "social security"—title to much property. But women seem afraid to trust women, even themselves, and almost ten out of ten of those who have inherited their wealth, entrust its potent management to men as lawyers, managers, or corporately in the trust companies, of which but one has yet named a woman to its Board. The married women, of course, 95 out of 100 of them, are dependent upon their husbands' income, but women who are their own direct income-earners are overwhelmingly on salaries or wages: few are own-workers.

Of course, this same shift to wage-earning status is depriving the male worker of his political independence, but it is more marked among women. In the U.S.S.R. where all are members of a union and employees of the state, this does not operate and women have swarmed into office. But Canada lacks, in any number, women of independent income and energetic interest as well in politics—the group who have done so much to "make" women's place in the public life of Britain. This pattern lends itself well to the procedure, beloved of the party managers, and makes the "husband-wife; father-daughter" technique perhaps the most single potent force in strangling women's power and freedom within the organized parties. By this the women and the women friends of "the family", (the candidate, the "prominent member" etc.) become the discreet, moderately articulate and politically ineffective outward and visible sign of the party's inward and spiritual graciousness towards "complete equality for women in all things" etc. etc. etc. The words may be found in any party's manifesto.

Most of the women so deployed do not even know they are decoys; others are as aware as Judas of what they are doing but lack the virtue of remorse. Many honestly and earnestly serve in the hard and humble routines in which they do believe they are saving the country by saving the party, imperilled by the equally devoted drudgery of their counter-parts in the enemy hosts. Their reward comes in the candidate's re-election, the naming of a woman here and there to an innocuous minority or an automatic post, or a trip to some conference or other.

These really good citizens, along with the immobilized thousands in our great women's organizations (pledged to non-political when they really mean non-party action) serve as sounding boards for "what the women want". Often their very motions are kites subtly given them to fly. Undoubtedly much of the enormous extension of state welfare provisions, impelled strongly however by a changing social economy, is the direct result of the power of the women's vote. Its unwieldy, ill co-ordinated, costly and confused erection, its administrative weakness, its deplorable auctioning are equally attributable to their tendency to exercise the power of the ballot without preceding or following it with the responsibility of the voter.

One end result is that neither within their own party organizations nor within many of the strong women's groups is there more than a minority, prepared to support informed and vigorous women who might "inconven-ience" the party leaders or the machine, might, above all, force clear-cut policy and substantial over-hauling. Of course they will ask for women—women just *per se* in the very top-flight posts, international assemblies, the cabinets, the Senate, etc. but they will not get out and support those who do plan strategy in the only places where the bridgeheads can be estab-lished. That is on the home salients of the ward association of the party, and in direct participation in the elective bodies on the local level—the school and library boards, the township, village, town, county and city councils. Nellie McClung put it briefly, as true 30 years ago. "We found out that the Local Council of Women could not be our medium. There were too many women in it who were afraid to be associated with any controversial subject. Their husbands would not let them 'go active'. It might imperil their jobs. The long tentacles of the political octopus reached far."

Canadian women could be lifted out of the cellar position they now occupy in western democracy within 24 months were even a small group of determined, informed women to assume responsibility for mobilizing and training a few "commandos". These would be women of all political faiths, and, at the moment, many of none—who would equip themselves to become the spearheads of advance in organizing and assuring the actual representation of women within their own parties, in "the machine" and as candidates, and at all levels of government, Dominion, provincial and municipal, the latter particularly.

All the provincial legislatures have four to five years of life now before them. The Dominion election is not likely to be invited until 1948, perhaps 1950; there are 2000 more reasons now for deferring it, annually, another year. The most momentous months in western civilization are upon us but Canadian women will have no effective part in their moulding. It is their own doing—the fruit of the easy compliance of the collaborationists; the disillusionment, disgust and sense of futility of others; the disinterest [sic] of the rest. It is a sad memorial to the dreams and aspirations of 1916.

SUGGESTED READING

Catherine Cleverdon's *The Woman Suffrage Movement in Canada* (second edition, Toronto, 1974) is the only complete account of the suffragist movement that has been written. Also useful is *Studies of the Royal Commission on the Status of Women*, 8 (Ottawa, 1971), which provides a general survey, while Chapter 12 of John Garner's *The Franchise and Politics in British North America, 1755-1867* (Toronto, 1968), describes the early history of women's voting rights. *The Report of the Royal Commission on the Status of Women* (Ottawa, 1970), is full of useful information. The most thorough guide to women's studies in general in Canada is found in the chapters written by Veronica Strong-Boag, and by Margrit Eichler and Lynn Primrose in *Women in Canada* (Toronto, 1973) edited by Marylee Stephenson.

The general historical context for the development of the women's movement is set out in Peter Waite, *Canada 1874-1896: Arduous Destiny* (Toronto, 1971) and R. C. Brown and Ramsay Cook, *Canada 1896-1921, A Nation Transformed* (Toronto, 1975). Richard Allen's *The Social Passion* (Toronto, 1971) is also valuable for background. Trevor Lloyd's *Suffragettes International* (London, 1971) provides a brief introduction to the international movement while William O'Neill's *Everyone was Brave* (Chicago, 1969) and Constance Rover's *Woman Suffrage and Party Politics in Great Britain* (London and Toronto, 1967) detail the history of the movements that had the most direct impact on Canada.

There are a number of specialized studies and articles that repay careful attention. Most important is the collection entitled *Women at Work, Ontario 1850-1930* (Toronto, 1975), which, while uneven in quality, is the best available study of the social history of women in Canada. To it should be added Suzanne Cross's article 'The Neglected Majority: The Changing Role of Women in Nineteenth Century Montreal', *Social History/Histoire Sociale*, 12 November 1973 vol. VI, 202-23, and Alison Prentice, 'The Feminization of Teaching in British North America and Canada, 1845-75', *Social History/Histoire Sociale*, 15 May 1975, vol. VII, 5-20. Jacques Henripin's *Trends and Factors of Fertility in Canada* (Ottawa, 1972) is enormously important in any attempt to understand the changing status of women and the family in Canada, as is Michael Katz's *The People of*

Hamilton, Canada West: Family and Class in a Mid-Nineteenth Century City (Cambridge, Mass., 1975). Michael Bliss' 'Pure Books on Avoided Subjects', *Canadian Historical Association, Historical Papers, 1970*, 89-108, is an important discussion of some aspects of sexual beliefs in Victorian Canada. James Gray's sprightly *Red Lights on the Prairies* (Toronto, 1973) is a popular account of prostitution.

Four articles add important details on the histroy of the suffragist movement: Joanne L. Thompson, 'The Influence of Dr. Emily Howard Stowe on the Woman Suffrage Movement in Canada', *Ontario History*, December 1962, vol. LIV, 4, 253-66; Jennifer Stoddart, 'The Woman Suffrage Bill in Quebec', in Marylee Stephenson, *Women in Canada* (Toronto, 1973), pp. 90-106; and June Menzies, 'Votes for Women in Saskatchewan', in Norman Ward and Duff Spafford, *Politics in Saskatchewan* (Toronto, 1968), pp. 78-92; Marie Lavigne, Yolande Pinard, and Jennifer Stoddart, 'La Fédération Nationale St-Jean-Baptiste et les Revendications Féministes au début du XXe Siècle', *Revue d'Histoire de L'Amérique Française;*, December 1975, vol. 29, 3, 253-74. There are also several unpublished works worthy of mention: Carol Lee Bacchi-Ferraro, 'The Ideas of Canadian Suffragists, 1890-1920', unpublished M.A. thesis, McGill University; Wendy Thorpe, 'Lady Aberdeen and the National Council of Women of Canada: A Study of a Social Reformer in Canada', unpublished M.A. Thesis, Queen's University, 1971; Veronica Strong-Boag, 'The Parliament of Women: The National Council of Women of Canada, 1893-1929', unpublished Ph.D. thesis, University of Toronto, 1975; Nancy Thompson, 'The Controversy over the Admission of Women to University College', unpublished M.A. thesis, University of Toronto, 1974; and D. A. Ronish, 'The Development of Higher Education for Women at McGill University from 1857 to 1899, with specific reference to the role of Sir John William Dawson', unpublished M. Ed. thesis, McGill University, 1972.

Rosa Shaw's *Proud Heritage* (Toronto, 1957) and Doris French's *High Button Bootstraps* (Toronto, 1968) provide helpful accounts of the National Council of Women of Canada and the Federation of Women Teachers' Associations of Ontario. Most other organizations have not been examined in detail. Consequently women's history can be most readily studied through biography and autobiography. Veronica Strong-Boag's edition of Nellie L. McClung's *In Times Like These* (Toronto, 1972) should be supplemented by Mrs McClung's two volumes of autobiography, *Clearing in the West* (Toronto, 1935) and *The Stream Runs Fast* (Toronto, 1945). Kennethe Haig's *Brave Harvest* (Toronto, 1945) describes the career of Cora Hind but barely mentions her feminist activities. Elsie Gregory MacGill's *My Mother the Judge* (Toronto, 1955) is one of the best suffragist biographies and includes a worthwhile account of the movement in British Columbia. Byrne Hope Sanders' *Emily Murphy: Crusader* (Toronto, 1945) is less satisfactory but nevertheless worth consulting. On Quebec two very different books are first rate: Claire Martin's *In an Iron Glove* (Toronto, 1968), and Thérèse Casgrain's *A Woman in a Man's World* (Toronto, 1972). John T. Saywell's *The Canadian Journal of Lady Aberdeen* (Toronto, 1960) is extremely interesting reading. Mary Quayle Innis, editor, *The Clear Spirit* (Toronto, 1967) presents twenty studies of varying quality of Canadian women. No one should neglect to read what is perhaps the most appealing of Canadian autobiographies, Emily Carr's *Growing Pains* (Toronto, 1946).